Chippewa Indians of Yesterday and Today

CHIPPEWA INDIANS

of Yesterday and Today

by
Sister M. CAROLISSA LEVI
F.S.P.A.

Illustrations by
PETER WHITEBIRD
Chippewa Indian

PAGEANT PRESS, INC.
New York, N. Y.

PUBLISHED BY PAGEANT PRESS, INC.

130 WEST 42ND STREET, NEW YORK 36, NEW YORK

First Edition

Library of Congress Catalog Number: 56-10616

MANUFACTURED IN THE UNITED STATES OF AMERICA

To M.P.H.

Our American Heritage—

these principles:

That all men
are created equal
that they are endowed by their Creator
with certain inalienable rights
that among these are
life, liberty, and the pursuit of happiness.

ACKNOWLEDGMENTS

To Mrs. Hildegard Thompson, Head of the Education Department, Indian Bureau, Washington, D. C., for writing the Preface to this book; to the Reverend Ladislas J. Siekaniec, O.F.M., instructor at Saint John College, Cleveland, Ohio, for valuable criticism of certain chapters; to Mr. Emmett J. Riley, present administrative officer, and to Mr. Jesse C. Cavill, former superintendent of the Great Lakes Indian Agency, for assistance in preparing the manuscript; to Dr. Richard Bardon, Duluth, Minnesota, for the loan of his father's historical manuscript; to Mr. Earle Holman, secretary of Langlade County Historical Society, for supplying data; to the late Sister M. Macaria Murphy, F.S.P.A., nearly half a century among the Chippewa, director of the historical research sponsored as a W.P.A. project by the Great Lakes Indian Agency from 1936 to 1940, for the compilation of the historical records on the Chippewa Indians which served both as guide and indispensable source for this work; to libraries and museums consulted for services rendered; to my Chippewa friends for courteously assisting me in many ways; to my community, the Franciscan Sisters of Perpetual Adoration, La Crosse, Wisconsin, for sponsoring this publication; to Sister M. Mileta Ludwig and Sister M. Hedwigis Overmoehle for the critical reading and correction of the manuscript and documentation; to all who helped in any way to bring this work to completion; to publishers of books, magazines, and newspapers referred to in these pages for granting permission to cite from their publications.

CONTENTS

Page

PREFACE

Chippewa Indians of Yesterday and Today is a much needed history of a great Indian Tribe. Relatively little information is readily available about the Chippewas, who at one time were among the three largest Indian groups north of Mexico. They belonged to the Algonquin language family and they occupied the Great Lakes region and portions of the Plains region on the North American continent. Today many of the Chippewa descendants still live in the same general areas. Others are scattered throughout the length and breadth of the land, occupying places of distinction in all walks of life.

Chippewas have, through their history, intermingled and intermarried with various European groups, the French, the German, the Scandinavians, the Dutch, the English, and others. Today the percentage of full blooded Chippewas is small. As history moves on, intermingling of Chippewas with other racial groups will continue with further obliteration of racial lines. Chippewa heritage is an important part of American heritage. It needs to be recorded not only for Chippewas but for other Americans as well. Sister M. Carolissa has produced a much needed factual record of the Chippewa people, both past and present. Her record brings together facts gleaned from careful and untiring research and presents them with an understanding that could only be gained by living in Christian neighborliness among the Chippewa people.

The Chippewas need this book. It gives them the recognition they so well deserve. The Chippewas can turn to this record to renew inner strength and confidence in themselves. This written record should give them a deep sense of pride, not only in the achievement of their forebears but more importantly in the contribution that they are making today to American life.

Those of us who are not Chippewa have much to gain from this record. We cannot read this history without developing a deeper understanding and appreciation of the Chippewa people.

The early explorers and settlers had a deep appreciation for the Chippewa people. The record states that they found them intelligent, stately, and pleasantly mannered. The Chippewas today have retained those same qualities and many others which are exemplified in our Chippewa friends and associates. Sister Carolissa captures Chippewa Indian character and records it to inspire and enlighten all Americans.

HILDEGARD THOMPSON

Chief, Branch Education
United States Department of the Interior
Bureau of Indian Affairs
Washington 25, D. C.

Peace or War

PART

I . . .

HISTORICAL AND RELIGIOUS BACKGROUND

THE FIRST AMERICANS

chapter 1

LONG BEFORE THE DAWN OF MODERN TIMES, American Indians had spread their numerous progeny over a large portion of the North American continent. Anthropologists tell us that the earliest American Indians may have made their appearance on the continent perhaps some twenty thousand years ago. These Indians of the red race, and not the white peoples who came later from Europe, are the real American natives. Ancestors of today's Indians welcomed the Mayflower Pilgrims to this land of opportunity.

The commonly accepted conclusion regarding the racial origin of the Indian points to Asiatic derivation. It is now generally admitted that the pathway through which North America was originally populated was by way of Siberia, which is separated from Alaska by less than fifty-four miles. Migration across Bering Strait could have been accomplished by means of boats or on the ice. For centuries, Eskimos living on both sides of Bering Strait used skin boats and open "dugout" boats hollowed from logs. In an announcement from the Smithsonian Institution, Dr. Ales Hrdlicka, the Grand Old Man of Anthropology, referring to his research in Alaska, stated:

The Peninsula was a regular sieve for movements of people from the north southward. There is a whole series of passes more or less easily practicable for even primitive people. About every 30 to 40 miles from east to west a good sized river extends for various distances from the north into the peninsula, ending in one or more lakes from which generally smaller streams lead farther southward to within a short distance of streams that run towards the Pacific. People such as the Eskimo or the Indian could readily, it was seen, have come along the western coasts, reached these passes and carried their skin boats over the few rapids and portages, after which they found themselves close to or within Shelikof Strait, facing the visible Kodiak Island, or in Cook's Inlet; and from both of these regions the way towards the northwest coast and the rest of the continent was open. This was plainly the most natural and the easiest way of procedure for all comers from the Bering Sea and northwestern Asia. The peopling of America therefore, as surmised before, took place not through Alaska but along its western coasts and through the Peninsula.[1]

The other possible route to the western hemisphere lay across the ice. At the present time, except in midsummer, the strait is more or less filled with floating blocks of ice. Geologists claim that ice sheets once covered the northern part of the continent; but even if ice conditions had never been more favorable than they are now, it would still have been possible for men to cross on foot or by dog-sled. As late as 1913, Mr. Matt Gottschalk of Nome, Alaska, crossed Bering Strait with a sled drawn by sixteen dogs. He estimated that he had travelled 200 miles, always heading back southward after being forced north by the fast moving ice.[2]

From the reconstruction of these routes, the Asiatic origins theory flows almost as a necessary corollary. Dr. Hrdlicka's discovery in 1932 of skeletons of an ancient oblong-headed people, deep under Kodiak's surface, adds weight to the theory. These skeletons, the anthropologist was convinced, will fix the California aborigines as the descendants of one of the earliest migration waves from Siberia into Alaska.[3] This discovery may furnish the final answer to one of the greatest enigmas of North America's prehistoric period.

Once these people had arrived on the continent, they found a favorable climate and a land abounding with animals and fish. No one questioned their title to the land. Through some manner unknown at the present time, they may have spread the news of their discovery to their fellow-tribesmen in Asia, and thus migration waves continued.

Another adherent to the Asiatic theory is the Reverend Chrysostom Verwyst, O.F.M., noted Chippewa missionary, scholar, and historian. He wrote as follows:

As to the origin of the Indian races, they are no doubt from Asia. We have seen in missionary periodicals photographic pictures of some Asiatic people, and we can truly say they so closely resemble our Indians that there is no doubt about their common origin. Father Grellon, who had labored amongst the Hurons of Canada and had left the country after the destruction of the Huron Mission in 1648-'49-'50, and went to Asia, relates in the "Lettres Edifiantes" that he met in central Asia, a Christian Huron woman and spoke to her in the language neither of them had spoken for years. This poor woman had been sold as a slave from tribe to tribe till she was brought far into the interior of Asia.

There is no doubt that in remote times Asiatic tribes, many of whom are still of a roving nomadic disposition, crossed Behring's Strait, and, once on American soil, pushed southward and in other directions. Moreover, the many islands in the Pacific Ocean seem to indicate that at a remote period there was a large continent, perhaps like Australia, between Asia and America. This may have become submerged in the course of time, ages ago, and perhaps many of the islands in said ocean are but portions of this continent. The ruins of Yucatan, Mexico, and Peru point to an Asiatic origin and civilization.[4]

But if the American Indians are all descended from the same ancestral stock, what explanation can be offered for the differences in aboriginal culture at the time of Columbus? Many of the differences are due to environment. The warm, moist climate of Mexico and Central America was favorable for the growth of food plants. Soft stone could be utilized for building purposes. These conditions encouraged a settled form of life and promoted a distinctive civilization. On the Great Plains, the buffalo provided food, clothing, and material for shelter. Near mountains and in ravines, numerous wild animals supplied many of the needs of its inhabitants. Along the Potomac and other eastern river valleys, the Indians combined limited agricultural pursuits with hunting, trapping, and fishing. On both the Atlantic and Pacific coasts, the communities subsisted largely on fish and oysters, as the large mounds of empty shells mutely testify. The Asiatic theory is thus further strengthened by the extent of Indian migrations on the North American continent, since even today some Asiatic tribes have a nomadic tendency.[5]

Another difficulty in regard to the Indian is to formulate a legal and socially sound definition of an Indian. Attempts to arrive at an agreement bring results that are sometimes tragic to the Indian. Because of frequent shifting in administration, the Office of Indian Affairs — now more than a hundred years old — has not yet clearly defined the status of the so-called Indian.[6]

Say "Indian" to many an American and he will conjure up an image of a tall, stately, copper-colored figure, displaying a feathered headdress, glowing with war paint and grease, brandishing a tomahawk, and emitting the blood-curdling yells of a scalp-hunting fiend on the warpath. Further probing into his subconscious may draw

forth ideas of tepees and be-shawled squaws with papooses strapped
to their backs. The sentimentally inclined may think of "Reservation Indians" squatting peaceably in the doorways of tent or hut,
weaving baskets or making souvenirs for the "Americans" who want
to "See America First," and possessing a limited monosyllabic vocabulary — "Ugh!"

Actually an Indian is neither a museum piece nor a wild West
exhibit, but a human being, endowed with a distinct personality.
Perhaps he is different from other peoples. Tom St. Germain, a Chippewa from Lac du Flambeau Reservation, thinks he is. While a
student at Tulane School of Medicine, New Orleans, and a member
of the army medical corps reserve, he made the following observations on the position of the Indian:

> The Indian is unique. First, because though conquered, he was
> not annihilated, nor colonized, and only partly absorbed. He is
> further unique in that he has been shelved with very little
> effort until recent years to make him economically independent
> and self-supporting.
>
> The relations of the Conqueror — the White — to the Con-
> quered, and Indian, in this country has been unique. Other
> nations have (1) annihilated the conquered, or (2) absorbed
> them, or (3) exploited them as "colonies." If the conquered are
> of an alien race, they are not absorbed to a great degree. None
> of these things has happened to the Indian.[7]

Possibly the difference between the Indian and the white man
may be learned somewhat from a comparative study of their manner of acting. For example, the Reverend Rudolph Hertz, for twenty
years a missionary to the Sioux in South Dakota, on one occasion
called a business meeting. He explained to a group of Indians that
exactly an hour would be devoted to the Council, forty-five minutes
to discussion and the final fifteen minutes to voting. Thereupon an
old Sioux arose and offered this sage comment: "The White man
acts, then talks about what he has done — and his heart is sad. The
Indian talks, thinks, talks some more, thinks yet again for a long
time, and then he talks some more. Then he acts — and his heart is
glad."

That the Indian can match wits with the white man can be
deduced from the following incident: In 1864, the legislature of
Minnesota demanded that the Ojibways should be removed from
their reservations. The Department selected a tract of land north of
Leech Lake and sent out a special commissioner to make the treaty.

The delegate solicited Bishop Whipple's aid in the negotiation. The Bishop informed the agent that the land selected for the Indian was the poorest in Minnesota and that no Indian would sign the treaty. The commissioner decided to proceed without the Bishop's help. Calling the Indians together, he said:

> My friends, your Great Father has heard how you have been wronged. He looked in the North, East, and the West, to find an honest man; and when he saw me, he said, "Here is an honest man; I will send him to my red children."
>
> Now, my friends, look at me. The winds of fifty-five winters have blown over my head, and have silvered it over with gray, and in all that time I have done no wrong to a single person. As your friend, I advise you to sign this treaty at once.

Old Shabaskong, a Mille Lacs chief, sprang to his feet, and, with a wave of his hand, said:

> Look at me, the winds of fifty-five winters have blown over my head, and have silvered it over with gray, but — they have not blown my brains away! I have done.

The council was ended.[8]

Irvin S. Cobb, with characteristic humor, sets forth the difference between the veneer of the white man's culture, when imperfectly absorbed by the young Indian, and the genuine culture of the native Indian:

> Everywhere in the West, the young Indian puts on the typical costume, featuring a Palm Beach suit and his fraternity pin, and escorts Princess Hot and Cold Running Water to the famous corn festival of his people, taking place at the nearest popcorn stand.
>
> But at a great intertribal ceremonial, we had thousands of real Indians in a pageant of barbaric savage beauty. Just now, an old Navajo said to me through an interpreter what could be translated thus: "The Indian once lived to satisfy his wants. The white man lives always to increase his desires."[9]

Historically, the first man to make an appraisal of the Indian was Christopher Columbus. In a letter to the King and Queen of Spain, he wrote: "I swear to your Majesties that there is not a better people in the world than these; more affectionate, affable, and mild. They love their neighbors as themselves, and they always speak smilingly."[10]

The centuries which have passed since this laudatory evaluation was penned have left their inevitable imprint upon the red man and his culture. Let William Frazier, an Indian from Round Valley, California, speak for his people today:

> We are not a dying race. We are not a miserable race. We are not a vanquished race. No race of people is dying, which in a generation can transform the blanket into a tailored suit, the tepee into a modern bungalow, the feathered headdress into a "The Yanks are coming." This we have done.
>
> There are today many Indians through the nation who are fitting examples for anyone to follow — Indians who have attained enviable stations in life — Indians who are a credit to their country and race.
>
> Into that great melting pot the world calls America, we are pouring no mean, degraded stream. Our contribution may be the rough ore, primitive, but fellow-countrymen, it brings no poisonous alloy from the older putrid melting pots of Europe and Asia.
>
> Oh, Americans! We are primitive; young — we bring to you the supple sinew, the trusting, open mind, the hope, the spirit, the eagerness, the noble purpose of youth; youth, uncowed by fear of failure, youth untainted by surfeit of success. We are eagerly grasping, we are ready.[11]

THE ALGONQUIN FAMILY TREE

chapter 2 THE CHIPPEWA INDIANS OF WISCONSIN, THE specific subject of this study, are of Algonquin lineage; hence a brief consideration of that great linguistic family is in order here.[1] When Columbus discovered America in 1492, the Algonquin territory stretched in an almost solid block from Labrador to the Rockies, and from Hudson Bay to the Cumberland River. This vast area was, however, checkered by Iroquois tribes living in and around the future state of New York and parts of New Foundland. Outlying Algonquin tribes comprised the Shawnee to the south and the Cheyenne and Arapaho to the west. The latter tribe had forced its way through the heart of the Sioux territory, across the Missouri, into the Black Hills, and westward as far as Colorado and Wyoming.

The noted historian of America's epoch of exploration and colonization, Francis Parkman, defines clearly the wide range of Algonquin habitation:

> The vast tract of wilderness from the Mississippi to the Atlantic and from the Carolinas to Hudson's Bay, was divided between two great families of tribes, distinguished by a radical difference of language. A part of Virginia, New Brunswick, Nova Scotia, and lower Canada was occupied, so far as occupied at all by tribes speaking Algonquin languages and dialects. They extended, moreover, along the shores of the Upper Lakes, and into the dreary Northern wastes beyond. They held Wisconsin, Michigan, Illinois, and Indiana, and detached bands ranged the lonely hunting-ground of Kentucky.[2]

David Bushnell, an authority on tribal migrations, holds that the Algonquins originated in the far Northwest and then skirted the shores of the Great Lakes before penetrating the country farther south. Long before the Iroquoian peoples arrived in regions south of the St. Lawrence, some Algonquin tribes had invaded the Tennessee mountains. Others had pushed onward to the Piedmont sections of Virginia and the Carolinas. Stone implements and weapons of great age found in these regions are readily distinguishable from others that were undoubtedly made by later historic tribes of the same areas. The older specimens were evidently fashioned during the early period of occupancy when numerous soapstone quarries were probably opened and worked.[3]

Explorations conducted by the archaeologist, Mark R. Harrington, in 1919 bear witness to three distinct periods of occupancy in the upper valley of the Tennessee. Because of the characteristic form of burial encountered, the first period was termed that of the "Round Grave People." Pottery and stone implements discovered are similar to those found from New England southward to Virginia. The widespread use of soapstone in these localities is another important similarity. The conclusion is that the "Round Grave People" were Algonquins closely related to those of the Middle Atlantic slope or tribes that had been profoundly influenced by the Algonquins.[4]

The Algonquins numbered several hundred tribes or "villages," each independent, although several villages sometimes banded together for protection. To the Algonquin family belong the Algonquins, properly so-called, and the following tribes: Montagnai, Abnaki, Pequot, Narragansett, Delaware, Ottawa, Chippewa, Illinois, Sac, Fox, Pottawotami, Menominee, Cree, Mohegan, Mohican, and Kickapoo.

The Indians with whom the European first came into contact were Algonquins. On this subject, Warren writes:

> The red men who first greeted our Pilgrim Fathers on the rockbound coast of Plymouth and who are so vitally connected with early history, were Algonquins (euphoniously termed by Schoolcraft as "Algics"). The people who treated with good William Penn for the site of the present great city of Philadelphia, and who named him "Me'guon," meaning in the Ojibway language, "a pen" or "feather," were of the Algic stock. The tribes over whom Powhatan, (signifying a dream) ruled as chief, and who are honored under the name of Pocahontas (names so closely connected with that of Captain John Smith, and the early Virginia colonists) belong to this widespread. family. . . . [5]

Despite an epidemic which had depleted their number by the thousands, the Algonquin population was densest in New England. Here were the Mohicans, Pequots, Narrangansetts, Wampanoags, Massachusetts, and Penacooks. These representative specimens of the Algonquin stock tilled the soil. They were thus spared, in some measure, the extremes of misery and degradation to which the wandering tribes were often reduced. Before the epidemic, Champlain and Smith had seen the region studded with wigwams and waving with fields of corn.[6]

Such were the conditions and the distribution of the Algonquin tribes in the early decades of the seventeenth century. Soon territorial disputes arose between the English and French colonists. In the resulting conflicts, the Iroquois allied themselves with the English, while the Algonquins sided with the French. Assisted by the English, the Iroquois compelled some of their Algonquin rivals to flee westward. Among these were the Chippewas whose migratory movement will now be traced.

THE CHIPPEWA INDIANS

chapter 3

BEFORE TRACING THE WESTWARD MOVEMENT OF the Chippewa Indians, it may be well to clarify the confusion that exists between the names "Chippewa" and "Ojibway." Which appellative is correct?

Warren, the noted chronicler of his race, finds a possible origin of the word Ojibway in the puckered seam which distinguishes the moccasins of the tribe. There is, however, a more plausible derivation, corroborated by reliable tribesmen. Since "Ojib" means puckered up and "ubway" means to roast, Warren draws the conclusion that "Ojibway" refers to the manner in which these Indians sometimes tortured their captives. Since Indian names are often derived from some peculiar custom or event, this particular group of Indians acquired the name "Ojibway."[1]

Schoolcraft, another writer of Chippewa history, offers a third theory for the origin of the tribal name "Ojibway." He also holds for the popular derivation of "Chippewa":

> They call themselves Od-jib-way, which is the plural of Odjibwa, a term which appears to denote a peculiarity in their voice, or manner of utterance. This word has been pronounced Chippewa by the Saxon race in America, and is thus recorded in our treaties and history. . . . The term "Chippewa" may be considered as inveterately fixed by modern usage, but in all disquisitions which have their philology or distinctive character in view, the true vernacular term Od-jib-wa, will be found to possess advantages to writers.[2]

Government officials consistently prefer the use of Chippewa to Ojibway. The name Chippewa will hereafter be used exclusively in this work to denote the particular group of Indians under consideration.

Both tradition and history assert that the Chippewa Indians came from the "Great Salt Water" in the east.[3] Three times they halted on their journey westward and erected lodges which they hoped would be permanent; first on the St. Lawrence River, then on the shores of Lake Huron, and lastly at Sault Ste. Marie at the junction of Lakes Superior, Michigan, and Huron. But the lure of the forest led them on to the Chequamegon Bay region on the southern shore of Lake Superior. From Chequamegon, the Chippewa spread like the branches of a tree. Some remained at Chequamegon; a large number migrated farther west; and some retraced their old route and settled around Sault Ste. Marie.

The abundant supply of fish made the Sault Ste. Marie and Chequamegon regions favored localities. Despite attacks by the Sioux Indians and superstitious beliefs which frequently caused them to desert their habitations for relatively long periods of time, the Chippewa gradually acquired all the land surrounding Lake Superior. They established villages at favorite sites until Chippewa habitations extended from Lake Superior to the treeless plains of the Dakotas. This far-flung nation of Indians was, nevertheless, closely united by customs, totemic relationship, language, and the tribal name Ojibway.

The first Chippewa settlement in Wisconsin is said to have been at La Pointe. Here food was plentiful. The creeks and the bay swarmed with fish; the lagoons, filled with tall rushes, were the homes of countless fowls; and wild rice grew in abundance.

In confirmation of the La Pointe claim, Huron Smith, an outstanding Wisconsin ethnologist, says:

The original habitation of the Ojibwe in Wisconsin is supposed to have been at La Pointe, a town no longer in existence, in Ashland County, near Lake Superior. The first reference to them in history is in the Jesuit Relation of 1640, when they resided at Ste. Sault Marie. It is thought that Nicolet met them either in 1634 or 1659. Father Allouez found them at Superior, Wisconsin in 1665-67.

According to Perrot, in 1670-71, those Ojibwe on the Lake Superior shore of Wisconsin cultivated corn and were living peaceably with their neighbors, the Sioux. About this time, they first obtained firearms, and pushed their way westward, fighting with the Sioux and the Meskwaki. The French established a trading post at Shangawawawnikong, afterwards La Pointe, in 1692, which was the most important Ojibwa settlement in Wisconsin.[4]

The village of La Pointe greatly antedated other early Wisconsin settlements such as Ashland and Superior. La Pointe was old before these cities were even dreamed of by white men. It harbored the first white settlers in Wisconsin, Pierre Esprit Radisson and Medard Chouart des Groseilliers, who in 1658, constructed at the head of the bay the first white man's habitation in Wisconsin.[5] These Frenchmen lived peaceably with their red neighbors and joined them in the big winter hunts.[6]

The intrepid missionary, Father Claude Allouez, arrived at La Pointe in 1665 to begin his work among the Chippewa. After two years of indefatigable labor, Father Allouez was succeeded by the zealous Father James Marquette. With admirable tact, the missionary maintained friendship with the Sioux, the inveterate enemies of the Chippewa. Then by treachery and folly, the Ottawas and Hurons, scattered among their Chippewa kinsmen, provoked war with the Sioux. These returned to Father Marquette all the presents that he had given to them and declared war upon the Chippewa. As a result, Father Marquette, the Hurons, the Ottawas, and some of the Chippewa were compelled to evacuate La Pointe in 1761 and flee eastward.[7]

MADELINE ISLAND, SEAT OF THE CHIPPEWA EMPIRE

chapter 4

LA POINTE ON THE CHEQUAMEGON PASSED INTO oblivion when the Sioux declared war upon the Chippewa tribes living in that area, but a greater La Pointe arose some years later on the Apostle Islands. A sketch of these islands will bring the Wisconsin Chippewa into clearer focus.

The Apostle Islands, sometimes called the Enchanted Isles of Keche-Gamme, lie scattered upon the waters of Lake Superior, in the vicinity of Bayfield Peninsula. Although named the Twelve Apostles by early missionaries, there are actually twenty-three islands ranging in size from a mere dot to Madeline with an area of 14,000 acres.[1] In 1774, Jesuit maps published in Paris, refer to the islands as the "Twelve Apostles." Jonathan Carver, the first English traveler to comment on these islands, also refers to them as the Twelve Apostle Islands in his journal written in 1778.[2] James

D. Doty, later territorial governor of Wisconsin, who accompanied Governor Lewis Cass on his official American expedition in 1820, wrote in his journal: "The islands, called by Charlevoix 'the 12 Apostles' extend about 20 miles from point Chebomegon."[3]

Geologists hold that these islands were once part of a mighty promontory which extended many miles out into the lake. The action of glaciers together with winds, waves, and currents cut channels through the promontory forming islands of fantastic shapes. Oak Island is nearly four hundred feet high; Madeline, the largest, is thirteen miles long and averages three miles in width. The coast of these islands is wild and bold; the rocks are in many places worn into grottoes, detached pillars and blocks, deep caverns, lofty arches, and graceful niches. At the slightest agitation of the waters, the sound of the waves reverberates through these rocks. The harmony of colors—the green of pine and spruce and the red and brown of sandstone rocks blended with the blue waters of Lake Superior — fashions these islands into one of Nature's fairy lands.

The Chippewa, however, have their own legendary explanation for the origin of these islands. Long ago, when the world was young, Menabosho, great demi-god of the Chippewa, once cornered his mortal enemy, Great Beaver, in Chequamegon Bay. Menabosho attempted to imprison the beaver by building a dam across the mouth of the bay. In his feverish haste, he let clods of earth slip from his fingers back into the lake. These clods became the Apostle Islands. One of these islands, "Mon-in-wan-e-kan-ing" translated "the place of the golden-breasted woodpecker," has played an important role both in romantic legend and stirring history.[4] When the Jesuits arrived in this region, they named this island St. Michel, an appellative it retained for more than a hundred years.[5] Schoolcraft, who passed through the region in 1820, called the same locality Michael's Island; doubtlessly, because he thought it had been named after Michel Cadotte.

On this island, a second La Pointe was built to supplant the La Pointe on Chequamegon. This new village became the seat of the Chippewa empire and the official headquarters for 12,000 Indians whose domain extended from Michigan westward to Lake Itasca and from Canada southward to Shell Lake, Wisconsin.

But why was St. Michel's island renamed Madeline? A brief survey of the activities of the early French fur traders will furnish the answer to this question.

Although the adventurers and traders, Radisson and Groseilliers, were the first white men in the Chequamegon region, Champlain, the founder of Quebec, had discovered St. Michel Island as early as 1618, the probable date assigned to an Algonquin punitory expedition against the Iroquois.[6] About the time that the Pilgrims were landing on Plymouth Rock, the Chippewa temporarily deserted the island. One reason advanced for this departure was the superstition of the natives. They had practiced cannibalism, eating the bodies of enemies slain in battle. The belief became prevalent that the spirits of these dead haunted the island.[7] Another reason given is that Champlain had given the Indians a supply of firearms; hence they could defend themselves while living on the mainland. This desertion is confirmed by Philip Means, a Smithsonian anthropologist, who maintains that the Chippewa occupied La Pointe (his name for St. Michel) uninterruptedly from 1490 until about 1620 when the island was deserted.[8]

France, in 1671, formally took possession of the Great Lakes country, including the present state of Wisconsin. This was done to offset the influence of Radisson and Groseilliers, who had associated themselves with the English.[9] Competition now entered the fur trading industry. To further strengthen their position, the French sent an envoy, Sieur du Lusson and Monsieur Cadeau, a trader, to negotiate with the tribes engaged in fur trading.[10] The bargaining was successful and many of the Chippewa returned to the island.

In 1693, Pierre le Sueur, an adventurous forest trader, was sent by the French to keep open the Bois Brule and St. Croix routes. This was a measure of expediency because the Fox Indians, partly through cupidity and partly because of injuries perpetrated by the French, made the route to Canada impossible.[11] Le Sueur built the first stockaded fort on St. Michel Island, placed strong palisades of cedar around it, and mounted a cannon for its defense. Of this fort, Philip Means writes: "In 1693 a French fort and an Ojibwa village were built on La Pointe Island, the site was occupied by the tribe with one or two interruptions until the nineteenth century."[12] French fur traders continued to occupy the island until 1763, the close of the French and Indian War.

Two years later, the British took over the fur trading industry under the leadership of Alexander Henry. The latter, noting the efficiency of John Baptiste Cadeau, son of Monsieur Cadeau, took him into partnership. About this time, for reasons not known, Cadeau's name was changed to Cadotte. On one of his trips to Sault Ste. Marie, Cadotte married an Indian woman. The marriage is recorded thus in the Parish Register at Mackinac:

I, the undersigned, missionary priest of the Society of Jesus, acting as rector, have received the mutual assent of Jean Baptiste Cadot, and Anastasia, a neophyte, a daughter of Nipissing, according to the rites of the Holy Roman Church, by which marriage has been legitimatized, Marie Renee, their daughter, about two and a half months old, in the presence of the undersigned witnesses and others, on the 28th of October, 1756, at Michillimackinak.[13]

The Chippewa wife of Cadotte was a woman of great energy and force of character, noted for the influence she exerted over her relatives, the chiefs of the tribe. She was equally successful in her dealings with other Indians. Accompanied only by Canadian *coureurs de bois* to propel her canoes, she journeyed to distant villages to further the interests of her husband. But Mrs. Cadotte is remembered chiefly because she was the mother of two sons, John Baptiste and Michel, names so linked with the Chippewa Indians that the historical importance of St. Michel Island is identified with the name of Cadotte.[14] The Parish Register records the baptism of Michel as follows:

August 13, 1764, I solemnly baptized in the church of this mission, Michel, legitimate son of Jean Baptiste Cadot and of Anastasia, his wife, born at Sault Ste. Marie on the 22nd of July last. . . . P. Du Jaunay, miss. of the society of Jesus.[15]

The Cadotte boys received a good education in Montreal. Later both engaged in the fur trading business, John Baptiste choosing northern Michigan as the scene of his labors and Michel selecting his father's location on St. Michel's Island. Here Michel married Equay-say-way, an Indian princess who was named Madeline at her baptism. Her father, Chief White Crane, pleased with the marriage, re-named the island Madeline in honor of his daughter.[16] From this time on, the fate of the Chippewa was indissolubly linked with that of the fur trade.

THE CHIPPEWA AND THE FUR TRADE

chapter 5

ROMANCE AND ADVENTURE CHARACTERIZED THE early days of the fur trading industry. During certain seasons the trading post presented a carefree, colorful appearance. The inherent love of the French for color was especially displayed in their attire. Beplumed red woolen caps perched jauntily on their heads. Under their blue capes, they wore gaudy beaded sashes from which hung gaily decorated pouches. Deerskin leggings and moccasins protected legs and feet.

Both *voyageurs* and *coureurs de bois* were hearty and gay. Long before the *voyageurs* appeared in sight, their singing could be heard; in fact, a good voice was considered a prerequisite for their success. These men were notorious for their boastfulness and their lack of conventional morality. They possessed, nevertheless, loyalty and faithfulness to their employers, qualities essential for successful fur trading.

Many of these traders had left Montreal because they wanted to be *les gens libres,* free men. The polished manners which they brought with them into the wilderness were used to advantage during the annual meeting with the Indians at the trading post. Business was conducted during the day and merry-making extended far into the night; one report says that at one post thirty gallons of rum were consumed during a single night's revels. Dancing to the music of bagpipe, violin, and flute lasted for days. Despite the handicaps of dress and rough floors, the fur traders danced with grace. The debonair Frenchman found an attractive partner in the dusky maiden of the forest. Then too, the company men from Montreal brought French cooks with them. Great banquets were held in the mess hall. The tables were loaded with delicacies almost unavailable to the woodsmen—bread, cakes, beef, ham, butter, peas, potatoes, tea, and wine.

There were French love and Indian fidelity, but there was also murder. White men with furs were shot down like deer in the forests and Indians with furs were filled with rum and then robbed. One of the principal objectives of the business was to get the Indians "consistently and persistently" drunk. In their desire to present the romantic side of early American life, historians tend to hide much of the hatred and the viciousness that marked the eighteenth and the nineteenth centuries. There was little honor in these fur traders' wars in which rum and bullets played an important role.[1]

The white man's fur trading enterprises with the Indians began with Etienne Brule whom Champlain had educated as an Indian interpreter. In 1610 Brule was sent to spend the winter among Algonquin tribes who lived along the upper reaches of the St. Lawrence River.[2] In company with a group of these Algonquins, Brule returned to Montreal the following spring with a supply of furs. Brule's reports to Champlain indicate that he later carried on trading activities with the Chippewa at the Sault. Moreover, he spent eight years at Huronia, a large Huron village. During this time, he married into the Huron tribe. Brule made extensive exploratory expeditions. From one of these tours, he returned with a nugget of copper—an indication that he was the first white man to see the Lake Superior mines. Unfortunately Brule's dissolute life brought disgrace upon the name of Frenchman. So great was the hatred aroused against Brule, that the Hurons murdered him in 1632.[3]

In 1638 Pierre Radisson and Medard Groseilliers began fur trading activities at La Pointe on the Chequamegon Bay. Two years later, they organized a trading party of one hundred canoes and set out for Montreal. After having traveled some distance, forty of the canoes turned back because of the hostility of the Iroquois. When the remaining sixty canoes reached Montreal with their cargoes, the governor confiscated most of the furs because Radisson and Groseilliers had gone to the Lake Superior territory contrary to his wishes.[4] In retaliation, the two traders joined forces with the English and became promoters of the Hudson Bay Company which was chartered in 1670 by Charles II.[5]

The French fur trade attained permanence through the activities of Sieur du Lusson and Monsieur Cadeau who paved the way for its flourishing establishment on Madeline Island. In 1693 a French trading post was built on this island near the village of La Pointe. In the winter of 1760-61, a dastardly murder committed at the post resulted in its dismantling and its temporary abandonment.[6]

In 1761, the fur trade had received a new impetus when Denys La Ronde built the first sailing vessel on Lake Superior, the "Ottawa," to transport copper to Canada. Later La Ronde, who held the first monopoly of the fur trade on Madeline Island, used the vessel to transport furs.[7]

After the French and Indian War, Alexander Henry, an Englishman, re-established the fur trade on Madeline Island. Before taking up his headquarters on the island, Henry spent a few days at the Sault during which time he took John Baptiste Cadeau, later known as Cadotte, into partnership. These men engaged successfully in the fur trade which was carried on in later years by John Baptiste and Michael, sons of John Baptiste Cadotte.

John Johnston, called "Irish Indian," entered the fur trading industry in the Chequamegon area in 1792. Here he married the daughter of the local Chippewa chief, Waubojeeg.[8] Johnston extended his fur trade to the Sault where he built a trading post in 1794. He lived at the Sault until his death in 1828.[9]

Michael Cadotte continued the fur trading activities of his father, John Baptiste Cadotte, by establishing on Madeline Island the first permanent settlement which is known today as the "Old Fort." He also built a trading post at Lac Courte Oreilles, placing John B. Corbin in charge.[10] After opening the fur trade resources in the Chippewa River district, Cadotte arranged with the Northwest Company for supplies. He purchased annually forty thousand dollars worth of goods which he distributed to the posts on the south shores of Lake Superior and on the Wisconsin, Chippewa, and St. Croix Rivers.

Michael Cadotte has the distinction of being the first fur trader in direct charge of the original post on Superior Bay. He was also the first fur trader to gain control of the industry at the sources of the Chippewa River. Year after year, he kept moving his posts farther to the west and to the north, leading the Chippewa into more prolific but also more dangerous hunting grounds. Some of these posts were built as far north as Winnipeg, Canada, and as far west as Thief River, Minnesota. Although Michael Cadotte's headquarters were on Madeline Island, it is a well established fact that one of his trading posts was at or near the present city of Chippewa Falls. Here, a son, also named Michael, was born in 1791.[11] Other trading posts in Wisconsin were at Yellow Lake, Snake River, and Pokaguma in the St. Croix area.

The younger John Baptiste Cadotte, upon his graduation from college, received forty thousand francs which he immediately invested in the Northwestern Fur Company. From his headquarters on Chequamegon Bay, he sent large numbers of beaver skins to the Montreal market. Cadotte's spendthrift habits and his generosity to

his Indian relatives cost him his fortune. Desiring to retrieve his
losses, John Cadotte decided to make the headwaters of the Mississippi the next scene of his labors, but he lacked the necessary
funds for the venture. Alexander Henry, who had been in partnership with Cadotte's father, gave him the needed financial assistance.
Cadotte's reputation for courage and fearlessness easily attracted to
him a large number of *coureurs du bois* and trappers and a few
Iroquois Indians to assist him in his undertaking. On this fur trading
route extending from Sault Ste. Marie to Cass Lake, Minnesota,
Cadotte collected a large quantity of furs. His prodigality, however,
again led him to bankruptcy and he was obliged to seek another
means of livelihood. Cadotte found employment with the Northwest
Fur Company and labored with such vigor and energy that he
regained the esteem and confidence of the firm. In order to give
Cadotte an opportunity to retrieve his fortunes and to pay his debts,
the Northwest Fur Company now entrusted to him the entire Fond
du Lac Department on a share basis.[12] This region included not
only the end of Lake Superior westward from Chequamegon but
also the district drained by the St. Louis River and its tributaries.[13]
This time Cadotte succeeded.

The influence of Michael Cadotte on the fur trade was ad-
vanced by the marriage of two of his daughters to Lyman and
Truman Warren.[14] After his marriage to Mary Cadotte, Lyman
Warren associated himself with Charles Ermatinger, a Scotch fur
trader. Some time later, the Warren brothers purchased Michael
Cadotte's fur trading interests at the Lac du Flambeau and the
Lac Courte Oreilles posts. In 1836, Lyman Warren, together with
Jean Brunet and Michael Dousman, built the first sawmill at
Chippewa Falls, Wisconsin. Warren continued, however, to work
in the fur trade, serving also, as subagent and farmer at a govern-
ment post located near Chippewa City.[15]

Truman Warren, after his marriage to Charlotte Cadotte, joined
his brother Lyman and Charles Ermatinger in the fur trading
business. He was active in Michigan territories, extending from
Mackinac to Detroit and also maintained Wisconsin posts at Lac du
Ermatinger Falls and still later, to Jim Falls, its present name.[16]
cut short by his death in 1825. A few years later, his widow married
James Ermatinger, son of Charles Ermatinger. In 1840, the Ermatingers came down the Chippewa River and established a trading
post at Vermillion Rapids about eleven miles north of the present
city of Chippewa Falls. The name of the settlement was changed to
Ermantinger Falls and still later, to Jim Falls, its present name.[16]

Thus the fur trading activities begun by Monsieur Cadeau were continued in an unbroken line by his descendants until this industry was superseded by other enterprises.

The American Fur Trade, as an industry of importance, extended over a period of more than two hundred years, reaching its zenith between the years 1820 to 1840. Although the French lost control of all their possessions in North America after the French and Indian War, Frenchmen, nevertheless, continued to be active in the fur trade either as independent fur traders or as partners with the English.[17]

The methods employed by John Jacob Astor, the head of the American Fur Company, to attain a monopoly of the fur trade were not always above reproach. At the 1815-16 session of Congress, through the influence of Mr. Astor, the Secretary of War designated certain points throughout the Indian country as most suitable for trading establishments and licenses to traders were confined to these localities. This was done to favor the American Fur Company, for if a license was granted to an adventurous trader not connected with the Company, he was only permitted to trade at some designated place already occupied by the American Fur Company. This rich company then sold their goods at half their real value and the new trader, unable to compete with them, finally left the field.[18]

However, Astor's policy in dealing with the Indians was superior to that exercised by the United States government. The agents of the latter had an idea, then prevalent, that the Indians wanted the cheapest goods in exchange for their furs. The British traders, on the other hand, had furnished the Indians with substantial goods and had taken special pains, when they had an inferior article, to call it American. Astor tried to secure suitable goods for the Indians in exchange for their furs.[19]

THE CHIPPEWA AND THE WHITE NATIONS

chapter 6

DURING THE THREE CENTURIES THAT FOLLOWED the Chippewa Indians' first contacts with the white man, five classes of people left their impact upon the tribe. These classes are represented by the explorer, the missionary, the trader, the settler, and the government agent. The relationships of the traders and these classes will be considered in the order of chronology.

With a view to future fur trade, Samuel Champlain, founder of New France, established friendly relations with the Chippewa at Sault Ste. Marie in 1609. The following year, Champlain dispatched a number of Frenchmen into Indian areas to acquire a knowledge of the Chippewa language. These men, among whom was Etienne Brule, acted as interpreters in fur trade transactions.

To further the interests of France, Champlain sent Jean Nicolet in 1634 to meet strange "People of the Sea," who lived in the country lying beyond Lake Huron. Nicolet's mission was to restore peace among warring tribes and to establish friendly relations between these tribes and the French. Although Nicolet, the discoverer and the first explorer of the region that now includes the state of Wisconsin, may not have come into direct contact with the Chippewa, he met other tribes of Algonquin lineage. Among these tribes were the Menominee, the Winnebago—People of the Sea—the Mascouten, and the Potawatomi. Since these tribes intermingled with the Chippewa, Nicolet's mission also had a direct bearing upon the Chippewa Indians.[1]

Another explorer of note to make contacts with the Chippewa was Nicholas Perrot, who was sent by the French envoy, Sieur de St. Lusson, in 1671, to invite the Chippewa to a great council of tribes at Sault Ste. Marie. The Chippewa response to the invitation was gratifying to the French. These contacts of French explorers with the Chippewa established relations advantageous to the fur trading enterprise.

The missionary group set a new pattern in white and Chippewa relations. The missionary was interested in the Indians as people —

in both their physical and spiritual welfare. He lived among them, ate their food, and instructed their children. The Indians sensed the difference between the motives of the missionary and those of the explorer; consequently, the missionary was called by some Indians, "the first good white man." The work of the missionary will be considered more fully in a later chapter.

The traders' livelihood depended upon the fur trade. Therefore, they maintained friendly relations with the natives. In exchange for pelts, the traders gave the Indians anything they liked or needed — ammunition, firearms, knives, axes, cloth, paint, mirrors, beads, and rum. Different tactics were used by the French and the English in this exchange — a fact that accounts for many later developments. Since the French had the earlier dealings with the Indians, their procedures will be considered first.

From that day in 1609, when Champlain joined his Huron-Algonquin neighbors on their warpath against the Iroquois, the French, both in principle and in practice, held to the policy of making friends with the Indians. The Indians were flattered, petted, and treated with ceremonial respect. But the very disposition of the French was perhaps the most effective force in establishing and maintaining the generally harmonious relations that marked this nation's dealings with the Chippewa.

In contrast with the English, the French made no attempt to extort huge cessions of land from the Indians. They applied to the tribe for the privilege of using the land, whether for residence or for passage. In 1671, when Nicholas Perrot was sent to the Chippewa village Shag-a-waum-ik-ong to invite the Indians to a council at Sault Ste. Marie, the Chippewa responded with alacrity. Warren describes the proceedings of the council thus:

> The envoy of the French king asked, in the name of his nation, for permission to trade in the country, and for free passage to and from their villages all times thereafter. He asked that the fires of the French and Ojibway nations might be made one, and everlasting. He promised the protection of the great French nation against all their enemies, and addressing himself to the Chippeway chieftain from La Pointe, he said:
> "Every morning you will look towards the rising of the sun and you shall see the fire of your French father reflecting towards you, to warm you and your people. If you are in trouble, you, the Crane, must arise in the skies and cry your far sounding voice, and I will hear you. The fires of your French father shall last forever, and warm his children." [2]

After this speech, Sieur de St. Lusson placed a heart-shaped gold medal on the breast of Ke-che-ne-zuh-yauh, chief of the Chippewa. This mark of honor conferred by the French envoy in the name of King Louis XIV, confirmed Ke-che-ne-zuh-yauh's right as chief of the Lake Superior Chippewa. The Indians received the "heart" of the French and accepted their proposals of peace, protection, and mutual support. From that day, the Chippewa called the French king "Father," and their lands were opened to French enterprise.[3]

Another factor contributing to French success was the intermarriage between the traders and their *engages*. The French adapted themselves so completely to the Indian mode of living that they actually participated in the assemblies and ceremonial practices of the Indians. Count Frontenac is said to have considerably livened the war dance by his participation in full war paint. The language of each race was easily learned by the other; in their meetings, bilingual conversation flowed freely and smoothly, and contributed greatly to their mutual enjoyment. So rapidly were the French absorbed into the Indian race that the stream of French immigration to the Chippewa has been likened to water poured on sand.

The Chippewa were generally hostile toward the English or "Shaug-un-aush." Parkman offers a plausible explanation for this hostility: The English, by their association with the Indians, became barbarians; unlike the French, they did not become Indians. Another reason for the enmity of the Chippewa was the defeat of the French by the English and the consequent loss of French dominion and power. This failure of the French was a mortifying blow to their allies, among whom were the Chippewa. Consequently when the victorious English established themselves in the forts and posts formerly owned and operated by the French, the Chippewa regarded them with poorly disguised hatred. There was a still further reason for this attitude. The English officers, unlike the French, treated the Indians with coldness and harshness; the brutal soldiers greeted them with oaths, menaces, and sometimes blows.[4] Because of this overbearing conduct on the part of the English, Pontiac's call for warriors to take up the hatchet against the English and restore French power was welcomed by the Chippewa, who formed a large contingent of Pontiac's valiant but fickle force. The subsequent defeat of Pontiac's war policy further intensified the scorn and the hatred that marked the respective relationships between the English and the Chippewa.

Following the Revolutionary War, the Americans, as a nation, did not take part to any great extent in the fur trade among the Chippewa until after the War of 1812. The Chippewa of the upper Mississippi date their first dealings with the Americans, "Long Knives," from the official visit of Lieutenant Zebulon Pike who had been sent to order the British from the Minnesota woods. Since the Chippewa had been trading principally with the British, all the chiefs wore badges and medals of Great Britain. When Pike reached Leech Lake, where the Northwest Fur Company was operating under British auspices, he hoisted for the first time, the stars and stripes over the trading post. On this occasion, the young Pillager chief and warrior, Esh-ka-bug-e-coshe, exchanged his British flag and medal for a United States flag and medal. Later the chief declared that he had ceased to be an Englishman and had become a "Long Knife." [5]

Some settlements, including Prairie du Chien and Mackinac, were the seat of much trouble; British malignity aroused a spirit of unrest. Some of the Indians concluded that while the "Long Knives" claimed to rule the Northwest, England had the long arm and bestowed gifts upon them. Since Washington was far away, there was no visible ruler to enforce law and order; consequently the Indians decided they could dispense with national authority. British trappers and fur traders continued to distribute rum, thus retaining the friendship of the Indians.

In 1820, the Federal government, to strengthen the notion that there was a United States, sent a special commission to the Lake Superior and the upper Mississippi regions. This delegation was to ascertain the true condition of the upper border country, interview the Indians, and inform them that they were allied to the United States. British traders, however, persisted in a campaign of insidious propaganda. As a result, the Indians went directly to the English for advice and made surprise attacks upon the Americans.

When the delegation reached St. Mary's River at the head of Lake Superior, it found the Chippewa so defiant of United States authority that they had hoisted the British flag over the chief's tent. General Cass, the leader of the commission, immediately acted with courage and decision. He stalked to the chief's tent, tore down the British flag, and threw it on the ground. [6] But for the intervention of a Chippewa woman who pacified the Indians, this incident might have resulted in disorder and bloodshed.

After interviewing the Indians in the Michigan area, the expedition proceeded to La Pointe on Madeline Island. Here the

Americans held an assembly with the Chippewa and assured them that the Americans were friends of the Red Men and that the United States was a well-disposed nation.

The impact of the westward movement upon Indian life was far reaching. White settlers wanted what the Indian needed for his existence, land and its natural resources. To the settler, the Indian was an obstacle to his exploitation of the land's natural wealth. The statement "The only Indian who is a good Indian, is a dead Indian," probably originated at this time. American settlers in Wisconsin were even less popular with the Chippewa than the English had been. Many dishonorable acts marked the westward progress of the Americans which began after Black Hawk's War in 1832. The on-coming settlers, confident of protection from the United States armed forces, provoked wars with the natives. The Indians, invariably the losers, were penalized by having their lands confiscated. Steadily the Indian territory diminished until the natives found themselves deprived of garden plots and game preserves. To this situation might be applied the words of Rufus Choate who remarked that the Pilgrims, upon reaching America, "first landed on their knees and then on the aborigines."

The fifth class of white men who dealt with the Indians were the government agents. In early days, government agents were army officers who officially represented the government but who also served the interests of the settlers by gradually helping to dispossess the Indians of their lands. When the Indian lands were taken over by the white settlers, the Indians were moved to reservations which were soon despoiled of many of their natural resources by the white men. Deprived of a means of livelihood, the Indians turned to the government agents for help. The effect of this system on Indian psychology was well summed up by Gus Big Man of the Crow tribe: "Once we had the buffalo. The buffalo gave us our food, our clothing, our houses, our tools, our fuel. Then the White Men came and killed our buffalo. Now the White Man is our buffalo." [7]

The results of this contact between the races was disappointing. It had been supposed that the Indian would adopt civilization, but the reverse frequently happened. The French fell under the spell of Indian habits and customs and the Indians acquired a variegated line of new and strange vices. In many instances, the English fur traders and settlers flung off the restraints of civilization and became barbarians; but, unlike the French, they did not become Indians.

Warren, the Chippewa historian, attributes the cause of this failure to the class of Frenchmen who mingled with the Chippewa.

He claims that they were nearly as illiterate, ignorant, and superstitious as the Indians themselves, and many were inferior to the red man in strength of character and in morality.[8]

John Bardon, pioneer and historian of Lake Superior country, viewed the results of this association of races in a different light. He wrote:

A gentleman asked me the other day if the Chippewa "Half-breed" developed the good or bad traits of the union of a white man and a Chippewa squaw. I told him as far as I could see, the offspring was on the whole benefited; that is, he received an education, and was better fitted to cope with the problems of the immediate times.[9]

Mr. Bardon mentioned several half-breeds who lived in Superior — the Gordons, Morrisons, Cournoyers, La Faves, and others — who possessed outstanding characters. Excellent Chippewa half-breeds were also found on Madeline Island among whom were the Cadottes, Warrens, and Ermatingers. Many of these were descendants of French-Indian parents, but Mr. Bardon affirmed that other nationalities, such as the Scotch, Irish, Germans, Scandinavians, Swiss, Finns, and even a Chinese who intermarried with the Chippewa produced promising progeny. But it may be safely stated that France was the first, last, and only white nation that ever gained the full confidence and complete good will of the Chippewa tribe in its entirety.

CHIPPEWA RELATIONS WITH THE IROQUOIS, THE FOX, AND THE SIOUX

chapter 7

BEFORE THE ARRIVAL OF THE WHITE MAN IN Wisconsin, several events of major importance greatly affected the Chippewa. First preserved by tradition, the account of these happenings was later put in writing by such Chippewa historians as William Warren and George Copway, who both wrote at a period when the incidents recorded were still fresh in the memory of the Chippewa.

As has been noted before, the Chippewa had emigrated from the East to the areas occupied by them at the time of their discovery by the white man. When the Chippewa settled in the Lake Superior area, they were surrounded by fierce enemies, the Fox and the Sioux. Moreover, the Chippewa were obliged to continue their ancient feud with the Iroquois, who occupied areas in the East.

The savage Iroquois who comprised the confederacy known as the Five Nations, had subjugated, incorporated, and destroyed or put to flight all the neighboring tribes. Although their war incursions extended even to the remote Illinois, the Iroquois were cautious about appearing in the Chippewa country. They had learned on several occasions that to wage war upon the Chippewa was to invite a reprisal upon themselves.

The final important battle between the Chippewa and the Iroquois occurred about 1750 on Lake Superior, a short distance above its outlet, now known as Point Iroquois. Ke-che-wash-keenh or Great Buffalo was chief of the Chippewa at La Pointe. The Chippewa, deciding to take the offensive, collected a war party on the shores of Lake Superior and proceeded eastward against the enemy. One evening they encamped on the lake shore a short distance from Sault Ste. Marie. After they had lighted their fires and prepared the evening meal, the sounds of distant revelry fell upon their alert ears. Scouts were immediately dispatched to investigate the noisy party whom the Chippewa supposed to be traders. But the scouts soon returned on the run with the information that a large war party of Iroquois were encamped on the other side of the point. These

Iroquois were drinking firewater and carousing, apparently with every sense of security.

The Chippewa quickly extinguished their fires, made the usual preparations for a desperate fight, and noiselessly surrounded the encampment of their boisterous enemies. The Chippewa waited until nearly all the Iroquois had drunk themselves insensible, and the remainder had fallen asleep. Then a signal was given for the onset and the Chippewa attacked the Iroquois with such fury that few escaped the Chippewa tomahawks and scalping knives. This Chippewa victory ended the long and fierce warfare between these two tribes. The Iroquois never again made an incursion into the country of the Lake Superior Chippewa.[1]

Simultaneously with the Iroquois conflict, arose the strife commonly known as the Sioux-Chippewa feud. This term is not entirely correct since it implies that only two distinct tribes were involved. Instead it was a conflict between the Chippewa and the Sioux and Foxes.

At every step of their westward advance along the southern shores of the Great Lakes, the Chippewa battled with the Foxes and the Sioux. Nevertheless, they pressed onward until they lit their fires on the sandy point of Chequamegon and finally encamped on Madeline Island. Although the highest point of the island is about two miles from the mainland, the Chippewa were not safe from the attacks of the Sioux. On one occasion, a war party of Sioux found its way to a point off the main shore of the lake. During the night, two of their number crossed the lake, each swimming by the side of a log. When they reached the island, they attacked a family who were fishing by torchlight. With four scalps and the canoe of their unfortunate victims, the Sioux departed. The next morning when the Chippewa discovered the mangled bodies of their dead, a determined band of warriors collected to avenge the deed. Their pursuit of the Sioux was long but unavailing. Similar skirmishes between the Chippewa and the Sioux continued for almost two centuries.

Shortly after the Iroquois had been vanquished, the Chippewa defeated the Foxes in a series of ambuscades. These Indians had drawn upon themselves the hatred of nearly every other tribe in the area because of their war-like propensities and provocative raids. The Chippewa drove them from the headwaters of the St. Croix and Chippewa Rivers southward to the Wisconsin River. About 1774, the Foxes made a last tribal effort to regain a portion of their former territory. Ascending the broad Mississippi in war canoes, they proceeded up the St. Croix River. Here they encountered a war party of Chippewa who immediately engaged them in conflict. After a short but severe contest, the Foxes were defeated. They withdrew southward far from the reach of the Chippewa war-clubs.[2]

One of the bloodiest battles recounted in the Sioux-Chippewa annals was fought on a balmy October day in 1842 on the shores of the Brule River. A messenger relayed to Chief Buffalo the information that the Sioux, under the leadership of the bloodthirsty Chief Old Crow, were headed for the Brule to give battle. Unfortunately the war party of the Chippewa under Chief Hole-in-the-Day was near the Mississippi and of no immediate assistance. But Chief Buffalo acted quickly and mustered about two hundred warriors. The Sioux held the west side of the river and the Chippewa, the east. Since both parties arrived at the Brule at sunset, pickets kept a careful watch during the night, fully aware that daylight would find them in combat.

At daybreak, the banks of the river bristled with savages armed with war clubs and knives. Clever Chief Buffalo had devised a cunning ruse. He had noticed an almost perpendicular bluff rising from 50 to 80 feet in height on the east side of the Brule. When the signal for battle was sounded, the Chippewa were to run toward the bluff, thus pretending weakness of numbers. The waters of the Brule at the east bank were about three feet deep and the bank was two or three feet above the water. Whether the Sioux were aware of this geographical feature is not known, but the Chippewa relied upon it for victory. The signal for battle was given. The Sioux, noting the simulated flight of the Chippewa, expected an easy victory.

A howling, surging mass of Sioux warriors rushed into the Brule, each trying to outrival the other in getting the greatest number of Chippewa scalps. They did not know that Chippewa braves lay concealed along the bank, awaiting the appearance of a Sioux scalp lock above the water. On came the Sioux, knives raised aloft, but the Chippewa disposed of them as fast as they came within reach. The Sioux, because of their position in the water, were unable to use their clubs and knives before they had scaled the banks of the river which soon ran red with the blood of the Sioux.[3]

An eyewitness of one of these Chippewa-Sioux encounters which took place near the present village of Danbury, Wisconsin, related the following:

> The main camp of the Chippewa in this area was on high bluffs overlooking the St. Croix River near the present village of Solon Springs. One day, Chippewa scouts spread the alarm that

Chippewa and Sioux

a large band of Sioux were headed for the village. The Chippewa worked day and night erecting mounds from which they
planned to fire upon the Sioux as they passed in their canoes.
But the Sioux detected their stratagem and pitched camp on an
island opposite the shore of the lake.

Sometime during the night, our warriors, under the leadership of Ya banse, divested themselves of everything but their
breechclouts and swam across the river to this island. The Sioux
guards were dispatched without alarming the village. Each
group then stealthily approached a wigwam. A signal was given
to begin the attack. Tomahawks were wielded unmercifully.
Some of the women and children were permitted to escape,
only to be captured later. Except for these few, the entire Sioux
party was massacred.

Early the next morning, the few survivors were loaded
into their canoes and told to proceed on their journey. Before
departing, they were given the following instructions: "Go!
Return to your people bearing this message. This land is ours;
ours to keep. Those who come within our boundaries will meet
the same fate as your party did. Your country begins below the
falls. Come no farther upstream than these falls. (The falls
mentioned are known as St. Croix Falls.) All the country above
the falls is ours." [4]

These signal victories of the Chippewa over the Sioux won for
the Chippewa the coveted inland lakes and streams which teemed
with fish and were lush with wild rice.[5] Gradually the Chippewa
gained possession of all the territory near the headwaters of the
Mississippi and the Rainy Lake country, an area embracing all the
territory between the western shore of Lake Superior and the
western plains.

As a peace overture, the Sioux,[6] at one time, endeavored to
enlist the aid of the Chippewa in a war against the United States.
Sioux emissaries contacted the Lake Superior Chippewa to ascertain
their opinion on the matter. The most influential Chippewa of this
area, assembled in council, gave the following reply to the Sioux
proposal:

The Chippewa cannot involve themselves in a war when the
cause of this conflict does not concern them. We have made
treaties with the United States which we promised will be in
force as long as the sun rises and sets, as long as the rivers flow,
and the grass grows. We have pledged ourselves to peace and

have smoked the pipe with the white man, and have taken his hand in friendship. We will not break our pledge. We are given no reason to fight. The war which the Sioux are engaged in now is their affair and not ours. So go in peace and tell your tribe of our decision.[7]

It is significant to note that the Lake Superior Chippewa never engaged in armed conflict with the United States army.

It remained for William F. Cody, Buffalo Bill, to bring the Chippewa and the Sioux together in a final and lasting peace at Ashland, Wisconsin. There they formally buried the hatchet on September 11, 1896, after an enmity of more than 200 years. Buffalo Bill, former Chief Scout of the United States army, and Lieutenant W. A. Mercer, Indian Agent at Ashland, called the peace council. About 400 Wisconsin Chippewa and 100 Ogallalla and Brule Sioux from the Dakotahs met on the grounds behind Buffalo Bill's circus tent.[8]

Chief Cloud, "Ana-wad," a Chippewa, opened the council by saying: "In days gone by, we were enemies, but now I come to you with a feeling in my mind as pure as the flag I carry (white). The members of my band present are only a small portion of our real number. My chiefs, also all of the braves, are pleased to have this opportunity of seeing you." [9]

Chief Flat Iron, whom Buffalo Bill characterized as "a son-of-a-gun on wheels," replied:

My friend, I give you what is in my mind. Thirty years ago, the Great Father wanted us to be peaceable, both Americans and Indians. There was trouble in those days, but we all go by one God. Why we had trouble among ourselves, we don't know. In our way, we introduced each other by the pipe. That means forever. At all times, the pipe is foremost. My people at home will be glad when I tell them of this day. . . . God knows that we are to make peace and He gave us a good day to meet.[10]

The peace pipe was passed and the Indians shook hands. To strengthen the bonds of friendship, a tableau was arranged in which a small Sioux girl and an equally diminutive Chippewa boy held hands.

At the conclusion of the peace council, Buffalo Bill remarked:

I am proud to have been instrumental in bringing together some of the representative men of the largest Indian tribes in the world. In over twenty-three years, the Sioux have smoked the pipe of peace only once with other tribes. Today's meeting has the greatest historical importance as it is held right on the scene of the ancient battlefields of these people.

This meeting will, in a sense, be a civilizer to the Sioux. When they return home, they will repeat every word the Chippewa said. You noticed that Flat Iron asked the Chippewa twice if they were getting aid from the government. The Chippewa told them that they do not receive annuities but support themselves. It will be a lesson to the Sioux. The Sioux are a prairie Indian and have not made as much progress in civilization as the Chippewa have.[11]

In 1939, a delegation of Chippewa and Sioux Indians met at Battle Hollow Park, Stillwater, Minnesota. After smoking the peace pipe, they participated in the dedication of a marker where these tribes had fought for the supremacy of the St. Croix valley. Father Philip Gordon, Chippewa Indian and Catholic priest at Centuria, Wisconsin, unveiled the monument.[12]

Thus ended the feud that had existed for centuries between the Sioux of the prairie and the Chippewa of the forest.

RELIGIOUS BELIEFS

chapter 8

THE CHIPPEWA, IN COMMON WITH ALL OTHER American aborigines, believed in the existence of a host of spirits or gods, both good and evil, all designated by the term "manitou." In addition to spirits, persons who appeared to be endowed with special characteristics or who had acquired special abilities or powers were regarded as manitous.[1] This worship of multiple gods by the Chippewa did not result in great ceremonial tribal gatherings such as took place among the agricultural and buffalo-hunting tribes, but rather developed into the practices of the Midewiwin secret society. Some of the Chippewa, however, believed in one god who was superior to and dominated all the others.

For the Chippewa, the skies were filled with the deities whom they worshipped, and the tenants of the forest were awakened by the whispers of the gods. Each mountain and valley, each lake and stream, sheltered some deity. However, the favorite resorts of the gods were the peaks of rocky cliffs or the clefts of craggy mountains. Waterfalls were the scene of their sporting activities. The chief god of the sky sometimes amused himself by hurling stars from their positions and thereby bringing perplexity and harm to the inhabitants of earth. This god of the skies could also be heard in the gentle breeze or in the howl of the tempest.

Constellations were the council gatherings of the gods. The brightest stars were the ruling spirits appointed by the Great Spirit as guardians of the lesser ones. Clusters of stars were the populous cities of the celestial inhabitants. Each star was associated with some strange event.[2]

Although the sun was the wigwam of the Great Spirit, few of the northern Indians ever held the idea that the sun was an object of worship. If the day was fair, when great councils were held or when medicine worship was in progress, the Chippewa thought that the Great Spirit smiled upon them. If the sky was cloudy, the Great Spirit was displeased. This Great Spirit, "Ke-sha-mon-e-doo," or Benevolent Spirit, governed the universe, ruling under different titles, such as the "god of war," and the "god of fish."[3]

Wigwam stories teemed with mention of high-born personages descending to earth to dwell among the people and vice versa, men ascending and dwelling in the skies. The Chippewa affirmed that animals sometimes received wings from heaven. Spirits of the forest clothed themselves with moss and, during a shower of rain, thousands of them found shelter in a flower. The Chippewa saw myriads of them sporting in the sun's rays and detected their tiny voices in the hum of an insect.

A medicine god presided over the most noted herbs of the earth. Men and women who considered themselves capable of learning the virtues of roots from this god, often fasted to gain his favor. During times of war, warriors carried certain roots with them to prevent injury from enemy fire balls. Indian youth underwent fastings of considerable length in order to gain the good will of the medicine god.

Young Indians were not allowed to speak the name of the Great Spirit without proper marks of reverence. George Copway, a Chippewa historian, wrote: "There was a time when they did not take the name of the Lord in vain, but this habit some have acquired since being civilized!" Both good and evil resulted from the conversation between the red man and the white man. The same author

continued: "As it is, there are children who, as soon as their tongues
get in shape, use them to blaspheme their Creator. I never heard a
man swear without it causing my blood to run cold. Why, pale face,
let me tell you, the Bad Spirit is a saint to such a man." [4]

Many Chippewa lived in a state of mental bondage to a class of
men who officiated as their priests or soothsayers. The latter founded
their claims to supernatural powers on early fastings, dreams, ascetic
habits, and often on charms and incantations. They were provided
with a bag of mystic objects, such as the hollow bones of some large
animals, carved representations of animals, bits of hair, hoofs, claws,
and sea shells. Some of these men acquired such a reputation for
sanctity that they turned their influence to political purposes, either
personally or through some popular warrior, as was the case of the
sachems Little Turtle and Tecumseh.[5]

William Warren offers the following exposition of Chippewa
belief:

It is a general fact that most people who have been discovered
living in a savage and unenlightened state, and even whole
nations living in partial civilization, have been found to be
idolators — having no just conception of a great first Cause or
Creator, invisible to human eyes, and pervading all space. With
the Ojibways it is not so; the fact of their firm belief and great
veneration, in an overruling Creator and Master of Life, has
been noticed by all who have had close intercourse with them
since their earliest discovery. It is true that they believe in a
multiplicity of spirits which pervade all nature, yet all these
are subordinate to the one Great Spirit of Good.

This belief is as natural (if not more so), as the belief of
the Catholics in their interceding saints, which in some respects
it resembles, for in the same light as intercessors between him
and the Great Spirit, does the more simple Red Man regard the
spirits which in his imagination pervade all creation. The never-
failing rigid fasts of first manhood, when they seek in dreams
for a guardian spirit, illustrates this belief more forcibly.

Ke-che-mun-e-do (Great Spirit) is the name used by the
Ojibways for the being equivalent to our God. They have another term which can hardly be surpassed by any one word in
the English language, for force, condensity, and expression,
namely: Ke-zha-mune-do, which means pitying, charitable,
overruling, guardian and merciful spirit; in fact, it expresses all
of the great attributes of the God of Israel. . . . There is nothing

to equal the veneration with which the Indian regards this unseen being. They seldom even ever mention his name unless in their Me-da-we and other religious rites and in their sacrificial feasts; and then an address to him, however trivial, is always accompanied with a sacrifice of tobacco or some other article deemed precious by the Indians. They never use his name in vain, and there is no word in their language expressive of a profane oath, or equivalent to the many words used in profane swearing by their more enlightened white brethren.[6]

The Chippewa believed that their home, after death, lay westward. In their terminology, they styled it "Ke-wa-kun-on," "homeward road"; oftener, it was called "Che-ba-kun-ah," "road of souls." Before consigning their dead to the grave, the old men addressed the deceased thus: "Ke-go-wa-se-kah," "You are going homeward." [7]

The Chippewa manner of burial was also an indication of religious belief. When a man was buried, all articles needed in life were buried with him — moccasins, blanket, flint, kettle, and gun. If a woman was buried, these articles were interred with her: moccasins, portage collar, blanket, kettle, and ax. The Chippewa believed that immediately after death, the soul stood on a deep beaten path which lay westward. The first object met by the soul was the great Oda-e-min (heart berry) or strawberry which stood on the roadside like a huge rock. The soul took a handful of this fruit for its journey.

Then the soul traveled until it reached a deep, rapid stream of water over which lay the much dreaded Go-go-gau-o-gun or rolling and sinking bridge. If, after having safely crossed this bridge, the soul chanced to look back, it would discover that the bridge had assumed the form of a huge serpent swimming, twisting, and untwisting its folds across the stream. After traveling over prairie country by day and camping by night, the soul after four days, arrived in the land of spirits. Here it found all its relatives assembled together with all mankind since creation — all rejoicing, singing, and dancing. This land, interspersed with lakes and streams, forests and prairies, abounded in fruits and game. It contained all that the red man coveted in life and that he considered essential to his happiness. Here he could enjoy the kind of life for which his manner of living on earth had fitted him.[8]

By way of summary, it may be said that the Chippewa recognized a Supreme Being to whom they offered reverence and worship. However, their warped ideas and superstitious practices made their cult almost unworthy of the name religion. Only the vivifying power of the Gospel of Christ could lift them from their degraded state.

THE CHIPPEWA RECEIVE THE GOSPEL

chapter 9

SCARCELY A HISTORIC SITE IN THE NORTHWEST can be named which a voyageur or a trader did not reach before the "Black Robe" or the "Brown Robe," yet the majority of the former left but a slight impression upon their environment in comparison with the permanent heritage of spiritual values and practical culture bequeathed by the latter. Since these emissaries of Christianity were concerned chiefly with redeeming the Indians from savagery and winning them to a Christian way of life, they disregarded the pangs of starvation and the bitterness of persecution to a degree almost beyond belief.

Although Francis Parkman's opinion of the missionaries and the motives which prompted their zeal is frequently clouded with prejudice, he has paid this tribute to them:

> Their story is replete with marvels — miracles of patient suffering and daring enterprise. They were the pioneers of northern America. We see them among the frozen forests of Acadia struggling on snowshoes with some wandering Algonquin horde or crouching in the crowded hunting lodge half stifled in the smoky den and battling with troops of famished dogs for the last morsel of sustenance. . . . Jesuit explorers traced the St. Lawrence to its source and said Mass among the solitude of Lake Superior where the boldest fur trader scarcely dared to follow.[1]

The first missionaries to visit the Northwest were Fathers Isaac Jogues and Charles Raymbaut, members of the Society of Jesus. In 1641, these intrepid heralds of the Gospel arrived on the shores of Lake Huron where some 2000 Algonquin Indians, among whom were the Chippewa, had assembled to celebrate a great "Feast of the Dead." The Chippewa were attracted to the Black Robes and invited them to visit their tribe. The missionaries accepted the invitation with joy. After a voyage of seventeen days in their frail canoe, Fathers Jogues and Raymbaut reached the rapids of Lake Michigan which they named Sault Ste. Marie. These two men could remain

but a short time with the Chippewa. Father Raymbaut died soon
after leaving them and Father Jogues entered upon his glorious
career among the Iroquois which ended in his martyrdom.[2]

The next attempt to evangelize the Algonquin Indians of the
Northwest was made in 1656. Fifty canoes carrying 250 Ottawa had
arrived in Quebec. When about to depart, these Indians requested
that missionaries accompany them and preach the gospel in their
country. Fathers Leonard Garreau, S.J., and Gabriel Dreuillettes,
S.J., complied with their request. Unfortunately these Ottawa fell
into an Iroquois ambush near Montreal and a number of Ottawa
were killed and others were seriously wounded. Father Garreau,
whose spine was broken by a bullet, was captured and dragged into
an Iroquois fort. After suffering intense pain for three days, he was
brought by his captors to Montreal where he died. The Ottawa who
escaped capture, secretly embarked during the night. They refused
Father Dreuillettes' plea to permit him to accompany them. Sixteen
years later, however, Father Dreuillettes was laboring with great
zeal among the Chippewa at Sault Ste. Marie.[3]

In 1659, explorations in the Northwest received a new impetus
when Msgr. de Laval placed the Jesuits in exclusive charge of the
Indian missions. Acting upon this charge, in 1660, Father René
Menard accompanied an Ottawa flotilla of sixty canoes which had
arrived at Three Rivers, Canada. Before starting on this journey,
Father Menard wrote to a friend:

> I write you probably the last word, and I desire it to be the
> seal of our friendship unto eternity. . . . In three or four months,
> you may put me into the Memento of the Dead, considering
> the manner of living of these people, and my age and weak
> constitution. Notwithstanding all this, I have felt such a power-
> ful attraction and have seen so little of nature in this under-
> taking, that I cannot doubt that I would have had eternal
> remorse had I missed this opportunity.[4]

The fifty-five year old Jesuit, whose health had been broken by
twenty years of toil in the missionary field, had to endure incredible
hardship on the way. For example, Father Menard was forced to
carry heavy packs over portages. He was also obliged to remain
barefoot, ready to jump into the cold water, in order to lighten the
canoe whenever the Indians judged it necessary.

The flotilla ascended the Ottawa and Mattawan Rivers, crossed
Lake Nipissing, descended French River to Georgian Bay, and then
followed a westward course from Lake Huron to Sault Ste. Marie

and Lake Superior. When they entered the Lake Superior region, Father Menard expected a slight cessation from his labors. Instead of experiencing relief, Father Menard faced new hardships. He wrote:

> . . . our canoe was smashed by a fallen tree, and that so completely that no hope of repairing was left. Everyone abandoned us, and we were left — three Indians and myself — without food and canoe. In that state we remained six days, living on filthy offal, which to keep off starvation we had to scratch up with our nails around an old abandoned lodge. To make soup, we pounded the bones that lay about. We picked up earth saturated with the blood of animals that had been killed there. In a word we made food of everything.[5]

Finally some Indians who were passing by assisted Father Menard and his companions to continue the journey. They arrived at Keweenaw Bay on October 15, 1660. A miserable hut constructed of fir branches was Menard's only protection against the bitter cold. The remains of fish, pulverized birch bark, and sometimes the delicacy of acorns, provided the daily fare. While at Keweenaw Bay, Father Menard heard of a powerful tribe, the Hurons, who lived two hundred leagues in the interior. He decided to visit them. The Indians at Keweenaw Bay endeavored to dissuade him from this perilous journey, but Father Menard replied: "God calls me; I must go there, should it even cost my life. . . . What! must God be served and our neighbor helped only then where there is nothing to suffer and no risk of one's life?"[6]

On July 13, 1661, Father Menard set out on his last journey. He and his French companion stopped fifteen days near a lake — probably in the Lac Vieux Desert area — waiting for the Huron guides who were to conduct them to their village. Provisions failed and they pushed on in a small canoe which they found in the brush. On or about August 10, 1661, Menard was murdered or he perished at a portage between the Wisconsin River and the headwaters of the Black and Copper Rivers.[7]

The work begun by these brave missionaries was continued by another Jesuit, Father Claude Allouez, called the pioneer missionary of Wisconsin, who labored for almost a quarter of a century among the Algonquins. He left Three Rivers, Canada, on August 8, 1665, in company with six Frenchmen and about 400 Indians of various tribes who had come to trade with the French. This journey, like that of Father Menard's, was one of almost unendurable hardship.

Medicine men, who were with the group, insulted and ridiculed Father Allouez on every possible occasion. Hunger and misery were his daily lot. Regarding the food provided on the trip, Allouez wrote: "I had to accustom myself to eat a certain moss which grows on rocks. It is a kind of leaf in the shape of a shell, which is always covered with caterpillars and spiders. When boiled, it makes an insipid, black, sticky broth which serves rather to keep death away than to impart life." [8]

After a tedious journey of almost two months, the party landed at Chequamegon Bay, a few miles northeast of the present city of Ashland, Wisconsin. Here Allouez built a chapel in honor of the Holy Spirit which he named La Pointe du Saint Esprit, the oldest name in Wisconsin today. It was a rude and primitive structure, but to the Indians, it was an object of intense admiration. A description of the Black Robe's marvelous tepee, dedicated to the Great Manitou, was spread along the trails of the plains and the paths of the forests. [9]

After the chapel had been built, Father Allouez began his missionary endeavors, but the Ottawas, in particular, resisted his efforts to Christianize them. Although Allouez was able to make himself understood by ten different tribes, he declared that it was necessary for him to ask God for patience, even before daylight, in order to suffer joyfully the contempt, raillery, importunity, and arrogance of the natives.

In 1667, Allouez went to Quebec for an assistant. He returned with Father Louis Nicholas whom the *Jesuit Relations* characterize as a "Strong, practical, everyday man and a tireless worker." Despite the persistent efforts of these two men, however, the Indians, in general, turned a deaf ear to their words.

Becoming weary of the insolence and obduracy of the natives and convinced of the hopelessness of his mission, Allouez announced his intention of departing. Immediately the Indians seemed to awaken from their spiritual torpor and they begged Allouez to remain. The missionary granted their request. The chief of the Kiskakonk tribe embraced Christianity and three other chiefs supported his views. Polygamy, pagan sacrifice rites, and superstitious practices were suppressed. Soon the chapel was crowded with eager listeners.

In the spring of 1669, Allouez returned to Quebec. During the three and a half years that he had labored at Chequamegon Bay, Allouez had baptized five hundred adults and children. He was succeeded by a man whose name was later to flash like a meteor across the sky — Father James Marquette.[10]

Father Marquette, who had been evangelizing the Indians at Sault Ste. Marie, arrived at Chequamegon on September 13, 1669. Some of the principal chiefs assembled in council and expressed their pleasure at again seeing a Black Robe. But Father Marquette informed them that he did not know their language perfectly and that Father Allouez, who was an exceptional linguist, had left them because they had shown little interest in Christianity. The Indians admitted that they deserved to be punished and showed by their conduct during the winter that they had resolved to improve.[11]

The seed sown by Father Allouez was only beginning to bear fruit when a new field of endeavor opened before Marquette. He encountered some Indians of the Illinois tribe who told him of a great river farther south. Marquette became interested in the possibilities offered by the "great river." An opportunity to see this river presented itself because of an unfortunate occurrence at La Pointe. The Sioux, termed the "Iroquois of the West" by the Jesuits, suddenly declared war upon the Indians of the Chequamegon area. Since the latter were unable to fight their enemies, flight was the only alternative. The Ottawa retreated to the Maitouline Islands. The Hurons, accompanied by Father Marquette, fled to Michillimackinac where Father Marquette founded the mission of St. Ignace. Thus in the spring of 1671, the mission at La Pointe was abandoned.[12]

At first thought, the labors of these early missionaries seems to have been almost useless. Subsequent contacts of these Indians and their descendants with later missionaries proved that the seed of the Gospel had not fallen on barren soil. In contrast with the attitude of their forebears toward Christianity, these later Indians responded with docility to the efforts of the missionaries on their behalf.

EARLY MISSIONARY ACTIVITIES ON MADELINE ISLAND

ONE HUNDRED FIFTY-NINE YEARS ELAPSED BEFORE
chapter 10   the light of the Gospel was again preached to the Chippewa in the vicinity of Chequamegon Bay. During the interim, French fur traders had settled on Madeline Island and a second La Pointe had come into existence; namely, the trading post on Madeline Island which was also called La Pointe.

In 1830, Lyman Warren, a Congregationalist, requested Frederick Ayer to establish a school on Madeline Island for the Indian children. The following year, Mr. Warren brought the Congregationalist missionary Sherman Hall and his wife to assist Mr. and Mrs. Frederick Ayer as catechists and teachers.[1] In 1832, Mr. Hall was joined by a classmate from Dartmouth College, the Reverend William T. Boutwell who collaborated with him in the construction of the famous "Old Mission House." [2]

The site chosen for the Mission House was about halfway between the Old Fort Settlement and the New Fort Settlement where the present (1954) village of La Pointe was just beginning to be built. The Mission House site was selected not only because of its practical relation to the Old and New Forts, but also because of its natural beauty. The settlers called the place "ne-sa-kee," meaning "the house at the foot of the hill." Traders named it "Middle Fort." After seventeen months of strenuous labor, the building was completed.[3] The formal dedication took place on August 30, 1833. The Old Mission was in charge of Mr. Hall until his departure for Crow Wing, Minnesota, in 1853.[4]

Contemporary missionaries of Mr. Hall and Mr. Boutwell were the Reverend and Mrs. Leonard Wheeler who, in 1841, arrived on Madeline Island from Vermont. Mr. Wheeler had been trained for the ministry at Andover Seminary and was a man of religious earnestness and executive ability. The Wheelers made their home at the Old Mission until Mr. Wheeler prevailed upon the government to exchange the Indian lands on Madeline Island for the Bad River Reservation. After this was effected, the Wheelers accompanied the Chippewa to the Bad River Reservation.[5]

The sincere efforts of these Protestant missionaries helped to break down pagan practices among the Chippewa. Knowledge of the one God supplanted the belief in many deities to whom the Chippewa had paid homage.

Outstanding among the Catholic missionaries who labored on Madeline Island was the well-known philologist, Bishop Frederic Baraga, who devoted thirty-six years of his life to the Chippewa and Ottawa Indians, chiefly at L'Anse and Keweenaw Bay, Michigan.

Frederic Baraga was born on June 29, 1797, in the castle of Malavas in the province of Carniola, Austria, fifty miles from the port of Trieste. Baraga's parents sent him to school at Laibach where he became a skillful artist under private tutors. At the age of 19, he entered the University of Vienna where he studied law together with the English, French, and Italian languages. Baraga completed his study of law in 1819, but instead of following the legal profession, he decided to become a missionary. He gave his castle with its adjoining lands to his sister Amalia and entered on a two-year course at the Seminary at Laibach. Baraga received Holy Orders in 1823 and then prepared for missionary work.[6]

When Father Baraga received word that Bishop Fenwick of Cincinnati, Ohio, had accepted him for missionary work among the North American Indians, he exclaimed: "Now at length I hear from afar a voice which invites me to come to the holy mission!" Hurriedly the young priest made preparations to leave his native land in order to begin the work that would make him the foremost figure in the early Catholic activity in Michigan, Wisconsin, and Minnesota.[7]

Father Baraga left Vienna on November 12, 1830 and arrived in Cincinnati on January 18, 1831. He immediately began the study of the English and Indian languages. On May 28, Father Baraga was sent to a little Indian settlement on the shores of Lake Michigan called "Arbre Croche," or Crooked Tree, now called Harbor Springs.[8] His reaction to this appointment was expressed in the following words: "Happy day which placed me among the Indians, with whom I will now remain uninterruptedly to the last breath of my life, if such be the most holy will of God!"[9] In his report to the Leopoldine Society, Father Baraga praised the docility, humility, piety, ready obedience, and child-like devotion of the Indians. They always called him by the endearing name of "Father" and treated him as good children behave towards a kind parent. After laboring at Arbre Croche for two years, Father Baraga was sent to a new wilderness, Grand River (Grand Rapids), Michigan, where he labored with great success.[10]

In 1835, Father Baraga was appointed to work among the Chippewa at La Pointe on Madeline Island, arriving there on July 27. When the expenses of his journey had been defrayed, he found that he had exactly three dollars left. Here the young missionary found that nearly all the Chippewa Indians were pagans. A few half-breeds who had been baptized at Mackinac Island and some French-Canadian traders married to Chippewa women formed the nucleus of the new Lake Superior mission. However, the people proved friendly and receptive to the faith and Father Baraga encouraged them to assist him in building a church. They worked with such good will that in seven days the structure was finished. On August 9, 1835, the first Mass was offered in the little church which was dedicated to St. Joseph.[11]

On September 28, Father Baraga remarked that since his arrival, he had experienced great consolation and much joy, but also many hardships and adversities. He had met with much opposition from evil-minded people, yet the conversion of a single pagan filled him with confidence and joy. Father Baraga found the climate rather disagreeable. He wrote: "Truly this is a dreary country. As early as September 22, we saw the snow-flakes falling and for several weeks past rooms are being heated." [12]

Between July 27 and December 28, Father Baraga baptized 184 persons. During the five months that had elapsed since the founding of the mission, only one death had occurred — that of a child two years old. This seemingly unimportant circumstance may have aided him greatly in his missionary labors. If many persons had died soon after Baptism, the people, who were extremely superstitious, would have attributed it to the Sacrament. In a letter written about this time, Father Baraga deplored his lack of assistance. He wrote:

> I feel grieved that I must continue this mission entirely alone, and that, moreover, I have not a cent of my own. A school would be very useful in this mission, but it is simply impossible for me to do two things—that is, keep school and properly perform my numerous missionary duties and visit the sick. For often I am in the huts of the Indians all day, where I always find something useful to do. I must necessarily omit one or the other. In this case, I rather omit keeping school than attending the mission, for, properly speaking, I am a missionary, and not a school-master. Of course, I would gladly do both, if possible.

That I have no money at all is also very hard, for I would gladly clothe, at least a little, the poor Indian children, who even now run about half-naked in winter, but I cannot give them a stitch of clothing. That is hard, but in the name of God, let it be so for the first year. I hope hereafter to get a teacher and also some assistance.[13]

Soon after his arrival at La Pointe, Father Baraga began the practice of rising at three o'clock in the summer and at four in the winter. He spent the first three hours of the day in prayer and meditation. That his devotion was effective is evidenced by the fact that during his first year at La Pointe, he baptized 255 persons, mostly adults. Since the number of converts had increased so rapidly, the church was already too small to accommodate them. Father Baraga, therefore decided to go to Europe to collect funds which would enable him to enlarge the church and to have published a Chippewa prayer book which he had written during the winter of 1835-36. On September 29, 1836, Father Baraga left La Pointe. Upon his arrival in Europe, he gave a report of his missionary labors to the Leopoldine Society which had previously given him funds for his missionary work. After receiving money from the Society and his friends, Father Baraga returned to America, arriving at La Pointe on October 8, 1837.

Father Baraga began his project, which entailed much care and labor since he was obliged to superintend the construction of both the church and the parsonage. The church and his residence were completed in 1838. Eighteen beautiful oil paintings decorated the interior of the church. The large painting over the high altar representing the Holy Family at work was painted in Laibach, and it was intended to remind the Indians of the great precept of their Maker: "In the sweat of thy brow, thou shalt eat thy bread." [14]

In a letter written to the Leopoldine Society, dated January, 1839, Father Baraga declared that he had nothing interesting to write as nearly all the pagans who had any leaning toward Christianity had been converted. The others seemed determined to refuse divine grace and persevered in their pagan customs.

The Mission was fast assuming the form of a well-regulated parish with a regular choir of Canadian and Chippewa singers. Adjoining the church was the cemetery with queer little houses built over the graves to which the Christian Indians had attached crosses to distinguish their graves from those of the pagans. Father Baraga stated that it could be truly said that the Indians showed more regard for their dead than many white people. They did not seem to have that aversion for the dead that white persons do, for they often built their wigwams close to their burial places.[15]

During the winter of 1838-39, Father Baraga composed *Gagikwe-masinaigan*, a sermon book which contained the epistles and gospels for the Sundays and holydays, a short history of the Old Testament, the Acts of the Apostles, and the epistles of St. Paul and those of the other Apostles. Three years previously, Father Baraga had composed *Anamie Masinaigan*, a prayer book in the Indian language; *The Life of Jesus*, also in Chippewa; and *History, Character, Life, and Manners of the North American Indians*, a work in the German language written for his benefactors in Europe.

On Sundays, Father Baraga preached five times in three or four different languages. His sermons, adapted to the capacity of his unlettered hearers, were generally short. Vincent Roy of Superior, Wisconsin, declared that Father Baraga had a sympathetic nature as the following anecdote shows:

> I recollect very distinctly on two or three different occasions while he (Father Baraga) was reading the gospel from the pulpit for the first or midnight mass at Christmas, in the Chippewa language, that the passage: "And wrapped Him up in swaddling clothes" would bring tears and three or four minutes would elapse before he could control himself, so as to be able to proceed. In fact, I remember one time that after reading those words he was so much affected that his sobs could be distinctly heard all over the church; he could not recover himself and was compelled to descend from the pulpit without completing the Gospel.[16]

Mr. Roy also related an incident to Father Chrysostom, the Chippewa missionary, which reveals the sensitive nature of Father Baraga. The good missionary used to dine at the home of Mrs. Lacomb, an aunt of Mr. Roy's. The meals were usually simple ones, consisting of corn, the shell of which had been removed by a lye preparation. On one occasion, Mrs. Lacomb informed Father Baraga that she had reached rockbottom in her provisions and that he should try to find another place to eat. The priest became excited and exclaimed: "Do you want to drive me away?" Mrs. Lacomb tried to explain, but Father Baraga left the house. The poor woman, weeping bitterly, followed the priest. After some explanation, Father Baraga was mollified, the woman was consoled, and the sparse meals were continued at her home as heretofore.[17]

By 1840, the church at La Pointe became too small to accommodate the Indians and the French-Canadians who thronged to attend divine services. Father Baraga again solicited funds from Europe and again his appeals met with a generous response. A new church was completed in July, 1841. In later years, interested persons attempted to palm off on tourists the story that this church at La Pointe had been built by Father Marquette.[18] However, the testimony of Mr. Roy, whose integrity cannot be doubted, proves beyond a doubt that the edifice was built by Father Baraga. Mr. Roy wrote:

> Lego and Belle Isle were both at La Pointe, when I was first there in 1839. I do not know whether they helped to build the first church in 1835. I understood that Joseph Defauld, the grandfather of Peter Defauld here, was the builder of the first church at Middle Fort. This church was taken down and removed about 1842 (1841) to where it now stands by Joseph Defauld (the same as above), who had the whole charge, besides thirty or forty assistants, all volunteers, those who could spare the time. I do not know where the material was obtained for the first building, but no doubt it was right on the ground. Material for the second building was all taken from the first, as above stated in the fore part of this paragraph, with the exception of the shingles and laths and mud and sand for plastering.[19]

An additional proof that this church was built by Father Baraga is found in an entry made by the missionary in the Baptismal Records at La Pointe.[20] The following notation appears in Father Baraga's own handwriting:

> In the year 1841 the undersigned missionary caused a new church to be constructed the old one being destroyed by him, which had been too badly constructed, and at the same time he placed it where it was nearer to the greater part of the Catholic congregation. In the month of July of the same year this church was finished, and on the first Sunday of August the undersigned missionary dedicated it to God under the name of the same St. Joseph.
>
> (Signed) Frederic Baraga,
> Missionary.[21]

After repeated importunities from Mr. Pierre Crebassa of L'Anse, Michigan, that he minister to the Chippewa there, Father Baraga agreed to leave La Pointe, if the Bishop gave his consent.

The permission was granted, and on October 4, 1843, Father Baraga left La Pointe. During his eight years of labor at La Pointe and Fond du Lac, Minnesota, Father Baraga had baptized 853 persons.[22]

Since no one had been sent to succeed him at La Pointe, Father Baraga returned in August, 1844, and spent one month in ministering to the needs of the Chippewa. On August 14, Bishop Henni of the Milwaukee diocese, to which La Pointe belonged at that time, administered the Sacrament of Confirmation to 120 persons. The Bishop remarked that the mission church at La Pointe was more elaborate than his cathedral in Milwaukee.

In the autumn of 1846, Father Baraga again returned to La Pointe to attend to the spiritual needs of his former congregation. After discharging these duties, Father Baraga engaged Louis Gaudin (Gordon), a half-breed, to accompany him to Grand Portage, Minnesota, where he intended to build a church. They had the use of a small fishing boat with a mast and a sail, but without keel or centre-board. Such a boat might function satisfactorily on a small body of water, but it could easily founder on a large lake. Nevertheless, Father Baraga and his guide set out on their perilous journey.

They waited at Sand Lake for a favorable wind to cross the lake, a distance of 40 miles. This short cut would save at least 100 miles of travel, but they would thereby expose themselves to great danger if a storm arose. As soon as conditions seemed favorable, they began to cross the lake. About midway, a heavy west wind arose and the frail boat tossed about on the lake. At the height of the storm, Gordon, thoroughly alarmed, exclaimed: "Nosse, ki ga-nibo-min, ganabatch," that is, "Father, perhaps we are going to perish!" Father Baraga, who was reading his office in an unconcerned manner, quietly replied: "Don't be afraid, Wizon (Louis); the priest will not die in the water. If he died here in the water, the people on the other shore, whither we are going, would be unfortunate." They sailed on.

When they reached the north shore, the danger was even greater because of the huge breakers. But they also passed through these unharmed and ran their boat into the mouth of a small river, now called Cross River. Full of gratitude for their miraculous escape, they at once erected a cross. "Wizon," said Father Baraga, "let us make a cross here so that the Christian Indians may know that the priest coming from La Pointe landed here." [23]

Father Otto Skolla, a Franciscan of the Strict Observance, the successor to Father Baraga, arrived at La Pointe on October 4, 1845. He found the Christian Indians gentle and peaceable. The missionary organized a temperance society among the natives, obliging its members to abstain from all intoxicating liquor for one or more years or for life. Up to 1850, he declared that he had more than 157 persons in the society. Former notorious drunkards kept their pledge faithfully and drunkenness had become an unheard-of vice.[24]

In 1850, the Indians were being urged to move to Sand Lake, Minnesota, and to other parts of that state. Many of them left so that scarcely ten families remained. Father Skolla reluctantly left La Pointe to labor among the Menominee Indians at Oconto and Wolf Rivers, east of Green Bay.

Subsequently, a number of Indians returned to La Pointe where they were ministered to by secular priests from 1853-1875. Among these clergymen were Fathers John Chebul, Angelus Van Paemel, Hugh Quigley, Francis Pfaller, George Keller, John Genin, Timothy Carie, August Benoit, and Anton T. Schuttelhofer. For almost three years, the Chippewa Indians were neglected. Then at the earnest request of Bishop Flasch, Franciscan Fathers of the Province of the Sacred Heart, St. Louis, Missouri, agreed to staff the Indian missions of the La Crosse diocese.

In 1878, when the first Franciscan Fathers, Reverend Casimir Vogt and John Gafron, arrived at Bayfield, Wisconsin, about 60 Indian and white families lived on Madeline Island. Mass was said at La Pointe and at Bayfield on alternate Sundays. Other Franciscan Fathers who labored at La Pointe were Fathers Chrysostom Verwyst, Servatius Altmicks, Eustace Vollmer, and Norbert Wilhelm.

Baptismal records at Bayfield, Wisconsin, show that from the years 1835 to 1904, 2,883 Indian children and 794 adult Indians were baptized, making a grand total of 3,677 baptisms. Sixty-nine years before, Father Baraga had remarked upon receiving 650 florins from the Leopoldine Society in Europe: "Ah, the salvation of a single soul is worth infinitely more than all the money of the world." [25] His efforts, together with those of other missionaries, were successful beyond all expectations.[26]

The story of the benefits resulting from the self-sacrifice of pioneer missionaries can never be fully recounted. John Collier, former Commissioner of Indian Affairs, on the occasion of a visit to Santa Barbara, California, paid the following tribute to the work of religious orders among the Indians:

No longer are the monastic orders acting as the makers and the correctors of states. The new emancipation of Indians — in many countries — is secular in its origin and impulse, today. But it is well for us secular workers to remember (and for sectarian workers more often and more earnestly to remember) that great record of saving and of creation, and of the mutual aid of races, of the past. It will give us patience. It will give us a bolder hope. It will discipline us, to remember the past. It will help us, perhaps, toward that "vision, without which the people perisheth." [27]

That some Indians have caught that "vision," is undoubtedly true. Perhaps no one has expressed it in more fitting language than Tom Whitecloud, a Chippewa Indian:

Oh, Father, whose voice I hear in the winds and whose breath gives life to all the world, hear me. I am a man before you, one of your many children — I am small and weak. I need your strength and wisdom. Let me walk in beauty, and make my eyes ever behold the red and purple sunsets. Make my hands respect the things You have made, my ears, sharp to hear Your voice. Make me wise, so that I may know the things You have taught my people — the lessons You have hidden in every leaf and rock. I seek strength, Father — not to be superior to my brothers, but to be able to fight my greatest enemy — myself. Make me ever ready to come to You with clean hands and straight eye, so that when life fades as the fading sunset, my spirit may come to You without shame. [28]

TREATIES WITH THE UNITED STATES GOVERNMENT

chapter 11   SINCE THE DECLARATION OF INDEPENDENCE TO recent times, the United States government has made treaties with the Indians. When the United States was in the throes of the Revolutionary War, it recognized the rights of Indians in a treaty concluded with the Delaware Nation at Fort Pitt, on September 17, 1778.[1]

The first treaty in which the Chippewa are mentioned was that of August 3, 1795, drawn up at Greenville, Ohio. Chief Kish-ke-tuh-wug, a Chippewa, was present at this treaty. As an old man, Kish-ke-tuh-wug, related the story of the treaty to his grand nephew, Chief James Stoddard (died in 1933), who in turn gave the following account of it to his friend, James M. Scott:

It was in the early part of May, 1795, that a group of Ottawa braves appeared at Madeline Island. They were delegated by Wyandot chiefs to invite the chiefs of the Lake Superior Chippewa to a grand council to be held in the near future at Greenville, Ohio. The Chippewa accepted the invitation.

The great council assembled in the open air. All the chiefs and speakers gathered in a large circle and with them were seated the "Che-mo-quo-mon" or the white men who were the representatives of the Great White Father in Washington and of the United States government. An official of the government, speaking through interpreters, said to the gathering:

"My friends and children of the Great White Father, I bid you a hearty welcome. I am thankful to God who rules our destinies that we are able to meet here for the purpose of considering matters that will open between us a passage-way for free intercourse in the consideration of your problems leading to perpetual peace among us. With your help we can put an end to the destructive wars of the past. We can settle all arguments, not with guns, but by thoughtful deliberation. As a representative of the Great White Father, sent here to commune with you, I am holding a document which means much both to your nations and the government of the United States. The signing of this document by your chiefs and the representatives of the government of the United States means much to every tribe assembled here. It means peace and freedom; and in consideration of your signing this document, the government of the United States agrees to give each of you a certain amount of cash, goods, and other considerations, annually, forever, as long as the sun shall shine on the American flag. The Indians under this treaty shall acknowledge themselves to be the subjects of the United States and shall enjoy the protection afforded by it. My signature shall confirm the words of this great document which shall bind the United States in the promises it sets forth."

The Wyandot chiefs and Buffalo, the Chippewa chief, were the principal speakers for the tribes who participated in this treaty. The government treaty purchased from the Indians two kinds of timber — white and Norway pine. Government representatives stated that the Great White Father desired this timber for the purpose of building bridges, vessels, furniture, and homes for his children — the Indians. The Indians consented to this with the understanding that the timber should be cut at least not lower than three feet from the ground, leaving these stumps and tops for the benefit of future generations. This timber stood on the lands ceded to the government under this treaty.[2]

After the adoption of the Constitution, one of the first official acts of Congress was concerned with its obligations to the American Indians, asserting that "the utmost good faith should be observed toward the Indians; and in their property and rights and liberty they shall never be invaded or disturbed unless in just and lawful ward authorized by Congress." [3]

President Jefferson continued this interest in the Indians by receiving as guests of the government a number of chiefs from the West. When they left the capital, President Jefferson gave them a letter to take home with them. As late as January 6, 1941, this letter was read in the House of Representatives by the Honorable Usher L. Burdick of North Dakota, in connection with Indian jurisdictional legislation. The letter, dated April 11, 1806, reads, in part, as follows:

This is the advice, my children, which I wish you to carry to your nation: Tell them that their father here receives them all into his bosom as his children; that he wishes to live always in peace and friendship with them, doing to them all the good in his power; that above all things he wishes to see them live in peace with one another, that their wives and children may be safe in their houses; that they may have leisure to provide food in plenty from the earth and to make clothing for themselves; that they may raise children and become strong and happy.

Tell them how many days' journey you have traveled among your white brethren from St. Louis to this place. . . . Tell your chiefs, your warriors, your women, and children that they will find in me an affectionate father, desirous to maintain peace and friendship among all his children, and like every good father unwilling to see quarreling and wrangling and fighting among his children; that we all will endeavor to put our trade with them on a fair and just footing, and so prevent their being cheated and imposed upon by bad men. And may the Great Spirit take you, my children, by the hand, conduct you back in health and safety to your families and give you to find them in health and happiness after your long absence.[4]

The Treaty of 1825 was, perhaps, the most important insofar as the Indians were concerned, since it established boundaries between the Fox, Sioux, Chippewa, Sauk, Winnebago, Potawatomi, and Ottawa Indians. Some accounts place the number of Indians present at the drawing up of this treaty in Prairie du Chien as high as 14,000.[5] James Otto Lewis, a Philadelphian of German descent, who accompanied Governor Lewis Cass on his western tours, relates that there were "upwards of 5,000" warriors present. Henry Schoolcraft, who was also present at the conference, declared that at the junction of the Wisconsin and Mississippi Rivers, the entire banks of the rivers for miles above and below the town (Prairie du Chien) were covered by Indian tents. A stretch nine miles long and as wide had been declared neutral ground and all the Indians had agreed not to harm each other within these bounds.[6]

Above the town, the Dakotahs had pitched their high pointed buffalo skin tents, embellished with flags, feathers, and implements. Wearing a magnificent robe of buffalo hide curiously worked with dyed porcupine quills and sweet grass, Wanita, the Yankton chief, carried a war flag of eagle and vulture feathers. The Dakotah bivouac presented the appearance of a Bedouin encampment. The Winnebagoes, who spoke the cognate dialect of the Dakotahs, were camped nearby and their lodges were similar in construction and decoration to those of their kinsmen.

The Chippewa were choice representatives of the Algonquin family. Large numbers of tall, war-like bands had come from La Pointe on Lake Superior and Sault Ste. Marie, from the sources of the Mississippi and from the valleys of the Chippewa and St. Croix Rivers. The Menominees, Pottawatomies, and Ottawas from Lake Michigan, cognate tribes of the Chippewa, mingled with them.

The tribes that attracted the greatest attention were the Iowas, the Sauks, and the Foxes. Although differing radically in language, yet they were leagued against the Sioux. They came to the meeting armed with guns, spears, clubs, and knives. The headdress of the warriors, consisting of red horse hair, was tied to the scalplock in such a way that it resembled the shape of an old Roman helmet. The rest of the head was completely shaved and painted. These Indians wore necklaces of grizzly bears' claws and tied tufts of red horse hair to their elbows. They wore a species of baldric and carried long iron-shod lances. The print of a hand in white clay marked the back and shoulders of some of the highly painted warriors. Some Indians carried feather flags, while others beat drums or sounded rattles.

As these tribes came across the channel to the fort, they landed in compact ranks, the very spirit of defiance. Their leader, Keokuk, stood as a prince, majestic and frowning. Seldom was the wild native pride of man in its savage state, flushed by the success of war and confident in the strength of his arm, so picturesquely shown. These warriors presented a spectacle of bold daring and martial prowess which awed the other tribes of the area. During the conference, they expressed their disapproval by defiant yells.

Keokuk, the watchful Fox, 24 years of age, always a friend of the white people, stood with his high crest of feathers and daring eye, like another Coriolanus. Whenever he spoke, he gestured with his lance at his enemies, the Sioux. It was evident that he wanted but the opportunity to even up old scores. Wapelo and the other chiefs backed him. Every Indian was ready to spring to the work of slaughter at the command of his chief. Keokuk was chief spokesman during the 30-day council.

General William Clark of St. Louis was associated with General Cass in the negotiations. Their one great object was to lay the foundations for permanent peace among the tribes by establishing boundaries. These agents of the government cooperated with the chiefs by making themselves familiar with Indian bark maps and drawings. The Indians realized that the treaty was for their welfare and they showed a hearty will to collaborate. The treaty, signed on August 19, 1825, at Prairie du Chien, Wisconsin, definitely defined the boundary lines between the Chippewa Indian territory and the other Indian tribes present.[7]

The United States government did not always adhere to the promise made in the Ordinance of 1787, but often forced land cessions upon the Indians. The earliest of these Indian land cessions in Wisconsin was brought about by the settlement of colonists in the lead mining area in the southwestern part of the state. These mines had long been known to the Indians. The French, with the Indians' consent, had already worked them with great profit. In 1819, the government induced the Chippewa, Ottawa, and the Potawatomi Indians to cede these mineral lands to the government. This cession included nearly all of the present Grant County, the western part of La Fayette County, and the southwestern corner of Iowa County.[8]

Another treaty which affected the Wisconsin Chippewa was framed on July 29, 1837, at St. Peter's on the Mississippi River. According to the terms of this treaty, the Chippewa parted with a vast territory held by them in northern Wisconsin. This land cession extended from the St. Croix River eastward to the present location of the cities of Crandon, Antigo, and Stevens Point, and from the vicinity of Stevens Point north to Rhinelander, and from Osceola and Eau Claire north to Lake St. Croix. Within this once great pine forest region are the headwaters of the Wisconsin River and large portions of the Chippewa, Flambeau, Namekagon, Black, and Yellow Rivers. In compensation, the Indians were promised an annuity of $35,000 for twenty years!

According to General Armstrong, the eagerness of the commissioners to effect a treaty was so great that the statements they made, so favorable to the Indians and so perfectly understood by them, were not afterwards incorporated in the treaty. The commissioners spoke thus to the Chippewa:

> The Great Father does not want your lands, it is too cold up here for farming. He just wants enough to build little towns where soldiers stop, mining camps for miners, sawmill sites, and logging camps. The timber that is best for you, the Great Father does not care about. The maple trees that you make your sugar from, the birch trees that you get bark from for your canoes and from which you get material for making oars and paddles, your Great Father cares nothing for. It is the pine and minerals that he wants and he has sent us here to make a bargain with you for them.[9]

The Chippewa were assured and they definitely understood that they were not to be disturbed in the possession of their lands so long as their men behaved themselves. They were also reminded that the Chippewa had always been good Indians and the Great Father thought much of them on that account. With these promises clearly understood, they signed the treaty.

In 1842, a third treaty was made with the Wisconsin Chippewa at La Pointe, Madeline Island. Robert Stewart, representing the government, negotiated this treaty in which the Chippewa of the St. Croix and Lake Superior areas ceded all that portion of their territory from the boundary of the former treaty of 1837 that lay along the south shore of Lake Superior to the Chocolate River in Michigan. The Indians had no idea that they were ceding away their lands. They supposed that they were simply selling the pine and minerals. The treaty stipulated that these Chippewa would receive an annuity of $31,700 for 25 years, payment to be made at La Pointe on Madeline Island.

The vigorous westward march of population after the War of 1812 brought with it new problems for the Indians. Many white pioneers were imbued with the idea that the possessions of the Indians existed for the convenience of the white man and were his for the taking. Any attempt on the part of the aboriginal owners to defend their ancestral homes was the signal for a declaration of war or a punitive expedition which invariably resulted in the defeat of the Indians. By the treaties of 1837 and 1842, the Chippewa understood that they were to be permitted to remain within the treaty boundaries and continue to enjoy the privileges of hunting, fishing, and ricing, and the making of maple sugar, provided they did not molest their white neighbors who were divesting the land of its timber and minerals. Then came the drastic Removal Order of 1849 which cancelled the Indians' right to hunt and to fish in the territory they had ceded and which also gave notification for their removal westward. According to Father Chrysostom Verwyst, Franciscan missionary, many Chippewa sought a refuge among their tribe in western Minnesota.

Resenting this command to abandon their burying grounds, so sacred to the Indian, the dissenters held councils and asked each other how they had understood the treaties. All had understood them the same way; that is, that they were never to be disturbed if they behaved themselves. In an effort to discover the reason for this sudden order to move, messengers were then sent to all the different bands to inquire if any depredations had been committed by their young men. This inquiry continued for a year, but the Indians could not ascertain any reason for the Removal Order.[10]

To make the Removal Order effective, William W. Warren was appointed in 1850 to conduct the male Chippewa Indians from the Chippewa River country to Sandy Lake, Minnesota, whither the government agency had been moved. The agent sent word to all the other Indians to come at the same time and see the country. If they liked it, they would all be removed the next year. Mr. Warren was in poor health and his mother, fearing the trip would be too strenuous for him, urged him not to go. He replied that he had started and did not wish to return. His sister, Julia, induced him to let her accompany him in order that she might assist him if he became ill and also to attend to the cooking since she would be the only woman in the party. After many entreaties, Julia was permitted to go. She describes the event as follows:

> There were a great many Indians on the Chippewa River at that time. In September, we started from our Uncle James Ermatinger's home at what is now Jim Falls, went first to Lac

Courte de Oreilles, where we had to wait a day for the Indians to gather. A great many came with their canoes.

Then we started from Lac Courte de Oreilles walking through the woods, the Indians packing their canoes on their backs, some others with big packs of provisions and other things. My brother had two men hired to pack our canoe and tent.

We walked all day and did not come to any lake or river to cross. We traveled in what was then the dense woods of northern Wisconsin. We came to the St. Croix River and stayed there for two days, then started for the mouth of the St. Louis River, near Lake Superior and camped near the sand bar near where the city of Duluth now stands. Some more Indians were waiting for us there. Altogether there were then about 900 in the party. We were now ready to start for Sandy Lake.

That night my brother was taken sick with hemorrhage of the lungs, and was not able to travel for four days, then we started up the river to Fond du Lac. Just before we started, my brother told the Indians he wished to say a few words. Then pointing to where Duluth now stands, he said that in this most desolate place will some day be a very great city, with a big harbor and many ships and pointing to the present city of Superior, he said there would be another city there. Said he would not live to see it but that some of the younger ones of us would. We all thought he was losing his mind.

From there we traveled toward Sandy Lake, and that was the hardest part of our journey, as we had to walk for about six days. Then the Indians went ahead of us and we camped all together on this side of the lake. All the Chippewas, with their families were waiting for us. In all there were several thousand, waiting to receive their payments. Had to wait three weeks for the money to come. It was then late in fall. The measles broke out among the children and many of them died, some of the grown folks as well. It was a sad time for us all.

Major Watrous held a council with the Indians in his front yard. I was there and heard every word. He urged the Indians to move and join the Mississippi Indians so they would be together on some reservation and the government would move them the following year. The head chief of the Chippewa River Indians, whose name was Kichi Makigan, Big Wolf, stood up and he was a fine looking Indian. He said they would not move. They would not leave their old homes, where their dead were laid, also they would never go to Sandy Lake again for their payments. So the removal at that time was a failure.[11]

The Treaty of 1842 had stipulated that the Indians were to receive their annuities at La Pointe for a period of 25 years. This part of the treaty was ignored. Non-compliance with the order to move away was a pretext to stop payment at La Pointe since a new agency had been established at Sandy Lake. The Chippewa were told to go there with their women and children and to remain there if they wished to receive their annuities.

In the autumn of 1851, after the return of the messengers who had been dispatched to discover possible causes for the Removal Order, the chiefs gathered in council. In order to discover the attitude of the government agent, they agreed that representatives from all parts of the area be sent to the agency. A delegation of some 500 men reached the new agency about September 10 of that year. They were informed by the agent that rations would be given them until the goods and money arrived from St. Paul.

During the latter part of the month, the new agency burnt down and word was circulated that the goods and money were burned. The agent immediately started down the river and was not seen for some time. When the ashes of the former agency had cooled, crowds of Indians and some white men made a thorough search for the melted coin that would have been there, if the agent's story had been true. They scraped and searched in vain. The only metal found in the ruins were two 50-cent silver pieces. The Indians camped around the agency and were fed on the very worst kind of sour, musty pork and corned beef, and the poorest quality of flour that could possibly be milled. In the course of the next month, no fewer than 150 Indians had died from eating this miserable food. Those who survived returned to La Pointe.

After the return of the remnant of the 500 Chippewa who had gone to Sandy Lake, councils were again held and dissatisfaction showed itself on every hand. The younger and more resolute members of the Chippewa made threats, declaring that if they tamely submitted to outrage, their condition would never improve. They realized that they had been imposed upon to sign treaties that they had not understood. When they had received annuities, they had received only what the agent had seen fit to give them; certainly not their due. On this one trip alone, 150 warriors had died as the result of being fed unwholesome food. They reasoned: "Is that what our Great Father intended? If so, we may as well remain here and be slaughtered where we can be buried by the side of our relatives and friends." [12]

Benjamin Armstrong, the adopted son of Chief Buffalo, saw that serious trouble would ensue if something was not done immediately. He told the Indians that if they would consent to let matters as they were for the present, he would go to Washington and tell the Great Father all their troubles. The Chippewa agreed. Mr. Armstrong, together with Chief Buffalo and four other Indians, left La Pointe, proceeding by way of the Great Lakes as far as Buffalo, New York, and then by rail to Washington.

En route they stopped at white settlements where Mr. Armstrong circulated a petition that the Chippewa be permitted to remain in their own country. Many signatures were obtained. Some of the signers, acquaintances of President Fillmore, affirmed that the President would recognize their signature, which he did. The birch bark canoe which the Indians were paddling, sailed along easily enough, but arbitrary agents employed by the government to administer Indian affairs, endeavored to turn them back. They persisted, however, and finally reached Buffalo, almost penniless. By selling Indian trinkets and putting the chief on exhibition, the party managed to obtain enough money to defray their expenses until they reached Washington.

Troubles began anew. They were refused an audience with those persons who might have been able to assist them. Finally through the kind assistance of Senator Briggs of New York, they arranged for an interview with President Fillmore. The Indians assembled at the appointed time. After smoking the peace pipe offered by Chief Buffalo, the Great White Father listened to their story. The Indians presented their petition, read it, and the meeting was adjourned. President Fillmore, deeply impressed by his visitors, directed that their expenses should be paid by the government and that they should have the freedom of the city for a week.

In a second interview, the President assured them that their request was granted. They were to remain in the territory in question and he, the President, would countermand the Removal Order. He furthermore instructed them that on their return to their homes, they should call an assembly of their people on Madeline Island to prepare for a new treaty in September, 1854. Their mission was accomplished. They had achieved what they had sought. An uprising was averted. With light hearts, they prepared for their homeward trip. Their fare was paid to St. Paul, which was as near as they could get to their homes by rail.

The return of the delegation was hailed with great joy at La Pointe. Runners were dispatched to notify the entire Chippewa tribe that the Washington trip had been successful.[13] Many who had left their homes in compliance with the Removal Act, now returned. Chippewa arrived on Madeline Island from all directions. Before the council met, it was agreed by all that no one would sign a treaty that did not give reservations to the Chippewa at different points of the area. Furthermore, these reservations were to be considered their bona fide homes. Maps were drawn of the different tracts that had been selected by the various chiefs.

After several days of deliberation, the council was opened by a speech given by Chief Na-gon-ab-nay, "The Dressing Bird," from the Lac Courte Oreilles band. Calmly facing the more warlike members of his tribe, even though he knew they had knives under their blankets, Chief Na-gon-ab-nay said that the march of the white man could no longer be stayed. He then made an eloquent plea to Commissioners Henry C. Gilbert and David B. Harriman that the White Father assure to his children their hunting grounds and rice fields, and protect them from the curse of the white man's firewater. Part of his speech was as follows:

My friends, I have been chosen by our chief, Buffalo, to speak to you. Our wishes are now on paper before you. Before this, it was not so. We have been many times deceived. We had no one to look out for us. The great father's officers made marks on paper with black liquor and quill. The Indians cannot do this. We depend upon our memory. When you talk, we all listen, then we talk it over many times. In this way, it is always fresh with us. This is the way we must keep our records.

In 1837, we were asked to sell our timber and minerals. In 1842, we were asked to do the same. Our white brothers told us the great father did not want the land. We should keep it to hunt on. By and by, we were told to go away; to leave our friends that were buried yesterday. Then we asked each what it meant. Does the great Father tell the truth? Does he keep his promises? We cannot help ourselves! We try to do as we agree in treaty. We ask you what this means. You do not tell from memory! You go to your black marks and say this is what those men put down: this is what they said when they made the treaty. The men we talk with don't come back; they do not come and you tell us they did not tell us so! We ask you where they are? You say you do not know or that they are dead and gone. This is what they told you; this is what they have done.

Now we have a friend who can make black marks on paper. When the council is over he will tell us what we have done. We know now what we are doing! If we get what we ask our chiefs will touch the pen, but if not, we will not touch it. I am told by our chief to tell you this: We will not touch the pen unless our friends say the paper is all right. . . .

My Fathers, look around you, upon the faces of my poor people. Sickness and hunger, whiskey, and war are killing us fast. We are dying and fading away. We drop to the ground like the trees before the axe of the white man; we are weak, you are strong. We are but foolish Indians; you have wisdom and knowledge in your head. We want your help and protection. We have no homes, no cattle, no lands, and we will not need them long. The winds shall moan around the last lodge of your red children. I grieve, but cannot turn our fate away. The sun, the moon, the rivers, the forests, we love so well, we must leave. I have no more to say to you, my Fathers.[14]

The treaty was signed on September 30, 1854. According to the terms of this treaty, the Chippewa ceded to the United States all the lands they had owned previous to this time, beginning at a point where the east branch of the Snake River runs in a straight line to the mouth of East Savannah River, up the St. Louis River to the mouth of East Swan River, up the Swan River to its source, then in a straight line to the most westerly bend of the Vermillion River and then down the Vermillion River to its mouth.[15]

The Chippewa were assigned two reservations in Michigan, L'Anse and Ontonagon; two in Minnesota, Fond du Lac and Grand Portage; and four in Wisconsin, Bad River, Lac Courte Oreilles, Lac du Flambeau, and Red Cliff or Buffalo Bay. The Indians were not to be removed from these reservation homes and were given the right to hunt and fish on the reservations whenever they desired, unless otherwise ordered by the President.

At this time, the Chippewa mutually agreed to separate into two divisions, making the Mississippi the dividing line between the Lake Superior Chippewa and the Mississippi Chippewa. Each Division was given the right to deal separately with the government. This treaty was the most important of all the tribal treaties affecting the Wisconsin Chippewa.

PART

II . . .

CHIPPEWA INDIANS OF TODAY

THE BAD RIVER RESERVATION

chapter 12   BAD RIVER RESERVATION, ORIGINALLY KNOWN AS La Pointe, occupies the northeastern section of Ashland County on the south shore of Lake Superior, ten miles east of Ashland, Wisconsin. The reservation lies in six townships and is ideally located from the standpoint of highways, transportation, and educational and general social facilities.[1]

The original land area comprised 124,234 acres which were allotted to 1,610 Chippewa. Only 60,627 acres remain of this area in Indian Allotment and heirship lands. Alienated and state swamp lands total 49,482 acres; 12,547 acres are United States title lands; and 1,578 acres are tribal property. This entire area was once heavily timbered with both pine and hardwood; it abounded in game, and the waters teemed with fish.[2]

The Bad River Reservation received its name from the principal river within its boundaries. The appellation "Bad River" was originally a misnomer. The Chippewa named this stream "Mashki Sibing," which means "Swamp River," because it flows through swampy lands. White people confusing the term "Mashki," meaning "Swamp," with "Matchi," meaning "Bad," called the stream "Bad River," instead of "Swamp River."[3]

Another version for the derivation of the name originated among the Indians. The name "Bad River" was not given to this body of water until after the white man came to log timber. The Bad River was treacherous and many white people drowned. Spring floods ruined their homes and swept their boats away. Later, the Indians suffered the same misfortunes. As an appeasement to the gods, the medicine men threw tobacco into the river. Ogi-ma-kwe is said to have beaten his water drum for four days in an effort to allay the wrath of the water god. But the manito was not pacified. Gradually the Indians also called the stream Bad River, for the term was no longer a misnomer.[4]

Odanah, the Chippewa name for village, is the only town on the reservation. Because of the fertility of the soil and the abundance of berries and wild rice, the area was originally known as "Old

Indian Gardens"; also as "Kie-tig-ga-ning," or Agricultural Paradise.
In 1831, when the historian, Schoolcraft, led his expedition up the
Bad River, he wrote of the splendid gardens that he saw in the
vicinity. From ancient times, the Chippewa visited Swamp River.
In the spring, they planted gardens and collected maple sugar. In
the autumn, they returned to harvest the produce of their gardens
and to gather wild rice.

The ancestors of many of the Chippewa on the Bad River
Reservation came from Madeline Island. "Spreading Eagle," or Ba-
bom-mi-go-ni-boy was perhaps the first Indian to make a permanent
home in the area. Selecting a suitable site, he built a large wigwam
in the vicinity of the present Chicago and Northwestern Railroad
bridge. After "Spreading Eagle" had brought his family, more
Indians followed in his wake. One of the first white men to reside
on the Bad River Reservation was Erwin Leihy, known among the
Indians as Neg-gig-goods, "a young otter." Mr. Leihy built a small
home at the foot of the falls and operated a small saw mill. An old
map of the Chequamegon area shows the location of this mill. Mr.
Leihy was never molested by the Indians because he never gave
them any cause for unfriendliness.

The first missionaries in this area were the Jesuits, Fathers
Claude Allouez and James Marquette. Although it is certain that
they evangelized in this region, yet there is some doubt that they
actually visited Bad River itself.[5] No explicit mention of such a
visit is made in the *Relations*. However, the Jesuits were accustomed
to go with the Indians on inland tramps, and it is probable that they
accompanied their neophytes on their biannual visits to Bad River.

When the Chippewa were transferred from Madeline Island to
the Bad River Reservation in 1854, they were accompanied by Mr.
and Mrs. Leonard Wheeler, Congregationalist missionaries, who
were then stationed on the island. At Bad River, these missionaries
continued to serve the Chippewa both spiritually and materially.
Mr. Wheeler had invented a windmill which furnished power to
grind the Indians' corn, thus contributing much to their physical
well-being.[6]

The first Catholic missionary on Bad River Reservation of whom
there is any certain record was the Reverend Angelus Van Paemel
who paid occasional visits to the Indians on the reservation from
1855 to 1859.[7]

After Father Paemel's departure from the Lake Superior country in 1859, Bad River was occasionally visited by other mission-

aries, among whom was Father Frederic Baraga. In 1860, he made the following entries in his journal:

June 5. Brought Holy Communion to Tchetchigwais very early in the morning; then said Mass, and then I set out for Bad River and arrived there in five hours. Stopped at Nawadjiwans, where I found a neat chapel upstairs. Immediately after my arrival, I went to visit sick Wabado. In the evening, prayers and sermon.

June 6. Last night I did not sleep much on account of the mosquitoes and crying of babies. After Mass I carried the Blessed Sacrament to sick Wabado, to whom I also gave Extreme Unction. It rains terribly from time to time.

June 7. Corpus Christi. At ten A.M. I had Mass and sermon, afterwards baptized two adults and four children. In the afternoon Vespers and sermon. Toward evening, I called Nawadjiwans and made arrangements with him for the upper story of his house.

June 8. Sailed from Bad River at 9 A.M. and arrived at La Pointe about 2 P.M.[8]

In 1868, Father John Chebul erected a church in Odanah for which the Indian agent, General Webb, donated a considerable amount of lumber. Since Father Chebul's missionary field included the whole of northern Wisconsin, his calls at Odanah were short and infrequent. During the summer of 1878, the faithful Chippewa, for a short time, welcomed the missionary, Father Chrysostom Verwyst. The first Franciscan to celebrate Mass on the reservation was Father Kilian Schlosser who visited the mission in the late summer or early autumn of the same year.[9] In October, Father Casimir Vogt, a Franciscan missionary, took charge of the Chippewa missions. From that time, Bad River had the services of a regular missionary, but not of a resident priest.

The first permanent Franciscan pastor in Odanah was the zealous Father John Gafron who arrived on December 23, 1878. Father John soon became proficient in the Chippewa language. Many pagans came great distances to hear his sermons. Perhaps Father John's greatest influence was exerted in the Indian homes. Sitting around the evening fires with the Indians, the missionary held them spellbound as in perfect Chippewa he told them stories from the Old and New Testament. In later years, when these Chippewa were asked what they remembered about Father John, whom they reverently called "Anamiegabaw," "Bowed in Prayer," they unhesitatingly replied, "his stories." [10]

In 1884, Father Chrysostom Verwyst was assigned to the Odanah mission. When the missionary visited the Chippewa, his bag always contained food for the healthy and medicine for the sick. If he was not always welcomed as an apostle, he would at least gain entrance as a benefactor. Father Chrysostom made few converts. The Midewiwin, the religion of the Chippewa, was so essentially a part of tribal life that it was difficult for the Indians to embrace Christianity. [11]

From 1889-1954, the following Franciscan Fathers have served the Bad River Chippewa: Fathers Bartholomew Feldman, Sylvester Bushkuhler, Eustace Vollmer, Odoric Derenthal, Optatus Loeffler, Bruno Forka, Barnabus Schaefer, Gaspar Thoennissen, John Meyer, Emeran Fox, Cyrinus Schneider, Symphorianus Northoff, Francis Werhard, Walbert Galerno, and Bertram Mitchell. In the summer of 1954, Father Lucien Trouy, O.F.M., was appointed pastor of the Catholic mission at Odanah.

In 1898, Reverend T. C. Thomas, a full-blood Chippewa, built a Methodist church at Odanah. In 1954, the Reverend Charles E. Browne was pastor of this church. [12]

Chippewa education on the Bad River Reservation has been conducted under various auspices. In 1859, Presbyterians opened the first school on the reservation. In addition to a moderately-sized school building, the Presbyterian mission property included 160 acres of land. Until 1883, this mission provided for the education of the Bad River Chippewa Indian children.

In 1881, under the direction of Father John Gafron, O.F.M., the Indians began the construction of another school building, named St. Mary. St. Mary School was opened on April 1, 1883, with Sister Emmanuela, a Franciscan Sister of Perpetual Adoration, as teacher. Twenty-five children attended school on the first day, but the enrollment soon reached forty.

The Chippewa children, unaccustomed to indoor life, naturally found the discipline of school life difficult. Sometimes, if the teacher turned her back, the children seized the opportune moment to disappear into the depths of the forest from which they did not return until the next day. At other times, the Indian children looked upon the recess bell as a signal for freedom. Frequently during these disappearances into the forest, the Chippewa children left on the trees some of the clothing that had been given to them at the mission. However, the brown-skinned Chippewa children soon learned to adapt themselves more or less to school life. Enrollment increased steadily.[13]

In 1909, approximately 300 children attended St. Mary School. The school was visited by Miss Evelyn Calef, teacher of domestic art in the public schools of Superior, Wisconsin. Her impressions of the school were given in the following words:

> The school which contains both white and Indian boys and girls has seven of the most beautiful class rooms in the entire country in which the children receive a thorough education covering not only the subject matter of the grades but the first year of high school work as well. The school spirit throughout all grades is splendid, teachers and pupils working together in a fine spirit of harmony and sympathy.
>
> Were this all to be said, it would still be worthy of mention, but the most noticeable thing is the great amount of practical knowledge which the students obtain. The boys gain this through their work on the farm which is connected with the institution. There is almost constant call for the handling of tools in the construction of new buildings and general repairs, while the engine-room and boiler-house furnish the opportunity to gain a knowledge of machinery. The younger boys who are too small to accomplish much in these lines are taught carpet weaving.
>
> The girls are taught fancy work of all kinds, Mexican drawn work a specialty, general housekeeping including cooking and sewing. In the sewing work there has been introduced the Taylor system of cutting and fitting whereby the girls learn to make every article of clothing from the simplest to the most elegant. . . .
>
> It has been said that, to be of value, education must prepare the student for life by living. Granting this, the St. Mary's Industrial Boarding School must be conceded to be a valuable educational institution because by its present system it is approximating just this end.[14]

The work of the school continued to progress satisfactorily. Evidence of this is a letter written in 1937 by Jesse C. Cavill, Superintendent of the Great Lakes Indian Agency. In part, it reads:

> Many fine reports have recently come to my attention regarding the good attendance of pupils in the Odanah schools and the splendid work that they are doing.

I have also read with interest, in the Ashland *Press*, Superior *Evening Telegram*, and the Duluth *News Tribune*, of the large number of pupils who have made the honor roll of perfect attendance in school; also of those who have won prizes at the recent Ashland Achievement Day in competition with County-wide 4-H Clubs. I think this is a splendid showing and the pupils are to be congratulated.

Many factors have contributed to the progress of the pupils. First of all, the pupils have worked hard to gain recognition. Secondly, the parents have made it possible for the children to attend school regularly. Thirdly, the teachers have made the school so interesting that the children have a desire to go to school. And lastly, the School Board has done well in selecting qualified teachers and providing necessary equipment for proper instruction.

The Odanah citizens should be proud of their school, and should do their part to keep up the good start that has been made.[15]

In 1946, Ann Hogan Pool, photographer for the Ashland *Daily Press*, visited St. Mary School. Regarding the school, Miss Pool wrote: "The Indian school, which has a total of 230 students attending, is almost spotless in its appearance and the bright, sunny school rooms lend an environment that all youngsters, the age of these Indian students should have." [16]

The life of the Chippewa on the Bad River Reservation is greatly influenced by certain physical characteristics of the area. One of these features is the numerous rivers on the Bad River Reservation — the Bad, Marengo, Potato, White, and other small streams. The village of Odanah is practically situated on a peninsula. Within the village limits, it is almost impossible to start out in any direction without encountering water.

The Bad River easily claims first place in point of picturesque interest. Perhaps the most inviting spot the tourist will find as he follows the river's winding course is Copper Falls, about three miles from the city of Mellen, Wisconsin. The student of Indian lore will also find many points of interest along its course. Although Bad River is noted for its scenic beauty, yet serious hardships and inconveniences, together with much damage and loss of property result when the stream overflows its banks. Then, too, when the numerous dams built on Bad River and its tributaries give way because of heavy rains or sudden thaws, the whole area is engulfed in a torrent of swirling waters.

The Artist's Favorite Haunt

Floods that caused serious damage occurred in July, 1909; in March, 1938; in September, 1941; and in June, 1946. The damage that followed in the wake of the 1946 flood seemed almost irreparable. Many homes were utterly ruined and debris that defied description littered the village streets. A corner of the newly erected St. Mary School was torn away.[17] With financial assistance from Ashland, surrounding towns, and other areas, the Chippewa again repaired the damage.

These reverses have seriously affected the living conditions of the Chippewa. An economic survey of the reservation in 1937 disclosed the following conditions: The homes varied from one-room shacks to ten-room frame buildings.[18] Nearly all these houses, approximately 40 years old, were in advanced stages of deterioration. The average home was a structure of four or five rooms, valued at approximately $325.00 and housing 1.62 families, or 1.25 persons to each room. When communicable diseases gained a foothold, this congested condition was a great handicap since even partial isolation was almost impossible. Less than a dozen families had the use of electricity. The remaining households used kerosene lamps. Thirty-two root cellars provided cooling facilities for the preservation of food, but many of these cellars were useless, since they were usually filled with water.

Seventy-two families owned sewing machines, fifty-eight families owned radios, and twenty-two families owned pianos, silent reminders of more prosperous days. In the rural areas of the reservation, four springs and eleven private wells provided the water supply. The village had six public wells.[19] Since 1937, with Indian Service assistance, twenty private wells have been dug. Running water in the home is still a rarity, yet children are kept surprisingly clean.

With the motto "Better Homes for Indians," rehabilitation plans initiated by the Great Lakes Indian Agency, changed the picture considerably. Under this plan, many new insulated homes, averaging four rooms each, were built between the years 1936 to 1939. Special care was exercised in building concrete foundations. The houses stood the test in the spring of 1939 when the flood waters rose, but did not penetrate into the concrete foundations. The Indians paid for all the materials. Labor was supplied by the Works Progress Administration.[20]

A 1944 survey of the reservation showed 160 homes, 28 root cellars, 34 barns, 19 hog houses, 38 poultry houses, 150 outdoor toilets, and one silo. Nearly one-fourth of the families own automobiles. Those who do not own cars and wish to leave the reservation, contact a car owner and offer to pay for the gas used during the trip. Greyhound Lines buses make stops at Odanah, but the nearest railroad service is at Ashland, Wisconsin. Although much improvement has been made, much remains to be desired in the line of modern plumbing, electric lighting, and other conveniences that help to make home life pleasant.

Social conditions on the reservation are at a rather low level. White people have exploited the Indians in the past, a fact which has created a definite prejudice in the minds of the Indians toward the white man. In return, because of the economic and social conditions existing on the reservation, there is condemnation of the Indian by white people living in surrounding areas. Much of the poverty prevalent on the reservation, however, is traceable to the great industrial development of the late nineteenth century when huge lumbering companies took advantage of the Indians.

From 1886 to 1894, contractors removed timber valued at $400,000 from allotted lands on the Bad River Reservation. During the years 1894 to 1922, the Stearns Lumber Company despoiled allotted lands of $6,813,373 worth of timber; the timber contracts of 1916 covered the more recently allotted Indian lands. Moreover, in 1908, fire damaged 163,000,000 board feet of lumber. In recent years, about 1000 cords of poplar, pulpwood, and boxwood are removed annually.[21]

The money which the Indians received from the sale of their timber in no wise represented its true value. Moreover, because the Indians had no experience in handling material wealth, the money was not spent wisely. Consequently, in 1954, Indian living standards are below the non-Indian level of the area. On the whole, however, the Chippewa of the Bad River Reservation have adopted the white man's way of life and live as a part of the general community. There are not a dozen persons on the reservation who cannot read and only a few who cannot write.

Until the new law of 1953 went into effect giving certain states the right to maintain law and order on the reservations located within these states, the Bad River Reservation was in many respects a "No Man's Land," where petty crimes and criminals went unpunished.[22] Two part-time policemen helped to preserve order, but the county court could not exercise jurisdiction by punishing petty crimes and misdemeanors committed on restricted Indian lands. Federal courts refused to consider cases, since there was no code which covered petty crimes.

In 1941, the population on Bad River Reservation was 1100, but the enrolled members numbered 1275. This included a small number of white residents who were engaged in business or who were married to Indians. There were 20 full blood Chippewa on the reservation. There are approximately 200 families living on the reservation whose average income varies from $400 to $2000. In 1942, the average income for five families was $400-499; for 150 families, $500-749; for 10 families, $1000-1499; and for two families, over $2000.[23]

Bad River Reservation, unlike some of the other Chippewa reservations, does not attract a large number of tourists. The Indians on this reservation must depend to a great extent upon the natural resources of the area for a livelihood. The swamp lands annually produce some 8,000 pounds of wild rice, which is used principally for home consumption. Approximately 2,500 quarts of cranberries are also gathered from marshy lands. In addition to these two crops, the swamp lands afford a natural habitat for muskrats and the sale of muskrat furs contributes no small part of the Indians' income. To increase the number of muskrats, the tribal council in 1942 secured a loan of $12,000 for a large muskrat farm. The plan was to sell from 15,000 to 25,000 muskrat pelts from which a total income of from $30,000 to $50,000 would be realized. Other fur-bearing animals whose pelts furnish additional income are bears and wolves. In 1943, the following wild life animals were killed: 300 deer, 1500 ducks and grouse, 100 mink, 25 beavers, 6000 muskrats, and 16,000 pounds of fish.[24]

Several attempts have been made to initiate farming projects on the reservation but with little success. Father Chrysostom, who knew Indian nature perhaps better than anyone, stated the following in regard to the Indian and farming:

> The idea that the Indian must first be induced to become a farmer in order to make of him a civilized man is absurd. All his Indian instincts revolt against it. He is quite willing to cultivate a small patch of land, to raise some potatoes, cabbage, onions, etc., but to farm on a large scale, as his white brother does, is disagreeable to him. The writer does not know of five Indians in northern Wisconsin who have as much as forty acres under cultivation. They are born hunters, fishermen, and, to a considerable extent, mechanics. The Indian is imitative, a sort of natural mechanic. Give him tools, and with very little instruction, he will do mechanical work as well as the average

white man; he will build houses, barns, make boats, etc., better than a great many whites, unless the latter be trained mechanics. If, instead of letting his pine be logged by thieving corporations, who will cheat him whenever they can, the government erected cheap sawmills and other factories for working up his timber into lumber, shingles, laths, staves, tubs, barrels, chairs, tables, etc., under the supervision of a few skilled and conscientious white mechanics, his large forest would have supported him for many a year. As it now is, his pine is fast disappearing, and then misery and starvation will be his lot.[25]

The truth of Father Chrysostom's statements, particularly in regard to the use of timber resources, is evident. On the Menominee reservation in Wisconsin, where the white man has not been permitted to exploit the forests, the Indian enjoys prosperity. What was true in 1900 in regard to farming holds in 1954. The Indian is not primarily a "dirt farmer," that is, he does not understand soil ingredients, the use of commercial fertilizers, and intensive cultivation of the soil. In his efforts to farm, the Indian will not exercise perseverance, a necessary quality for a farmer. However, intermarriage with white persons has somewhat changed this attitude.

The soil on Bad River Reservation is largely of two types, clay and a sandy loam which has been improved by plant growth and decay. Under proper management, the soil is productive, but agriculture has been hampered by the cost of clearing the land.

The typical farm on the Bad River Reservation is composed of a 60-acre tract, half of which is seeded in barley, oats, and hay. The remaining acres may support one cow, two horses, and forty chickens. In 1943, there were 504 acres planted in oats, corn, clover, alfalfa, hay, corn fodder, beans, potatoes, fruits, and garden crops. This acreage represents a total of about one-half the acres of tillable land on the reservation. The value of these crops was $4,798, an average of $9.52 per acre. During the same year, there were 106 head of dairy cattle, 32 horses, 17 swine, and 1480 chickens on the reservation.[26]

Although the Chippewa are not favorably disposed toward farming, they have shown initiative, ability, and progress in gardening. About 130 families have gardens ranging from small plots to several acres. The average-sized garden is about one-eighth of an acre.

In 1922, another industry took root on the reservation when

one of the Beauregard brothers captured a swarm of bees.[27] In 1937, that swarm had increased to eighty hives and the brothers marketed 1100 pounds of honey. In spite of a long and severe winter that was followed by a poor summer which necessitated a long hand-feeding period, the total amount of honey produced that year was 3,163 pounds.[28]

The utilization of red clay for ceramics offers a possibility for increasing the income of the Bad River Chippewa. A sample of the clay found on the reservation was sent to Madison, Wisconsin, where it was tested on a comparative basis with a good standard clay. The University laboratory specialists reported the following: "Odanah clay is one of the best all-round Wisconsin clays for ceramic purposes. So far in our tests we have not combined the Odanah clay with any other clay bodies, but this could be done to make the clay better for some of the ceramic purposes."[29] The erection of a ceramic factory on this reservation would be a worthwhile project.

That the Chippewa Indians on the Bad River Reservation have much latent talent is evidenced by the success of various organizations which were gradually introduced into the community. But intelligent and persevering leadership is needed to continue the activities that have been initiated. Crafts and agricultural interests are promoted by 4-H Club work which was begun in 1937. Two years later, the Odanah 4-H Club with an enrollment of 109 members had the distinction of being the largest of its kind in the state of Wisconsin.[30] Both Girl and Boy Scout Troops were organized in 1937. A second Boy Scout Troop was organized at St. Mary's gymnasium in 1946.[31] Various other organizations, such as the St. Mary School Alumni, Mothers' Club, and Parent-Teachers' Associations flourished for a time and then were discontinued.

Recreational activities on the reservation are varied. The chief forms are fishing, hunting, athletics, walking, visiting, dancing, reading, radio, and motion pictures. In 1936, a recreational program was launched at Odanah with Frank Smart, a Chippewa, as director. The project, which functioned during the winter months, carried on activities suitable for both young and old — including dramatics, arts and crafts, basketball, indoor baseball, music, and social recreations of various kinds.[32]

Two years later, Mr. Smart directed a three-day pageant depicting the progress of the Bad River Chippewa in civilization. The pageant portrayed the hopes, the dreams, the frustrations, and the endless endeavor of a race in competition with the mad rush of civilization. Interwoven throughout the pageant were the dances of the Indians as executed by them long before their contact with the white race.[33] One of the main features of this pageant was a 30 piece Indian band under the direction of Eric Engblom. This band had the unique distinction of being the only all-Indian band in Wisconsin.[34]

Music is a form of recreation that is especially enjoyed by the Chippewa. In 1938, a novel band was originated on the Bad River Reservation by John Webster, Anthony Rabideau, Michael Durant, Clarence Cloud, and Vincent Bender. These five Chippewa exchanged their tom-toms and drums for the um-pah-pah of basshorns, clarinets, and trombones. Dubbing themselves the "Hungry Five," the men devoted themselves to playing German waltzes and marches, thereby relegating war dances and pow-wow music to the background.[35]

In 1938 bands from Lac du Flambeau, Lac Courte Oreilles, and Bad River formed a 50 piece unit. They gave a concert at Odanah under the direction of Eric Engblom, educational supervisor of the Great Lakes Indian Agency. A spirit of competition was engendered among the groups when individual numbers were given by the Flambeau and Odanah performers.[36]

Indian Thespians made their debut at Ashland, Wisconsin, in 1937 at the traditional festival held in thanksgiving after the wild rice and garden produce were harvested. These Odanah Indians, under the direction of Matt Zak of Ashland, were organized under the name "The Lake Superior Chippewa Tribe Company." Before the troupe left Ashland in November on a tour to various cities, they staged a ceremonial feast. Chief Sounding Winds led the ceremony in which all the traditional customs were carried out, including the Pipe Ceremonial and the display of the Sacred Dream Drum.

When Milwaukee celebrated its centenary in 1946, Chippewa performers from Odanah were one of the highlights of the occasion. Mr. John B. Chapple of Ashland, Wisconsin, was in charge of the performers. On the Centurama stage, Chief Antoine Starr executed the famous horse dance. Philip Deragon, William Gokey, and Lawrence Sweet, St. Mary's School dancers, delighted the audiences with their interpretation of Indian dances. Edna Cloud, Marie Livingston, and Clara Blackbird, known as the "Andrews Sisters of the Chippewa," because of their three-part harmony, sang Indian favorites. Edna Cloud, "Princess La-La-Wa-La," sang the opening and closing theme song — "Indian Love Call." [37]

In 1951, local Indian dancers and singers were invited to participate in the Chicagoland Music Festival at Soldiers' Field. About 60 Chippewa from Odanah and the surrounding area participated. Unabashed before the immense crowd, eighteen-month old Elizabeth Shinway, four-year old Johnny Bender, and tiny Philip Gordon danced in perfect rhythm to the drum beats. George and Joan Starr, children of Chief Antoine Starr, sang with unsurpassed harmony "It Is No Secret What God Can Do." Chief Starr gave a classic interpretation of the Horse Dance. The noted Chippewa soloist, Edna Cloud, "Princess La-La-Wa-La," delighted the audience with "Indian Love Call." The grand finale, the "Dance of Victory," was led by Chief Antoine Starr. Chief Me-Gee-See carried the feather flag of the Chippewa; while Mrs. Lillian Craig, Gold Star Mother of Ashland, carried the American flag; Chief De Coteau of Manitowish Waters, whose picture was carried by *Look* as that of a typical Indian chief, unfurled a Chippewa buckskin banner painted by the Chippewa boy artist, Joseph Whitebird. Perhaps this was the largest audience to witness an Indian program in the history of the United States. According to some spectators, this demonstration was hailed as "The greatest show in Chicago's history," "even greater than the performances in the days of Buffalo Bill." [38]

THE LAC COURTE OREILLES RESERVATION

chapter 13

THE LAC COURTE OREILLES CHIPPEWA RESERVATION, located in Sawyer County in the northwestern part of Wisconsin, is about ten miles east of Hayward, Wisconsin. The twin cities of St. Paul and Minneapolis, Minnesota, are about 125 miles southwest of the reservation. The original land area of the reservation was 69,136 acres, but about 14,437 acres, the most desirable lands near the lakes, have been alienated. A total of 41,000 acres are allotted lands and 510 acres are tribal lands. Since 1935, purchases of land under the Resettlement Administration have increased government owned lands to 13,183 acres, so that the total area of the reservation is now 54,699 acres. In 1944, there were 46,351 acres of cut-over timber land and 6,960 acres of commercial timber land. The Indians farmed 300 acres and used 500 acres for open grazing purposes. Tribal rolls of 1953 showed an enrollment of 1700 Chippewa but 1200 was the actual population on the reservation. One hundred of these Chippewa were full-blooded Indians.[1]

Contrary to some opinions, the meaning of "Courte Oreilles," "short or cropped ears," does not infer that these Indians mutilated their ears. The term actually means that the Indians' ears were of natural size since they had not been elongated by the wearing of heavy rings or other adornments. The name may also refer to a small lake which has a form similar to an ear. The Chippewa named the settlement "Odah-wah-sah-ga-e-gun," Ottaway Lake. Many years before its settlement by the Chippewa, a party of hunters had found the frozen body of an Ottawa on the lake shore.[2]

The settlement of Lac Courte Oreilles has an interesting background. In 1745, three Chippewa hunters of the daring and fearless Bear Clan, braved the attacks of the Dakotahs by planting their wigwams on the shores of Lac Courte Oreilles. During the course of the winter hunt, a child of the band died and was buried in the woods. The strange fascination which hung over the silent grave of the little one caused the bereaved parents to defy all dangers and remain near the burial place of their child. Other Chippewa followed. They settled in such large numbers that the Dakotahs were driven back and the area became a Chippewa settlement.[3]

During the latter part of the eighteenth century, Michael Cadotte established a trading post at Lac Courte Oreilles. In 1800, this post was placed in charge of John Baptist Corbin, an educated Frenchman from Canada. The post prospered until the Shaw-nee Prophet, a brother of Tecumseh, sent word to the Chippewa that the Great Spirit bade them return to the primitive usages and customs of their ancestors. The Prophet commanded that all usages which the evil white race had introduced were to be discontinued. In compliance with the Prophet's instructions, some young Indians proposed to destroy the supplies in the post. The influence of Chief Mons-on-ne at first checked the ardor of the young men, but an act committed by John Corbin added fuel to the fire enkindled by the Prophet.

Corbin had married a Chippewa woman who was related to an influential family of the village. During the excitement mentioned above, Corbin gave his wife a severe beating and sent her back to her parents. This act exasperated the Indians. They broke into the trading post and confiscated all the supplies. To save his life, Corbin was obliged to flee to La Pointe through a pathless wilderness of a hundred miles.

Later the Chippewa realized that the Prophet had perpetrated a great fraud. The chiefs and medicine men hung their heads in shame whenever his name was mentioned. Peace was restored through the influence of Michael Cadotte, and Corbin returned to Lac Courte Oreilles.[4] In 1818, the trading post operated under the auspices of the Astor Fur Company, but Corbin remained in charge. He lived to the ripe old age of ninety-nine years and was buried on the reservation. Some of Corbin's descendants still live on the reservation. Numerous tombstones in the cemetery bear witness to the generations of Corbins who have lived among the Chippewa.

About the year 1850, the Presbyterian Mission Society sent a native missionary to the Lac Courte Oreilles Reservation, but his six-year effort to gain souls was practically fruitless.[5] Father John Chebul, who attended to the most necessary spiritual needs of these Indians from 1860-1871, was somewhat more successful.[6] This was due partly to John Corbin, whose reformed Christian life influenced many of the Indians to adopt the religion of the white man.[7]

Father Chrysostom performed the functions of his ministry in the home of a Corbin, probably that of Louis Vincent Corbin. He writes of himself: "He preached and read and talked Chippewa all day long. Finally the root of his tongue became sore from pronouncing those endlessly long Indian words and he had to quit."[8]

When the Franciscan Fathers arrived in Bayfield, Wisconsin, in 1878, they included Lac Courte Oreilles in their missionary itinerary. Fathers Casimir Vogt and John Gafron, in turn, ministered to the Chippewa of this reservation. The number of Christians increased and a church building became imperative. In 1881, at the request of the missionaries, the government granted a ten-acre tract of land for the exclusive use of church and school purposes. Since the Indians had little or no money to erect buildings, Father Casimir collected the necessary funds in lumber camps. When the church was completed in 1883, the Most Reverend Bishop Kilian Flasch of La Crosse, Wisconsin, administered Confirmation to a large number of Indians on the reservation.

In addition to Fathers Chrysostom Verwyst, Casimir Vogt, and John Gafron, Franciscan missionaries who attended to the spiritual needs of the Lac Courte Oreilles Chippewa included Fathers Odoric Derenthal, Sylvester Bushkuhler, and Optatus Loeffler. Their service extended from 1878 to 1914. Then Father Philip Gordon, the only

Catholic Chippewa priest in the United States at the time, was appointed to minister to his tribesmen. His service extended from January, 1914 to September, 1914, when the mission was again placed in charge of the Franciscans.

In January, 1918, Father Gordon was reappointed pastor on the Lac Courte Oreilles Reservation. During his six years pastorate, Father Gordon collected funds for the erection of the beautiful stone church which stands at Reserve as a monument to his zeal and priestly endeavor. Since 1924, the Franciscan missionaries have served the Lac Courte Oreilles Chippewa except from 1925-1934 when Father Ignatius Kinney, a zealous and sacrificing secular priest, was pastor.

From the outset, the education of the Indian children was of major interest to the missionaries. They employed Dominic Ducharme as teacher paying him from their own scant salary. Mr. Frank Oshoge permitted the use of a room in his home, free of charge, for classes. Louis Corbin boarded the teacher at the low rate of from ten to twenty cents per day.

As soon as circumstances permitted, a school and Sisters' home were built. In 1886, Franciscan Sisters from Greenfield Park, Milwaukee, agreed to take charge of the school without remuneration. The following winter, through the efforts of the Catholic Indian Mission Bureau, the government agreed to pay $7.50 for each child per quarter. For several years, attendance was satisfactory; but by 1900, it seemed impossible to retain the children in school because of the roving disposition of the parents. Then, too, the neighboring schools of Bad River, Bayfield, Keshena, and Hayward attracted the children of Lac Courte Oreilles. The problem appeared insurmountable to the Sisters, and in the autumn of 1903, they left abruptly. Four years later, Bishop Augustine Schinner of Superior, Wisconsin, again secured the services of these Sisters and the mission school was reopened.[9]

Regular state, county, and local school services are now available to all the Lac Courte Oreilles children. In 1943, there were 337 children of school age on the reservation. Of these, 206 attended public schools; 91, the mission school; 22, government schools; and the remainder, special schools. The education of these Chippewa compares favorably with that of their white neighbors. Ninety-nine percent of them can read and ninety percent can both read and write.[10]

In 1903, a railroad was built to the village of Reserve and a sawmill was erected there which gave employment to many of the

Indians. Unfortunately, at that time, the Chippewa did not know the value of money and spent it for trifles or worse, whiskey. Father Chrysostom, at this time, concisely summed up the situation in the following words: "The three great enemies of the Indian are money, whiskey, and the white man." [11]

There are three small villages, almost entirely Indian, located on the reservation — New Post, White Post, and Reserve. All the Indians live in homes of frame, shiplap, or tarpaper construction. Few of the homes have electricity, telephones, or modern plumbing. One of the greatest needs on the reservation is more wells. Some Indian families are obliged to carry water from creeks or wells a distance of from one-fourth to one-half miles. For many years, one old couple carried water for a distance of nearly two miles. [12] Carrying water for washing and cooking in cold, blizzardy weather is a severe hardship. The attempts of the Chippewa to maintain cleanliness can be appreciated when the deplorable conditions under which they live are considered.

Many dwellings, built long ago, afford their occupants little protection against the inclemency of the weather. Numerous homes are equipped with old stoves whose burnt-out grates and broken ovens are scarcely serviceable. Sleeping facilities are inadequate. In one home, with a family of nine, there was but one bed. "Make-ups" on the floors served as couches for those who could not get into the one bed. Quilts and blankets are a dire need in many homes.

A 1943 survey of the reservation revealed these facts: 286 homes, 29 barns, 2 hog houses, 18 poultry buildings, 1 silo, 282 outdoor toilets, and 190 storage cellars. Machinery is scarce, but many of the Indians have cars; most of them old. [13]

In 1934, an all-Indian unit built a twelve-mile truck trail through the dense underbrush known as the "big sugar brush." The trail, the first road in the area, begins two miles south of New Post and ends at Signor, three miles south of Reserve. It enables the Indians to travel by auto where formerly they could go only on foot. Lovely springs along the trail have been curbed for permanent use. Tests reveal that the spring water is free from contamination.

A bridge has also been built over the famous Pipestone Creek to which the Indians journeyed to procure pipestone. Over the nearby Pipestone Falls, waters pour down with a roar that can be heard long before the cataract is seen. Tourists make long camping trips to view the beauty of Pipestone Falls. [14]

One of the chief sources of income on the Lac Courte Oreilles Reservation is the tourist industry. Many vacationists visit the reservation to observe Indian life. Numerous lakes on the area furnish excellent fishing facilities. Muskullenge, bass, pike, and crappies are caught in abundance. From fifteen to twenty Indians serve as guides to tourist fishermen. The grounds surrounding the summer cottages are cared for by from twenty to thirty men. A number of women and girls are engaged in the domestic work. Ceremonial dances, for which spectators are charged a nominal fee, are held each week.[15]

During the summer months, wild blackberries, raspberries, and blueberries form part of the family diet. Wild rice, harvested in the late summer or early autumn, is used mainly for home consumption, although a small amount is sold. In 1943, 259 acres of land yielded crops valued at $12,580. These crops included alfalfa, corn silage, timothy-clover hay, wild hay, beans for canning, fruit, vegetables, and potatoes. Because of the numerous forest fires which have devastated parts of the reservation, much of the soil supports nothing better than brush or small aspen.

When winter closes in, from thirty to fifty men engage in trapping bears, beavers, and muskrats. No estimate is available of the monetary value of this industry to the reservation. The men also cut timber, mostly for pulp. In 1942, this industry netted the Chippewa $6,000. The women contribute their share to the family income by their handicraft. They are expert bead workers, birch bark craft makers, and moccasin and buckskin specialists.

Despite their efforts, economic conditions are at a low ebb. In 1942, the average family income for 222 families was $479; eight families received less than $300; and only one family realized an income of more than $2,000. The lakes on the reservation are well stocked with fish, but the Indians cannot subsist on one type of food. Wild game, the once great source of meat, is no longer plentiful. The Federal government and the tribal council have made an attempt to bring employment facilities and opportunities to the Chippewa on the reservation. In 1950, a loan of $10,500 was made to the tribe to finance a thirty-two acre cranberry marsh project. This project now furnishes a substantial cash income for the Chippewa.

During the fiscal year 1943, the Great Lakes Indian Agency Social Worker and the Education Field Agent spent about 15% of their time on the Lac Courte Oreilles Reservation. Other social workers on the reservation were Field Aid and Federal Health officials. In addition to the services rendered by the Great Lakes Indian Agency staff, these Indians received parallel services from the Sawyer County Children's Worker, as well as the services of representatives of the Division of Child Welfare, Division of Vocational Rehabilitation, Division of Crippled Children, and the Sawyer County Juvenile Judge.

Lac Courte Oreilles Chippewa Indians follow the customs of their non-Indian neighbors in dress, food, and conduct; but there is a strong tendency to ignore civil and religious marriage ceremonies in favor of the so-called Indian custom of common consent of man and woman.

That some of the Indians on the Lac Courte Oreilles Reservation retain old customs is evident from a four-day celebration held at Reserve in 1937. The tribal leader thus explained the reason for this festival to a newspaper reporter:

> We meet twice a year to observe a spring and fall festival of religious tradition, especially, for our older Indian pioneers. Here we feel families can gather to exchange social greetings and be better acquainted. Many of our homes are scattered over a large territory and a meeting like this brings friends together for a few days.
>
> We celebrate the bountiful harvest and are thankful for the fruits of the field, the berries, the vegetables, and the things that help us to live.[16]

The Chippewa held services in a long, narrow enclosure carefully constructed of the bent and twisted boughs of white and Norway pine. Pine needles, which were massed together, formed a dark green wall about three feet high. In addition to the social activities of the festival, the Chippewa also pray.

THE LAC DU FLAMBEAU RESERVATION

chapter 14   THE LAC DU FLAMBEAU RESERVATION IS LOCATED
in the northeastern part of Wisconsin in Vilas,
Iron, and Oneida Counties. In addition to the
Chicago and Northwestern Railroad which crosses the reservation
from the northwest to the southeast, Highway Number 51 and three
trunk highways make the reservation easily accessible.[1]

The beauty of Flambeau Lake, its setting in a virgin pine forest,
and its accessibility, early made the area a favorite rendezvous for
the Chippewa. Because of the custom of spearing fish by torch light,
the Indians named the locality "Waus-wag-im-ing," "Lake of the
Torches." Another explanation for the name is to be found in the
legend of fire balls which the aborigines believed to be Indian medicine men traveling on their missions of good or evil. These supposed
fire balls were frequently seen along the lake shores opposite the
spectators. When the French traders arrived, they made a thorough
investigation of this phenomena. These traders discovered that the
fire balls were nothing else than the "will-o'-the-wisps," which
originated in gaseous, boggy swamplands. The French, noting the
reflection of the camp fires on the waters, called the settlement the
French equivalent of the original Indian name, Lac du Flambeau.[2]

Grandeur marks the winter season in the Lac du Flambeau
country. The pine trees, covered with soft, glistening snow, branch
out like great white flowers. Many of the lakes are frozen, but the
swift Flambeau River refuses to sleep and rushes on. That the
Flambeau country is equally attractive in summer, is attested by
the 15,000 tourists who annually enjoy its land, lakes, and rivers.

The original acreage of Lac du Flambeau Reservation was
81,386, but only 40,219 acres now remain in Indian ownership. The
allotment of 80 acres to each male Indian twenty-one years of age
or over began as early as 1888 and continued until 1933. Under the
Allotment Act of 1903, 600 Allotments were made with little regard
to value, location, or possible use. Allotment tract books show that
22,706 acres have been alienated. Principally because of an old
Federal Land Grant Act, 18,361 acres of swamp land are claimed

by the state of Wisconsin. The most valuable lands along the lake shore have nearly all been alienated to white owners.[3]

Approximately 950 Indians live on the Lac du Flambeau Reservation, although tribal rolls show a population of 1,115. Of this number, 328 are fullbloods. Transition from Indian culture to white civilization has been slow. Many of the Indians on this reservation retain traits of tribal culture in language, religion, and dress. A 1943 survey showed that there were 319 Indian children of school age on the reservation. Of this number, 222 attended the reservation school and 47, the local public school. The remaining 50 attended schools outside the reservation.[4]

From 1854 to 1860, the spiritual needs of the Indians were provided by missionaries from Chippewa Falls. A certain Father Coffee had the honor of being the first missionary on this reservation. His successors were Fathers Benedict Smedding, Peter Abelen, and Charles Goldsmith.[5] In 1862, Father John Chebul included the Indians in his missionary itinerary. Although there are few records of Father Chebul's ministrations at Lac du Flambeau, yet his labors must have been successful since Father Chrysostom, in later years, referred to the "many converts of Father Chebul." His stay, however, was brief. Missionaries did not visit the reservation again for about fifteen years.

In February, 1879, the Flambeau Indians sent a messenger to Bayfield, Wisconsin, inviting the Franciscans to their reservation. Father Casimir, accompanied by John Denomie of the Bad River Reservation and Michael Bressette of Bayfield, set out for Flambeau on March 4, 1879. Father Casimir conducted a week's mission at Flambeau with the aid of his Indian guides, who served as interpreters. Many of the Chippewa showed a keen interest in the religious services. Michael Bressette taught the Indians the Chippewa alphabet and also hymns in their language.

After Father Casimir's departure, some of the Indians met each night to practice reading Chippewa. When the priest returned four months later, he was agreeably surprised to hear the Chippewa read in their own language. Until 1881, Fathers Casimir and Gafron attended the mission, travelling on foot, a distance of two hundred miles. In 1883, Father Casimir built a church which was dedicated by Bishop Kilian Flasch on July 24. The Reverend Charles Goldsmith, a former missionary to the reservation, rode on horseback from Chippewa Falls to attend the dedication. Sometime later, Father Goldsmith wrote a letter describing the event. His letter reads in part, as follows:

The Franciscan Father Chrysostom preached a sermon in Indian. It sounds musical indeed, despite its gutturals. The people were in their holiday attire, and one could not but notice the extreme cleanliness of the Chippewas, both male and female. Their air of somber recollection, not to say piety, in the church, the fervor with which they joined in prayer and song, together with the polite, the generous, respectful manner with which they treated their clergy, was noticeable and praiseworthy indeed. . . .[6]

Although Lac du Flambeau again became a mission of the Notre Dame parish at Chippewa Falls, during the next years, Franciscan Fathers agreed to visit the reservation four times a year.[7]

When Father Chrysostom returned to Lac du Flambeau in 1886, he found poverty and sickness prevalent among the Indians. An epidemic of measles was raging and many of the Indians were dying of the disease. The two missionaries, Fathers John Gafron and Chrysostom Verwyst, served these Chippewa alternately for several years. They were succeeded by Father Odoric Derenthal. Lac du Flambeau was a difficult mission. The Chippewa on this reservation clung tenaciously to their ancestral ideas. Pagan dances and other religious observances presented an obstacle that only time, zealous work, and silent prayer could overcome. Prudence and tact, too, played their part in gaining for Christianity these hearts and minds steeped in paganism.[8] Father Lawrence Henninger, O.F.M., the resident pastor at Lac du Flambeau in 1954, continues the traditional Franciscan assistance to these Chippewa.

Recreational activities on the reservation are similar to those enjoyed by white people. During the summer months, baseball is one of the principal sports. In July, 1934, an unusual Field Day was sponsored by the Indian Emergency Conservation Camp located on Flambeau Lake. Besides hundreds of tourists, more than 2,500 conservation workers and their families attended. An Indian band concert opened the day's festivities. Track sports, pole vaulting, boxing, baseball, canoe races, and log rolling were the principal activities. Although no records were broken, the contestants exhibited true Indian skill. In the evening, ceremonial dances in colorful Indian regalia delighted the hundreds of visitors who had never before seen such an interpretation of native art. The camp manager, J. H. Broker, an Indian, summarized the value of the exhibition as follows: "The Field Day event has created an added interest among the boys here. I have since noticed more have come out to the athletic field to do something; so, whatever effort was put forth on last Saturday has assuredly taken root and is certain to result in better morale and production." [9]

Lac du Flambeau again sponsored a Field Day in 1937. This was one of the largest Indian gatherings in Wisconsin since the signing of the 1854 Treaty on Madeline Island. Jesse C. Cavill, Superintendent of the Great Lakes Indian Agency, awarded medals to the winners.[10]

The village of Flambeau has a Parent-Teachers' Association, a Lions' Club, a Chamber of Commerce, and a Ladies' Aid Organization. The younger members of the community are organized into Boy and Girl Scout Troops.[11] Since the men have few organizations, they imitate their white brothers by gathering in front of stores for recreation. Here they discuss the weather, indulge in village gossip, speak of the latest move of the Indian Bureau, or perhaps philosophize on the fate of the nation. Unlike their white brothers, they do not discuss income taxes.

An example of the Chippewa Indian's idea of the qualifications necessary for public office was given during a meeting held to nominate tribal council members. A young Indian, a Wisconsin University student, requested that men should not be chosen because of their education, intelligence, or success, but, rather because they had the interests of the tribe at heart. Furthermore, men should not be chosen who would use the office to increase their personal prestige, but men who would work for the prestige of the tribe. Finally, men must be chosen who would work hard, unselfishly, and earnestly.[12]

An unusual industry was developed on the Lac du Flambeau Reservation as an aftermath to the 1929 depression. An aged Chippewa woman, desperate for an income, wanted to make articles that required less time and provided more income than the usual headdresses, bands, and belts which she ordinarily made. She asked Frank Smart, a Bad River Chippewa, then stationed at Flambeau as government easement officer, for advice.

The idea occurred to Mr. Smart that if the rabbit's foot was regarded as a good luck charm, why not combine the Indian jeebic or good luck charm with the rabbit's foot? He advised the woman to do this. The woman enclosed jeebic roots within the tiny beaded figure to which she attached the traditional rabbit's foot.

Supervisors of the Civilian Conservation Camp at Flambeau were intrigued by the talisman. They organized a club entitled "The Grand Order of Jeebics," and purchased all the jeebics the woman had made. Other women made jeebics. The jeebics became so popular that before the end of the year, more than 1000 had been sold. The jeebic fad spread. In 1933, during the World Fair at Chicago, jeebics were sold on the souvenir stand at the Indian village and thus became a national success. In 1952, jeebics in the form of turtles, gingerbread men, tiny moccasins, totem poles, and pert little Indian faces were on sale at Flambeau. Since most jeebics sell for a dollar, the industry provides lucrative employment for skilled handicraft workers.

Another skill exercised by the Lac du Flambeau Chippewa is the designing and construction of rustic furniture. According to Benjamin Gauthier, a Chippewa, the designer's selection of the wood is made in view of the finished article. The customer furnishes no plans or specifications. The wood artist builds as he envisions the completed article. During the tourist season, much rustic furniture is sold.[13]

In 1946, Chippewa handicraft was given further opportunity for development when the Simpson Electric Meter Manufacturing Company established a branch assembly line on the reservation. The instruments made by this company require dexterity and skill. The management of the company believed that Indians had just such qualities. Business considerations, not sentiment, led the company to set up a small plant in an abandoned school at Flambeau.

The plant soon expanded and it now gives employment to about 150 persons, 95% of whom are Indians, who have easily adapted themselves to the intricate work.[14] The difficulties of establishing habits of regularity and punctuality have also been overcome. Because of this project, some of these Indians for the first time in their lives have a steady income — as high as $1,200 per year. This income may seem small, but if compared to the income of the majority of the Chippewa Indians, it is high.[15]

Another example of Indian skill was the construction of Pokegama Bridge over Pokegama and Flambeau Lakes. This bridge was planned and constructed by the Lac du Flambeau Chippewa. Ted Stucklager, grandson of John Drumbeater, drew every line of the plans.[16]

The tourist industry is also a source of income for the Chippewa on Lac du Flambeau. In 1938, comfortable summer cabins, equipped for housekeeping, were built on the shores of Fence Lake, the largest lake on the reservation.[17] Attractive rustic markers, fashioned in the shapes of canoes, arrowheads, tomahawks, and wigwams, direct tourists to the lakes, streams, waysides, and other points of interest.[18] Caretakers and domestic workers find employment on the grounds and in the cottages. Guide work is also important on the reservation.[19]

Since economic conditions have improved on the reservation, living standards have risen. Health conditions have improved, as will be noted in a later chapter. An air of prosperity not generally found on the other Chippewa reservations prevails at Lac du Flambeau.

THE RED CLIFF RESERVATION

chapter 15

SCENIC RED CLIFF RESERVATION IS LOCATED three miles north of Bayfield, Wisconsin, on the southern shore of Lake Superior. Originally, the settlement was known as "Wi-kwe-ang," which means "bay." Since numerous buffalo once roamed throughout the area, the name of the reservation was lengthened into "Buffalo Bay." The word "Buffalo" may also have been appended as a tribute to Chief Buffalo and his warriors, to whom the land was assigned by the Treaty of 1854.[1]

In 1897, a firm known as the Red Cliff Lumber Company, erected on the reservation a saw mill, a store, a postoffice, and other buildings. From that time on, the reservation has been called Red Cliff. This name is singularly appropriate since red sandstone cliffs jut out into Lake Superior.[2]

After the reservation was re-named by white people, the Chippewa designated the site as "Pa-sa-bi-kong," a name which refers to a cliff about three miles from the village, now called Pageant Grounds. According to the Chippewa legend, Wenaboozho, a demigod, lived a few miles north of Red Cliff. One day at L'Anse, Michigan, Wenaboozho's grandmother caught a beaver. She shouted to Wenaboozho for help in killing the animal. Wenaboozho requested his grandmother to hold the beaver until he had finished the construction of a canoe. The Indians point out the black rocks that held the bark of the canoe in place during its construction.[3]

The area of Red Cliff Reservation, the smallest of the four

original Chippewa reservations in Wisconsin, was 13,652 acres. After the passage of the Allotment Act, 9,796 acres were alienated. In 1934, 4,716 acres were again added, thus bringing the present acreage to 8,572. Of this total tract, 3,856 acres are allotted to individuals and 4,716 acres are in tribal ownership. The Chippewa population on Red Cliff Reservation is 324, but the tribal rolls show a membership of 653; none of which are full blood Indians.[4]

Father Chrysostom Verwyst, pastor at Bayfield, Wisconsin, attended to Red Cliff Reservation since it was part of the Bayfield parish.[5] When the Franciscan missionaries arrived in this area, they assumed charge of Red Cliff. Father Casimir Vogt was the first Franciscan to read Mass in the little log chapel at Red Cliff. From that time on, 1878 until 1910, Franciscans from Bayfield ministered to these Chippewa. In 1910, a resident pastor was appointed for Red Cliff.[6]

A striking delineation of the spirit that hovers over Red Cliff was given by Father Oscar Rascher who came to Red Cliff in 1930. He wrote:

> To one even only slightly acquainted with the history of Chequamegon Bay, there is a story in these words: the evergreen, the mission, and the Indian. It is a story of vast silent forests, of life and light in the midst of darkness, and of the plain realities of human life.
>
> The wilderness and heroic mission fields are but shadows of memory, for the fur, fishing, and lumber and mining industries have in turn throttled the wilderness to snatch from it their tribute of passing gain. But the spirit of the wilderness still hovers over the Northland. If you would feel its presence, then come in spirit to this Indian village on the shore of Lake Superior.
>
> Picture yourself here by the winter fire as the wind drives off the inland sea to hurl itself against the trees which strive to hold the barriers of the ancient forest. You will find a note of sorrow in its clamor, for it plays a game of make-believe. The forests are gone. But the boisterous wind tugs and hauls with the shrinking woodlands, making believe that his strong playfellow of olden days, the forest, still laughs at his coming.[7]

The first school to which the Chippewa children from Red Cliff had access was a rented house that lay half-way between Bayfield and Red Cliff. This school opened its humble door on October 5, 1880 with Sister Nazaria, a member of the Franciscan Sisters of

Mary Immaculate, as teacher. One year later, at the request of government officials, a Catholic school was opened on the reservation. The Sisters who lived at Bayfield made the daily trip to Red Cliff with horse and buggy.[8]

After 1895, the Sisters lived at Red Cliff during the week returning to Bayfield each Friday night. Generally, they walked the three miles that separated Red Cliff from Bayfield. The clayey mud sometimes claimed their rubbers. Occasionally, a kind friend offered his hay rack or his wagon as a mode of conveyance. Later, the Sisters availed themselves of the luxury of a caboose on the Bayfield Transfer Railroad which operated for some time between the two places.[9] Among the teachers who have rendered outstanding service on the Red Cliff Reservation is Sister Victoria who has labored there uninterruptedly for a period of 64 years.[10]

In 1953, about 80 children attended the mission school, a substantial brick building erected by the donations of benefactors. The remainder of the children on the reservation attend a public school.

The Red Cliff band of Indians were the first Chippewa to vote on the adoption of a constitution and by-laws preparatory to making application for a charter of incorporation under the provisions of the Indian Reorganization Act of 1934. The eligible voters, 293 in number, met on April 18, 1936, at the voting precincts of Bayfield, Wisconsin, and Red Cliff. The election boards manifested a deep sense of responsibility and discharged their duties with intelligence and efficiency. The vote for adoption was almost unanimous. Did these Chippewa realize what they were doing? Jesse C. Cavill, former Superintendent of the Great Lakes Indian Agency, answers the question thus:

> If anyone ever doubted the adaptability of the Chippewa Indians to our form of democratic government, to have been present and witnessed the conducting of this election would have at once dissipated any such doubts. There was not the least disorder among the voters, no heated arguments and discussion. There was no electioneering and no excitement. All were calm, serious, and self-possessed.
>
> The Indians came to the polls quietly with grave determination written upon their countenances. They seemed to feel that they were entering upon a new adventure — one destined to stimulate among them productive cooperation and individual enterprise. They were imbued with the desire to achieve through organization the creation of new incentives for group self-help and to re-awaken their old-time Indian civic pride and

consciousness and to make possible the development of capable, progressive leadership.

These Indians have evidently been doing a lot of serious and intelligent thinking and they have arrived at the conclusion that cooperative community organization is for the benefit and advancement of the community as a whole. They seemed to understand that the prime object of the Indian Reorganization Act is to give to the Indian tribes a share in the management and administration of their own affairs and a responsibility in their economic and social development. There is great hope for the improvement of the social and economic condition of this band of Indians through the instrumentality of their newly adopted Constitution and By-laws and their eventual incorporation as a chartered community.[11]

The Red Cliff Chippewa held another meeting to discuss the credit provisions of the Reorganization Act. Since the only light available was furnished by a kerosene lamp, the secretary sat close to a table to read the minutes of the previous meeting. The council members sat on stiff-backed chairs, their light being the moonbeams that streamed into the room. The waves of Lake Superior, dashing against the rocks, accompanied the low murmur of their voices.

A number of reasons were advanced why the Chippewa wanted credit funds—far too large a percentage of them were on relief projects. They needed help to become self-supporting. Many Chippewa living on the reservation remembered that money had been plentiful during the years of timber operations. Until 1929, they had succeeded in making a living without a great deal of difficulty. As late as 1933, most of them were engaged in occupations which made them self-supporting. The decline of the logging and fishing industries had since thrown many Indians on public relief. Their case seemed desperate until the Indian Reorganization Act presented a ray of hope. Now they looked forward to a time when they could again become independent economically—a desire which was expressed repeatedly. Credit funds would enable them to develop their lands.

It was late when the meeting adjourned. The Chippewa were convinced that they must proceed carefully, recalling sad experiences of former treaty-making. Their teamwork was splendid. Although they did not always agree, yet when a decision was made, each member backed the decision and helped to put it into effect. The credit agent, Albert Huber, remarked: "They have so little and need so much." [12]

The Chippewa were not disappointed in their hopes for credit. In 1936, the Chippewa of Minnesota, Michigan, and Wisconsin, sent representatives to Washington to discuss general business relations and common problems. As a result of the meeting, Jesse C. Cavill, Superintendent of the Great Lakes Indian Agency, secured a loan of $16,500 for the Red Cliff Chippewa.[13]

The Indian standard of living at Red Cliff is but a little lower than that of ordinary white people in the area. Culture is part Indian and part white. Most of the homes are of frame construction and stand badly in need of repairs and paint. Storm windows and screens are at a premium and plumbing facilities and electricity are rarities.

In 1944, approximately fifty-eight acres were utilized for garden purposes, forage crops, cereal grains, beans, and tree fruits. Wild berries, such as blueberries, blackberries, and strawberries help to vary the summer diet. During the herring season, many of the Indians work in the fisheries. In the winter, pulp cutting, hunting, and trapping furnish a meager income. In 1942, the average income of 102 families was $583.70. Six families received an income of $100-199; seventy-five families received $500-749; and one family received $1500-1999.[14]

One hundred years ago, the cold winter winds dashed against a dense forest of trees on Red Cliff. Today the boisterous blasts play havoc with the depleted woodlands. The best timber was cut prior to 1923, yet there still remain a few evergreen trees to send their spires heavenward. Their colors blend with the green of summer, the scarlet and gold of autumn, and the white of winter. Although human beings cannot subsist on scenic beauty, yet this loveliness is not lost on the Indian and it helps him to bear his economic burden.

SAKAOGON OR MOLE LAKE RESERVATION

THE TERM "LOST TRIBES" WAS APPLIED TO TWO groups of Chippewa Indians whose status within the Chippewa tribe had never been officially determined prior to 1938. Identified as the Mole Lake and St. Croix bands, these Chippewa Indians now live on reservations.

Under provisions of the 1934 Reorganization Act, 1745 acres of land were purchased for the Mole Lake "Lost Tribe." This area lies in southwestern Forest County, near Crandon, Wisconsin. On this reservation, in 1938, lived 106 Chippewa, of whom 18 were full bloods. The number of unenrolled Chippewa was estimated at 200.[1]

In 1930, a roll was taken of the "Lost Tribe" in the Mole Lake area in order to determine if these Indians could be identified with existing reservation Indians. The census showed a total of 212 Indians. Thirteen of these were entitled to tribal rights with the Lac du Flambeau Indians.[2] However, there were good reasons for believing that this "Lost Tribe" was once part of the larger group of Lake Superior Indians. They had wandered away from the main group and stubbornly formed a separate division.

Acording to legend, Mee-gee-see, their chief, was prevented from attending the treaty council on Madeline Island. He sent his speaker, Ni-gig, to observe and report the proceedings. Without proper authority, Ni-gig signed a treaty which promised the Chippewa cash, equipment, and lands. The following year when Mee-gee-see met with the Indian commissioner, the latter denied that he had made any treaty with Ni-gig. However, he promised to set aside a grant for the band the next year. He drew up a map which gave the Chippewa approximately 20 square miles of land in the Summit, Pelican, Metonga, and Pickerel Lakes area.

The agent gave Mee-gee-see a copy of the plat, retaining the original for government files. But on the return trip from Washington, the boat sank in the Great Lakes with everyone aboard.

That autumn, as was their custom, the Sakaogon band followed the deer herds east to the swamps of Peshtigo, and, as usual, a trader, named Bill Johnson, grubstaked the tribe against the winter's trapping returns. Unfortunately, the story relates, the Chippewa were unable to pay the $1,200 debt because of the winter's severity. Johnson slipped into the chief's tepee and requisitioned the map as security for the loan. Before the Indians were able to redeem the map, the trader became ill. He gave the map in payment to a man named Straus who cared for him until his death. Straus later committed suicide, leaving only rumors of the map's disposal. As a result, the Sakaogon Indians were without a vestige of evidence to press their claim.[3]

During the chieftainship of the Great Martin, "Ki-chi-waw-be-sha-shi," the Post Lake band numbered 700 Chippewa.[4] Great Martin, a signer of the first treaty between the United States and the Chippewa of this area, was the father of Mee-gee-see, the Great Eagle. Mee-gee-see was intimately connected with the history of Langlade County. His daughter, Ma-dwa-ji-wan-no-quay, "Maid of the Forest," married William Ackley, Antigo's first white settler. Two sons were born to this marriage, Charles and De Witt. In 1947, Charles Ackley declared that his grandfather, Chief Mee-gee-see, had stated that the Mole Lake band had been promised a tract of land twelve miles square touching on Post, Pelican, and Mole Lakes.[5]

Charles Ackley was prominently connected with Langlade County activities for many years. In 1947, Ackley claimed that he was 95 years of age. He based this claim on his recollection of the year that his father told him he had reached manhood. Langdale County, however, records his birth date as October 20, 1857. If the record was correct, Ackley was 90 years of age instead of 95.[6] Mr. Ackley died in 1952. The following account of his funeral appeared in the Antigo *Daily Journal:*

> With a rite never before performed in such a setting, and which Antigo probably will never see again, Charles Ackley, centenarian resident of Langlade County, son of its first permanent white settler, and grandson of Chippewa Chief Great Eagle was accorded the burial honors of the ancient Medawe ceremonial. . . .
>
> William Miracle, an elder member of the Mole Lake Band of Chippewas, took his position beside the casket and gave an address in the language of his people, making from time to time, the gestures appropriate. Chief Willard Ackley then took his place to give a free English version of what had been said by Miracle, who is the religious spokesman of the band, and

leads the tribal dances that form part of their religious expression.

The previous speaker, Chief Ackley said, had addressed the spirit of the departed, telling him that he was going into the presence of his Creator to be accorded a place at his right hand. He had lived well while he was with us, and he was entering the "happy hunting ground" where would be found all that is good on earth. In the joys before him he would not feel the want of his relatives on earth, and he was urged to go forward, entering into all of his privileges.

After summarizing the address by Miracle, Chief Ackley gave a short review of the history of his band, telling of Great Martin, the great-grandfather of Charles, of his grandfather, Great Eagle, his daughter, Maid of the Forest, the mother of Charles, and his white father, W. L. Ackley. References were also made to his later elder brothers, Ed (Missabe) and De Witt, one living to the age of 90 and the other to the age of 85. . . .

With a prayer in Chippewa, Chief Ackley completed his part. The service closed with a Chippewa burial chant by Charles Van Zile while all present stood.

While the curtains were drawn, the newly-made moccasins for the heavenward journey were placed on his feet. Also buried with the body were a small buckskin bag containing a key, a pipe, and three matches, two for his pipe, and one for light should he lose his way.[7]

As the above account shows, old pagan ideas are still a part of the life of these Chippewa.

In 1937, Mrs. Grace Shaw Ross of Crandon, Wisconsin, gave a resume of the early Mole Lake Indians. When the Shaw family moved to Mole Lake, the Chippewa Indians in the vicinity numbered about 400. The Shaws were friendly toward the Chippewa and endeavored to have them settle on a permanent area. The nearest village at the time was Pelican Lake, 22 miles away. Mrs. Ross described the situation thus:

We had always wondered that so many Indians remained here. They seemed to be kind of a lost tribe, as they had no government aid of any kind. About seven years after we located here, we tried to send some of the stray Indian children away to school, as they had no education of any kind. When the government agent came here to take them to Carlisle, and even furnished tickets for them to go, the tribe held a council. They refused to send any children, even orphans, as they said Uncle Sam had not done as he agreed with them in former years.

Then it was discovered that they had been promised all this land here for a reservation. They produced a treaty signed by Franklin Pierce, giving them this land. My father saw this treaty. It seems their agent who was to finish this treaty and secure the land for them, went to Washington to complete the deal. He was drowned on the lakes in returning. They never got the land, but still remained here.

When my father found this out, he wrote to the government about it for them. The government said they had at this time deeded the land to the Northwestern Railway Co., as a land grant. They could not now let them have this land but would give them each an 80 of land in Minnesota. But this they would not accept. They said all their people were buried here, and they would not leave this place where they had always lived.

Ever since that time, the tribe has been working to get a reservation established in this part of the country, but so far have not succeeded. The government has given them some aid at different times, distributing flour and clothing. For many years they were destitute, but now their children have been somewhat educated and can work.

The treaty signed by Franklin Pierce was finally lost in some way by the tribe, but they still have some emblems given them by the government.[8]

Mrs. Ross's statement regarding a treaty substantiates the Indians' claim to such a treaty.[9]

Before the reservation was incorporated, the Mole Lake Chippewa lived in extreme poverty. Except for a cook stove, there was little or no furniture in their tar paper shacks. These Chippewa welcomed the Reorganization Act and accepted a Constitution on October 8, 1938.[10] Since the Mole Lake Indians were now recognized as a distinct Chippewa band, Works Progress Administration built eighteen log houses for their use.[11]

The principal means of gaining a livelihood for this group are boat building, gathering wild rice and wreath greens, and selling souvenir bows and arrows, and other novelties. The soil, a sandy loam with gravel outcroppings, yields fair crops of potatoes and vegetables, oats, clover, and timothy hay. Game on the reservation includes deer, muskrats, and wild fowl. In 1944, eight families annually received an income of $2,000-1200 and four families $400 or less. Excepting four persons, all the Mole Lake Indians speak, read, and write the English language.[12] Since they have become an organized band of Indians, the stigma "Lost Tribe" has been removed.

THE ST. CROIX RESERVATION

chapter 17

THE ST. CROIX RESERVATION LIES IN BURNETT and Polk Counties, but many Indians belonging to the St. Croix band are scattered over Washburn, Barron, and Douglas Counties, an area which the Chippewa have occupied since 1700.

In 1854, after the Chippewa Indians of the Lake Superior area were placed on reservations, the St. Croix nomadic band refused to settle on any of the four designated reservations. Consequently, they were landless until recent years.

Chief Buck, "Ya Banse," was the leader of this group. A legendary account relates that at the 1854 Treaty parley, Chief Buck asked for land in the St. Croix area. Before the grant was settled, Chief Buck died at Little Rice Lake. Before his death, the Chief exacted from his people the promise to remain in the St. Croix area. He assured them that the government would keep its pledge to reserve for them the land that he had chosen. Two years later, the Indian chiefs again met at Madeline Island. Since Chief Buck had not appointed a representative for his people, the former claims of the St. Croix Indians were ignored. They were left landless.[1]

After the Allotment Act of 1887 was passed, this band of Indians made several attempts to identify themselves with Indians on reservations, but they were unsuccessful. Their lot has not been a happy one. The St. Croix Indians observed that the government provided reservation Indians with schools, hospitals, and other benefits. They, the "Lost Tribe," eked out a miserable existence as squatters on cut-over lands or on tax-delinquent land belonging to various counties.[2]

Finally, John Lonestar of Shell Lake, with thirteen other representatives of the "Lost Tribe," made a trip to Washington, D. C.

The delegation asked for official recognition as members of the Chippewa tribe. Their request was granted. They were organized as a Chippewa band under the Indian Reorganization Act of 1934. This recognition gave them title to lands that the government might set aside for them.

As a representative of the Indian Office, Frank Smart was ordered to take a government roll of the St. Croix Indians at Danbury, Wisconsin, in order that the band could receive some of the benefits of the Reorganization Act.[3] While taking the census, Mr. Smart noticed the dilapidated condition of the homes in the area. In 1938, through cooperation between the Great Lakes Indian Agency, the Burnett County Board, and the district Works Progress Administration, new homes were built at Danbury. A similar project was developed for the Ya Banse Community at Sand Lake near Hayward and at Round Lake near Luck.[4] When possible, the officials purchased land at the place where the Indians were living. With rare exceptions, the families were given the privilege of choosing the community in which they wished to live.[5]

The old settlers of Cumberland tell many stories of the Indians of this area. In early days, the Indians had hunting drives on an island near the present town of Cumberland. The men went southward and the women and children, together with a goodly number of dogs, scattered northward. With great whooping and screaming, the women thrashed through the woods driving the wild animals toward the men who killed them. When the white families settled on the island, the Indians brought blueberries, raspberries, fish, and bead work to trade for flour and other commodities which the white man had. The logging camps and settlers' homes were always open to hungry Indians. Frequently, on the next day, the redskin appeared at his host's door with an offering of gratitude — a fine fish or a choice bit of game.[6]

Semi-annually, members of the St. Croix band meet at Sand Lake for a ceremonial dance. In 1937, in a setting of sylvan beauty, John King, "Big Man," and John Kasabin, "Top of the Earth," summoned their followers to a fenced-in enclosure where the dance was held. The dancers, wearing native costumes, performed tribal dances as their forefathers had done centuries ago. This pageantry was meaningful to the Chippewa, but unintelligible to ordinary spectators.[7]

The total area of the St. Croix Reservation is 1328 acres. The principal crops grown on the reservation are hay, beans, and corn. Road construction, pulp cutting, cranberry farming, and collecting wild rice provide other means of livelihood. There is no data on the annual income of these Chippewa.

There were 160 enrolled members on the reservation in 1938, but the membership may reach 400. In 1942, the constitutions of the band were accepted under the Indian Reorganization Act. The tribal council consists of five members, both men and women. The standard of living at the St. Croix Reservation is low. Culture is part Indian and part white. Conditions were greatly improved by the building projects extending from 1938-1941. Fifty small houses were built for the group.[8]

PART

III . . .

INDIAN PROBLEMS

INDIAN ECONOMIC PROBLEMS

chapter 18

FOR MORE THAN FOUR HUNDRED YEARS, THE Indians of North America have been exposed to the civilization of the white man, and for more than one hundred and fifty years, the government of the United States has been endeavoring to solve the Indian problem. The question has been a burning one to humanitarians and a perplexing one to statesmen. After the expenditure of millions of dollars by the government, (although little of the amount expended actually reached the Indian) and the unselfish efforts of churches and philanthropic organizations, schools and hospitals, the United States is still confronted with an unsolved Indian problem.

During this more than a century of effort, much of which has admittedly been misdirected, white men have been trying to fit the Indian into their civilization. But they have been rolling the stones of progress up the steep mountainside of material civilization, only to have them, in the end, come tumbling down upon their own heads. By way of extenuation, many plead that the great majority of people have persisted in regarding the Indian as an alien, or as a ward of the Federal government to whom society at large owes no obligation and for whom the state in which the Indian lives acknowledges no responsibility.

The American Indian inherently possesses many desirable qualities and is generally regarded by those who know and understand him, as loyal and patriotic, and of all the non-Caucasian races, the most adaptable to the American form of government. Nevertheless, the fact remains that many Americans regard him as "a quaintly picturesque and unwashed portion of the primeval landscape," or as an interesting study for ethnologists, or perhaps, the hero of a "Leather-Stocking Tale."

Comparatively few people see in the Indian the germ of a useful and desirable citizen or look upon him as a human being, possessed of the same feelings, emotions, and sense of justice as the rest of mankind. The great majority of real Indians, those of more than one-half Indian blood, are not, as a rule, given the same degree of social justice and the same equality of opportunity enjoyed by other citizens. Their application for a job results in a refusal with the remark that there are no jobs for Indians. The government will take care of them. When Indians see members of other non-Caucasian races forging ahead and occupying positions of trust and responsibility, they must intuitively feel that being an Indian establishes their status in the minds of others as irresponsible, shiftless types of people with no ambition, desire, or capacity for improvement. This indifferent, uninterested, and unjust attitude on the part of the white population must be changed to one of active interest and cooperation, before conditions will materially improve. Moreover, the Indian must be induced to show a greater desire and willingness to improve his own condition by his own efforts.[1]

The lack of opportunity for his people in their native land was bemoaned by Chief White Cloud, a venerable patriarch of the Iowa tribe. As Chief White Cloud walked the streets of the Kansas town that bears his name, he discussed the future of his people. The husky old Indian chief pointed out that the government had established fine schools and colleges for his people, but that Indian youths were not allowed to find a place in industry and everyday life. He said: "The native land of the Indian now regards him as a foreigner. The Indian of today has little to look forward to." [2]

That the Indian can be brought to show a greater desire and willingness to improve his own condition was illustrated by an article which appeared in *Indian Education*, entitled "The Overstuffed Chair." An Indian Service Field employee had purchased an upholstered chair for his living room. One day, a young Indian called and was offered the place of honor in the new chair. The Indian's evident enjoyment of the chair prompted the host to ask him if he would like to own such a chair. He replied enthusiastically that he would but frankly admitted that he had no money. The white man told him to go home and plant an extra half acre in potatoes. The money received from these potatoes at harvest time should be spent for the new chair. The Indian followed the advice, and he, too, had an upholstered chair.[3]

A frequent accusation brought against the American Indian is that of laziness, shiftlessness, and general incompetency. To substantiate this statement, fingers are pointed at some of the Indians who adorn agency areas, gracefully doing nothing, except returning for rations or other charity. It cannot be denied that many Indians today find life pointless. They follow the line of least resistance by adopting a hand to mouth existence, with very little to put into the latter. What was the status of the Indian before he came under the influence of the white man? Florina Denomie, a Chippewa on the Bad River Reservation, interviewed an old Indian, James La Fernier, and asked him to answer the question. The following was his explanation regarding the self-support of Indians:

I have heard many statements made concerning the condition of the Indian before he came within the influence of civilization, and those who had the administration of his affairs were wont to magnify his uncivilized state, regarding him as an untamed animal more than as a human being, and the big issue thus created gave birth to the so-called Indian Problem.

That the Indian was a "problem" was only a condition of the mind of those who were appointed his guardians, and, as a matter of fact, he needed no guardian to look after him. True, he was hampered by the new mode of life brought about by the advance of civilization. The Indian faced new conditions which were foreign to him, many of his inherent rights were taken from him, and for a time he became an alien in the country of his birth.

My own experience has proved to me that the Indian was better off sixty or seventy years ago than he is today in so far as his ability to provide the necessities of life for himself and his family is concerned. The forest held unlimited game, the lakes and rivers plenty of fish, and there was an abundance of fur-bearing animals. The former provided for his table, the latter clothing and the sale of the surplus fur furnished the means to secure other things which the munificence of nature failed to provide.

It was not easy for the Indian to fit himself into the pattern of civilization. The removal of timber from the forest caused the migration of game to more remote parts, and the hamper of game laws, restricting his freedom to hunt where he pleased, all contributed to make adequate provision for his maintenance a difficult and complex problem. Yet, where conditions were equal, he was able to stand up with his white brother and earn his bread by the sweat of his brow.

All in all, the Chippewa is not lazy and he is eager to do all he can to better his condition, and having the heritage of the hardiness of his ancestors, he is equal to any task he is called upon to perform.

I repeat, the Indian was self-supporting in primitive days.

Today all he asks for is an opportunity to work to make him self-sustaining.[4]

This so-called Indian laziness was analyzed many years ago at a Carlisle graduation by Charles D. Carter, an Indian representative in Congress from Oklahoma. Mr. Carter answered the charges leveled against the Indian on the ground of laziness by stating that the apparent laziness was rather a lack of aggressiveness and initiative. He declared that, fundamentally, the Indian is not lazy. He never hesitates to exert himself in the pursuit of his real desires. In his more civilized state, when a task is set before him and he understands the responsibility as his own, he will complete the work with as much speed and efficiency as any person of a different race.[5]

The problem of securing a livelihood in his environment, basic to all peoples, presents many difficulties for the Chippewa. Fundamentally, they are a rural people. Until comparatively recent times, these Indians practiced an extensive culture of the land, rather than an intensive one. The Indian had large areas at his command which supported him with little labor on his part. The land abounded with fish, game, berries, nuts, and other natural products. The Indian's methods may appear inefficient, yet they were efficient enough to maintain his survival and to afford the leisure and the kind of life that he apparently desired. At least, his economy did not call for exploitation of resources to the detriment of future generations.

As the Indian was pushed back into limited areas, he could no longer depend to so great an extent on the bounties of nature for his subsistence. Buffalo gave way to cattle. Small areas had to be developed and intensively cultivated. Markets, price systems, values, and other mechanisms of modern economy were foreign terms to him and he faced a bewildering condition of life. The need to obtain a livelihood remained, but the methods to attain it were entirely different. The basic needs of food, clothing, and shelter had to be met, but the new economy failed to supply them satisfactorily. Thus the "Indian Problem" resulted.

As time went on, because of need and greed, the white man also encroached upon the limited areas set aside for the Indian. Lumber companies moved in, cut the Indians' pine, built stores that carried goods suitable for the wealthy, and gave the Indians coupon books in payment for their lumber. The Indians took the coupon books to the stores where they received the best of everything, all of which was paid for with a small scrap of paper. They did not worry about spending money. When nearly all the lumber was slashed from the forests, the lumber companies moved out as millionaire concerns. The Indians remained — paupers! The companies looked for more lands to cut over, leaving the Indians, as some one has expressed it "to hunt, root, or die." If the Indian was fortunate enough to have claim to any fund held in trust by the government, he was allowed to invest it in high-priced machinery, cattle, horses, and dynamite. The dynamite helped to blow up the only crop most of them ever raised in this section of the country, a crop of stumps left by the lumber companies.[6]

The transition of the Indian to the prevailing economy brings other problems such as that of creating new wants which only cash money can satisfy. One solution is to teach the Indian to use his diminished resources in such a manner that his increased wants can be supplied. Economic development programs must be such that the Indian understands their nature. He must help to formulate plans and procedures which, with assistance, he can carry out. However, on some reservations, resources are inadequate, even with efficient development, to supply a satisfactory standard of living.

In 1935, Congress in order to further the economic independence of Indians, passed the Arts and Crafts Bill. This act provided for the setting up of an Arts and Crafts Board to serve without compensation for the purposes of developing and improving Indian art and craft products, of organizing Indian producers of such goods, and of finding wider markets for the improved product. This Board was also given the power to protect Indian-made goods by the use of government marks of certification as to their Indian origin. It was also given the power to prosecute those who used this mark on goods not genuinely Indian-made or who imitated the label.[7]

The American Indian has proved that he is entitled to recognition among our most skilled workmen, and in some lines he has shown that he is superior to his white brother. In logging days, much work requiring skill and experience was done by Indians. They read maps; estimated timber; sealed, decked, and loaded logs; and sluiced and drove logs down the river. As lumbering operations progressed, Indians were engaged as graders, head sawers, and re-saw operators. In the planing mill, Indians were engaged in the setting up of blades — work that required special skill.[8]

The mechanical skill of the Chippewa Indians is now, (1954) being utilized in the ship yards at Manitowoc, Wisconsin, whither a number of Indians have migrated as a result of an Indian Service Placement and Relocation Program. Emmett Riley, Administrative Officer of the Indian Agency, furnished the following information regarding this plan:

The purpose of the Indian Service Placement and Relocation Program is to assist and encourage unemployed Indians to move voluntarily to areas where they will have full time, year around employment, so that the Indian can become self-supporting on a standard of living compatible with decency and health and to become a part of the social and economic life of the nation.

The Chippewas of Northern Wisconsin did not need much encouragement to take advantage of this program. Many of them had worked away from the reservation for years but always returned to the reservation for Indian Service medical care, education, etc. In the past many never left the reservations until the family funds were almost exhausted so that families were unable to move with the wage earner.

Assistance from the Placement Program has helped many families to move to industrial areas where the head of the family had full time employment. . . . All did not remain at their first relocation, some moved from Chicago to Milwaukee. As would be expected, some returned to the reservations, to date we can account for four families and sixteen unattached persons returning to the reservations. In addition to the number relocated with assistance from the Placement Program, we estimate that approximately 60 persons have moved to industrial centers without contacting the Placement Officer.[9]

During the years July 1, 1951 to June 30, 1953, this program has relocated thirty-one families and unattached persons, representing a total of 244 persons. Ninety-one persons were moved to Milwaukee; seventy-three to Manitowoc; sixty-one to Chicago; fourteen to Minneapolis and St. Paul; and a family of five to the state of Washington.[10]

This program is similar to that of the government program for displaced persons from European countries. The Indian Agency, through the state employment bureau and other agencies, first secures for the wage earner housing facilities and employment. Transportation and moving costs are defrayed by the agency which also assists the Indians financially until their first pay day. No attempt is made to place the Indians in colonies, but they are located where they will feel satisfied and will be able to be incorporated into the community.[11]

The economic plight of the Indian remains his most serious problem. What has the United States government done to alleviate it? The Congressional Record of March 16, 1943, contained this information:

> During the past 20 years the United States government has spent $643,000,000 on the American Indian and we are presently employing over 8,000 people in the Indian Service. The Indians are living on some 100 reservations. How many Indians are there now? According to the latest census, 333,969. Thus we find one government employee in the Indian Service for about every 40 Indians. If Indians average 5 to a family, this means 1 employee for every 8 Indian families.[12]

How much of this vast sum of $643,000,000 actually reached the Indian? An investigation was made by William Madison, secretary-treasurer of the Society of American Indians, on conditions among the Indians in South Dakota. Mr. Madison visited "Two Woman Armstrong," who was living in an old, dilapidated log shack on a reservation. Mr. Madison described the situation thus:

> This old log shack, which is her home, has a dirt roof and a dirt floor. She said that she had no articles of furniture, and no food on the premises and that when she asked the subagent at Wolf Point for help and food, he did nothing for her and advised her that she could drown her gophers for meat to eat.[13]

Conditions similar to the one cited were multiplied on that particular reservation. A like poverty is not found on the Wisconsin Chippewa reservations. The Placement and Relocation Program now in force is alleviating economic conditions to a great extent.

INDIAN EDUCATION

chapter 19

WHAT IS THE OBJECTIVE OF INDIAN EDUCATION and how shall the attainment of this objective be measured? In view of the investigations that show the economic plight of the Chippewa Indians, undoubtedly, one of the great objectives should be the attainment of self-supporting and self-respecting citizenship.

In their native state, Indian children were not educated in reading and number work as in our American schools. They were taught the type of education that would enable them to lead "a good life"; an education that inculcated skill in the arts and crafts necessary to make their lives livable and happy.[1] In colonial days, commissioners from Virginia informed six tribes of Indians that they would be pleased to provide for the education of a limited number of Indian youths. The government would provide for their needs and instruct them in all the knowledge of the white race. After the period of silence demanded by their notion of politeness, the Indians replied:

We know that you highly esteem the kind of learning taught in those colleges and that the maintenance of our young men while with you would be very expensive to you. We are convinced therefore that you mean to do us good by your proposal, and we thank you heartily. But you, who are wise, must know that different nations have different conceptions of things; and you will therefore not take it amiss if our ideas of this kind of education happens not to be the same as yours. We have had some experience of it.

Several of our young people were formerly brought up at the colleges of the northern provinces. They were instructed in all your sciences; but when they came back to us, they were bad runners, ignorant of every means of living in the woods, unable to bear either cold or hunger, knew neither how to build a cabin, take a deer, nor kill an enemy; spoke our language imperfectly; were therefore totally good for nothing.

We are, therefore, not the less obliged by your kind offer, though we decline accepting it; and to show our grateful sense of it, if the gentlemen of Virginia will send us a dozen of their sons, we will take great care of their education, instruct them in all we know, and make men of them.[2]

This reply of the Indians to the Virginians is well worth considering. Certain "learnings," although not always listed as such in our modern text books, are fundamental for Indian education. Among these learnings are care for one's sick body so as to protect others from infection, learning to conserve one's health and strength after illness, learning the feeling of self-respect that comes from economic independence — these are fundamental "learnings" that should not be overlooked.

Nevertheless, there is a basic core of things that all children must learn if they are to live under modern American conditions. This basic core includes the ability to speak and to understand the English language; to read with fluency and understanding; to communicate intelligently both in writing and speaking; to have some mastery of number combinations; and to acquire the ability to do straight thinking. The development of arts and crafts is not a solution that will cure all the economic ills under which the Indian suffers.

A highly significant event in adult Indian educational circles in the United States took place on the Bad River Reservation on July 12, 1940. Forty workers from the Indian division of the Civilian Conservation Corps were presented with diplomas representing successful completion of the eighth grade state accredited course.

To meet for one class weekly, the enrollees "banked" one-half hour a day for five days a week, with the accumulated half-hours serving as their classroom time for a period of eight months. They were taught by two Works Progress Administration teachers, Harry Kotleski and Ethel St. Arnold. Before graduation, the students passed the regular Stanford Achievement Tests and the diplomas were signed by both the county superintendent of schools and the state superintendent of public instruction. These were the first eighth grade diplomas issued to any Indian Conservation Civilian Corps in the nation. Included in the class were Indians from Bad River, Lac du Flambeau, Lac Courte Oreilles, and Red Cliff Reservations. Dr. J. D. Brownell, President of Northland College, Ashland, Wisconsin, delivered the principal address and presented the diplomas.[3]

That the Indian has splendid latent abilities is evident from a test conducted by Dr. Grace Arthur, formerly of the Amherst H. Wilder Child Guidance Clinic of St. Paul, Minnesota. One of Dr. Arthur's experiments was with Chippewa Indian children on the Red Lake Reservation in Minnesota. Dr. Arthur selected children with the highest percentage of Indian blood. Many of them were full blood Chippewa, with a limited English vocabulary and no experiences of any life outside their lake and forest environment. At first, they were shy. But they became friendly and were soon at ease.

These children, according to Dr. Arthur, were spontaneous, full of laughter, and more alive than city-bred children. Dr. Arthur describes one day's experience as follows:

> One day when I was going through a routine test procedure, I started to touch a wrong block. The motion was checked almost before it was begun. I am sure none of my adult friends, and probably none of our clinic children would have detected it. But glancing up, I found myself looking into a pair of black eyes brimming with laughter. This nine-year-old was apparently fully aware not only of the error, but of the fact that I thought it had been checked too quickly for her to have sensed it. Ears were as keen as eyes. It was never necessary to repeat instructions, or to urge these children to "look," or "listen." [4]

Similar tests were also conducted with the high school pupils at Red Lake. The results of these tests were equally interesting. Dr. Arthur writes:

> With the high-school pupils, I found the same tolerant humor that I have learned to expect from my adult Indian friends. One brilliant boy, in giving the difference between laziness and idleness during the Binet examination, said with an amused smile, "Laziness is sort of natural, but idleness is more accidental: you don't happen to have anything to do." In the same test, another pupil, in comparing poverty and misery, said: "Poverty, you haven't got anything. Misery, you are disgusted with what you've got."
>
> One girl had been somewhat defensive at the beginning of the examination. When she had finished, she gathered up the pencils, which had grown somewhat dull with use, took them to the pencil sharpener near the window, sharpened them, laid them before me on the table, glanced at me to make sure I understood this wordless apology, and quickly left the room. With the continual traffic in words of our present civilization, it

is restful to be with people who can, upon occasion, do business so comfortably without them.[5]

Dr. Arthur also experimented with Haskell Institute students, Lawrence, Kansas, a school which Indian students from all tribes in the United States attend. She reported:

A code test which I had demonstrated in a form that was correct from the position of the student, was carried out by one girl so that it was inverted from her point of view, in order that it might be right side up for me. When I looked surprised, she explained that as I had been nice enough to draw it upside down from my point of view so that it would be right side up for her, she was returning the courtesy. After a week of this kind of experience, I was not surprised to hear a teacher say that the most effective way to correct any kind of undesirable behavior in these girls was simply to tell them that it was not in good taste.

Results with the Kohs block-design test were astonishingly good. Difficult patterns that our white high-school students often are unable to copy within a four-minute time limit were reproduced in less than the required time by the majority of this group. On the Binet Scale, many responses indicated clear insight into the emotional verities. One student wrote: "Envy is hate. You don't like somebody because they do something better than you." It was interesting that in this group, envy was always described as a reaction to superior skill, never as an emotional response to greater material possessions.[6]

The results of the tests conducted by Dr. Arthur show that on the revised point scale of performance tests, the highest ratings were earned by students with the highest percentage of Indian blood. The averages, as compared with averages obtained from a middle-class American white population, indicate that Indian boys and girls, tested at high-school level, are definitely superior. These tests show that Indians have rapid and accurate observation, keen insight, steady nerves, and good motor coordination — qualities that should enable them to succeed in many fields that demand a high order of ability.[7]

Are Indian children hard to teach? Mrs. Juanita Bell, who entered the Indian Service as a primary teacher at Colorado River in 1931 and taught intermittently throughout the Southwest until her resignation in 1943, did not think so. Her penetrating understanding of Indian culture is revealed by the following poem which she wrote:

LITTLE INDIAN SPEAKS

People said, "Indian Children are hard to teach.
Don't expect them to talk."
One day stubby little Roy said,
"Last night the moon went all the way with me,
When I went out to walk."

People said, "Indian Children are very silent,
Their only words are no and yes."
But small ragged Pansy confided softly,
"My dress is old, but at night the moon is kind,
Then I wear a beautiful moon-colored dress."

People said, "Indian Children are dumb,
They seldom make a reply."
Clearly I hear wee Delores answer,
"Yes, the sunset is so good. I think God is throwing a bright
    shawl around the shoulders of the sky."

People said, "Indian Children have no affection.
They just don't care for anyone."
Then I feel Ramon's tiny hand and hear him whisper,
"A wild animal races in me since my mother sleeps under the
    ground.
Will it always run and run?"

People said, "Indian Children are rude.
They don't seem very bright."
Then I remember Joe Henry's remark,
"The tree is hanging down her head because the sun is staring
    at her. White people always stare.
They do not know that it is not polite."

People said, "Indian Children never take you in.
Outside their thoughts you'll always stand."
I have forgotten the idle words that People said,
But treasure the day when iron doors swung wide,
And I slipped into the heart of Pima Land.[8]

As Mrs. Bell has clearly shown, Indian children have the same mental and emotional outlook on life's problems that white children experience. With proper guidance, Indian children profit from an adequate educational program.

HEALTH ON CHIPPEWA RESERVATIONS

chapter 20   HEALTH CONDITIONS ARE, TO A GREAT EXTENT, dependent upon economic conditions. Since the majority of the Chippewa Indians in Wisconsin are undernourished and live in homes with inadequate sanitation facilities, health offers a problem of major importance. Prior to the coming of the white man, the health of the Chippewa was generally good, except when an epidemic spread through the community. Then the Indian was helpless.

It must be kept in mind, moreover, that among many Indians, the concept of illness was connected with religion. There was a conviction that illness was often due to transgression against supernatural powers, to violations of religious rites and traditional rules. The continued efforts of missionaries have not yet succeeded in dispelling these errors. The four leading causes of death among Wisconsin Indians are accidents, pneumonia, premature births, and tuberculosis. Since the chief causes of death among the white population are heart disease, cancer, and cerebral hemorrhage, it can readily be seen that the causes of Indian mortality are more preventable than those of the white man.[1]

As a step towards decreasing preventable deaths among the Indians, a Free Chest Clinic was conducted by the Wisconsin Anti-Tuberculosis Association in 1923, at Odanah, Wisconsin. The Milwaukee *Journal* carried this report of the clinic:

> "White man — he funny man —
> Tell Indian 'go in house.'
> Indian live in house.
> Indian get consumption.
> White man tell Indian
> 'Live outdoors.'
> White man — he funny man."

So said an old Indian chief to a government doctor. But the funny white man's health educational campaign, and especially the gospel of fresh air, is reaching his red brother. This fact was revealed in the free chest clinic held on the Bad River Reservation in Ashland County by the Wisconsin Anti-Tuberculosis Association in co-operation with the Wisconsin League of Women Voters, and is borne out in the statement of Dr. H. A. Sincock, Superior, former government physician on the reservation for twelve years, who assisted State Association physicians with the examinations.

"There is a marked improvement in health conditions among the Indians over that which prevailed when I came to the reservation fourteen years ago," said Dr. Sincock. "Indians have yet to learn the food value of milk; their homes are overcrowded and medical care is inadequate."

That these Chippewa have felt the ravages of tuberculosis, the white man's disease that came to them with civilization, is revealed in the clinic records. More than one-fifth of the 629 Indians examined came from families where at least one member had been a victim, and several had suffered the loss of one or both parents and a number of sisters or brothers from the disease.

Approximately 16 per cent of the 215 adults examined had tuberculosis and over 4 per cent of the 414 children examined were afflicted. Thirteen were found to be in need of sanatorial treatment. The children will be sent to the government sanatorium for adult tuberculosis Indians. Efforts will be made to take the adults to Pure Air Sanatorium, the Tri-County Institution for Ashland, Iron, and Bayfield Counties.

"Send us a doctor," was the plea of many of the Indian mothers to the clinic workers. Repeated attempts of the government agent to get a doctor to locate on the reservation have been unsuccessful, the monthly salary of fifty dollars paid by the government offering small inducement to a physician to start a practice in this little Indian settlement.

"This clinic was a most gratifying experience," says Dr. T. L. Harrington, one of the examiners. "One impression that stands out above all others was the number of splendid, sturdy, deep-chested, broad-shouldered young men and women I examined. America's first citizens are a strong and sturdy race, with alert minds and great possibilities. Nothing could give our Association more satisfaction than the knowledge that the ravages of tuberculosis have been checked among the red men, who seem to be particularly susceptible to this disease." [2]

In 1930, a second clinic was held for all the Indians of Bayfield, Odanah, and Red Cliff. Federal, state and local doctors and nurses conducted the examinations. The authorities were well pleased with the cooperation of the Indians.[3]

Undoubtedly the "health history" of the Chippewa reservations follows much the same pattern. A brief study of the records on the Bad River Reservation reveal that soon after the opening of St. Mary's School in 1883, black measles began to take their toll. In 1894, shortly after the construction of a sawmill, a resident physician was secured for the reservation whose services were paid jointly by the lumber company and the Federal government. The local doctors best remembered by the Odanah Chippewa for their efficient and kindly services were Dr. Judson Meyers and Dr. Henry Sincock.[4] Both of these doctors later became outstanding figures in the medical service of Superior, Wisconsin.

In 1923, after the departure of the lumber company, the company doctor also left the reservation. A physician stationed at Lac du Flambeau made weekly trips to Odanah, and a state doctor and county nurses also made periodic visits to the reservation. But these services were inadequate. However, Ashland physicians always responded to urgent calls.

Beginning with 1939, conditions approached the ideal. A practicing physician and surgeon from Ashland came to Odanah twice a week. The doctor was assisted in his work by a state nurse who spent three days of each week on the reservation.[5] In addition to the weekly clinic, the Federal government, at regular intervals, held special clinics providing chest, and eye, ear, nose, and throat services by specialists.[6]

Although many efforts have been made to stamp out tuberculosis among the Indians, the death rate from tuberculosis in 1940 was ten times that of white persons. To combat the disease, the Federal government X-rayed one-fifth of the Indian population in one year. Mantoux tests are given regularly to tubercular contacts. If a positive reaction is shown, the patient is taken to the Indian Hospital at Hayward for an X-ray. Indians requiring hospital care for tuberculosis may go to a Federal Indian sanitarium in Minnesota or to county or state tuberculosis sanitaria. The cost of hospitalization in county institutions is borne jointly by the state and county. In some instances, the Bureau of Indian Affairs has arranged to cover the cost of the county's portion for this hospital care. The county and the state share equally the cost of an Indian patient in state sanitariums. In some counties, authorities are unwilling to send Indians to tuberculosis sanatoria because little remuneration is made by the Indians in property taxes.[7]

In 1952, Dr. Edward W. Seaforth summarized health conditions on the Lac du Flambeau Reservation as follows:

Since my discharge from the U. S. army in July 1946, I have been employed by the Department of the Interior, Bureau of Indian Affairs, as a physician for the Indians on the Lac du Flambeau Reservation in Northern Wisconsin.

I took up my work in July 1946, under the most discouraging conditions. I will try to give you a cross section of general conditions existing on the Lac du Flambeau Reservation from 1946 through 1952.

(1) HOUSING

An average of more than three persons per room, without regard to size of the rooms. The majority of these homes are old and dilapidated, with lack of light, inadequate ventilation and heat, very little screening against flies and mosquitoes, and sanitary privies negligible in number. Such overcrowding affords the maximum opportunity for the spread of tuberculosis, pneumonia, common colds, influenza and numerous other diseases which are spread from one person to another, on account of too close contact.

(2) FOOD

In the homes of many of the patients I attended there appeared to be nothing to eat but potatoes three times a day, supplemented with fish and bread in some instances. This inadequate diet frequently results in malnutrition, scurvy, skin diseases, dental caries, and tuberculosis. These people needed to have a suitable quality and quantity of food – a balanced ration – to build up and maintain vital resistance to disease.

Isolated as the Indians are, far away from industrial and farming centers, they cannot have a plentiful supply unless it can be obtained from the products of their own soil. This cannot be done so long as they remain crowded in small villages miles away from their tillable soil lands. This ways and means of a food supply and resettlement, however, is a problem for the Extension and Home Economics Departments.

(3) MEDICAL

The average death rate prior to 1942 was twenty two (22) deaths a year (Indian population 1000).

From 1946 to 1952 the average death rate is nine (9) deaths a year (Indian population 1250).

During 1946 to 1952 two hundred and thirty six (236) births. Only one of these babies died at birth, due to congenital malformation. Two others died of pneumonia before six months of age. The others are all living today. There were no maternal deaths.

CONDITIONS REVERSED

During the past two years conditions have reversed, due partly to the fact that some one hundred (100) Indians are employed at the Simpson Electric Company in Lac du Flambeau. Housing conditions have improved, there is evidence of better food and nutrition, better clothing, and better observance of the laws of health. With more medical funds appropriated by Congress, it is possible to have modern drugs available.

Most of the Indians employed by the Simpson Electric Company carry health insurance and are able to take care of their own medical needs.

An intensive tuberculosis case finding and follow up program has been carried on the past two years.

At the present time there are five tuberculosis cases in sanatoria. No known active cases at large on the reservation.

Immunization centers for protection against smallpox, whooping cough and diphtheria, are held each month.

CONCLUSION

The Indians of Lac du Flambeau Reservation are, in my opinion, as strong and healthy today as the people of any other similar community having the same standard of living.[8]

The conditions existing on the Lac du Flambeau reservation are largely typical of those found on other Wisconsin Chippewa reservations. The significant point of the physician's report is that, with improved economic conditions, the health problems have decreased.

In 1954, the weekly clinics on the reservations, the part time contract doctors, and the public health nurse, together with the dental officer, are instrumental in keeping diseases at a minimum among the Indians. Services of regular county nurses are available[9] to all persons regardless of race. In counties which have regular set-ups for the prevention of smallpox, diphtheria, and whooping

cough, vaccination and immunization are provided to the Indians
on the same basis as to other persons. County, state, and Federal
social workers continue to unite their efforts with those of the school
and church for the betterment of moral, social, and sanitary conditions in the homes.[10]

THE LIQUOR QUESTION

chapter 21

THE INDIAN LIQUOR PROBLEM DATES BACK TO THE
coming of the fur trader. When the Indian arrived at a trading post, pelts were exchanged
for tobacco, cloth, and anything that the hunt did not furnish, including whiskey. The traders soon learned that the Indians were
easy to deal with when under the influence of whiskey. Consequently, liquor became one of the main items used in the exchange
of furs among the Indians. If the Indian wanted to purchase a gun,
the price was a stack of beaver hides equal to the height of the gun.
As this mode of exchange became a recognized standard, the height
of the gun kept increasing! However, the gun-trading barter did not
succeed with the Indian uninfluenced by liquor.

Many of the older Chippewa Indians recall that a similar system was used in the distribution of annuities at La Pointe and other
places. Under the influence of liquor, the Indian returned to the
white man nearly all the goods he had received in annuities.[1]

At the earnest request of the more far-sighted Indians who
desired protection from avaricious white men, a clause prohibiting
the introduction of liquor on reservations was incorporated into the
1854 Treaty. This provision was strengthened further by a Federal
Law passed in 1892, prohibiting liquor traffic on Indian lands. The
law also forbade the sale of alcoholic beverages to Indians who
were not on the reservation.

These regulations, however, failed to accomplish their intended
result. Under the system employed, many violators of the law, both
white persons and Indians, were heavily fined or imprisoned. In
some instances, the infliction of both penalties was authorized by

law. Despicable and under-handed methods were sometimes used
to obtain convictions. Sometimes Indians of low character were
ordered by officials to buy liquor, and later inform Federal agents
where it had been purchased. This use of Indians as decoys created
an atmosphere of hostility towards all Indians since they were
considered treacherous and untrustworthy.

A social stigma was attached to the Indian when he was
refused admission to bar rooms and other public places where alcoholic drinks were sold. This prohibition forced the Indian to keep
aloof from the general public and obliged him to seek the company
of undesirable white or Indian associates. An Indian who desired to
drink alcoholic beverages, sometimes procured liquor by hiring a
white man or a mixed blood to buy it for him. In some cases, he
turned to commercial mixtures, such as denatured alcohol, bay rum,
patent medicines, and the like.

An Indian who indulged rarely, moderately, or not at all, was
often placed in the same class as the immoderate drinker who was
not troubled about social stigma. The white man often pointed his
finger at an intoxicated Indian although he himself indulged in
like manner.

This discrimination against the Indian has been the cause of
deep resentment. An ex-service man of World War II living on the
Lac Courte Oreilles Reservation voiced his opinion in a letter to the
Evening Telegram in the following words:

> I heard an attorney say one time as he was defending a case
> for an Indian fellow, "I wish to say that this man is a Chippewa
> Indian and he is entitled to anything that a white man is en-
> titled to." But doesn't that mean, too, that he should be entitled
> to go into a tavern once in a while and get a glass of beer? It's
> about time Uncle Sam should be looking into this, especially
> when our Indian soldier boys return from overseas.[2]

In 1946, United States District Attorney Charles H. Cashin
denounced the terrible conditions existing on Indian reservations
which he attributed to the use of liquor. He stated that World
War II veterans, under the influence of liquor, were causing havoc
on the reservations. His indictment brought strong protests from
veterans of both World Wars I and II. The joint refutation of World
War I veteran, James White, Jr., and that of World War II veteran,
Gus Whitebird of the Bad River Reservation, totaled some 1100
words. After calling attention to certain articles in the Bill of Rights,
the two veterans pointed out the splendid service rendered by the

Indians during both World Wars. They refuted several charges made by the district attorney regarding the manner of living of the Indian and then discussed the moot liquor question. Part of their letter published in the Ashland *Daily Press* reads as follows:

> The Indian Liquor Laws, namely since 1802 — Section 2139, United States Revised Statutes, as amended June 15, 1938 (52 Stat. 696) and many other statutes are enforced upon the Indian, and are creating a hatred between the whites and the Indian. Even the veterans who are in uniform are not recognized as citizens, but are always humiliated whenever they enter public taverns for a bottle of beer. The bartenders like to patronize the veteran in uniform, by showing their patriotic respect for the uniform, regardless if it's on an Indian. But authorities enforce these liquor regulations to the letter upon the people, so that the proprietor cannot have the Indian permitted in the premises. . . . Time has come when the veteran Indian be given some consideration of his future status. He fought side by side with his white comrades, as a soldier, not separate and apart. Whenever legislation is effected to repeal these laws, many politicians employed under these statutes will be cast out of their feathered nests. This, however, will eliminate the expense of the Federal government and the taxpayer.[3]

That the liquor situation presents a real problem in connection with Indian life is evident. It is interesting to note that liquor traffic among Indians has been carried on almost entirely by white persons. During the 1940 calendar year, under Federal law, only 36 Indians were charged with selling liquor to Indians, while 634 white persons were arrested on that complaint.[4]

The ban against the purchase of liquor by Indians in taverns was removed by the passage of Bill 1063 on August 15, 1953.[5] The provisions of this bill also permit the sale of liquor on the reservations, if the tribal authorities desire it. Whether the passage of this new law will improve the liquor situation remains to be seen.

LAW ENFORCEMENT

chapter 22

LAW ENFORCEMENT ON RESERVATIONS AFFECTS not only the Chippewa in residence there, but also anyone living in neighboring areas. Several factors are responsible for the problems that arise regarding law and order among Indians. In allotted areas, the coming of the white man and his ideas of government have tended to destroy native social organization. Many Indian groups have also suffered an almost complete destruction of their native economy, thereby removing the very core of native social organization with its controls and discipline. Moreover, many Indian groups which have been reduced to economic dependency by the greed of their white neighbors, have resorted to drinking and other forms of escape. In like manner, the tendency of the general public toward lawlessness, combined with the notion that crime is permissible if one can avoid detection, has left its mark on the Indian. However, the great majority of Indians are law-abiding and Indian offenses are usually minor ones. Available statistics indicate that the Federal offenses for which Indians are most frequently convicted are larceny, theft, burglary, violation of Federal liquor laws, and a relatively few cases of criminal homicide.[1]

Under the provisions of the Indian Reorganization Act of 1934, Indian courts were established by many tribal councils, acting under authority of their own constitutions. In 1952, Lac du Flambeau was the only Chippewa reservation in Wisconsin with a tribal court, a policeman, and an active law enforcement system, operating with a code of law and order.

Prior to August, 1953, Wisconsin Indian court cases came under Federal authority, the United States Attorney trying crime cases committed by or against Indians in Indian country. These cases were brought to the United States Attorney by Federal Bureau Investigation agents or by the Bureau of Indian Affairs' agents. In general, minor offenses were not prosecuted by United States attorneys since Federal law made no provision for their prosecution.

The Federal government permitted tribal law to retain jurisdiction in the field of minor misdemeanors. Federal jurisdiction was almost exclusive in regards to violations of liquor laws by Indians.[2]

Several interesting court cases referring to the priority of the Federal Government over the state government have occurred among the Chippewa Indians. In 1938, the Indian rights' question, as it affected the Chippewa of the Great Lakes area, flared up as the result of the arrest of two leading tribesmen of the L'Anse Vieux region. Irate and "rights-conscious," the two Indians were on the warpath in an attempt to clarify a tangled situation that had grown out of their arrest and the subsequent conviction of one of them. The case in question was the illegal sale of a rabbit that had brought 60 cents, and the removal of a seal from a deer for the purpose of sale.

William Spruce and John Loonsfoot, the two Indians, claimed that two strangers approached them saying they were "city hunters," who had had no luck. They bought drinks for the Indians and then questioned them as to where they could purchase a rabbit and a deer. Spruce charged that the two men induced him to meet them at his own home, on trust lands. After he had accepted the 60 cents for the rabbit, the strangers flashed badges and placed him under arrest.

Loonsfoot, to whom Spruce had innocently directed the disguised conservation officers, was arrested by the same men after he had removed the seal from the deer he had shot. Pleading guilty, because it was the easiest thing he could do, Loonsfoot served 30 days in the Baraga County jail.

Although the Indians were within their rights according to treaty privileges of 1854, conservation officials refused to comment on this particular case. In the case of litigation already undertaken in lower courts regarding similar cases, conservation officials cited the game laws of the state. A high tribe member indicated that the Indians were ready for a decisive test case, but that the courts, to date, had rejected controversy on the issue. On the other hand, court action was reportedly halted in some cases because of the inability of the Indians to finance their claims. Leo J. Brennan, Baraga County prosecutor, had announced that the state would undertake a test case but he was unsuccessful because the Indians refused to litigate the case.[3]

How does an Indian become a citizen no longer subject to Federal court jurisdiction and how does an Indian cease to be a ward of the Federal government? Federal District Judge Ferdinand

A. Geiger of Milwaukee ordered two Indian attorneys to file briefs covering a response to the question. The Indian attorneys were defending two Indians, Paul Moore and Jerry Pero, who had been sentenced to life imprisonment for the murder on February 9, 1927, of Willard F. Marks, a Bad River Reservation druggist. The Ashland County Circuit Court had tried the case.

In November, 1935, Attorneys Thomas L. St. Germaine, a Chippewa from Lac du Flambeau Reservation, and William J. Kershaw, a Menominee Indian, instituted habeas corpus proceedings on the grounds that the Indian youths were wards of the Federal government and, as such, should have been tried in Federal court. District Attorney G. Arthur Johnson stated that the Federal court refused to try the case, therefore the trial was referred to a state court. The District Attorney claimed that, although Pero was a Chippewa Indian enrolled on the Bad River Reservation, he had a Certificate of Competency which placed him on the same status as a white man. Moore, the other Indian, had never been enrolled on the Bad River Reservation and had migrated there from St. Croix Falls, Wisconsin. Johnson concluded his statements by saying: "Federal courts have jurisdiction only when the crime committed involves an Indian ward of the government and is committed on restricted lands. In this case, the crime was committed upon restricted lands, but did not involve an Indian ward of the Federal government." [4]

Federal District Judge Geiger ordered the men released on a writ of habeas corpus. The Indian attorneys, St. Germaine and Kershaw had won the petition for the habeas corpus on the ground that as Chippewa Indians, Moore and Pero were wards of the Federal government and therefore only a Federal court had jurisdiction over them. Federal jurisdiction also arises, they argued, from the fact that the murder occurred within the boundaries of the reservation which is United States territory under supervision and control of the Indian Bureau of the Department of the Interior. Thus did the Indian lawyers reply to Federal District Judge Ferdinand A. Geiger's question. The Indians were later tried in a Federal court, but the sentence remained the same. [5]

What is the solution to crime prevention among Indians? Antoine Roubideaux, a Sioux of South Dakota, and chairman of the Rosebud Tribal Council, offers the following advice:

Only by turning our minds and hearts to God again and our fellowmen we can find ourselves. Then, by mutual understanding and putting our ideas together, work out our economic and industrial programs. By agreements and cooperative efforts put over our economic and industrial enterprises. These ought to occupy our minds more than anything else.[6]

Wayne L. Morse, while Dean of the University of Oregon School of Law, maintained much the same position in his article "Crime Prevention Among Indians":

Raising the general economic status and providing enlarged opportunities for vocational training would certainly help the situation. It will be noticed that most of the crimes committed by the Indians, . . . are due to economic causes. But the answer does not lie alone in the solution of problems surrounding poverty, inadequate housing, disease, and political corruption. Crime is a result of complex forces in which the attitudes and behavior characteristics of delinquency are fostered. Not only the agencies which deal with criminal justice, but all social institutions — the community, the home, the school, the recreation center, the church, and the welfare agencies, must cooperate in waging an adequate program for crime prevention.[7]

Perhaps the best solution has been offered by Mark L. Burns, Superintendent of the Consolidated Chippewa Agency in Minnesota. He said:

Since the home is the basis of all civilization, any attempt to improve Indian homes will be reflected in raising the standards of living for Indian families, educate Indian children, and better prepare them for the struggle to gain a livelihood, whether it be on the reservation or on the outside in white communities.[8]

PART

IV . . .

CHIPPEWA INDIAN CUSTOMS OF YESTERDAY AND TODAY

PERSONAL APPEARANCE, FAMILY LIFE, AND CHARACTER OF THE CHIPPEWA

chapter 23

THE SPLENDID PHYSIQUE OF THE CHIPPEWA MEN marked them as Nature's aristocracy. Their height ranged from six feet four inches to six feet eight inches. The Indian men had well-developed chests and sinewy frames. In contrast to these properties of great strength, they generally had small, shapely hands. Keen black eyes were matched by an abundance of black hair which did not turn gray at an early age. Sometimes the warrior's hair at the age of seventy-five was as black and as thick as it had been in his youth. Bald heads were a rarity. The Chippewa men usually had white, even teeth until past middle age, although they took no care of them. Their voices were usually high-pitched and resonant. Poise and grace marked their springy step.[1]

The women's appearance, in many respects, presented a direct contrast to that of the men. Instead of walking with an elastic step, they trudged along with a heavy, plodding motion, devoid of all grace. Their heavy gait may have been the result of the enormous packs, which for generations, they had had to carry. All their lives, many of the women had carried burdens weighing as high as 200 pounds.

The Chippewa man, in early days, rarely carried a pack, if there was a woman to do it. He put the pack upon the woman, while he strode magnificently ahead, carrying his bow and arrows; later a gun. Both parties considered this procedure as proper and natural. Often the baby, securely tied to keep it from falling, was perched high above the mother's head, on top of an enormous pack. When on a journey, the woman carried birch bark for the wigwam, rush mats for sleeping purposes, cooking utensils, and food. The canoe, weighing 80 to 100 pounds, was inverted and carried for miles over portages by the woman, while the warrior carried the light trappings. Sometimes, the Indian found it easier to move the entire family to the game supply than to bring the food home.[2]

In spite of her drudgery, the Chippewa woman exercised some of the rights enjoyed by modern women. She controlled, to a certain extent, the choice of leaders among the tribes. In assemblies, she was treated with respect and esteem.

The Indian woman was a devoted and careful mother, who gave tireless devotion and self-sacrificing service to her husband, her children, and her home. According to the age-old customs of the Chippewa, the woman's life was an industrious one, leaving her no time for idleness or discontent. She carried out her husband's slightest wish. When he came home from the hunt, it was her duty to remove his moccasins and to clean and dry them.

The Chippewa woman was the agriculturist of the tribe. She cleared the fields with the aid of fire and with the help of children, dependents, and guests. Sometimes the old men and the crippled assisted with the work. Woman planted corn, beans, potatoes, pumpkins, squash, and other crops. During the growing season, she carefully cared for the plants. When the crops had matured, she harvested them and stored away the surplus. The Chippewa woman gathered berries, nuts, grass seeds, wild rice, and other edibles. She was also a fisher-woman.

In addition to her role as breadwinner, the Chippewa woman was adept in the textile industry. She wove baskets, mats, and scarfs; she braided rugs, sewed clothing, and embroidered. The dressing and curing of skins and hides of animals was done by the woman. She also designed and made all the tools required in the various processes of tanning hides.

Mother and daughter were close companions. The daughter learned to do many things by watching and helping her mother. Indian children were reared in keeping with certain customs. When a woman became a grandmother, she watched over the behavior of her grandchildren. She was kind but firm in her admonitions and claimed that anyone who tried to live up to these teachings would reach a ripe old age.[3]

It was the custom of primitive Indians to arrange marriages for their children. When selecting a husband for a girl, the parents measured their choice by the man's hunting ability, for they judged that a good hunter would also be a good provider. The marriage consent of the youths was obtained through fear or respect for their elders. The youth was always older than the maiden.

After providing the young man's wigwam with new rush mats, his mother or one of his kin moved the bride's effects with those of the groom to the lodge. The bridegroom's kin then escorted the bride from her parent's wigwam to the bridal lodge and the couple was considered married. Instructions to the young couple by the older people concluded the ceremony.

Divorces among the Chippewa were usually announced at a public dance or meeting. The brave seeking a separation, took a double blanket, made a public statement that he was dissolving his marriage, and tore the blanket in half. He rolled one half of the blanket and threw it outside; the other half, he kept. The couple were then considered divorced. If there was a reconciliation later, the husband took clothing and other articles to the next dance. He publicly stated that at the last dance, he had dissolved his marriage to give his companion a scare. She had since come to her senses and had returned to him. He made amends by offering gifts of clothing. The marriage was thereby re-established.[4]

The early Chippewa, as a rule, were a monogamous people, although the taking of two wives was not considered out of the ordinary. Historians usually state that this practice was the result of a man's success as a hunter. They claimed that a good hunter considered that one woman was not capable of caring for the meats, hides, lodges, and gardens. If a man did these tasks, he would have been subjected to the ridicule of other men and particularly to that of the women of the tribe. Therefore, he took another wife.[5]

Rudolph Kurz, speaking of his personal experiences in a long life spent among Indians, wrote: "Polygamy among Indians is not a sign of sensuality, but simply shows their system of labor. I have known many Indians who had only one wife, and never had any other." [6] Father Baraga frequently complained of drunkenness and other vices among the Chippewa, but he made no allusion to polygamy. If polygamy had been common among the Chippewa, the missionary would have denounced the vice as frequently and as earnestly as he did the other failings of the Chippewa.

The Indian language reveals no word for "orphan." Since many children lost one or both parents, there was some social organization in every tribe that cared for such cases. Society, in general, was not hardened and the child was not deprived of the joys of homelife. Since relatives formed a closely-knit group with mutual bonds of affection, loyalty, and responsibility, parentless Indian children were cared for by their family or kinship group. Children were never formally adopted according to the white sense of that term. Except in the case of a partial adoption in memory of a departed child, adoption was reserved to making outsiders members of the tribe. Since the introduction of individual property subject to inheritance, Indian adoption is now subject to legal regulations.[7]

On hot summer evenings, the children of the Chippewa who lived along the shores of the upper lakes, frequently assembled before their parents' lodges and amused themselves by chants of various kinds intermingled with shouts and dancing. The chants were often addressed to the firefly, since the air literally sparkled with the phosphorescent light of these tiny creatures.[8]

Contrary to a common opinion, the Chippewa were not silent and reserved in their domestic life. From morning until night, there were continual jests and laughter in the wigwam. After an old woman had made some droll remark, the children repeated it and laughed at it. Other members of the family retold it, adding some ludicrous detail. Thus the lodge resounded with merriment. As long as the Chippewa had something to eat and no one in the family was seriously ill, he was happy and cheerful.[9]

Visitors observed little ceremony in entering a wigwam. Whether during the daytime or at night, they raised the blanket which hung over the doorway and went in without further ado. If the family viewed the visitor with favor, they might say: "Nind ubimin, nind ubimin," "We are at home, we are at home," — words which constituted a welcome. If nothing was said, neither considered it a breach of etiquette. When the master of the house wished to treat his visitor with great respect, he rose from his seat which was directly opposite the opening or door. Carefully, he brushed away any dust from the mat upon which he had been seated, and invited his guest to sit thereon.[10]

A visitor, in some respects, was regarded as a newspaper. He was expected to relate anything of interest that he had heard, especially if, as was often the case in early days, the next wigwam was five or ten miles away. The family and the visitor discussed deaths, sickness, and the affairs of other Indians generally. If the visitor had come from a strange village, he told the news of that village. The Chippewa were interested in all the other Indians. Generally each Indian man and often his wife, knew individually the men and women of all the other Indian villages within a radius of fifty to a hundred miles. Thus the host learned the current happenings among his fellow tribesmen, but generally the first item he inquired about was the place of the annual payment — its nearness or its remoteness.

The Chippewa had no regular hours for eating. They ate when they were hungry or when the mother had prepared the food. Without questioning, a visitor was given food as long as there was any in the wigwam. When the dish was set before him, it was considered good etiquette for the visitor to say "Oonghondijita." Roughly translated, this means, "O, this goes to the right spot." A white visitor was expected to pay from ten to twenty-five cents for a meal; an Indian took the favor as a matter of course. Even if the visitor had never done a stroke of work or if he had just returned from losing a gambling game, he shared the food of the others without question. If the host wished to show great respect to the visitor, the food was placed on a white cotton cloth.[11]

The assurance of a long life was one of the rewards promised to a faithful observer of the Midewiwin or Grand Medicine Society. Therefore, old age was a mark of distinction among the Chippewa. Statistics prove that many Indians attained to a great age, but it is difficult, in many instances, to secure the accurate age of an Indian.

In early day, dates were not recorded as such. Events were remembered by being associated with happenings of significance or with some phenomenon of nature, such as an eclipse of the moon. "I shall be married fifty years next berry-picking time," is a typical response to a query regarding the age of a person well-up in years. Events in the lives of persons were frequently placed according to the developmental period: "before I could walk," "when I was already an old woman." [12]

Perhaps "the Grand Old Man" of the Chippewa Indians was John Smith, of Cass Lake, Minnesota. The June, 1939, issue of *The American Indian* reported that Smith died at the age of 129 years.[13] The Leech Lake sub-agency records showed that he was 118 or 119 years of age at the time of his death in 1922. But the agency records may not have been correct. According to a 1937 report, the Commission at the Agency, at the time of John Smith's enrollment, guessed his age.[14]

Another historic character was Seymour January, the last of the Solon Springs Chippewa who for 98 years had watched upper Wisconsin change from a Chippewa hunting paradise to a white man's work-a-day world. Michael James, "Tchmens," grandfather of Mrs. Frank La Fernier on the Bad River Reservation, lived to the approximate age of 103 years. Mrs. Delia Diver, "Qui-ka-ba-no-kwe," "Dawn Woman or Towards East Woman," was regarded as the oldest woman in Ashland County at the time of her death in 1940. Newspapers reported her age as 98 years.[15]

The early Chippewa was strongly attached to the area of his birth and he generally lived and died in his native village. Since he knew nearly every tree and stream of water for miles around, the thought of leaving his native settlement filled him with dread. Large numbers of Chippewa were not tempted by the offer of four or five years' rations and machinery with which to farm in more fertile regions. The Chippewa reasoned thus: "Here I have a good supply of fish, venison, wild rice, and berries. If I go to a place where there are none of these things and where I must plough and work for a living, perhaps I shall have a hard time. I will not be tempted by these offers." [16]

By way of summary, the following analysis of Chippewa character, written in 1897 by Reverend Joseph Gilfillan, is given for the reader's perusal:

> In one respect the Indian is remarkable. He is such a reader of character. There is no use trying to deceive him. He seems to look right through a person, "sizes him up," as the phrase goes, much more accurately than we can. They are very accurate judges of a person's social standing.
>
> What does the Indian think of the white man? We show them our electric lights and our other wonders, and think they will fall down and worship us as superior beings. It is not so. The Indian, it is true, sees his white brother do many wonderful things. But put the white man in his circumstance, and he is a miserably helpless creature, far inferior to the Indian. He does not know how to make a camp, how to protect himself from the cold, how to find the game. Put an Indian and a white man into the woods; the white man can see nothing and will starve to death, the Indian can find a good living. In the Indian's country and in the same circumstances, the white man needs the constant help of his red brother to keep him alive. . . . In brief, the Indian sees that he is just as superior in his sphere as the white man is in his. The Indian has a far higher opinion of himself than the white man of himself. "Do you not know" said one of our Indian clergymen to me "that the Indian thinks his body God?" That translated into our idiom means that he has a very high idea of his own personality. Consequently the one who treats him with very great respect is the one who gains his esteem and love.
>
> It is strange also that with the Indian, amiability is the test by which he judges. One of themselves may do anything, no matter how outrageously bad, even according to their own standard, and he will not lose caste in the least. He will associ-

ate with the others precisely as before, without a thought on his part, or on theirs, of there being any difference. But if he loses his temper, or, as we say, "gets mad" he has utterly fallen in the Indians' estimation. To lose control of one's self, to get in a passion, to scold, is with the Indian the unpardonable sin. I cannot remember ever to have seen an Ojibway in a passion.

The Ojibways have certainly many strong points. Their speech is clean. I can hear more bad language among my own people in half an hour than I have heard among the Ojibway in over twenty-four years. They never swear, and I have heard very little obscene language. Once at Sandy Lake I did hear such language; almost every word was foul, but I saw they were only imitating some of the scum of the frontier, whom they have met, and that they thought it was smart. That is saying a great deal for them, cleanness of speech.

And they are far more honest than the whites. I have inquired everywhere among the lumbermen, for hundreds of miles, and the testimony is always the same, namely, that where the Indians are they can leave things lying about and nothing is taken. But when the whites came there was a sad change. From Bemidji through Pokegama Lake to Mille Lacs, the testimony is always the same. They have also more respect for the law, and more fear of the law, when they know a thing to be law than the whites have.

Among the poor Ojibways, life and property are absolutely safe. There has been no instance of any man or woman having robbed or "held up" another, red or white, in a quarter of a century. They would never think of such a thing, and it makes no difference how much money a man may be known to have on him, he is perfectly safe. A helpless woman or child might go from end to end of their country by day or night, and would never be molested.

Among the Indians one has a feeling of absolute security in person and property. During the twenty-four years I have never carried a gun or pistol when travelling among them, and that was almost constantly, in a circuit of three hundred miles, except once for fear of wolves; and never have I had firearms in my house except once, when some white tramps were reported to be meditating an attack, of whom the Indians also were mortally afraid.

My family and I never received anything but kindness from the Indians, and never felt one moment's apprehension.

Once we were gone for three months, and the house, unten-
anted, and filled with things they needed, stood by the roadside. When we came back it was untouched. All of us, when
among the whites, at certain times and in certain places, fear
and are on our guard; when we want absolute security, we go
among the poor Ojibways.[17]

INDIVIDUAL NAMES AND SURNAMES

chapter 24

IN THEIR ABORIGINAL STATE, THE CHIPPEWA WERE
not grouped in families under common surnames. The individual was given a name which
identified him, but it did not designate his family or lineage. The
instances in which a name denoted lineage were extremely rare.
The tracing of lineage was left to the memories of the individuals
or to the whole tribe. The genealogy of a person was kept for at
least a century. After the Chippewa had adopted the customs of
white civilization, surnames were given to them.

The majority of the Chippewa received their personal names
during their childhood in conjunction with the ceremony "bestowing a name." However, there are instances where an individual name
was acquired by virtue of prowess in the occupations or pursuits of
the tribe. The "bestowing of a name" was the Indian equivalent of
the ceremony of Baptism as practiced by Christian nations. The
event was marked by speeches, solemnity, and feasting, which characterized all important social activities of the Indians.

At the feast, the host requested the guests to name the child.
Usually, a name thus bestowed, had its origin in a dream and referred to some outstanding quality of the vision in the dream. This
act of bestowing a name created a bond of kinship between the
"namer" and the recipient of the name, a kinship considered equivalent to blood relationship of a close degree. In some instances, the
name given to the child was the personal name of another individual. A close bond was created between the person so honored
and his namesake, "Ni-a-we-e."[1]

Names bestowed with ceremony in childhood were deemed sacred. Out of respect for the spirit under whose favor the names were supposed to have been selected, the Indians seldom pronounced these names. As an endearment, a mother frequently called a male child a bird or young one. By way of reproach, she addressed him as bad boy or evil doer. These names often adhered to an individual throughout life. Parents also avoided the true name by saying, "my son," "my younger son," "my elder son," "my younger daughter," "my elder daughter." [2]

In the early days of the Bad River Reservation, a Presbyterian Mission conducted a small school on the reservation. The teachers experienced difficulty with the Indian names of their pupils or sometimes with the lack of them. To overcome this handicap, they gave their pupils the names of biblical and historical characters, and, sometimes of acquaintances. In some cases, different surnames were given, by mistake, to members of the same family. Some of the children discarded these names upon leaving school. Among the names of noted white persons which have been retained are Greeley, Webster, and Jackson.

Other surnames originated purely as nicknames. When the Reverend Manypenny left the Bad River Reservation, he gave his tall silk hat to one of the Indians who had manifested a special admiration for it. When this old Indian was seen wearing the hat, the other Indians greeted him as "Manypenny." The name remained with him and was inherited as a surname by his descendants to the present time. [3]

The surname "Messenger" is said to have originated with George Messenger's father, who until his death, was one of the chiefs on the Bad River Reservation. The old man, in his youth, was a fast runner. During Civil War service, he was selected as a messenger. Thus he was designated "Messenger" by his comrades. The name remained with him and has been inherited by his descendants.

The complexities of civilization made it imperative that the Chippewa use surnames. The lack of a family title often proved confusing in business negotiations and in attempts to establish or to prove lineage. The Chippewa personal names, of which Gitchi Wabisheshi, (Big Martin), Mis-kwa-kwi-wi-sens, (Red Boy), are examples, were both difficult to pronounce and to remember. To offset the inconveniences caused by these original names, the Chippewa, in some cases, readily adopted surnames. In certain localities, Indian names were lost sight of by intermarriage with white persons. Then, too, many of the Chippewa translated their names into

English with pleasing results, as: Bird, Rice, Lake, White, and Cloud. For some, English translations resulted in fanciful-sounding names, as Big Boy, Two Birds, and Loon's Foot, all surnames of large Chippewa families today. Some Chippewa retained as surnames the title of one of their earlier kin in pure Chippewa pronunciation as Chingway or Ramesay. Others have adopted an Anglicized version, as Jimens or James for Tchemens.[4]

TOTEMS AND TOTEMIC RELATIONSHIPS

chapter **25**

ONE OF THE DISTINGUISHING CHARACTERISTICS prevalent among the Chippewa Indians was their division into clans according to the Totemic System. The Totemic System is not peculiar to the Indian tribes, since it is at the root of nearly every primitive religion. Since the totem had for its basis the belief that all men have a kinship with animals or plants, it probably had a deeper influence on Indian character than any other element in his culture.

The Totemic System or relationship was traced back to several grand families, each known and perpetuated by a symbol representing some bird, animal, fish, or reptile. The totem symbols invariably descended from the male. After having made known their clan or totem, it was a common occurrence for individuals to make claims of kinship. A person of the first, second, or third totemic affinity was cordially received and held in high esteem by the acknowledging kinsmen.[1]

The principal totems of the Chippewa were the crane, loon, bear, marten, wolf, and catfish. Approximately four-fifths of the Chippewa belonged to these totems. Other animal totems were the beaver, moose, lion, lynx, raccoon, and reindeer. The eagle, black duck, gull, goose, and hawk were prized as bird totems. Among the lesser fish totems were the pike, sucker, perch, bullhead, and sturgeon. In later years, the chicken was the totem of children whose mother was an Indian woman and the father a white man, but not a Frenchman. Since the white settlers had these fowl, the "chicken totem" became acceptable. Because the lion appeared on the French Royal Coat of Arms, it was the totem for children of Indian-French descent.[2]

Animal exemplars of the several totems were regarded with great reverence. Many instances are told of Indians' refusing to kill or molest their totem symbol. One old Indian was guiding a white man in a boat along the lake shore. Suddenly, they saw a deer run from the woods and plunge into the water. Shortly after the deer had disappeared, a huge timber wolf, apparently chasing the deer by scent, came to the water's edge, and sniffed the water. The white man lifted his rifle to shoot the wolf. The old Indian promptly intervened, exclaiming sharply, "eh! eh! gigo. Mi ow nin-dodaim," meaning "Don't, that is my dodaim!" Another aged Indian woman whose totem was the bear, was highly pleased with a gift of a "teddy bear." The Indians frequently had some part of their totem symbols, such as the teeth, claws, and skin in their possession. Sometimes they made effigies of the animal. Always they regarded their totem in the sense of a guardian spirit.[3]

Since animal totems were looked upon with such great respect, there was a tradition among the Indians that if an Indian insulted the totem of another Indian, he must apologize or make amends in some way for the indiscretion. James Scott, a Chippewa from the Bad River Reservation, explained what happened to him when he inadvertently insulted the totem of an Indian woman:

> About fifteen years ago, (1925) a feast was held at Da-dac-ko-mosh Frost's house, which I attended. In addition to the meats, potatoes, and other foods, platters of fruit were served. I took a bunch of grapes, and on leaving, I had four of the grapes with me. I handed them to a lady named Ma-ge-com-e-go-kwe, and told her in a friendly spirit to eat them, little thinking that she would resent this, and consider it as an insult to her totem. She misconstrued my friendly intention as an insinuation that her totem was hungry, and felt it her duty to protect the honor of her totem. Accordingly, a feast was held. The purpose of feasts of this nature was to rectify wrongs of the one whose totem had been insulted. The offender was required to eat everything that was set before him. He was, however, allowed to call upon his totem and take members of his own clan to help him.
>
> Shortly after this, Frank Gishkad came to me and, after giving me some tobacco, told me that I was invited to a feast at Ma-ge-com-e-go-kwe's home. He cautioned me to attend. I did

not know what the feast was for, but James Stoddard and many of my friends knew its purpose. They also attended the feast.

When I arrived, I found the setting a perfect tribute, if the spirit in which it was offered had been different. I saw a large pile of blankets and quilts — all for me. An immense dish filled with food was set before me. I was in luck, however, since many others of my clan, the duck clan, were present and they came to my rescue. One of the rules was that if the insulter did not turn his plate upside down on the table, after eating, a still larger feast would be served. I did nothing, however, I merely tasted the food, since I felt hurt and thought the procedure of this woman was unwarranted. I rose from the table and left, nor did I touch any of the gifts intended for me. If Ma-ge-com-e-go-kwe had indicated her displeasure in some other manner, I should have been glad to make apologies, although she had absolutely no occasion to take offence. Certainly my act in giving her the grapes could have been easily explained. But she had the satisfaction that she had spared no effort to appease her totem, since big feasts like this one, are according to Indian belief, especially pleasing to the totems.[4]

At the time of the offense, a warning was generally given to the delinquent. If he said, for instance, that the fish was dry and gave it a toss, the insulted person might answer with a grunt, "Wait, I shall see that my totem becomes moist." If the offended person did not want to create a scene, he interviewed the violator alone. The offender had to acknowledge the wrong he had committed against this person's totem. Furthermore, he promised that he would never commit such a grave mistake again. When this was done, the affair ended. However, if the offended party had discussed the matter with other clan members, then it was no longer his personal concern. The clan members were obliged to see that the insult was avenged.

Reparation for a totem insult was a "gorging feast." All clan members contributed food. The food donated was determined by the kind of food eaten by the totem. If the totem of the offended person was a fish, some fish were placed into a bowl or pan over which alcohol or some other beverage was poured. After the offending person had eaten the fish, he drank the liquid in the bowl. The bowl was refilled and emptied again by the offender. At the conclusion of the gorging, an old man arose, expressing his regret that his fellow clansman should have been so thoughtless as to belittle another's totem. He asked that in the future, all respect the totems of others and thus avoid disturbances. The old man's apology in behalf of his clan member was accepted and the insult was repaired.[5]

The extent to which the early Chippewa believed that the totem assisted him is almost unbelievable. The following incident is supposed to have happened to August Whitebird's grandfather:

In his early boyhood, Ogeemageezship (Whitebird's grandfather), went through all the trials and hardships of a hereditary chief's life. His fasting was of the most strenuous type. Already in boyhood, he showed signs of becoming the well-loved and forceful chief he became. During his fasting, he dreamed about a buffalo. The buffalo told him: "Ogeemageezship, whenever you are in trouble, look to me for help. All through your life, I will be your guiding light. I will come to your aid when you need it. You must never be afraid to ask my help at any time." With these words, the buffalo vanished from his dream. The boy awoke with renewed vigor and the ambition to carry the responsibility placed on him as hereditary chief.

When he grew into manhood, he was regarded as one of the foremost leaders of the tribe. One day, when he was camping with his family and a group of Indians who were picking berries, he decided to hunt for small game. Taking a rifle, he started out. Suddenly he came upon a large black bear that had been feeding on berries in the vicinity. The bear began to walk away, then suddenly turned and charged. Ogeemageezship, seeing no escape, fired at the bear, but the bullet scarcely penetrated the bear's thick hide. This made the bear furious. Taking his small hatchet in hand, the chief waited for the charge. When the bear was at close range, Ogeemageezship struck at it but missed, and the hatchet slipped away from his grasp. The warrior began to fight with his rifle. The campers, hearing the noise, rushed to the rescue. They came upon a large bear that had just been slain. Nearby lay Ogeemageezship, cut, battered, and unconscious.

Close inspection of the scene of conflict revealed large hoof tracks like those of a buffalo. It was assumed that these tracks were those of buffalo. Ogeemageezship had called upon the buffalo to come to his aid and they had responded. This story was verified by old residents of Odanah and many testify (1937) that they saw the buffalo's hoof prints on the ground.[6]

As recently as 1937, a totem pole ceremony was enacted on the Bad River Reservation in connection with Midewiwin ceremonies. James Scott reported that the straw matting on the floor was covered with white sheeting. Four tobacco bowls, fashioned from turtle backs, were set in the center of the spread. Indian foods, such as hominy, wild rice, maple sugar, fish, venison, and berries were placed on one end of the matting. Medicine bags made of the skins of various fur-bearing animals and fowls were laid side by side on the matting. Bundles made from strips of colored cloth with a tobacco offering attached were set near the medicine bags. A large stone ceremonial pipe, filled with kinnikinick, was presented to the master of the secret order who later passed it to the other men present.

After smoking the pipe, the master of the secret order spoke to the assembled Indians as follows: "You people heard what was announced yesterday afternoon by Waishke Martin at the medicine ceremonial dance. She begged me not to mention the names of the two men who gave her the information because 'small-town talk' is dangerous. She was told that voices of unseen persons had been heard. Similar voices were heard in earlier days when an epidemic of black measles spread so rapidly that the almost incessant tolling of the mission church bell announced the death of Catholics. The firing of a gun proclaimed that one of the pagan Chippewa had fallen a victim to the deadly scourge. Punishment had come upon the Chippewa people because they had neglected their duty to Gitche Manitou, the Great Spirit. Perhaps the present voices are warnings that a misfortune of similar nature is imminent." [7]

After the speech, the master of the secret order asked a blessing on the food. At the conclusion of the feast, the master requested his associates to prepare powerful medicine which the people must keep in readiness in case of another epidemic. Herbs were ground into powder, as prescribed by ritual. After the medicine was prepared, each person was given a small portion.

The master of the secret order continued the meeting by asking the Great Spirit to guide the people and to preserve them from accidents as they journeyed through life. He ordered that half of the bundles be hung or tied to the totem pole as an offering to the Great Spirit. This pole, 40 feet in height, stood within 20 feet of the Newagon home. The bundles containing the offerings of tobacco and clothing were tied, one above the other, half-way up the totem pole. Because of the difficulty in reaching the upper part of the pole, the remaining bundles were thrown into the Kakagon River. The "medicine" was carefully preserved in medicine bags.[8]

In general, among Wisconsin Chippewa, at the present time, the totem is regarded as a conservation expediency. If fish is one's totem, it is incumbent upon the person who has that totem to see that fish are not wasted.[9]

CHIPPEWA ADOPTIONS

chapter 26   SEVERAL KINDS OF ADOPTION PREVAILED AMONG the Chippewa. The most common, in times past, but now regulated by law enacted by Congress in 1940, was that which took place when death occurred in a family. A mutual agreement was made between two families. The family of the deceased adopted a son or daughter from another family, through the family ceremony adoption, one of the Chippewa's most solemn ceremonies. The adopted child took the place of the dead one and was treated with the same affection as the deceased member whom he represented.

In 1936, Robert Wilson gave an account of his own adoption into a Chippewa family:

> One of the most vivid pictures of my boyhood days, which I recall with singular pleasure, was my adoption by a family which had lost their only son by drowning. As the lost boy and I were about the same age and size, and I resembled him closely, this family chose me as their adopted son. This is how it happened:
>
> On June 16, 1925, Joseph Martin, aged seven, was having real sport sailing an old raft on the Bad River. Possibly it was in an attempt to jump from the raft to the shore that he missed his footing and slipped into the river. Unable to swim, he sank to the bottom of the stream. Some hours later his body was recovered and in a few days a small mound covered his mortal remains.

The paternal grandmother of the drowned lad prepared for the adoption of a young boy to replace her grandson. I was selected for this role. My parents were requested to bring me to the Martin home. I was given all the dead boy's clothes and was urged to make frequent visits to his parents. I went frequently to the Martin home and was received each time with kindness.

One year later, in accordance with Chippewa custom, a sumptuous anniversary feast was given in memory of the drowned Martin lad. My parents were invited and my father asked me to accompany him. From the moment we arrived at the Martin home until we departed, I was the object of special attention and favors. I was immediately ushered into a side room and given one of the most beautiful beaded costumes I have ever seen. Gladly I donned the regalia.

Then I was ushered into a large room where all the old men of the tribe were seated and I was given a seat of honor among them. Speeches were made by the old men. Since they spoke in Chippewa, I did not understand what was said, but I learned afterward that they explained the old custom of keeping the anniversary of a deceased person.

After the speeches ended, the dance of commemoration took place. I was the leader of every dance. Then a feast followed during which I sat at the head of the table as guest of honor. Waboose, Joe Baker, an old medicine man, gave a speech which made me the owner of the beautiful costume that I wore. I was also given a complete outfit of citizen's clothes. My father gave the acceptance speech in my stead. For three or four hours, I, a lad of ten summers, had been honored as a king. I went away happy as a lark, the proud possessor of an Indian costume which I still possess and prize highly.[1]

The Chippewa have adopted Indians of different tribes and even white men as bona-fide members. Captives who displayed extraordinary bravery or who had performed some notable feat were adopted with the consent of tribal chiefs. The person adopted was thenceforth accorded all the rights and privileges of the tribe. After the segregation of Indians on reservations, the ceremony of adoption became more formal and also more rare. Now it is only by a majority vote of the Tribal Council that such an official adoption can take place. However, the Indian Office at Washington reserves the right to confirm or to reject such an adoption.

Beginning in 1901 and continuing for some years, a number of orphans, averaging two or three years in age, were sent to the Lake Superior country by a New York City society. At least twelve of these children were placed in homes of mixed blood.

In recognition of some deed of valor or achievement, adult white men were sometimes adopted into the tribe. Ceremonies of this form of adoption closely resemble those of the so-called Adoption Ceremony, but they do not equal them either in duration or in solemnity. These adoption ceremonies are a public expression of the high esteem in which the adopted individual is held by the adopting tribe. One of the most notable adoptions of the Lac Courte Oreilles Chippewa tribe was that of the Reverend Francis C. Young, of Chicago, author of the patriotic prayer-poem, entitled *Our Nation's Prayer*. From 1921 to 1937, Father Young had spent his summer vacations on Lac Courte Oreilles Reservation. During one of these vacations, Father Young constructed most of the furnishings of his rustic lodge, "The Angelus." When the lodge was completed, Chief Peter Wolfe conducted colorful induction ceremonies at "The Angelus," making the Chicago priest an honorary chief. He was given the name "Nago mo Inini Me Ka Te wika na i e" which in ordinary parlance means "Singing Man Black Robe," or poet priest.[2]

The same Chippewa band also adopted Colonel Carl R. Gray, Jr., executive vice president of the Omaha road. The ritual was part of a Sunday afternoon program on the Minnesota Sportsmen's Show on November 14, 1937. Chief Oconomcai, Johnny Frog, presented the tribal war bonnet to Colonel Gray. This headdress, the hand work of the Chippewa, contained a number of eagle feathers. Since the Chippewa no longer kill eagles, they had sent to western states for the plumage. Mr. Gray was given the Indian name "Bewabik-Go Gaba-shigo Gunshe," meaning "The Iron Horse." [3]

On August 15, 1938, at Ashland, Wisconsin, the Chippewa of the Bad River Reservation bestowed tribal honors on Admiral William D. Leahy, Chief of the United States Naval Operations, and on Commander Daniel J. Doherty, National Commander of the American Legion. The gifts presented by the Chippewa represented their sincere esteem: the eagle feather headdress signified that the recipient was considered a leader; the moccasins indicated the donors' desire that the wearer tread softly and comfortably, side by side with the Indian in seeking and preserving a lasting peace; the calumet signified and sealed everlasting friendship between the donors and the recipients. In recognition of his untiring efforts to make the United States Navy outstanding, Admiral Leahy was given the name "Kitchi Be Ba Mash," meaning "Great Sailor." [4] Commander Doherty was accorded this honor because of his efforts to promote world-wide peace. He was given an Indian name which meant "Big Chief of the Peace Time Army." [5]

Rarely does European royalty acquire another title on American soil. Such was the unusual distinction afforded to Prince Olav of Norway upon the occasion of his adoption by the Chippewa Indians. The adoption took place in Superior, Wisconsin, with the Lac Courte Oreilles Indians in charge of the ceremonies. Frank Smart of the Bad River Reservation acted as interpreter. Prince Olav was christened "O-sha-wa-sh-ko-gi-jib," or "Chief Blue Sky." The royal couple were the recipients of many gifts from the Chippewa. After receiving a gift, the Prince said, "Tak skal du ha!" — a Norwegian "Thank you!" phrase. The Prince wasn't prepared for the answer, which was: "Ja!" [6]

The adoption of John B. Chapple, editor of the Ashland *Daily Press,* was a gesture of gratitude on the part of the Bad River Chippewa Indians. The ceremony was performed by Chief James Jacco in the presence of a number of Chippewa leaders. Mr. Chapple was given the appropriate name "Minno-Gee-Shik," or "Nice Day, Happy Day." The public announcement of the adoption took place on March 25, 1951, at the Odanah community hall where 400 persons had assembled to honor Mr. Chapple. For three or four hours, the crowd enjoyed a full-scale revival of Chippewa dances, the first of its kind in ten years. [7]

The adoption of Colonel Robert R. McCormick, editor and publisher of The Chicago *Tribune,* by the Chippewa of the Bad River Reservation was the occasion of the largest gathering of Chippewa at Ashland since the signing of the Sioux-Chippewa treaty in 1896. The ceremony began at St. Mary's Indian School on the Bad River Reservation where Colonel McCormick was greeted by tribal leaders and 300 Indian children. Chief James White bestowed the Indian title "Mee-Gee-See," which means "The Eagle, the Strong One, the One of Courage," upon Colonel McCormick. Calling attention to the eagle symbology in Colonel McCormick's Chippewa name, Chief Antoine Starr of the Bad River Council initiated the adoption and dance ceremonies. Chief Starr said that the eagle is peculiarly significant in the name of Mee-Gee-See because it is a part of the great seal of the United States government. This bestowing of the name "eagle" is the highest honor that can be given to anyone by the tribe.

In order to accommodate thousands of spectators, Colonel McCormick's final adoption ceremony took place in Dodd Gymnasium in Ashland, Wisconsin. Chief Flaming Arrow, Jesse Martin, performed the feather dance signifying that the adopted brother had the word "eagle" in his name. At the close of the dance, the ceremonial pipe, gaudy with feathers and leather thong wrappings, was passed from chief to chief. After the smoking of the pipe, Chief White bestowed his own Indian name on Colonel McCormick and the adoption ceremony was completed. Colonel McCormick, upon whose brow rested a magnificent eagle feather ceremonial headdress, joined the Chippewa in a friendship dance.[8]

Not all the Chippewa favor the adoption of palefaces into their tribe. At a mass meeting held at Cass Lake, Minnesota, some of the Chippewa adopted a resolution protesting against the "indiscriminate adoption of white men into the Chippewa tribe." It was alleged that some Indians, seeking their own political advancement, adopted white men into the tribe.[9]

On July 8, 1940, Congress enacted a uniform law for the adoption of minor Indians. In effect, this law abolishes the old Indian custom of adoption. This law applies to all Indians in the United States who have adopted children in the past or who contemplate adoption in the future, with the exception of the Five Civilized Tribes and the Osages. At the time of the passage of the law, there were many persons, then adults, who had been adopted by Indian custom many years previously. If there was no adoption through a decree of a state court, the Indian had to take up the matter with the Superintendent of the Indian agency, the Tribal Court, or the Tribal Authority that provided a method of adoption. In all cases, a record must be kept.[10]

chapter 27 AMONG THE CHIPPEWA, AS AMONG ALL OTHER Indian tribes, feasts formed an important element of community life. These feasts ranged in importance from those of childhood playmates to the sacred ceremonial feasts of the tribe.[1]

The invitation to a feast was simple. After pulling aside the blanket door of the wigwam, the inviter, without further ado, announced, "You are invited to a feast." Each member of the household picked up a wooden mug, a dish, and a spoon and set out for the feast.[2] If a guest neglected to comply with the rule of supplying his own tableware, the host, in a joking manner, taught him an impressive lesson by serving him from the largest container or kettle that he owned. If he was clever enough to evade the penalty, the negligent person was not obliged to gorge himself. He could outwit his host by inducing friends to partake of the food served him. His cleverness was rewarded with presents of bead work, moccasins, medicine bags, or other articles that the host had in readiness.

Marie Livingston, a Chippewa woman, tells the story of what happened to her father and a friend, who as young men, deliberately neglected to bring their tableware to a feast.

When they entered the wigwam, the feast was in full swing. Some of the older men warned them of what was in store, as it was apparent to all the guests that they had come without the necessary articles. Soon the waitress came and asked for their tableware. They replied that they had none. They were ordered to be seated and a large dish pan of food with two spoons in it was set before them. My father's friend remarked: "Now we are in for it." My father sized up the food, then took some tobacco and offered it to his friends. They accepted it and passed some to their friends. The tobacco was understood to signify an invitation to partake of the dish pan of food which consisted of layers of meat, rice, soup, and maple sugar. A half pail of hemlock tea was placed nearby. The recipients of the tobacco had a merry time as they partook of the food. In a short time, the pan was empty.

Since the host had been outwitted, he spread a blanket on the floor on which he piled yard goods, medicine bags, moccasins, belts, and beadwork. In a short talk, he lauded the two youths for their resourcefulness. My father thanked him and graciously refused the gifts. The host replied that the custom must be kept. My father thanked him again and accepted a pair of moccasins and a medicine bag. His friend did likewise. The remainder of the gifts was divided among those who had partaken of the food.[3]

One of the principal feasts of the Chippewa was given to placate the anger of the gods. The older Chippewa believed that a succession of several infant deaths in a family was due to the evil influence of angry manitoes. They also believed that malicious human beings caused deaths by the use of "bad medicine." After such a misfortune had occurred in a family, the parents consulted the "shake lodge," through jugglers, to determine in what respect they had erred. Invariably, the manitoes of the "Shake Lodge" informed the parents that in their youth, they had dreamed of certain manitoes and had failed to give them gifts. Therefore, the manitoes had concluded that the parents preferred to sacrifice their children's lives rather than to make the customary offerings.

When another child was born in the family, the parents, acting upon the information previously received, gave a feast to appease the angered manitoes. At the celebration, a spokesman for the unfortunate parents besought the manitoes to cease all punishment. The parents were urged to make offerings of food, tobacco, and clothing at stated times. If the manitoes accepted the offerings, the child's life was saved.

If the cause of the deaths was through the "bad medicine" of an evil person, the malicious person was given two alternatives: either to desist from the evil work or to take the punishment of the shake lodge manitoes.

After their conversion to Christianity, some parents also observed an Indian rite which was carried on in the nature of a feast following the baptism of an infant. If the child was a boy, the mother was careful to include three aged women among the guests. After the visitors had assembled, the mother told the aged women that it was their privilege to choose a name for the baby in addition to his Christian name. The old women, after expressing their appreciation for the favor, related the dreams that had come to them during the period of their youthful fasting. The dream that offered the best possibilities for the selection of a name was chosen. The following account of a dream is a typical one:

The dream, one old woman affirmed, had come to her many times while she had fasted. She had seen a number of young men in council. One young man gave such excellent advice that he was given an honorary seat and declared a leader. In another dream, the old woman saw many men in a boat. One of the men who sat ahead of the others seemed to be the leader. In a third dream, the aged woman saw one star guiding a great number of other stars. Because the woman had seen a leader in each dream, she decided to name the child, "Netami," the leader or guide.

Sometimes, medicine men also bestowed names upon boys. This rite created a strong bond of friendship between the boy and the medicine man. If the boy became ill, the medicine man prescribed a remedy, and visited him daily. He also bestowed gifts upon the boy.[4]

One year after an Indian's death, an anniversary feast was held. Such anniversary feasts are no longer common, but one was held on the Bad River Reservation on November 2, 1938. This feast combined both pagan and Christian elements. Several days before the feast took place, the host appointed an old Indian to invite the guests. According to Chippewa etiquette, tobacco was presented to invited guests.

Just before the meal was served, the master of ceremonies arose and addressed the guests: "I suppose you know why this food is given to us. It is in remembrance of our beloved dead: parents, relatives, and friends. Each one of you here represents some one of our deceased. We shall take these few moments to think of them." Lights were dimmed and a profound silence followed. Then the speaker continued in a low voice: "All who are gathered here tonight should thank the Great Manito for letting us meet today. It is hard to tell how many of us will be here next year. Let us give thanks for all this good food we are about to eat." As soon as he had finished speaking, he walked to the stove, opened a package of tobacco and shook its contents into the fire as an offering to the Great Manitoes. The lights were again turned up.

To please the totems of all persons present as well as those of the deceased, a wide variety of game was served: venison, bear meat, rabbit, porcupine, partridge, grouse, and duck. Other foods served were chicken and beef, wild rice, hominy, corn-on-cob, potatoes, cabbage, carrots, pickles, cake, cookies, and bread.

Later the table was re-set and food placed thereon for the spirits of the dead. It was believed that the spirits actually partook of this food. The next morning, the food that remained on the table was collected and burned or buried in ground set apart where no one walked over it. The food could not be given to animals.[5]

A Chippewa feast still popular today is the New Year Feast during which the Indians hold "open house." No one remembers when the feast originated, but it is well established among the Great Lakes' Indians. When anyone enters an Indian home at this time, social, political, and financial inequalities, and all animosity are forgotten. The host greets his guests as they enter and presents them with a gift, usually some produce of the soil. The Great Spirit is also invoked to bless those who have called. This annual celebration is really part of an old Thanksgiving feast, usually carried out at the phase of the moon called Gitchi Man-i-do, or Great Spirit.[6]

The Chippewa realized that wild rice, berries, nuts, fish, venison, and other products of the forest, soil, and streams were part of the Great Spirit's bounty. In recognition of these blessings, different bands united in a ceremony of thanksgiving which assumed the nature of a feast. Other thanksgiving feasts were held at different times of the year. The Indians living in the wild rice areas held a festival in honor of their Manito in mid-summer. The Thanksgiving offering for maple sugar usually took place at the conclusion of the sugar season.[7]

Feasting played an important part in Midewiwin ceremonies. At these feasts, it was customary to eat dog flesh, not because of its edible quality, but to please the Great Spirit and thus win favors from him. The religious significance of this custom is found in the comparison of the relationship between a man and his dog and those of the Great Spirit with his subject, man. Man may scold his dog, beat him, and chase him from the house, but the faithful animal always returns to renew friendship with his master. Man, too, may stray from the narrow path, but if he repents of his evil, he is again restored to friendship with the Great Spirit.

A special feast was sacred to the bear, a favorite animal of the Chippewa. Marie Livingston described one of these celebrations thus:

In 1931, my husband and I took a trip, visiting friends and renewing old acquaintances among the different Indian settlements in Minnesota. One of these places was Sandy Lake, where ten Chippewa families lived. I was particularly impressed when these Indians asked me to what clan my grandfather belonged. When I told them that he was of the Bear Clan, I was no longer considered a stranger, but a relative. They called me "Gitchi-gami-kwe," "Lake Superior woman."

During my visit there, I was invited to several homes, where I found that these Indians still adhered to the old Indian customs. In one home, I was invited to the "Feast of the Bear Paw."

The home was a one-room structure. Although they had a table and chairs, all were seated on the floor which was covered with rush mats. The food was served in large pans. It consisted of things that the bear is supposed to relish — whiskey, baked beans, wild rice with raisins, maple sugar, and syrup. There were no plates, but the host provided each guest with a cup and spoon.

The centers of the mats were decorated with bead work, ribbons of many colors, and tobacco intermingled with bear paws, neck chains of bear paws, and many small deer-skin pouches of "medicine." Loose bear claws floated in the whiskey bowl.

A brief talk was given by an old man stating that the food was placed on the floor as an offering of thanks to the bear for protection. Although fierce and quick-tempered, the bear is the only animal that has offered the Indian herbs and shown him any kindness. The medicines acquired from the bear are especially beneficial. The knowledge to prepare and use these medicines was given to the bear in a dream.

After this talk, we began our feast. We ate with a spoon from the large pans. The whiskey was served in cups. I was handed a cupful but did not wish to drink it. An old man, noticing my embarrassment, told me that I was not obliged to drink it. He said that if I touched my lips to the cup, I might then give the cup to someone else. I followed this suggestion and gave the whiskey to the person next to me.

When the meal was finished, we rose, shook hands with our host, thanked him for his kindness, and returned to our homes.[8]

It is significant to note that the Indian has not instituted one feast in thanksgiving for military success. It is of equal significance that there was not a tribe in the 200 or more tribal groups in the

United States that did not hold thanksgiving ceremonies. The Seneca Indians had nine Thanksgiving days and they still retain this custom. Each spring at planting time, they held a thanksgiving festival. Their motives for gratitude are expressed in the following prayer which is also representative of the sentiments of the Chippewa:

> Now is the season of growing things. Now we give thanks to our Creator.
> Now we sprinkle tobacco on fire. Now smoke arises, it lifts our words to Him.
> Now we speak to Hahwenniyu, the great ruler, the great life, one Great Spirit.
> Now He listens to the words of the people here assembled.
>
> We thank Him for return of planting season.
> We thank Him that He has again permitted us to see it.
> We thank Him that we again take part in ceremony.
> We thank Him that He has given us the earth, our mother, from whose breast all things grow.
>
> We thank Him that He has given us seed to give back to our mother.
> We thank Him for rivers and waters that flow.
> For herbs and plants, and all fruit-bearing trees and bushes that grow.
> We thank Him that our supporters of life — corn, beans, squash — fail us not.
> That famine is not permitted to enter our lodge doors.
>
> Continue to listen, Hahwenniyu: Again we speak.
> We thank Him that our old men and our old women,
> Our young men and our young women and children are here.
> We thank Him that the eyes of the people are turned to Hahwenniyu.
>
> We thank Him that the minds of the people remember the great wisdom, the one Great Creator,
> Who makes all things to grow.
> Now smoke rises, He has seen it.
> Now we have spoken, He has heard it.
> It is done, Naiewhyie.[9]

CHIPPEWA SONGS AND DANCES

chapter 28

Music, closely associated with the life of every race, was and is still one of the greatest pleasures of the Chippewa. In times past, when a Chippewa returned from a visit to another reservation, the first question asked was, "What new songs did you learn?"

Many of the songs sung on the reservations are very old; a few are of recent origin. The Chippewa still celebrate important events with song.

The Chippewa singer preserves the history of his songs by prefacing them with brief sketches concerning their origin and theme. If a song originated in a different locality, the fact is mentioned. After the completion of a song, the vocalist again addresses his audience, repeating the title of the song and its theme. Because of this method, the words of the song become closely associated with the melody. The melody of Chippewa songs is considered more important than the words. Therefore, it is not unusual to find the same words occurring only once in a single song. Although it is customary to compose new words for old tunes, the substituted words are generally similar in meaning to the old ones.[1]

Wigwam lullaby chants possess a particular delicacy. Imagine a play-loving girl trying to put a restless child to sleep in an Indian cradle board. As the keen-eyed, black-haired baby hangs its head over the side of the cradle, the elder sister imitates the child's own piping tones as she sings:

> Who is this?
> Who is this?
> Eye-light bringing
> To the roof of my lodge.

Then imitating the tones of the screech owl, the girl answers her own questions:

> It is I
> Coming.

> It is I
> Coming.
> Down! Down![2]

Chippewa who have attained prominence in song writing are Odjib-we and Princess O-mi-mi. Odjib-we, the last warrior of the Mississippi band of Minnesota Chippewa, composed and sang songs which were associated with his own war experiences. These songs realistically pictured the war customs of his people.[3]

Princess O-mi-mi, Mary Wiggins-Killoren, has also attained national prominence by composing and singing her own songs. Her writings include a booklet entitled, "Poems From Life," many of which are included in her repertory. The following selection is characteristic of Chippewa moods and sentiment:

THE NORTH WOODS

In the North Woods close beside the Gitchi-Gume
There among the pines I long to be
> The birds are singing gay
> Happy all the live-long day.

On the deer trails close beside the Gitchi-Gume
> There the paths of the deer,
> Lead me to the waters clear.

Then the cares and worldly schemes
Are all lost and gone it seems.
> And you put on thoughts anew
> Bringing back the good and true.

In the wild woods by the lakes of old Wisconsin
In the North Woods by the streams
> There is where I love to dream
> Where the whip-poor-wills are calling
> At the time the night shades falling
> And the quiet gentle breeze
> Softly singing through the trees,
With graceful white birch and stately pine,
Carry a thought to me Divine,
Then the Great Spirit is near you know
And you feel the Gitchi-Man-i-tou.[4]

New customs have brought new songs to the Indian, but, with few exceptions, he has not yet adopted the white man's custom of

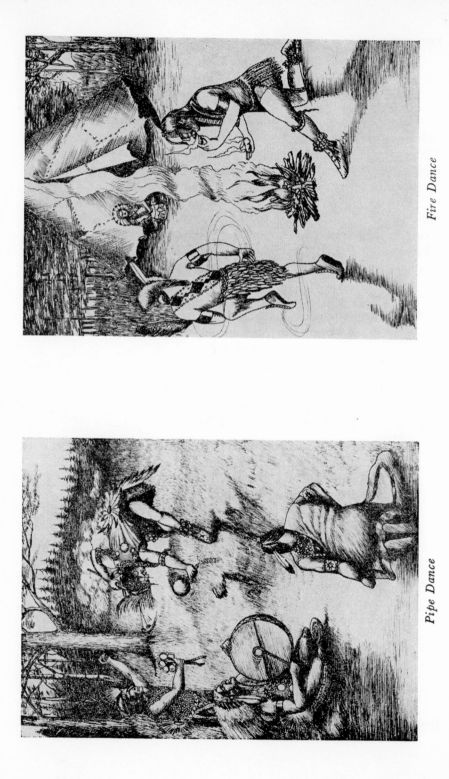

Fire Dance

Pipe Dance

singing for the approval of an audience. Song is still for the benefit of all. A Chippewa desires excellence in singing so that he may be a leader of the drum singers.[5]

Chippewa songs are usually accompanied by drums or rattles.[6] From the earliest times, drums were used by the Algonquin Indians. In John Smith's days, Powhatan's Indians used the drum almost exclusively for military purposes. Although drums were used by the Chippewa for centuries, the first ceremonial drum of the tribe originated at Devil's Lake, North Dakota, in 1878. According to the story of a young Sioux girl, a venerable old man gave her detailed instructions for its construction.[7] During a truce, the Sioux taught the Chippewa how to make a ceremonial drum.

After the introduction of the ceremonial dream drum, the Sioux began a dance known as the Pow-wow Dance.[8] In accordance with instructions from the spirits, the Sioux[9] taught the Chippewa how to dance the Pow-wow. By 1880, the Pow-wow Dance was in its hey-day on the Chippewa reservations. The Chippewa reverenced the dance as a gift from the Great Spirit. According to custom, the Pow-wow Dance closed with a Give-away Dance during which there was an exchange of gifts ranging in value from ponies to a pair of moccasins.

Chippewa Indians are noted for the variety of their dances and for the gracefulness of their performances. Dancing for the early Chippewa was more than a mere means of expressing happiness. Since many Indian dances were connected with religious beliefs, they were fraught with symbolism and mystic meaning. In later years, a number of dances with no religious significance originated.

Among the North American Indian dances, the Calumet is one of the most ancient. It was the peace dance of the Indians at their inter-tribal meetings and it was also performed when peace pacts were made or renewed with white people. Among the Chippewa, this dance is known as "Opwag-unun-nimiwin," or Pipe Dance. The motions of the dance tend to ease tension and to foster a spirit of good will. The dance has lost its significance in modern times.

Usually accompanied by singing, the Pipe Dance is performed as a solo dance.[10] During the dance, the speed of the drum beats is increased as the dance progresses. The performer, carrying a pipe in his right hand and shaking a rattle in his left hand, twists and turns his body into a variety of positions. A string of bells attached to his ankles adds a delicate touch to the rhythm.[11]

The Fire Dance, as originally performed, was largely a test dance to detect the potency of medicine. While herbs were boiled,

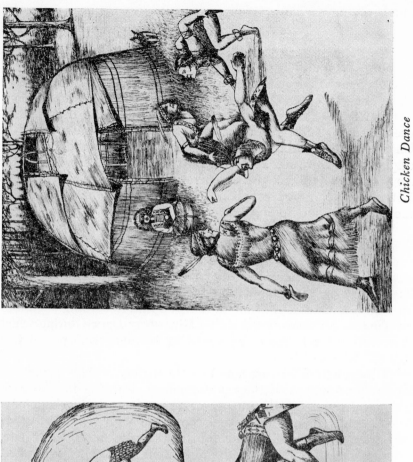

Chicken Dance

Scalp Dance

the tester and his companions danced to the accompaniment of songs. After the boiling and refining of the medicine, a severe test was undergone by the dancer to determine the strength of the medicine. While continuing his dance, the performer held hot coals in his hands and a live coal in his mouth. If the medicine had been properly mixed, the dancer was uninjured. Then the medicine was carefully preserved for future use.[12] Hot coals are no longer used in the dance.

The Scalp Dance, popular among the primitive Chippewa, was so named because the motions of the dance simulated the scalping process. Shortly before the dance, a deer head was cooked and placed in the center of the dancing court. A waiter, while dancing around the court, selected four warriors and led them to the deer head. After the warriors were seated around the deer head, a speaker addressed the spectators and the warriors, telling them the origin of the Scalp Dance. The warriors partook of the deer head and returned to their places. Then the first warrior selected danced around the bones of the deer head. His motions indicated the capture and scalping of an enemy. In the meantime, the spectators sang to drum accompaniment. At the conclusion of the song, the dancer tapped the deer head bones with his war hatchet and told the assembly of his latest experience on the battle front.[13] He embellished his story to arouse his audience to a high pitch of excitement. Each of the warriors danced in turn and concluded the dance by relating his war experiences. In modern times, this dance is kept alive only as a matter of Indian history.

Many Indian dances are imitations of animal movements. The brothers George, Henry, and Joseph Martin, Chippewa on the Bad River Reservation, originated the Chicken Dance as an Indian celebration dance. This dance combined original movements with legendary elements and remnants of pow-wow songs. Sometimes as many as a hundred persons engage in the dance. The participants cackle and crow in imitation of hens and roosters. When the men meet who represent the roosters, they engage in a fight, keeping time with the beating of drums. The crowing and cackling continues during the entire dance.

According to legend,[14] the idea for the Deer Dance occurred to an Indian hunter while he was on a hunting trip. One day, while enjoying a smoke in his lodge, he heard faint sounds of an unfamiliar dance. The next morning, the hunter decided to explore the surrounding area. He suddenly found himself in a deep valley. Although he heard singing and the beating of drums, he saw no

Hunter's Dance

Deer Dance

dancers. Instead, he saw before him hundreds of deer in the glen. The hunter left his former lodge and migrated to the valley of plenty.

The following autumn, the hunter again set out on a hunting trip in the direction of his former location. One calm evening, the hunter heard sounds similar to those he had heard the previous year. He followed the sound. As the huntsman advanced, he recognized the sounds as dream drum beats. He proceeded cautiously. To his amazement, he discovered a large group of deer facing each other rubbing their horns together. The deer were dancing in their own fashion. The knocking of horns had produced the drumlike effect.

When the hunter returned to his village, he told the people of his unusual experience. The listeners encouraged the hunter to imitate the actions of the deer. He did so. Thus the Deer Dance originated. The men, representing the buck deer, dance with their heads held downward, indicating that they are ready to battle with the other buck deer. Whenever they come close together, they lock horns, figuratively, and a battle ensues. The battlers, however, keep dancing in perfect time with the music. The women, also, perform the Deer Dance. They do not follow their usual method of dancing in a circle, but cross back and forth. The Deer Dance is a favorite number at big Indian celebrations.

Another legend[15] reports that "O-sow-wa-de," a tall, lanky Courte Indian, originated the Hunters' Dance. One day, while "O-sow-wa-de" lay asleep under a huge pine tree, he dreamt that a man invited him to a dance. The lad was delighted and accepted the invitation. When he and his companion arrived at the scene of the dance, they entered a lodge and seated themselves in the center. After some time, the boy was given a drum and invited to join in the merriment. As the dancing progressed, "O-sow-wa-de" noticed that some of the warriors wore huge war bonnets. He was pleased with the dance and experienced keen sorrow when he awoke from his dream. "O-sow-wa-de" had this dream several times. During one of the dreams, the scene suddenly changed. Instead of Indian dancers, he saw a great herd of deer. The war bonnets that he had imagined he had seen in his first dream were the horns of deer. "O-sow-wa-de" was frightened and tried to escape. But an albino doe beckoned to him and said in a tone of great sweetness: "You have won great power and you shall henceforth command all the beasts of the forests." This dream is the basis of the Hunters' Dance which is now used as a specialty dance.

The Wisconsin Chippewa learned the Hoop Dance from the

Forty-Nine Dance

Hoop Dance

Minnesota Chippewa. The dancer, in the course of his performance, jumps through a hoop.[16] Some of the dancers use two or more hoops in this intricate dance. Fast time pow-wow songs are the usual accompaniment for hoop dancers.

The Forty-Nine Dance dates back to the days of World War I. John Chingaway, a Chippewa from the Bad River Reservation, was appointed recruiting officer for Company E, 6th Nebraska Infantry. Of the 150 men that compose Company E, 139 were either Omaha, Winnebago, Sioux, Sac and Fox, Iowa, or Chippewa Indians. After a short period of training, the Company was disorganized and trained groups for scout duty were sent overseas. The members remained across for about one year and then returned.

Of the 61 Winnebagoes who had engaged in the war, only 49 returned. During a big celebration held in their honor, the soldiers who were not disabled danced. Other joined. Finally, only the veterans were dancing. When the dance was completed, an old Winnebago arose and suggested that this dance be known as the "Forty-Nine Dance." [17] In 1923, Chief Decorah from Black River Falls, Wisconsin, taught the Chippewa the Forty-Nine Dance.[18]

The Horse Dance also passed from the Winnebago Indians to the Chippewa. The dance movement, classical despite its common-place name, centers around the experiences of Indians with wild horses. A horse tail is attached to the back of the dancer who performs his actions to the rhythm of any fast-time pow-wow music.[19]

Since many members of the Chippewa tribe prefer to learn the less difficult dances of the white people, the ranks of accomplished Chippewa dancers are rapidly being depleted. Unless the Indians themselves foster an interest in their traditions, many of their tribal dances will be lost in the mad whirl of twentieth century "jazz" and "swing" rhythms.[20]

Horse Dance

GAMES AND ATHLETICS

CHIPPEWA PROWESS AND SUCCESS IN ATHLETIC
chapter 29   games is attributable to the vigorous outdoor life
of the Indians. Two types of games prevailed
among the Indians of the Great Lakes area: those requiring skill
and endurance combined with dexterity, and games of chance.[1]

America's oldest and roughest game was lacrosse, having been
played by the Indians before the coming of the white man.[2] In
primitive days, this game was part of a religious ceremony which
marked the close of the sugar-making season. There are various
legends concerning the origin of lacrosse. According to one Chippewa legend, the manner of playing the game was revealed to an
Indian boy in a dream.

The legend relates that on an exceptionally pleasant day, an
Indian lad took a nap in his canoe. After he had fallen asleep, the
canoe, released by the tide, drifted into the deep waters of Sha-ga-
wa-me-gunk. In his dream, the boy beheld a great open valley and
large numbers of Indians coming toward him. One of the younger
members of the group invited him to join the crowd. Proceeding to
a place where food was being served, they requested him to partake
of the repast. After the meal, they were summoned to a wigwam
where a medicine man was preparing "medicine" for a great game.
To insure success in the game, clubs were held over the smoking
"medicine."

After the clubs had been "medicined," the players assembled
in two formations. Two poles were erected on the plain. At a given
signal from the medicine man, a ball was thrown into the air. The
game began with great shouts and beating of drums. When the
excitement was at its highest, the Chippewa lad hit a pole with the
ball. His success was cheered with loud cries.

When the Chippewa boy awoke from his dream, he related it
to the leading men of the tribe. The Chippewa declaring that the
thunder birds had spoken, began to play the game.

The game was an intensely exciting one. Nothing stopped the
players in their rush after the ball. Neither brushwood, fallen timber,

"Medicine" Applied to Racquets

or stumps; neither bogs, swamps, or rivers proved a barrier. The onrush of the players resembled the stampede of a buffalo herd.[3]

The rules for the women's game, "chaw-ha," are similar to those for the men's game of lacrosse. The action is less vigorous and the distance between the goals, shorter.[4]

The moccasin game is played with four moccasins and four bullets. The players divide into two teams. A bullet, one of which is marked, is hidden under each of the moccasins by one player. During the hiding process, his assistant, really a cheer leader, beats on a drum and sings. The words of the song tend to confuse the player who is trying to guess the location of the marked bullet. If the opponent guesses correctly the location of the marked bullet, he scores a point for his side. Then he hides the bullets. If he fails to find the marked bullet in four attempts, (the shots are shifted each time) he loses. The score of the game is marked with small sticks. A total of ten sticks is required to win a game. Since this is a game of chance, the betting of cattle, blankets, and other articles is common. Sometimes an Indian will bet the shoes he is wearing, if he has nothing else with which to meet the bet of his competitors. Relatives and friends who dance to bring good luck to the players, receive a share of the wagered articles.[5]

Athletic sports are popular forms of recreation among Indian boys and men. The chief sports among the Chippewa are baseball, football, basketball, boxing, archery, and log rolling.

The Chippewa on the Bad River Reservation claim Charles Albert Bender, "Chief Bender," Carlisle Indian School's greatest baseball star, as one of their native sons. Classed by sport authorities as one of the greatest pitchers of the era of great pitchers, Bender made his baseball debut with the Philadelphia Athletics in 1903. In divining the other team's signals, "Chief Bender" was considered the keenest man in baseball. His "fast ball" was nearly as speedy as that of the famed Walter Johnson. Because of his skill in deceiving his opponents, he was the despair of batsmen. When hostile fans whooped derisively in imitation of Indians, "Chief Bender" delighted in walking close to the stands and shouting scornfully, "Foreigners!" [6]

Other Chippewa Indians who have attained fame on the baseball diamond are "Chief Cadreau," and Antoine Starr. In 1912, Cadreau pitched for the Northwestern League in Spokane, Washington. The *Spokesman Review* of that city wrote of his baseball technique in the following terms:

To Chief Cadreau goes the honor of pitching his second no-run, no-hit game of the season, Tacoma being the victims of a magnificent exhibition of pitching. The way the break came as a no-hit game was about the only thing that could win for Spokane, and the Chief's performance is all the more creditable that it was a pinch case. Cadreau got the big hand every time he came to bat and every time he walked off the field. He retired the whole side on strikeouts in the third inning and got a wild ovation. Again he brought the stands down on a beautiful pickup and throw of Crittenden's freak bounder.[7]

Antoine Starr, the famous Chippewa dancer, formerly of Odanah, played with the Chicago White Sox before his induction into the army in World War I.

Lawrence Johnson, renowned football player, was one of the greatest defensive pivot men of the West. He attended St. Mary's School in Odanah until he was eight years old under the name Lawrence Walkijohn. After playing with the Boston Redskins in the National League, from 1933 to 1936, Lawrence Johnson, also known as Bob Johnson, joined the New York Yankees. In 1939, Johnson arrived in Superior, Wisconsin, with the New York Giants. Scarcely had the "Chief" found a room in the State Teachers' College dormitory before he produced a brilliantly colored Indian war bonnet and other Indian regalia. His arrival was discovered when a booming voice shook the rafters of the college. His physique matched his voice. The "Chief" was more than six feet in height and weighed 225 pounds. His shoulders were said to stretch "from one side of the room to the other." According to Coach Steve Owen, Johnson was one of the biggest and toughest boys in the National Professional Football League. Whenever Johnson had a few days off, he could be found mapping out a hunting or a fishing trip.[8]

Chippewa skill in basketball is well-known. The Odanah team, composed of former high school students, scored its greatest victory when it edged the All-Star Globe Trotters, a traveling Negro quintet by a score of 42-39.[9]

Boxing is another sport in which the Chippewa excel. As a boxer, Johnny Arbuckle, although not always successful, carried far the reputation of northern Wisconsin. While a student at Haskell Institute, Lawrence, Kansas, Arbuckle was chosen to represent Haskell on the Missouri Amateur Athletic Union team from Wichita and in the National Amateur Athletic Union classic in San Francisco. He lost in the former bout to Emmett Murphy of Great Falls, Montana. As a member of the Missouri Valley team, Arbuckle fought

Moccasin Game

two other bouts at San Bernardino and Ontario, California.[10] Private Walter Dashner, one of the seven sons of Mr. and Mrs. Edward Dashner of Odanah, won a silver cup for himself and another for his company in a boxing tournament at Fort Benning, Georgia.[11] Odanah boxers won two of the eight novice championship contests held at Eau Claire, Wisconsin.

Chippewa excellence in archery has become almost proverbial. In 1941, John Smart, "Wa-bi-mong" was proclaimed the second greatest archer in the nation. John was a member of the famous all-Indian Company E of Camp Robinson, Arkansas, one of the most publicized groups of the United States Selective Service Army. While in the army, Smart won second place in the first national tournament in Chicago, and in the second national contest in St. Louis.[12]

A sport that requires special skill is log rolling. The "birler" has to be fast and nimble to manipulate the fast moving logs in a swirling stream. In 1925, William Beauregard, a colorful Chippewa lumberjack of Odanah, defeated Joseph Stauber of Marinette, Wisconsin, in a record-breaking birling match which lasted two hours and forty-seven minutes. The next year, Beauregard won the Indian championship of the United States at Washburn, Wisconsin, defeating a group of 22 competitors. In 1937, Beauregard traveled with a log-rolling show throughout Canada and the United States.

Spherical objects have a special attraction for Chippewa of all ages. Younger members of the reservation are adepts with marbles. In 1944, James Boyd, a thirteen-year old student at St. Mary's School, was the winner of the county marble tournament, with Patrick Moore, aged nine, also a student at St. Mary's, as a runner-up.[13] After this victory, Boyd participated in the state marble tournament at Milwaukee, Wisconsin. Here he won sixth place against eleven other entrants. But he did not feel too badly over his defeat because the tournament was the occasion for his first ride on a train and his first trip away from the Chequamegon area.[14]

The following year, Gerald White, an eleven-year old student at St. Mary's, was first place winner in the county marble tournament. As a guest of the Milwaukee *Journal* and the Wisconsin Recreation Association, he entered the state marble contest at Milwaukee.[15] Fourteen districts throughout the state were represented. Although Gerald did not win first place in the state tournament, (he tied for ninth place) he found the trip to Milwaukee a pleasant experience.

CHIPPEWA DOCTORS, MEDICINES, AND MEDICATIONS

chapter 30 MEDICINES PLAYED AN IMPORTANT ROLE IN INDIAN life, since medicines were intimately connected with Chippewa religious ceremonies. The Chippewa consulted one of two classes of men for relief or cure in physical distress. One was the medicine man, a pseudo-psychiatrist, whose methods will be considered in connection with the Midewiwin secret society. The other was the Indian doctor who tried to cure the patient by the use of herbs, roots, and various barks.[1]

The Indian doctor learned the beneficial uses of natural remedies through traditional accounts or from experience. There was no mystery connected with his methods. After making a diagnosis, he prescribed the medicine he thought would effect a cure. The forests and plains were his drugstore. According to Matthew W. Stirling, chief of the Bureau of American Ethnology, the Indians' knowledge of medicine was questionable. In 1937, he wrote:

> It is very generally believed that there are many "lost arts" in connection with Indian civilizations. Among these might be listed the belief that Indian doctors had knowledge of certain specific medicines, usually of a vegetable nature, that were particularly potent, and that the "secret" of these is now only in the possession of an occasional old person or has been entirely lost. This idea received a great deal of stimulation during the halcyon days of patent medicine, when Indian remedies were much in vogue.
>
> As a matter of fact, the Indian believed most sickness to be caused by the activity of evil spirits which could be moved only by sorcery. Therefore the priest was the physician and the treatment consisted in frightening or luring away these spirits. In many tribes there was a crude knowledge of the therapeutic use of certain plants, but even in these instances their application was deeply rooted in magic. The sweathouse which operated somewhat on the principle of a Turkish bath was in gen-

eral use among the Indians, but its use could scarcely be termed a curative measure.[2]

By way of answer, White Bison De Forest, a seventy-seven year old Indian, requested that his point of view be presented to the public. Defending the Indians' use of medicine, he wrote:

> . . . no family doctor can conduct his practices, his calling as a family doctor of medicine, without using medicine *discovered by Indians.* I will agree they did not know about tinctures, or fluid extracts and they did not have machines for making pills and powder, but the healing power was there just the same; the idea was there. Mr. Stirling refers to Indians knowing about hot water and turkish baths, but states you could not say both had any curative power. You started something there, Mr. Stirling. Please give me some credit. United States Government should answer that one with the millions of dollars they spend at Hot Springs, Arkansas and what is claimed by Doctors for it; also Virginia Hot Springs; that were both used by Indians before white man, and are used to this day by rich Indians. . . .
>
> Was you to Chicago World Fair, Mr. Stirling? Did you see the wonderful display of medicines that Indian gave to white man? Did you know Indians knew liver was good, not five years ago like white doctor gets credit for finding out, but years? Did you ever hear about the rich man get a North Wood guide Indian man: He cook fish; Indian keep liver and dark meat and give white man all nice white meat. Indian do all the heavy work and is strong; white man eat white meat and is not strong. You say Indians never knew about healing with herbs. What about Cascara Sagrada, bark of California? It is now used by every doctor and every hospital in America? What about Quinine; Winter Green, and the starting point of your aspirin or Salicylic Acid; Nux-Vomica-Dog Button (Strychnine). White man's school never any way discover Digitalis (Foxglove).[3]

Claiming that he knew hundreds of others, De Forest enumerated thirty-four other herbs, roots, and barks commonly used as medicine. The old Indian also declared that his statements were to inform young Indians, wearing fancy trimmings of white men, that the old Indians did know *Herbs.*[4]

In reply to De Forest's defense of Indian medicines, Mr. Stirling wrote: "The Indians, like the early Europeans, used herbs so extensively for medicinal purposes that there were very few plants that were not put to use in some manner and it was inevitable that some of these have later been demonstrated to contain certain beneficial principles." Mr. Stirling further stated that quinine was never used by the North American Indians. The plant is a native of South America and was first used by Spaniards. He claimed that his article was written mainly to clear a popular misconception among white people regarding the Indians' knowledge of efficacious and mysterious medicines not generally know to others.[5]

Huron Smith, noted ethnologist, taking a different view of the Indian's knowledge of plants, wrote:

> The Ojibwe are probably the best informed and the strictest observers of the medicine lodge ceremonies in the country. Their knowledge of plants both in their own environment and far away is probably the best of any group of Indians. While their flora is not so rich in species as that of Indians farther south, they make trips far away from their home to obtain necessary plants.
>
> It is worth noting that they understand the proper time to gather the plant part. At times, the medicinal qualities are inert, undeveloped or dispersed by being too old. Much of the knowledge of white men originated from studying the Indian plant uses, in the early days. Eclectic practitioners sought the Indian herbs and observed carefully what parts of the plants were used. This mass of early information was sifted scientifically by the students of medicine, and finally tested physiologically on animals. Perhaps sixty-five per cent of their remedies were found to be potent and are included in our pharmacopoeia; the other thirty-five per cent were discovered to be valueless medicinally.[6]

The Indian doctor had a ready cure for the ordinary ills of life. Even tuberculosis, one of the diseases brought to the Indians by civilized methods of living, has been cured through treatment prescribed by the Indian doctor.

Chippewa remedies were cathartics, expectorants, diuretics, emetics, tonics, teas, emulsions, ointments, lotions, narcotics to induce sleep, and sweat baths. Ceremony and superstition were practiced with the selection of plants and herbs for medicinal purposes. One of these superstitions was connected with "wa-ba-dow."

High in the branches of some pine trees, scarcely discernible from the ground, grew the mythical "wa-ba-dow," a cylindrical-shaped parasite about a foot or more in length. When the wind blew, the "wa-ba-dow" emitted a sound which could be heard for nearly a mile. "Wa-ba-dow" was sometimes used as a medicine, or its presence on the tree also signified that herbs were growing near the tree. Since the only way "wa-ba-dow" could be located was by following the direction of the sound heard only on windy days, it was difficult to find.

Generations past, Chippewa Indians abstained from food and drink for several days before they collected herbs for medicine or other purposes. They sat in a pine tree waiting for the spirits to tell them the kind of herbs to use and its particular use.[7]

The Chippewa named many roots and herbs after birds, fishes, beasts, and reptiles. The following legend relates the origin of this practice:

Many years ago, three owl cousins lived in the wilderness posing as men. Throughout the summer, they enjoyed their chosen role, but when winter set in, their food resources became very low. The cousins, therefore, agreed to hunt for their living. Each morning the owl-men went on the hunt, returning late at night. By the time spring came, one of the cousins was very much underweight. Upon being questioned by one of the cousins concerning his condition, he replied that since he was not accustomed to continuous, strenuous activity, he found the hunt extremely exhausting. The truth of the matter was that he was starving because he had given up the hunt. The eldest of the owl cousins, wiser than the other owls, was not to be deceived. He also questioned his cousin to determine the cause of his trouble.

Since he was no longer able to endure the pangs of hunger, the starving owl decided to confide in his wise cousin. He related that one day while hunting, he had crossed a meadow but he was not permitted to proceed farther, because the occupant of a log cabin at the end of the meadow had challenged him to a wrestling match. He was assured that if he succeeded in throwing his opponent, he would become a skillful hunter. The owl-man, afraid to accept the challenge, had stopped hunting.

After satisfying the starving cousin's hunger, the wise owl advised him to wrestle with the occupant of the cabin. If he felt himself worsted, he was to say: "If my cousin were only here, you could not throw me." That would be the cue for the wise one to come to his rescue.

Everything happened as the wise cousin had anticipated. During the wrestling contest, the owl realizing that he would soon be overcome, gave his cousin the cue planned. While the wise cousin was grappling with the adversary, the underweight one hurried to the man's cabin, seized a medicine bag, and ran home. After the defeat of his opponent, the wise owl also hastened home to examine the medicine bag. The owl cousins gave a feast for all the animals of the forest. During the feast, they divided among the animals the herbs and roots of the medicine bag. Each root or herb received the name of the bird, beast, fish, or reptile that accepted it.[8] Thus ends the tale.

In addition to prescribing herbs, roots, and barks for the alleviation of pain and sickness, the Indian doctor also practiced minor surgery. For a headache of long duration, a small incision was made at the temple with a sharp piece of flint. The doctor then placed the mouth of a horn over this incision and drew the blood from the wound. When it was thought that a sufficient amount of blood had been drawn, a fomentation containing healing properties was applied to the cut in order to check further bleeding. This treatment is said to have given almost instant relief, even in the most stubborn cases.

Susan Buffalo, Mrs. John Gurnoe, a direct descendant of the great Chief Buffalo, claimed that on Red Cliff Reservation, "bleeding" was also a common remedy for blood-poisoning, bruises, rheumatism, dizziness, and high blood pressure. For bruises and blood poisoning, the incision was made directly on the injured or infected part. The Indians called this remedy "pai-pai-shewain."

Rheumatism was treated by massaging the affected parts of the body. Then several needles were forced into the skin over the rheumatic area. The blood which oozed from the perforated skin was scraped off and medicine was applied to the pricks for absorption.[9]

John Bardon, Douglas County historian, related the following story of an Indian surgery:

On one of these trips, we ran on to a kind of a recluse Indian Medicine Man, named "Wa-bay-may-sha-way," who had frozen his left hand the previous winter. It refused to heal, and gangrene having set in, he concluded to 'operate.' He placed his hand on a log and with a hatchet in the other hand, he cut off the damaged fingers. He had his frying pan red-hot and seared the wound. He completely recovered and we knew him for many years after.[10]

The Chippewa custom of taking sweat baths dates from primitive times. The sweat house had a framework similar to that of a wigwam and was covered with matting, skins, or bark. In later years, canvas and blankets were used. The sides of the bath house were airtight, but there was a small section at the top which could be uncovered. Red hot stones were set in the center of the sweat lodge. The patient sprinkled the stones with a liquid made from boiled barks and evergreen boughs. The steam induced profuse perspiration. Since the treatment was weakening if not properly regulated, the patient left the bath when he thought the treatment had produced the desired effect.

After the bath, the patient rubbed his skin briskly or bathed it with cold water. Except in cases of serious illness, the patient resumed his duties in a short time.

This form of treatment was considered beneficial for sufferers from persistent coughs, asthma, pneumonia, hay fever, and rheumatism. It was also regarded as a mental stimulus and was used for a general toning up of the body. For checking a cold or fever, "na-me-wuckons," a wild mint, was used as a hot tea to induce sweating.[11]

Emetics were used in the treatment of digestive disturbances, colds, and headaches. The patient took copious draughts of a liquid composed of approximately nine parts of lukewarm water and one part medicine. Either a finger or a feather was introduced into the throat to further the process of regurgitation. According to the Chippewa, this had to be done about two minutes after the liquid had been swallowed. Sometimes salt was added to a quart of lukewarm water as an emetic. The patient shook himself vigorously to agitate the solution, whereupon vomiting was induced. The older Chippewa still prefer this treatment to palliative medicine prescribed by a physician.[12]

Indian doctors and medicinal herbs and roots are no longer part of the Chippewa pattern of life. The Indian depends upon the white doctor for aid in physical distress. Efforts have been made to teach the Indian the value of proper foods and rest, and the necessity of proper ventilation, but owing to his poverty, the Indian cannot always meet the health standards of modern civilization. In some cases, he is unable to build properly ventilated houses or to provide nourishing food for his family. He is therefore not physically able to cope with certain diseases, especially tuberculosis.

BURIAL AND MOURNING CUSTOMS, SPIRIT BUNDLES, AND GRAVE HOUSES

chapter 31

THE CHIPPEWA INDIANS' BELIEF IN THE EXISTENCE of the soul and a hereafter, together with a high respect for the mortal remains of the dead, account for particular tribal burial customs. Prior to the influence of the missionaries and to the introduction of tools for excavating, the Chippewa of Wisconsin, Minnesota, Montana, and the Dakotas, wrapped the dead body in a robe, enclosed it in birch bark, and then placed it on a scaffold or in a tree. Skeletons were buried only after the flesh had decayed. Bones found in burial mounds frequently indicate long exposure to the air. Their discovery is one proof of scaffold burial.[1] Cremation among the Chippewas was considered sacrilegious.

When death occurred in a family, members of the household put charcoal on their faces and in their food. Family groups were notified by messengers and, in later times, by a gun salute fired into the air four successive times. It was customary in the eighteenth century, and even in some instances it is so at the present time, to keep a four-day and night vigil over the dead. Since the early Indians did not have the services of a doctor, they considered the delay necessary to prevent too early burial. There were, however, variations from this custom, even to the extent of burial immediately after death.

The body of the deceased was washed and dressed in its best clothing. A decorated animal skin, representing the clan or totem of the departed one, was hung near the corpse or placed in its hands. If the deceased was a mide medicine man, his mide bag was also buried with him, unless he had provided otherwise for its disposal. The coffin was made of sheets of heavy birch bark which were securely tied around the corpse with wigub or fancy scarfs. Before putting the body into the coffin, it was placed on a cot enclosed by four blankets fastened to boards, curtain fashion. If mourners wished to view the body, they lifted one side of a blanket.

Before burial, the Chippewa always gave a farewell feast in honor of the deceased. Prior to the meal, words similar to these were spoken by a prominent member of the family: "My dear relatives, we are dining here today to bid one of our departed relatives a farewell. Let us all be happy and not show our grief, but let us bid him goodbye in a cheerful manner. He has passed on to the Happy Hunting Ground and some day we will all be happily united."

The feast over, the burial ceremony began with the beating of drums and singing, and the performance of the Brave Dance. This dance symbolized the courage with which the deceased should go forth to meet his fate. During this ceremony, the officiating brave placed food, wearing apparel, hunting equipment, and trinkets in the coffin. This was in accordance with the Chippewa belief that after death the soul departs on a four-day journey toward the setting sun.

Before the coffin was closed, a grand medicine man delivered the ceremonial burial oration. Although it was believed that the spirit had left the body and could not communicate with the living, yet the Chippewa held that the soul was cognizant of all that occurred around it. Therefore, the medicine man cautioned the dead not to cast regretful glances upon those he was leaving. Neither was he to tarry, since he had finished with all earthly things. He must not be disturbed by the tears of the living. In a short time, they, too, must go to the setting sun.

The medicine man then turned to the mourners and admonished them not to weep for the dead since it would make his departure from this earth more difficult to have his clothing saturated with the tears of the living. In a short time, they too would join him. During the oration, rattles were shaken occasionally. When the speech was finished, the drums were again beaten and all the mourners danced for about ten minutes.

When the dance was finished, the medicine man chanted in a low tone the ceremonial song of the dead. During the singing of the farewell song, the corpse was taken through a window or an opening that had been made on the east side of the house or wigwam; never through the regular entrance. The Chippewa did this to prevent the dead from treading the paths of the living, for they feared he might cast a shadow on them. It was also believed that if the body was taken through the door, an evil spirit would follow it and cast a spell on the deceased person's family. By taking the body through a window or an opening, the evil spirit was foiled. This practice is still followed by a few of the Lac du Flambeau Chippewa.[2]

The ancient custom was to carry the corpse to the cemetery. During the funeral procession, singing, accompanied by drums and rattles, was carried on in a low tone. When the funeral party arrived at the cemetery, the Chippewa danced again. After the body was lowered into the grave, the officiating medicine man gave a farewell speech. The Chippewa usually buried their dead in shallow graves.

A wooden marker was driven into the ground above the grave. The inverted totem symbol of the deceased was painted on the marker, so that the deceased could be identified by other members of the clan. If the deceased was a woman, the husband walked on a board placed lengthwise over her grave. After the funeral, he usually remained in seclusion for a short time.

If it was suspected that the deceased was the victim of an evil medicine man, friends or relatives watched over the grave for four nights. Often the Indian who had used witchcraft on the dead while living, tried to retrieve his "medicine" from the body after burial. During this period of vigilance, a small fire was kindled at sunset and at sunrise to ward off evil-doers who might wish to violate the grave. Furthermore, it was believed that fires would provide comfort to the soul of the dead during his rest in camp, as it was thought that the soul traveled only in the daytime.[3]

After the mourners had eaten their first meal following the funeral, an older member of the family gave instructions to them somewhat as follows: A mourner should not be idle. Labor helps one to forget his grief; it becomes a consoler. Idleness during grief tends to laziness, shiftlessness, and the destruction of good habits. Too much sleep, especially during day-time, sickness excepted, should not be indulged in. One should rise with the sun and retire at sunset. If a mourner acquires the habit of remaining in bed after sunrise, he will gradually become listless and weak, and will have to spend the remainder of his life in bed.

On the anniversary of the death, a Memorial Feast was given by the mourners to friends and relatives. An invitation was also extended to all who had attended the "wake" or the funeral of the deceased. Unless someone dreamed of the deceased, offerings were no longer placed on the grave after the first anniversary of the death. If the departed had appeared to them in ragged garments, clothing was placed on the grave. If the deceased appeared hungry, food was taken to the grave. This practice still prevails among the followers of the Midewiwin.[4]

As late as 1937, some Chippewa still hesitated to have the

bodies of their deceased taken to an undertaker's establishment. Marie Livingston thus explained the reason for the objection:

Many years ago, when the Indians welcomed the white men into their midst, they regarded them as trustworthy brothers. Later when the white man began to mistreat and encroach upon their rights, the Indians looked upon them as evil conspirators, always seeking to outwit the lowly Indian. In time, the Indians came to look upon all white men as enemies.

The Indians believed that white doctors were merely experimenting on their fellow tribesmen. They felt that the doctors were not interested in curing the Indians. Indians believed that when an Indian went to a hospital, he was as good as dead — very few did return alive.

Generally the doctor appointed as a government physician was an inexperienced man who stayed just long enough to confirm the Indian's opinion that he came to the reservation for the sole purpose of acquiring experience.

Never before the coming of the white man were the Indians deprived of seeing their dead. When this was refused, the Indians thought that it was from some evil purpose. Such an incident was that of a young Chippewa girl who went to a hospital for an operation. She died there and the relatives were informed that she had died of a contagious disease.

When the coffin arrived at the home, it had an order tacked on it, forbidding the opening of the casket, and stating that anyone caught breaking the seal would be prosecuted. The weight and size of the casket caused the Indians to become suspicious. No one ever admitted that the casket was opened, yet they always contended that the body of the girl was never sent home. From that time, the Indians would not let their dead out of their sight long enough to be taken to an undertaker's establishment for embalming until recent years.[5]

The ancient custom of requiring a widow or a bereaved mother to carry a small wrapped dish tied around the waist was a common practice among the pagan Chippewa. Immediately following her bereavement, a relative or a close friend of the deceased presented this dish to the woman. She was obliged to carry the dish one year, until the ceremony of "releasing the mourner." If the woman was invited to a meal or a feast, or even in her own home, she took food from the table and placed it on the dish. The dish was handed to some person, who either ate the food or burned it. According to Chippewa belief, this was feeding the soul of the departed.

Another old custom of the Chippewa was that of cutting some hair from the dead. If the deceased was a married man, the hair was tied, wrapped in buckskin, and given to the widow. It was the duty of the widow to add something to the hair, anything from a ribbon to a blanket. These goods represented the price he or she must pay to the parents'-in-law at the feast of "Releasing the Mourner."

The mourner showed respect for this "spirit bundle," by guarding it carefully. He reserved a place for it at night. He carried it with him when traveling. If a man went hunting, another watched over it during his absence. If, at the end of the year of mourning, the "in-laws" were satisfied that the bereaved had satisfactorily fulfilled the tribal customs, the favor was returned by giving the mourner his freedom or a substitute mate. If the relatives regarded a bereaved man with esteem because of his kindness to his former wife and his ability as a provider, there was no alternative choice — he was given another wife.

If his behavior had been satisfactory, the mourner was given a simple feast sometime before the term of mourning had expired. At this feast, friends each donated one article of clothing, generally of a brilliant color. Red was preferred because it indicated freedom.[6]

At the releasing ceremonial, the mourner, if a woman, was seated on a new blanket and dressed in the donor's contribution of clothing. Her face was washed. Her hair which had hung loose before, was oiled with a pomade of bear grease and neatly braided. The spirit bundle was removed. A spokesman gave an oration on behalf of the mourner, explaining why she should be released. However, the woman was not entirely freed from the obligation of mourning, until she had given an anniversary dinner. But she could, however, again participate in dances from which she had been barred during the period of mourning.

The Indians believed that during the first year after a death, the spirit of the deceased returned several times to its earthly abode. It jealously observed the family and did not leave permanently until after the anniversary celebration. If a widow ignored the traditional mourning custom and decked herself with ornaments or wore brilliantly colored clothing, especially red, she invited trouble. Such display was considered an insult to her parents-in-law. Two or more women waited for an opportunity to waylay the offender. They beat her severely. She was regarded with disfavor by all. If a widower erred, the women tore the garments from his body and he became the jest and laughing stock of the community. It was against the dignity of the braves to take part in such affairs.

According to a story related by Quikabanokwe, an old Chippewa woman, a certain woman married the youngest of three brothers before her mourning period had elapsed. After their marriage, the couple went on a hunting excursion for their winter supply of meat. The other brothers, humiliated and angry, bided their time.

One day, when the canoes of the trappers and hunters began to arrive, the brothers saw their erring brother's canoe. They watched the brother beach the heavily-laden canoe, after which he proceeded with his pack toward the village. The woman also stepped from the canoe, adjusted the tumpline across her forehead and lifted her pack, preparing to follow. In the meantime, the two brothers had stationed themselves on either side of the trail. As the woman passed, bent under her heavy load, they drew their knives and cut the pack strap. Each man seized one of the woman's ears and cut it off. Her nose was likewise cut off and most of her hair. This was her punishment for refusing to adhere to tribal custom.[7]

Chippewa honored their dead in cemeteries by building grave "houses" over the burying places of the deceased. Time and the elements have destroyed most of these relics of ancient times. These houses conformed to four general types, but they were all approximately three and one-half feet high and about two and one-half feet wide, with shelves on the outside.

In one type, the rear planks were placed perpendicular to the ground, signifying that the person in the grave either went to the Happy Hunting Grounds above, or to the evil hunting grounds below. This reference to evil hunting grounds was due to Christian influence. The totem of the deceased was carved on a board. The front was built the same as the rear but it had an opening about one and one-half feet high and two feet wide. The opening was to allow the spirit of the dead to come and go, and also to permit friends to leave food on the grave.

The rear of the second type of grave house was like the first, except that it showed no totem. In the front, there were two small openings and a shelf. The two openings signified that the dead belonged to the bird clan. One of the openings was for the spirit of the dead and the other was for the birds to make their homes in the house. Food for the deceased was placed on the shelf.

The front and rear of the third type were identical with the first, but drawers were placed in the openings. The spirit passed in and out of the house through the drawers.

A fourth type had no openings. This was because the house had been built over the grave sometime after the burial, and it was believed that the spirit had already left the grave. The house was built for the convenience of the spirit when it returned to receive gifts which were placed on the shelves.[8] Only a small number of these grave houses remain; reminders of the days when Indians believed that their dead set out for the "Happy Hunting Grounds." The dust of these vestiges of the past has mingled with that of the bodies in whose memory they were erected.[9]

DREAMS AND FASTINGS

chapter 32

ALTHOUGH ALL PRIMITIVE PEOPLES HAVE DREAM stories, to the Indian, dreams were media through which he received preternatural powers. These powers, he affirmed, enabled him to foretell future events, to control diseases, and to exercise the office of priest or leader. Through the observance of some rite involving personal privation, the Indians sought dreams or visions.[1]

When a child was old enough to reason, the parents tested him to discover if he would be gifted with unusual powers. The test was a simple one. When all the family were at table, the parents set two dishes before the child. One dish contained food for the meal; the other, charcoal. The child might ignore the dish of charcoal and he might continue to do this for many years — in some instances, he never recognized the dish of charcoal. If he took the charcoal dish, one side of his face was marked with charcoal and he began the fast.

The fasting was done in a secluded woodland, usually during the sugar season. A blanket was the only protection allowed. The length of time the youth fasted was the determining factor for the amount of power he would receive. An Indian might fast two or three days and receive a power, but he could not expect to receive

as great powers as one who had fasted for ten or more days. If a
youth persevered to the fifth day, a small amount of food was given
him. He was allowed to wash and comb, and to mark the opposite
side of his face with charcoal. He was then ready to finish his dream
trial.[2]

At the end of his trial, if the youth had not been favored with
a dream or vision, or if he was not satisfied with his revelations, he
could enter upon another period of fasting. In some instances, the
fast continued for twenty days.[3] From experience, older Indians had
learned that one who had fasted too long became mentally unbal-
anced. Therefore, if a youth undertook an additional ten-day ordeal,
he was given a small amount of food each fifth day during this time.[4]

Girls also fasted, dreamed, and received powers. In any dream
perplexity, they usually went for guidance to a man who had
dreamed about the same object. Angeline Cedaroot, "Nashinaquay,"
an elderly Chippewa woman, was asked if she thought that girls
received as much power as boys. Her reply was:

No, I would not say it was as powerful, but they did have medicine which they used to their advantage. My old grandmother,
Nokomis, had some powerful medicine which I will tell you
about.

The name of my grandmother's medicine was Wa-ba-no-
waisk. When she was a young girl, she acquired this medicine
through strenuous fasting. She had a dream which meant for
her to begin her fast. She took charcoal from the campfire and
marked her face with it. She then walked through the camp to
let the people know what she was about to do. Finding an ideal
spot in a tree, she began her fast. She did not eat or drink for
ten days. During the day, she came down from the tree and
roamed the vicinity. At night, she returned to the tree to sleep.
On the tenth day, she returned home, feeling fresh, with an
abundance of renewed vigor.

The powers she acquired on her stay in the woods enabled
her to walk on fire, pick up and handle live coals without being
burnt. This power was given her so that in case the time came
when she would be endangered by fire, she would escape unharmed.

Nokomis not only acted as a "Florence Nightingale" in
battles, but would take a gun into battle and her very presence
won many battles. The Sioux were frightened by the presence
of an "Amazon" in the Chippewa ranks. In a battle near St.

Paul, the Sioux surrendered when they saw Nokomis with the Chippewa. They were afraid of a woman warrior. When she placed Wa-ba-no-waisk on wounded soldiers, they were made immediately fit for battle.[5]

Indians customarily preserved the memory of their dreams by picture writing. Many Chippewa on the Bad River Reservation wrote their dreams on a large flat rock. They believed that if the dreams were preserved, the writer would secure greater power. To please bird totems, the writing was done before the birds had disappeared in the autumn and vegetation had ceased its growth. On the Lac du Flambeau Reservation, a few Chippewa youths still observe fasting. Their dreams, designating their totem, are written on pieces of cloth attached to a pole standing near the front of the dwelling.

According to the Chippewa, the dream trial did not prove beneficial to every youth who underwent the ordeal. Should the dreamer be so unfortunate as to see a Windigo, an "ice spirit," in his dream, he was liable to be transformed into an ice spirit or Windigo himself. If anyone turned into a Windigo, he became self-conscious, and was not considered responsible for his actions. Intense cold weather, together with insufficient food, also caused the transformation into a Windigo. Indian women frightened their children into submission by telling them stories of the "ice spirit."

One of these Windigo stories is concerned with the evils which befell a family consisting of father, mother, and one child. Because the father was a good provider, the family often had a surplus of food, which the mother stored away for future use. A jealous, evil-minded person begrudged this family's good fortune. He used "bad medicine" to discredit the man's reputation as a generous provider. The family's good fortune changed. Although the man spent his entire time hunting, he was unsuccessful. For a time, the family lived on the supplies they had stored, but these gradually dwindled. Then the husband became moody and refused to hunt, saying that it was useless. After the weather had become intensely cold, the man's countenance wore a strange, forlorn look. His wife became alarmed. She began to gather firewood so that they would at least have fuel.

One day while gathering wood, the woman noticed heavy smoke pouring from the wigwam. She returned hastily to discover that her husband had killed their only child and was cooking the flesh. Not wishing to antagonize her husband, for she knew that he had undergone the transformation of the Windigo, she pretended that she did not notice anything amiss. However, she determined to leave the wigwam. In order to prevent her husband from following her, she hid his snowshoes. She escaped that night. Although exhausted and nearly starved, fear kept her moving onward.

Finally, she saw an Indian village. After the Indians had heard her story, they called a council to discuss the best means of meeting the situation. During the "gosa-bun-damo-winini," the trance-man's swoon, he saw the unfortunate man moving toward the village. To enlist the aid of spiritual powers, all who had undergone the dream trial went into seclusion. After some time, the spirits informed them that only a person who had dreamed of the ice spirit could combat the dreaded Windigo. A shrunken and stooped old woman was the only person who had seen the ice transformed into a gigantic being. She willingly offered her services. The council was requested to bring her a certain kind of club and to have an antidote in readiness for her after she had met the Windigo. She cautioned them not to disobey her. If they did, she, too, would become a dangerous Windigo.

The old woman stood poised before the opening of the first wigwam in the village, ready to offer combat to the Windigo. The first and second blows had no telling effect, but the third accomplished the desired result. During the encounter, a kettle of grease was kept boiling. After the old woman's task was accomplished, she let the boiling grease sizzle slowly down her throat. The greasy antidote prevented her from becoming a Windigo.[6]

Stories, similar to the Windigo, tended to increase superstition among the Chippewa. However, the fasting among youth today, almost a thing of the past, is not practiced with its former rigor. The totem of the fasting youth is of conservation significance. Animal, fish, bird, and plant totems are not wantonly destroyed.

THE MIDEWIWIN OR GRAND MEDICINE SOCIETY

chapter 33

THE MIDEWIWIN WAS A SECRET ORGANIZATION IN which the members, as they gained proficiency in the society, were advanced successively through eight degrees. The discipline was rigid. The fraternity surrounded its ritual with great secrecy, and regulated the religious and social conduct of the community. In their efforts to Christianize and civilize the Indians, missionaries and white teachers found that the Midewiwin society was their greatest opponent. If the term "pagan" was applied to an Indian community, it usually signified that the Mide was in control.[1]

According to some Chippewa, the chief purpose of the Midewiwin was not to worship the gods, but to preserve the knowledge of herbs for the prolongation of life. The Midewiwin maintained that the span of life was extended by right living supplemented by the use of herbs given by the Mide Manido. Odinigun, a member of the society said, "In the old days, the Indian lived out the full length of days."[2]

The Midewiwin taught that wrong doing deserved punishment. Moreover, membership in the society did not exempt a member from suffering the penalty of his mis-deeds. Lying, stealing, and the use of liquor were strictly forbidden. Men must practice patience, be moderate in speech, quiet in manner, deliberate in action, gentle of voice, and courteous to old people. The power of the Mide was exercised through music and medicine. In addition to the mi-gis, a small white shell, each member of the Midewiwin carried in his Mide bag herbs and other substances supposed to have medicinal properties. In his treatment of the sick, a Midewiwin first sang a ceremonial song and then prescribed his medicine.[3]

The Midewiwin had its own method of punishing offenders within its realm. If necessary, subtle poisons might be used. Some Chippewa claim that the Midewiwin were also able to call down curses on those who displeased them. A certain man who had offended a Midewiwin medicine man was warned that misfortune would soon befall him. In a short time, his little daughter died.[4]

The society held its meetings in a special lodge. Its size was determined by the number of persons who attended the meetings. Warren stated that the lodge in which he attended a meeting was approximately 100 feet long and 15 feet wide. Long poles which crossed two feet from the top were driven into the ground. The sides of the lodge were partially covered with green boughs. Pieces of calico, handkerchiefs, blankets, and other objects were hung on a horizontal pole extending the entire length of the lodge. These were the offerings of candidates who were about to be initiated into the mysteries of the Midewiwin society.[5]

For three days and nights prior to the day of worship, the beats of the great medicine drum resounded through the forest. During the two days preceding this worship, great preparations were made. Young and old decorated themselves fantastically with paints, feathers, and animal skins. Although children were sometimes allowed to join the society, generally the privilege was reserved to older members of the tribe. For a year or more, before an Indian was received into the society, he was given a series of instructions regarding the responsibilities he was about to assume. In case of a very sick person, the elders held a consultation and generally decided to initiate such a person at once in order that his health might be improved through the intervention of the Mide gods.[6]

During the medicine worship ceremonial, usually held in spring, only members of the society were permitted within the lodge. The men and women sat in rows along the sides of the lodge, each holding in his hand the "me-da-wi-aun," or medicine bag. This bag was made of bird, otter, beaver, or mink skins. It might also be a wild cat paw or the skin of a rattlesnake. Since Chippewa tradition relates that the four Manido appeared in the sky at dawn, with the morning sun shining on their faces and a live otter in their hands, the otter bag was preferred.[7] In each mide bag were herbs and charms.

Candidates sat on mats facing the center of the lodge where the "me-da-wautig," a cedar post, daubed with vermilion and ornamented with tufts of birds' down, had been planted. Initiation rites were supposed to instil a "spirit power" into the neophyte received into the order.

Four "we-kauns," initiating priests, surrounded the candidates with their medicine bags, rattles, and drums. After addressing a few remarks to the candidates in a low voice, one of the "we-kauns" took from his medicine sack the migis, a small white sea shell, the chief emblem of the Midewiwin rite. Holding this shell in the palm of his hand, the "we-kaun" slowly walked around the inside of the lodge, displaying the shell to the onlookers.[8] He was followed by his fellow we-kauns swinging their rattles and chanting in deep guttural tones. After circling the lodge in this manner, they returned to the candidates and saluted them. Then they quietly walked to the western end of the lodge where the leader delivered a loud and spirited address.[9]

The candidate was given instructions regarding the use of a few simple herbs which he was expected to carry in his medicine bag. In later and higher degrees, the instructions were concerned with Mide mysteries, the properties of herbs, and the nature of vegetable poisonings. Each degree had its special songs and its special kind of Mide bag. Fear of death, either by poison or violence, sealed the lips of the Midewiwin members.[10]

The Indians understood that a Midewiwin session was a time to test the wits and the skill of the participants. No spectator or participant could safely enter the lodge without "zinso-o-win," a protective medicine which was kept in the medicine bag. The Indians claimed that persons who did not carry the protective medicine sometimes died of the violent nausea caused by the Midewiwin council.

The Chippewa advance the following story [11] to prove that a protective medicine was necessary in the medicine lodge. Neganibenazekwe had been initiated into the society when she was very young, but she never affiliated herself with the society or attended any of its ceremonies. At one time, when the society was initiating candidates, a friend urged her to attend the ceremonial. Not wishing to offend her friend by a refusal, Neganibenazekwe explained that she no longer carried protective medicine. Her friend tossed her a weasel skin bag and said, "I'll loan you this, if that's all that keeps you from going."

Neganibenazekwe accepted the medicine bag without question and accompanied her friend. The ceremonies had already begun when they arrived. In a short time, Neganibenazekwe felt ill and fell into a deep swoon. Upon recovering consciousness, she found the chief medicine man blowing a medical spray into her face. When she had completely recovered, the medicine man, an acquaintance of hers, gave her a lecture, warning against attending Midewiwin ceremonies without the protection of "zinso-o-win." The weasel bag

that she carried had been empty. Her companion was also repri-
manded for urging her friend to attend the medicine lodge without
protective medicine.

Teachings and records of the grand medicine council were
written on birch bark rolls. The rolls were strengthened by strips
of wood placed on opposite ends of the bark and securely fastened
in place. The inner side of the roll contained the records and teachings of the society. The outer side usually had a number of circles
which corresponded to the number of degrees or lodges represented
in the teachings. If an old man presented a young man for initiation
into the Midewiwin, he showed him this roll and explained the
teachings written thereon. If a child was to be initiated, the old
man showed the roll to the child's parents and explained the teachings to them.

The path of life from youth to old age was shown by phases on
the rolls. Seven tangents represented the seven temptations of man.
The first tangent represented the first temptation which comes to a
young man. If he yielded to it, he would not live long. The second
tangent represented the second temptation which had the same
penalty attached to it. With the third temptation, the element of
religious responsibility appeared. The person was asked, "How did
you act when you were initiated into the Midewiwin? Were you
respectful to the older members and did you faithfully fulfill all
your obligations?" The fourth tangent represented a temptation
coming to a man in middle age. With the fifth temptation, the
person began to reflect upon his own length of days and asked
himself: "Have you ever been disrespectful of old age?" The sixth
temptation returned to religious ideas and asked whether all religious obligations had been fulfilled. The seventh temptation was
said to be the hardest of all. If a man could resist it, he would live
to the allotted age of man. At this time, an evil spirit came to him.
If he had smiled during a Midewiwin ceremony, he had to reckon
with this spirit.[12]

In 1937, a medicine dance was held on the Bad River Reservation at a former pagan center. The ceremonial services were reported by James Scott, an eyewitness:

> On that day, Mrs. Alex Newagon entered the fourth degree of
> the secret order of the medicine lodge. The master of the secret
> order and all his associates wore beaded costumes, symbolizing
> some secret in the design language. One of the designs was a
> wheat design signifying a knowledge of herbs.
>
> "Ob-waud," William Webster and Waiske Martin pre-

sented Mrs. Newagon with four kinds of herbs. Since the medicine lodge embraces eight degrees, each degree is represented by a special design. Twelve associates attend the first degree and these increase in number by four for every new degree. When the final degree is taken, forty associates are in attendance for this grand occasion. The purpose of the associates is to give the candidate special instructions. The degrees in the medicine lodge become harder as the person advances. Those who have attained the eight degrees are few in number. At this date, it would be difficult to find more than two in the entire Chippewa country.[13]

Although the Grand Medicine Society has lost its original significance among modern Chippewa, remnants of the ceremonials survive. Superstitions are so deeply ingrained in the Indian that it takes many years before they are eradicated.[14]

MEDICINE MEN AND THEIR POWERS

chapter 34

THE CHIPPEWA OF THE PAST SPENT THEIR LIVES in an environment rife with superstitious beliefs. Stories of ghosts, grotesque beasts, evil manitoes, together with the preternatural manifestations of conjurers and medicine men, created an atmosphere of dread. Because of awe-inspiring feats of legerdemain and divination, the medicine men exercised a malignant power over the minds of the Indians. According to the Indians, wicked medicine men abused gifts which they had received during their days of fasting. At that time, the manitoes had given the young men powers beyond those of ordinary human beings.[1]

Nearly all ailments were regarded as curable through rattle-shaking and incantations of medicine men who were also aided by charms, fetishes, and amulets, the potency of which allegedly covered a wide range.[2] Medicine men were hired to cast spells, as well as to remove those which had been inflicted by other members of the profession. Both in peace and in war, the members of the "medicine fraternity" exerted an influence which greatly affected the tribe. Many of the great war leaders were medicine men—Pontiac, Tecumseh, Sitting Bull, Black Hawk, and King Philip. Frequently the medicine men were aided by "prophets" who rallied the Indians to their cause by injecting a wave of "religion" into the tribe, making them fanatics to a particular cause.[3]

Among the Chippewa, there were several types of shamans or medicine men—medicine men proper, jugglers, and conjurers or seers. Many of the medicine men were connected with the Midewiwin Society and had practical knowledge of the medicinal value of herbs, barks, and roots. Jugglers or wabenos practiced medical magic and professed to draw out the affliction with instruments, usually tubular bones, which they swallowed and regurgitated. The sickness thus drawn out was usually represented as a bug, a strand of hair, or a variety of other objects, including live fish. Incantations, rattle-shaking, and drum-beating were the stock-in-trade of these healers. Conjurers or seers were said to derive their power from the thunder god. Their specialties were divination by means of dreams and consultation with the spirits of the "Shake Lodge" ritual.

In administering natural remedies, the medicine men of the Midewiwin Society usually intermixed enough jugglery to impress ignorant Indians. The belief was general that an evil medicine man could detach his spirit from his body and prowl about on nocturnal visits. This was done under the disguise of an animal which appeared as a "fireball" that alternately dimmed and glowed with the respiration of the beast. It was also claimed that while in this state, the medicine man was exceedingly weak. A slight blow at the "fireball" was sufficient to cause his death. Only persons who had a "protective medicine" could come into close contact with a "fireball" and retain his senses. The medicine man who had the evil power of the "fireball" could accomplish harm by merely touching the person or he could use a form of the "fireball" called the "bear walk."[4]

The medicine man who assumed the form of a fireball had the power of using different animals in his work and was capable of flying in the air. Unless he was frustrated by a "healer," a medicine man who worked for the good of his fellow beings, the fireball generally accomplished the death of a victim. After the death of a victim, the medicine man was obliged to extract from the dead body the medicine he had used to cause the death of the person. This had to be done during the time of the wake or at the cemetery, or immediately after the burial. If the medicine man failed in recovering the "medicine," death was his fate.

The appearance of a fire ball, "be-ba-ma-so-ko-neg," always created fear and a foreboding of evil. When a fire ball entered a dwelling, a member of the household was marked for misfortune. The unfortunate person could be afflicted in any manner the evil doer chose — severe pains, deformity, insanity, and even death. During this time, the body of the medicine man resembled a corpse. When the animal under which he veiled himself was struck, it emitted sounds peculiar to such an animal. The Chippewa claimed that close proximity to the fire ball usually caused a temporary state of amnesia and paralysis, unless the person was protected by an amulet or some other talismanic object.

When it became evident that a person was under the influence of sorcery, the relatives or friends attempted to secure the relief of the afflicted person. To shoot or to strike the luminous object would in all probability cause the death of the person whose spirit was incorporated therein, that is, the medicine man. This course of action was seldom resorted to because the condition of the affected person would then remain permanent. If the perpetrator was known, he was presented with many gifts. The acceptance of these gifts carried with it the obligation of a return payment. Upon being discovered and forced to recognize the custom of placation by gifts, the complete recovery of the victim followed.

If, in addition to the restoration of the afflicted, revenge upon the evil doer was sought, the services of other medicine men or women were employed. A "shake lodge" was erected in the forest and by incantations and other conjurations, the spirit of the evil doer was forced to enter the lodge. Upon request of their employers, the hired medicine men or women could bring deformity or even death to evil medicine men.

According to the belief of the Chippewa, a bad medicine man realized that his own life was in constant jeopardy, whenever he traveled under the guise of the fire ball. If he was outwitted, he paid the forfeit of his own life. At such a time, it was said, even the toss of a handkerchief or a slight switching meant his death. Although the fire ball walker carried a protective medicine that had a stupefying effect upon his enemies or other persons whom he might meet, it sometimes failed because of the stronger will power of his opponent. When he started out on his nefarious course, he exposed himself to frustration since everyone knew the weakness of the fire ball. However, the evil doer was rarely detected. If he was captured, he begged his captors to spare his life and to keep his identity a secret. He offered half his medicine, his knowledge of the fire ball, or even his entire worldly goods if his life was spared.[5]

Medicine Man

Pagan Indians were firm in their belief of the fire ball. Even a Christian Indian, Dan Morrison, declared that the fire ball was a reality. He said:

I might mention an incident that happened in my own family. During the life of my mother, she told me many times that she saw fire balls moving around on Madeline Island in the early days of the settlement. The appearance of the fire ball was usually a forerunner of death in the family living in the vicinity visited by the fire ball.

My father, who was on the old St. Paul road one night, was much astonished to find himself confronted by a fire ball. Upon investigation, he discovered that the light was caused by a piece of phosphorus wood! This is one of the arguments advanced by many that belief in the Indian fire ball is merely the product of a distorted mind. Fantastic as it may seem, however, many Indians believe in the fire ball, claim to have observed it, and experienced its far-reaching effects. The power to command the movement and use of the fire ball lies within only the most powerful medicine men. In point of mystery, it is co-related with the shake lodge, though the use of the latter is often employed to offset the effects of the former.[6]

Many years ago, according to the accounts of old pagan Indians, fire balls were frequently seen on the Bad River Reservation. Christian Indians who lived among the pagan Indians tried to forget these superstitious practices, but sometimes happenings occurred which apparently confirmed pagan beliefs, as the following instance shows.

Two Christian families were living a short distance apart. In one of the houses, there lived a young Indian couple with two small children; in the other, another young couple and an old mother. Sometime before, the family with the two children had been forced to testify in a land litigation concerning heirship lands belonging to a pagan Indian. The pagan, an old medicine man, lost the case. Much wrought up, the old man burst into angry tears, pointed an accusing finger at the man who had testified against him and said: "My friend, I have just lost something that I value very much, and it will not be long before you, too, will lose something you now prize very highly."

Sometime after this occurrence, the old mother arose at dawn. She happened to glance at the neighbor's house and was astonished to see a peculiar bluish light moving up and down over the house. Instantly, she realized that it was a fire ball. The other members of the house hastened outdoors, the young woman carrying a loaded gun. She fired over the top of the house and the fire ball disappeared. A few minutes later, they saw an otter running towards the woods.

After a hurried breakfast, the old mother hastened to the neighbor's home where she found the young parents in great distress. One of the children was paralyzed on one side of his body and he was unable to utter a sound. Although doctors were called to help the child, their remedies were useless and the child died one month later. Some years later, a three-year old child of this same family showed symptoms of a similar nature. A government physician treated the boy, but finally declared the case hopeless. This child also died. These deaths were attributed to the evil influence of the medicine man.[7]

In the early 1900's, according to a Chippewa story, Ma-gi-dens, a wicked medicine woman, lived at Odanah. Although she had attended St. Mary's School, she returned to Indian superstition in later years. Using the Christian religion as a shield, she became an adept follower of the fire ball craft. Thus she kept her friends and neighbors ignorant of her true character.

One night, a young man arrived in the village to visit friends. As he walked along, he sighted a brilliant ball of fire which traveled over the tree tops. At regular intervals, it dimmed its light to a mere point. The young man remembered that his grandmother had told him about the fire ball and he pitied the creature, who, for evil purposes, was jeopardizing her own life. He did not carry placating "medicine," but, on the spur of the moment, he decided to chase the fire ball. During the pursuit, the fire died out and the fire ball assumed the form of a bear. When the young man overtook the bear, he recognized old Ma-gi-dens. She immediately offered the young man half of her medicine and also instructions how to work the fire ball, if he spared her life and kept her identity a secret. The young man scoffed at the offer. Since her business was treachery, perhaps at the first opportunity, she would harm him.

Ma-gi-dens begged the young man to accept her offer and promised to do him no harm. Finally, he promised and escorted her home. She divided her "medicine" and showed him how to work the fire ball. The young man took the roots and herbs and buried them in the woods. According to the Chippewa, he was able to perform the fire ball, but his cautious grandmother warned him not to do so.[8]

Another fire ball story relates that many years ago, when the road to Ashland was little more than an Indian trail, an old Indian, Charles Bressette, was returning from Ashland to his home. The night was dark and the bushes and trees presented weird shapes. Bressette picked up a stout stick for protection against any danger that might befall him. When he was about two miles from the village, he saw a fire ball, weaving in and out among the trees. Bressette, a daring man, pursued the fire ball, and caught up to it. With one blow he brought it to the ground. The fire ball suddenly changed into the form of an old woman. The woman begged Bressette not to mention the happening to anyone. He promised, and to his astonishment, the woman suddenly disappeared.[9]

If ordinary means of communication were not available, medicine men were also credited with the power of thought transference. Before there were railroads on the Chippewa reservations, all communication between the different bands was carried on through messengers. It so happened that the Indians on the Bad River Reservation had business to transact with the Indians of the St. Croix band. A council was to be held in two days, but the distance was too great to notify these Indians by messengers in the intervening time.

An old medicine man, long since passed to the "Happy Hunting Grounds," was informed of the predicament. He volunteered to notify Aniquod-donse, a medicine man, who lived along the banks of the St. Croix River. Although the local medicine man did not leave the reservation, yet the St. Croix Indians arrived in time for the council, a two-days' journey.

Indians familiar with the so-called powers of the medicine men affirm that the notification of this council was accomplished by the local medicine man either through an exchange of dreams with the St. Croix medicine man or that he sent a spirit messenger to contact Aniquod-donse, who notified the other Indians.

That the medicine men sometimes took advantage of the ignorance of the Indians is evident from the following story told by a Chippewa on the Bad River Reservation:

A certain medicine man went to more civilized parts of the region. On his return, he called for a medicine dance to thank the spirits for his safe return and also to convey to the other members of the lodge his findings. But he did not reveal his possession of matches which were then unknown among the Chippewa. They had just been placed on the market in the locality he had visited. Realizing that it would be a long time before matches would be introduced on the reservation, the medicine man saw an opportunity of increasing his prestige. He also saw a chance to secure a few more possessions.

During the dance, the medicine man stated that the spirits had empowered him to make fire easier than the old way of using flint and stone. He had some magic sticks which were very precious. With great ceremony, he struck a match on a hard surface producing fire as if out of the air. The crowd was awe-struck. The medicine man informed them that he would exchange a stick of the magic for one blanket. His supply of "magic sticks" was soon exhausted. Thus he became the possessor of a large number of blankets, sufficient to keep him warm for many moons.[10]

Although it is not too difficult to understand how the medicine man deceived the other Indians, how he permitted himself to be hood-winked is less comprehensible. The Minnesota Historical Society reports the following incident:

> When an old friend of mine, named Shakopee, who was a medicine man, became sick at the Redwood Agency, I sent my doctor down to see him. I was then represented by Dr. Daniels, now one of the most prominent physicians in the state, living at St. Peter. He reported that he was sick with typhoid fever, and that all he needed was good nursing, good food, and rest. I had the facilities for all these conditions, and sent an ambulance to take him to my agency. But he positively refused, and had the medicine men drum and rattle beans over him until he died.
>
> Now, this had always been to me a problem; do these savages actually believe in their medicine, and that they get gunlocks, snakes, frogs, and such things out of their patients? Or would they rather die under the same treatment than confess their frauds by accepting civilized methods?
>
> I confess that I have never been able to solve the problem, and when my old friend, Shakopee, stuck to the barbaric treatment until death, I rather inclined to the opinion that they were really in earnest. It is an interesting question, and, having given the facts, I turn the psychological part of it over to the thinkers.[11]

William P. Bigboy, a Bad River Chippewa, claimed that some medicine men had "good medicine." Bigboy related the story of Wagaszick, a medicine man, thus:

> As is generally the case, especially among the older Indians, Wagaszick, was a good story teller. He became a favorite with

some of the younger people who enjoyed his stories of olden days. The medicine man told how the Indians eked out their existence and how they tried to keep in good health.

At one time, Wagaszick was asked how he became a medicine man. He replied: "In my young days, nearly all the people were pagans and members of the Midewiwin. When I came to the age of reason, I, too, was prepared for my eventual entrance into the lodge. I was put on a fast in order to determine what work or degrees I would be able to take. I fasted nine days before a dream came to me. I dreamt of water. My grandfather was much pleased with my dream and he told me to prepare to be a medicine man and help the sick to become well."

Wagaszick was forced to work at an early age and had no opportunity to study medicine until he became too old to work. Then he applied himself earnestly to study medicine. His remedies were so successful that his services were in constant demand, not only in Odanah, but in other settlements as well.[12]

The powers of the medicine man were seldom disputed and the general belief of the Chippewa in their medicine men was sacred. Nothing that the medicine man did was questioned. However, the age of the medicine man is gone. Bearskin, the last of the Lac du Flambeau medicine men, died in 1937. The Chippewa now depend upon white physicians almost exclusively. Chippewa boys who served in the medical corps during World War II, have brought back to the reservations medical knowledge that strengthens respect for the white doctor's skill.

INDIAN JUGGLERY AND THE
DJISAKIN OR SHAKE LODGE

chapter 35

IN ADDITION TO MEDICINE MEN, THE CHIPPEWA also employed the juggler to help them in solving their problems. Jugglers supposedly exercised their powers through the medium of the shake lodge.[1]

A shake lodge was constructed of four, six, or eight poles about three inches thick and from eight to ten feet long. The poles were arranged to form a conical-shaped structure, which was covered with birch bark or mats. Bells were hung from the highest point of the lodge. Spruce branches were spread on the ground within. The lodge was open at the top, but there was no door. When the juggler or "tchisakiwiwini" wished to enter, he shoved aside the mats.

Before the juggler entered the shake lodge, he addressed the buffalo, the bear, and the bird manitoes, saying: "You have been good to me, granting me to perform this wonderful work. You have given me the power to do it and now I kindly call you here. The Indians who are here have engaged me. They like to listen to you when you speak." After entering the lodge, he sang: "Bi pindigen nin wigiwaming," "Come enter into my house," repeating this invitation several times.

Inside the lodge, the juggler lay prone upon the ground. The manitoes announced their coming by little sparks of fire which appeared above the lodge. As soon as one little fire spark was seen above the lodge, the structure began to move gently. When several lights had appeared, the lodge moved rapidly from right to left, forward and backward, and finally swayed quickly in a circle.

In the meantime, the Indians who had come for assistance, sat around the outside of the lodge. From time to time, they threw tobacco into a fire as an offering to the manitoes. Prior to this meeting, they had agreed among themselves who should be the first to confer with the manitoes. When the swaying of the lodge indicated that the manitoes had arrived, the first spokesman addressed the manitoes thus: "We have engaged our friend, the juggler, to call you. Indeed, we are in trouble. What shall we do?" (If the trouble was a case of sickness, the ailing person was generally lying in a nearby wigwam.) "Is there anything that will make our comrade well?" [2]

Then two manitoes answered; one spoke Chippewa, the other, Agima-manito, used a language which the Indians did not understand. Through a manito interpreter, the agima-manito said: "Yes, there is something you ought to do." The Indian outside the lodge inquired, "What is it? Tell it to me." The chief manito, Oshkabenwis, might advise the sick man either take the roots of a certain herb as a medicine or join the Indian religion.

Sometimes Indians inquired about their absent friends: "How is he? When will he come?" If an Indian was angry at some person, he spoke to the manitoes thus: "I put this tobacco here. I want you to get that Indian's soul. I want it here, to be tortured." The Indian did not mention the person's name, but he disclosed where the person lived. After Oshkabenwis had caused the enemy's soul to appear, the angered Indian asked: "Why did you do that?" The soul might answer: "I did not do it purposely. Have pity on me. I will not do it again. Let me go." [3]

During the ceremonial for the cure of a sick person, the juggler sometimes swallowed several bones about three inches long. After this feat, he approached the patient, made certain gestures, and expelled the bones. After the juggler had ejected the bones, objects, such as particles of glass and strands of human hair were sometimes expelled by the sick person. If this occurred, the Chippewa claimed that the sick person was instantly cured. This ceremonial was a four-night procedure. If it was not successful, the juggler tried to find the evil medicine man who had caused the illness.

Chippewa on the Bad River Reservation relate many and varied stories concerning the shake lodge. Marie Livingston described her experiences thus:

> The ancient mystery that surrounds the superstitions of the shake lodge or "djisakiwin," is a problem that has perplexed many. Being an Indian and having heard all about the shake lodge, I have my personal opinion about the "powers" that be. I married a man who believed in, and practiced the mysteries of the djisakin, and I often witnessed his performances. I have heard voices, snortings, thumpings, and felt the wind created by the operation of the shake lodge. I have even answered the voices that had spoken to me, yet I was skeptical about the whole business.

I often jokingly accused my husband of faking the entire performance, of shaking the lodge by his own physical force, as he was a husky man, and to this, he would answer: "Sometime, I am going to show you that I do not use my physical strength to shake the lodge."

A few days later, I noticed that he was busy and upon my inquiring as to what he was doing, he answered, "I am making a small djisakin to convince you that I have nothing to do with the shaking of the lodge, be it large or small." I then kept close observation on his work to make sure he did not pull a "fast one," and have the laugh on me.

The miniature lodge stood two feet high and twelve inches in diameter. This was securely fixed onto a board six feet in length, which he securely nailed to the floor. That night, after the children had gone to bed, my husband instructed me as to what I was to do.

I inspected the shake lodge and found there were no wires attached that my husband might pull, and I sat down on the board near the lodge. He gave me a rattle, lowered the light, and then sat down about ten feet away from the shake lodge. He smoked, talked, and chanted a beautiful song, meanwhile keeping a slow beat on his drum. While he was doing this, he gave me a signal to start the rattler. Before doing so, I felt the movement of the board I sat on, and when I shook the rattle, the miniature lodge was swaying from side to side. I was mystified and I am still just as perplexed as the next one, although I did not admit to my husband that there was some kind of force at work. I still cannot say I believe, as far as I am concerned, the question remains unsolved with all of its perplexities.[4]

Frank Frost claimed that in 1923, he was a victim of the wrath of an aged Lac du Flambeau Indian who had the reputation of being a "medicine charm" hunter. A number of hunters had camped together, among whom was the Flambeau Indian. Strange reports had been circulated concerning him. On the last day of the hunt, Frank Frost was in the rear of the group, "cat footing" his way. As he approached a clearing, he heard the snapping of bushes. Through the opening, he saw a doe. He lowered his rifle and fired. When he moved forward to claim his prey, a buck came running up. Frank also shot the buck and realized that he was on a deer runway. Seven more deer appeared and fell victims of his gun.

A few days later, Frost met the Lac du Flambeau Indian hunter who sneeringly remarked: "The hunters of today use hunting charms to get their game, and it was not skill on your part. Perhaps you shall not live to go hunting again next year."

Some days later, Frost was hunting again. In the evening, while preparing his food, he heard the jingle of djisakin bells, weird songs, and drum beats. He realized that a juggler was at work nearby. He tried to distract himself by preparing for the next day's hunt, but the annoying sounds gave him no rest. He broke camp and went home in the middle of the night.

The following evening, while searching in the woods for a lost cow, he again heard strange songs and drum beats. Immediately, he returned home and told his wife that he was being subjected to the evil power of the shake lodge. As night approached, Frost began to speak as though in answer to someone, although no one seemed to be speaking to him. Thoroughly alarmed, his wife informed Federal officials. After investigating the matter, the officials made arrangements to send Mr. Frost to a mental hospital. At this juncture, Frank's father, "De-dakum-osh," a good medicine man, obtained permission to keep his son under close observation. At the end of five days, under "De-dakum-osh's" care, the patient showed marked improvement. Finally, he became normal again.[5]

Perhaps one of the most mysterious accounts regarding the power of the shake lodge is based on the activities of John Sky, reputedly the most powerful juggler of later years. Antoine Couture, a Bad River Chippewa, had been missing for about twenty days. His family and relatives were untiring in their efforts to locate him, but every attempt had ended in failure. As a last resource, they requested John Sky to perform the shake lodge rite.

After the shake lodge was constructed, a large fire was enkindled near the djisakin to hasten the arrival of the spirits. Swinging a large switch vigorously, one of the Chippewa circled the lodge four times. Then the juggler entered the lodge which soon began to shake violently. Sounds like those of rushing wind were heard. Then came a thud followed by profound silence. Next, an almost inaudible voice, that of mi-she-kwe, the "snapping turtle," was heard. Because mi-she-kwe was a messenger, his presence was required at every ritual of the djisakin. Mi-she-kwe asked for a song to accompany his dance.

When the dance was over, John Sky asked mi-she-kwe if he could tell the whereabouts of the missing man. Mi-she-kwe replied that it was impossible for him to give the information; he could call Oshkabenwis, the chief manito. The latter stated that the lost man

Juggler Attempting a Cure

Shake Lodge

was dead and that his body was in the ground, near the bank of a river. Little credence was given to this information of the manito. After some effort to find the body, the search was abandoned.

Nine days later, the same group again consulted the djisakin. Oshkabenwis now stated that the body was in the river and it would be found in four days. Four days later, Indians working in the Stearns' lumber yard, heard a shout from a group of white men who were working on the river. They had found the body of an Indian which was recognized as that of Antoine Couture.[6]

According to Parkman's writings, the Chippewa consulted mi-she-kwe the turtle, in important affairs. Parkman wrote the following:

> The Ojibways had been debating whether they should go to Detroit to the assistance of Pontiac . . . but distrusting mere human wisdom in a crisis so important, they resolved before taking a decisive step to invoke the superior intelligence of the great turtle, the chief of the spirits. The juggler's tipi and performance are then described, and it is said: A low, feeble sound, like the whine of a young puppy, was next heard . . . upon which the warriors . . . hailed it as the voice of the great turtle, the spirit who never lied.[7]

In 1894, Henry Bressette drowned in the Bad River Falls, but his body could not be found. Ma-da-ga-mi, "Moving Water," a respected juggler was requested to perform a shake lodge rite to recover the lost body. The ceremony lasted twenty-two days and nights. Sometimes such ceremonies lasted an entire summer.

A wigwam had been erected a distance from the shake lodge which housed from forty-five to fifty Indians. Ceremonial dances were held daily. The evening before the body was found, Ma-da-ga-mi predicted that only one more day would be spent in using his power to call the spirit of Bash-kwo-dash for assistance.[8] Frank Bressette was appointed runner to Ashland to buy supplies consisting of whiskey, red, yellow, and green ribbons, and broadcloth. These articles were to be used with the "medicine."

Since food was becoming scarce, the men left camp and soon returned with some pike. After the fish had been dressed, two old women put it in a large pan on a nearby hill. Immediately the pan overturned and the fish scattered on the ground. Alarmed at this happening, the women fled from the scene. Ma-da-ga-mi heard the commotion and hurried from his lodge. Greatly disturbed, he informed the women that the hill belonged to Bash-kwo-dash now on his way to the lodge. The women had trespassed on sacred ground and he had caused this disturbance to discourage another similar happening.

Ma-da-ga-mi returned to the lodge. Suddenly a strong wind shook the lodge, flapped the side covers high in the air and a voice boldly announced that the body would soon be found. The juggler informed Chief Ana-kwad, who immediately retired into his tent to await the dream which would inform him of the location of the body. In a short time, Ana-kwad awoke and called to the Indians to follow him. Without hesitation, Chief Ana-kwad went toward a river. The body lay in full view near the shore.[9]

John Frost related the circumstances of an alleged cure of the shake lodge. A little girl who had been left in the care of his parents became ill. The local doctor diagnosed the case as incurable. A juggler was consulted. He declared that the girl had not reached the end of her life's path. He would cure her. In order to obtain good results, the Indians gave the juggler tobacco and a hunting outfit consisting of a gun, cartridges, belt, and hunting knife.

Friends built a shake lodge in the woods and the weird ritual began. The people in the sick room had been told that if success attended the juggler's efforts, a swishing noise would be heard in the sick room, the child would move its arms, and health would be restored. While the rites were in progress, the signs indicating a cure were manifested. The girl recovered. The white doctor listened for the tolling of the church bell announcing the girl's death, but it did not ring for many a year.[10]

The following account relates the experiences of a well-known man in Odanah, of one-eighth Indian blood, who requested that his name be withheld. Born and reared among white people, he was a Christian and did not believe in Indian medicine. For a time he acted as policeman on the reservation. On one occasion, he was about to arrest an intoxicated young Indian. An old Indian woman demanded that he desist or she would "get him." Disregarding the threat, he lodged the drunken man in jail until he was sober.

Shortly after this occurrence, the policeman began to suffer from persistent headaches which became almost intolerable. He consulted several doctors, but they were unable to diagnose the case. Upon the advice of friends, he consulted a juggler. The latter declared that he needed two assistants, because strong medicine was required.

A shake lodge was erected. The patient lay in a wigwam nearby. After kindling a fire, the jugglers sang, beat drums, and shook rattles. The wigwam swayed as though a heavy wind were blowing and the sick man heard a woman wailing. A juggler told the sick man to speak to the woman. Not knowing the Chippewa language, he requested his wife to speak in his stead. She asked the woman why she was punishing her husband and what medicine would cure him. The woman replied that she was avenging the arrest of a young Indian. Then she gave the name of the man who could prescribe the right medicine. The juggler asked the patient what punishment should be meted out to the old woman they had in their power. He requested that she be released. The prescribed medicine relieved the headaches.[11]

Edward Peavy, a Chippewa from Nett Lake, Minnesota, while a student at Haskell Institute, Lawrence, Kansas, related the following story of the occult powers of a juggler:

I had an interesting experience while I was in Nett Lake. A lady hired a juggler to help locate her friend who had been missing for two weeks. A close friend of mine and I had heard about this juggler's intention of performing a djisakin to find out the information that the lady desired.

We located his shake lodge and decided to wait for him and watch while he performed his djisaki. We loitered near the spot where his shake lodge was erected. On the evening of the second day, we were rewarded by his arrival. We concealed ourselves in a spot where we were sure the juggler could not see us, although we could watch his every movement.

He carried a large pack on his back of birch bark and woven rushes. After starting a fire, he removed furs, bells, and a drum from his pack. Some of the furs he placed in the lodge, others he donned for his ceremonial dress. After this, he put the bells in the lodge, and with drum in hand, sat on the ground near the opening of the wigwam and began to sing.

After singing for some time, he glanced curiously about him. Apparently satisfied, he resumed his singing. Soon, in disgust, he said: "Ga-we-sa," meaning, "I can't do it." Then he spoke in English: "I want the persons who are watching me to come out into the open or leave immediately." Although we were rather frightened, we remained quiet. He continued: "Will you two boys either come over here near me or get out? I can't work with eyes peering at me."

Let me tell you, we got out. I am a firm believer in the Bible and in Christian teachings, yet I cannot understand how it was possible for the juggler to know that we were staring at him, as we were so well concealed that he could not, humanly speaking, have known we were there.[12]

Some believers in the shake lodge also maintained that through its ceremonies messages could be delivered at a distance. Mrs. Joseph Barbano, while on a visit to friends at Nett Lake, Minnesota, related a story of an Indian's only son who was dying. The father wished to inform his brother of his son's illness, but the brother lived at a considerable distance. Through the shake lodge, the father delivered the request. The man arrived that same night. He stated the time that he had received the message, and it coincided with the time that the message was sent.[13]

Strange as these reports of the shake lodge appear, yet white persons of integrity attest to the reality of similar ones. Parkman wrote:

There was a peculiar practice of divination very general in the Algonquin family of tribes among some of whom it still subsists. A small, conical lodge was made by planting poles in a circle, lashing the tops together at the height of about seven feet from the ground, and closely covering them with hides. The prophet crawled in, and closed the aperture after him.

He then beat his drums and sang his magic songs to summon the spirits, whose weak, shrill voices were soon heard, mingled with his lugubrious chanting while at intervals the juggler paused to interpret their communications to the attentive crowd seated on the ground without.

During the whole scene, the lodge swayed to and fro with a violence which has astonished many a civilized beholder, and which some of the Jesuits explain by the ready solution of a genuine diabolical intervention.[14]

This practice was first observed by Champlain. From his time to the present, numerous writers have remarked it. Le Jeune, in the Relation of 1637, treats of it at some length.[15]

In 1900, Father Chrysostom Verwyst, while visiting with Tchibinges, a fervent Christian, inquired the cause of the movements of the shake lodge. The old Indian, a former juggler, replied that he spoke to the gods and the lodge swung. Incredulously, the priest said: "You made it swing. You took it with your hands and shook it and made it swing."

The aged Indian looked at him sternly, almost indignantly, and said: "Nosse, Father, look at me. My hair is gray. I am an old man. Do you think I would tell a lie to you—a priest? No, never. But I thought myself. There is something wrong in this thing. I got afraid, quit it, and was baptized."[16]

That the shake lodge did move is evident from the accounts of spectators. How this was accomplished is a moot question. According to Frank Bressette, a Chippewa Indian, the djisakin of the present day is but an imitation of earlier performances. In earlier days, the ceremony was so weird and the feeling of expectation so tense, that the heart and soul of each Indian was in it. Real fires, not lighted by human hands, shot from the shake lodge.

WITCHCRAFT AND CHARMS

chapter 36 WITCHCRAFT IS DEFINED AS THE ACT OF CONTROL-ling the will and the well-being of another person by occult means, usually to his detriment. Anyone, the Chippewa declared, could practice witchcraft, if he used the proper formula.

Indian lore explains the existence of witches thus: Many years ago, some old Indian women looked upon as witches, were supposed to have obtained occult powers by entering into compacts with evil spirits. In exchange for this power, the women surrendered both body and soul to the wicked spirits. As soon as the bargain was concluded, wicked spirits entered the bodies of the evil women. With the aid of these wicked spirits, the witches could assume different forms of animals, such as cats, dogs, owls, and snakes. Furthermore, under these forms, witches could cross lakes, rivers, and high mountains without difficulty. Human beings with unusual powers were another cause of superstition prevalent among the Chippewa.

The mode of bewitching was similar to that employed by wizards of both Europe and New England. The wizard secured some personal belongings of his victim, such as a hair, some of his saliva, a piece of his clothing, or some of his implements. A small figure of the victim was outlined in sand, clay, or ashes. If the wizard wished to cause a sore throat in his victim, he placed saliva on the throat of the figure that he had made and tortured this figure. The person, whose effigy was thus tortured, then suffered from a sore throat and might even "spit himself" to death. A few hairs placed on the effigy's head, might cause the person whom the effigy represented to have a severe headache.[1]

Among the many witchcraft stories that survive among the Chippewa, one tells of an old woman who lived with her nine-year old grandson near Mole Lake, Wisconsin, and who was found guilty of practicing witchcraft. She was regarded by the Indians of the surrounding area as a dangerous character. Her little grandson often wondered why she left him alone at night. To solve the problem, he decided to watch his grandmother and to follow her when she left the house.

On the first night of his vigil, the boy retired early. He cut a hole in the coverlet through which he could watch his grandmother's proceedings. The old woman, likewise, retired early, but as the boy had anticipated, she arose about midnight. Thinking that her grandson was asleep, she removed a black box from a recess in the wall. She opened the box and untied several small packages which were wrapped in buckskin. The contents of the packages glowed with beautiful rainbow colors. After rubbing some of this material over her body, the old woman returned the bags to the box, placed the box in her bosom, and left the hut. The lad followed her cautiously, for he knew that detection would mean severe punishment.

About a quarter of a mile from the woman's hut, lay a huge boulder. When the woman reached the boulder, she stopped and again anointed her body. After standing silently for a few moments, she made four circles around the boulder. Then she turned the rock to one side, apparently with no effort. From the bed of the boulder, she removed a kettle covered with bear skin. The contents of the kettle appeared to be some kind of "medicine." When she straightened up, she held in her hand an object resembling a clock. To this object was attached a neck band which, when adjusted, hung exactly at the center of the woman's breast. The boulder was then returned to its place.

The woman started toward a home where a child lay dangerously ill. As she walked, the charm that she wore around her neck cast a bright light similar to that of a flashlight. When she reached the home, she entered without ceremony. Everyone in the house appeared to be in a sort of hypnotic state; even the cats and dogs seemed to be similarly affected. At her approach, the sick child cried out in terror. After the woman had sprayed the little one with a liquid, the child ceased crying and became rigid and unconscious.[2]

Upon observing this phenomenon, the boy hurried home. In spite of his speed, he barely had time to jump into bed and cover up, before the witch returned. In a state of great excitement, she went to his bed, struck him across the legs with her cane and demanded, "Where have you been, my boy?" At first he pretended to be only half awake, unconscious of the blows rained on his legs. Then leaping from the bed, he ran to the wall and made a pretense of climbing but fell to the floor. Regretfully, the old grandmother picked him up, kissed him, and muttered to herself, "What made me do this to my little son?" Then she poured cold water over the boy's face to revive him. The boy rubbed his eyes as if coming out of a daze. He threw his arms around his grandmother's neck and cried, "Grandma, someone is after me." The old woman replied, "There, there, nobody is going to hurt you as long as I am here with you." In a low tone, she muttered, "I am positive that it was not my imagination. I know I saw someone entering my home."

The following morning, the boy showed his grandmother long blue streaks across his limbs. He remarked: "This is the place where a bad animal bit me last night." She replied: "Never mind that, my son; forget about it. It won't happen again." The old woman appeared to be on the verge of a collapse.

A few days later, the grandmother was invited to a medicine lodge ceremonial dance. On the morning of the dance, the old lady rose early, collected a few articles, and told her grandson that he might follow her later in the day. Then she crossed the lake in her canoe.

After finishing some small tasks, the boy wondered if he could do the marvelous things he had seen his grandmother perform. When he opened the packages of "medicine" in the black box, a peculiar odor emanated from the contents. After the boy had rubbed his body with the "medicine," he felt fearless and daring. Placing the box in his bosom, he started toward the boulder.

When the lad arrived at the giant rock, he went through the same movements that he had seen his grandmother perform. He, too, raised the rock without difficulty. After adjusting the neck piece, he replaced the boulder. Then the boy walked along a wagon road which led toward Crandon. At regular intervals, the neck charm threw a light ahead of him. When he came to a field where a farmer was working, the latter noticed that his dog was acting in a strange manner. As the farmer walked toward the road, he experienced a premonition of impending evil. Then he noticed a moving object carrying a peculiar light. The farmer ran home, returning with a loaded gun. When he was about to fire, a small Indian boy dressed in a bear skin met his gaze. The man dropped his gun, dashed for

A Witch's Stock In Trade

A Witch Suspect

the boy, and demanded what the queer regalia meant. The lad seemed utterly exhausted and unable to make a reply.

The man carried the boy to his home and revived him. The farmer questioned the lad, but he could not speak enough English to answer the questions. A hired man was sent in search of an Indian interpreter. When the man returned with the Indian, the latter immediately recognized the significance of the boy's dress. He told the boy to remove the costume. When this was done, the boy related all the happenings of the past few days.

Since there had been several instances of supposed witchcraft in the vicinity, the farmer felt that a solution was at hand. He took the lad to Crandon where he related his story. Regarding the information as a joke, the town officials requested the boy to demonstrate his unusual powers. Accompanied by others who wished to enjoy the joke, skeptical town officials went to the large rock. In utter amazement, the crowd watched the boy as he lifted the huge boulder. Although they could not understand how this was accomplished, they all agreed that the practice must be discontinued. After hearing of the old lady's visit to the home, they arrested her and brought her to trial.

The old woman pleaded guilty, saying, "Yes, I am the cause of all the mysterious deaths which have occurred among many of my people." Rising, she pointed a finger at the officers and said: "You fools fell into an ocean of luck that you caught me with empty hands." During all this time the boy was not allowed to see his grandmother. The officials feared that the old woman might become a raving maniac if she learned who had disclosed her secret. The following morning, the woman was found dead in her cell.

A report of this occurrence was sent to F. W. Horne, District Attorney of Forest County, Crandon, Wisconsin, to ascertain his opinion of the matter. He offered the following explanation:

I have talked to several old persons and they say, "Yes, it is a fact, that there was an old woman who practiced witchery." Of course, you and I realize that this witchery business is a superstition, more or less.

The old lady's name was "Kawehasnoquay." She died around 1886. An old man who knew her described her to me as a very bad looking character. She had a hard, wicked face with a wide, protruding jaw. The Indians shunned her and were afraid of her. They attribute several deaths to her. That is, deaths that were outright murders, aside from her witchery.

For instance, her daughter married a man and I talked to this man's brother and this old witch decided that it was bad for her daughter to have this husband so she had a man shoot him.

Then again, they found another man with a piece of haywire around his neck and tied to a tree, dead, and she has been attributed to having him murdered.

I asked an Indian that was about seventy years old if he ever saw her bewitch anyone and he said, "yes," he did. He said that he saw her come up to a man and begin to make motions with her hands and the man stiffened up as if he were dead. The next day he sort of came out of the spell but said that he was not well and in a short time, he went insane and died.

Another man told me that she would make motions and talk to the Indians and they would become wild as if they were drunk. A man told me that for several nights way back in the 1870's, he heard a drum beating all night, so he decided to see what was the matter. The old woman's husband was beating a drum very softly and slowly and she was going through a lot of motions having a medicine dance. In the doorway was a dead dog hung up by the neck. Her husband told this man that there was a boy who had been possessed with a devil and was sick. She had driven the devil out of the boy and into the dog and they had hung the dog.

I did not find out anything about the grandson, but I did find that she had a daughter whom they called "Old Kate." The daughter is still alive, but very old. Her name is Kate Motzfeldt. She lives at Odanah with her daughter Jennie, on a reservation that is right in your territory. . . .

This old Kawehasnoquay, I was told, could not speak English. She was very old and crippled. . . . I realize that this whole thing is more or less tradition, still it naturally is part of the history making up the Chippewa existence, habits, tradition, etc.[3]

Some women, not regarded as witches, are said to have displayed unusual powers. Marie Livingston related this story of an Indian living on the Lac Courte Oreilles Reservation:

Mis-za-be-coo-ence, "Solid Rock Mass," was a lad who lived with his grandmother at Lac Courte Oreilles. His father had died when he was a small child and his mother, Win-dee-gook, "Cannibal" in the English tongue, had married again. Mis-za-be-coo-ence had lived with his grandmother from the time of his mother's second marriage. He loved his grandmother as she was very kind to him and he grew up to be a husky lad.

As was the custom among the Chippewa, the sugar season was the usual time to put youths to a test. When this season had arrived, one morning the grandmother prepared a dish of food with charcoal and handed the dish to her grandson. The youth understood what was required, and told his grandmother that it was time that he used the charcoal. He then prepared himself according to the custom, and went into the woods for the fast.

A the end of the ten day period, he was dissatisfied and continued for fifteen days longer. Then his grandmother urged him to discontinue his fast, as she feared the long duration would unbalance him mentally. After the fast was over, it became known throughout the neighboring settlements that Mis-za-be-coo-ence had endured the dream trial and was therefore considered a desirable matrimonial "catch."

Two women called on the grandmother, each with the purpose of arranging a marriage for the grandson to her daughter. The grandson, sensitive and shy after his prolonged fast, did not look with favor on either of the proposed wives. He ignored the women and spent his time hunting and lingering alone in the forest until darkness covered the settlement. The two women became very angry and began to quarrel over the suitability of their daughters for the young man. One of them asserted that neither her daughter nor the daughter of the other woman would marry the young man, and, also that he would never marry anyone else.

One evening as Mis-za-be-coo-ence came in late from the hunt and sat down to his meal, two yellow dogs came in and began to fight at his feet. He pushed his food aside, arose, took a look at the fight and ran out. After this he was never the same person and for days he went without food.

Then he began to relate stories of his travels; the people humored him for they knew that he was no longer responsible for the tales he told. At meal time, he demanded large amounts of maple sugar. One day his grandmother did not give him all he craved. He became so enraged that he killed her.

After this his own people feared and hated him and even his own relatives tried to get rid of him. But neither arrows nor shots seemed to have any effect on him. His love for his younger brother caused him to abduct the lad. The little boy, in later years, told strange stories of his adventures with his brother. It is not known what eventually became of the unfortunate Mis-za-be-coo-ence.[4]

Although a witch doctor had the power to cast evil spells or charms, he also had the power to cure victims of spells or charms. John Whitefeather, a Lac Courte Oreilles Chippewa, declared that the frequent wry mouth or twisted face among the Indians was caused by some witch doctor. The distortion could be cured, if the victim paid a good medicine man more than his enemy had paid an evil witch doctor to bring on the affliction. Sometimes a medicine man who had caused such misfortunes had to leave the village in order to save his life. This happened to Anawabi, a medicine man. A boy had died of pneumonia and the parents claimed that Anawabi had taken his breath away. Anawabi protested that he was miles away from the boy at the time and had not even thought about him. However, he made a hurried trip to Oklahoma, remaining there several years until the anger of the parents had subsided.[5]

Although charms were used by witches for their heinous pursuits, charms were also used for less unworthy purposes. Preparation of medicine charms was tedious work requiring at least a year for the completion of the charm. The collection of flowers, foliage, herbs, insects, reptiles, and phosphorus began in early spring and lasted throughout the summer until late autumn. The following spring, the Chippewa erected a wigwam, strewed cedar boughs on the inside and built a fire of medicine incense in the center. Except on rare occasions, young people were not permitted to participate in this ritual. If they were allowed to attend the ceremony, either a medicine man or a juggler testified that the youths possessed some remarkable gift.

After the collection had been dried near the medicine fire, it was pulverized. The bulk was divided into as many individual packs as there were Indians present at the ceremony. Then the participants performed a dance in honor of Medicine gitchi manito.

In one instance, on the Bad River Reservation, all the participants of this ceremony followed the leader in single file to Birch, a distance of eight miles. Although the procedure, "gi-gwa-dabun-owod," took place on a dark night, there seemed to be illumination along the path that the Indians traveled. When they returned to the ritual lodge, each individual pack of "medicine" was labeled for good or for evil purposes. The Indians gave thanks to gitchi manito for permitting them to complete their work. At a later date, each participant was required to contribute to a feast offering.[6]

Although many of the ingredients of "good medicine" are known, yet, strange to say, those of "bad medicine" have not been revealed. According to some of the Chippewa Indians, the charms were of undisputed power. If they wished to catch deer in a hurry, they called deer with a whistle rubbed with chewed roots of boneset and milkweed. If a hunting party came across deer tracks, they smoked finely powdered root of wild aster. As they proceeded farther along the trail, they paused at intervals to smoke the charm. Finally, the deer appeared sniffing the aroma and the Chippewa had their quarry. Fishnets were often sprinkled with a mixture of dried and grated roots of sweet flag and wild sarsaparilla. Sweet flag had a distinctive scent which attracted fish.[7]

Certain success in muskrat trapping followed in the train of the Chippewa who used a charm made from dogwood. A hazel twig smeared with chewed roots of dogwood was placed in an upright position over a submerged muskrat trap. The odor of the dogwood was so enticing that muskrats would devour a trapped comrade to get a bite of the wood.

The Chippewa not only cast spells upon animals, but also upon persons. An Indian, who had a grievance to settle, secured the assistance of a medicine man. Together they cleared a small piece of ground, smoothing off the area to the bare soil. Using a stick, an outline of the victim was drawn. After a short chant, the medicine man tossed a bag of "bad medicine" on some part of the figure. Regardless of where the person was at that particular time, he immediately received a sharp pain in that part of the body where the medicine had been cast. In some instances, bad medicine was thrown on the ground where an enemy walked, or bad medicine was hidden in his clothes. In either case, the Chippewa claimed that the person became paralyzed. If the death of the victim was the desired end, a figurine was attached to a twig by a thread and exposed to the forces of the wind, sun, and rain. Unless the victim was protected by a counter charm, he died at the exact instant these forces caused the thread to break.

Counter charms were the wild pea and the fumes of mugwort. The roots of the wild pea were rolled in pieces of birch bark. No amount of "bad medicine" thrown in the pathway of a Chippewa could injure him while he carried this charm. If an Indian sensed that someone was trying to cast a bad spell over him, he immediately collected dry flowers of white mugwort. Then he built a fire in his back yard. When the fire had burned down to embers, he tossed the mugwort on it. The person stood in the fumes which arose and his body was made immune to the evil spell.

Snakes, too, avoided "charmed" paths. The Chippewa powdered the roots of plantain and mixed the substance with vermillion.

No reptile came near the path of the one who carried this medicine charm.[8]

Among the Chippewa, witchcraft as practiced in early days, is a thing of the past. However, certain elements of superstition remain, especially in regard to charms. But these, too, are fast being relegated to obscurity and oblivion.[9]

INDIAN PROPHECIES

chapter 37

IN GENERAL, INDIAN PROPHECIES WERE CONFINED to weather predictions.[1] The weather, especially the winter season, played an important part in the life of the early Indian. The kind of winter he must prepare for was a matter of deep concern to him. Primitive Indians found Nature an open book which guided them wisely.

In some instances, the dining table of the Indian afforded the means for a forecast. If a rabbit's shoulder blades were transparent, the winter would be mild; if there were dark blotches in the bones, it would be severe.

If rabbits' fur turned white after the first snow-storm, an early winter might be expected. If the rabbits' fur did not turn white after the first snowfall, a long, mild winter could be anticipated. If squirrels gathered and stored food early in the autumn, winter was near at hand.

During the latter part of September and the early part of October, the Chippewa watched the activities of the bear. If bear tracks were seen immediately after the first snowfall, it was usually the sign of a mild winter.

Even the muskrat played his part in weather forecasts. If muskrats began gathering food for winter in August or if they built their winter houses unusually large and heavy, their activities were interpreted as presages of an early, cold winter. Muskrat observation was generally made during ricing time.

One sign the Chippewa looked forward to with interest was the southward migration of geese or "ni-kug." If the geese flew low, a long winter was predicted; if they flew high, autumn would be long, the winter proportionately short. Early disappearance of crows meant that winter was near.

Another bird which the Indians watched was the partridge, "bine." The drumming of partridges in October was a warning that the winter would be cold. If the birds drummed again in December, the winter would be very cold with an abundance of snow, especially during the months of January and February.

The Chippewa regarded the knocking of woodpeckers on trees as an unfailing sign of warm weather. If knocking occurred during sugar-making time, they said: "The birds are locking up the sap. Sugar-making is almost over and the sap will stop running in a day or so."

A deer seeking shelter in a pine grove or heavy brush presaged a storm. If chickens ran for shelter when it started to sprinkle, only a shower was expected. If they kept on eating, then more rain would fall. Well-filled crops of grouse or partridge signified bad weather, because these birds do not venture out for food during a storm, but provide for themselves in advance. When the flicker cried mournfully, the Chippewa expected rain; as they did, also, when flies and mosquitoes were unusually troublesome.

The Chippewa also scanned the heavens for weather signs. When patches of blue sky were seen on cloudy days, sunshine was expected to follow soon. When "sundogs" were seen, the Chippewa said: "The sun is wearing feathers and it will become intensely cold." When the Aurora Borealis was seen, Chippewa expected south winds within the next twelve hours.

If the new moon was in a vertical position, the Chippewa declared: "The moon cannot keep moisture or water." They, therefore, anticipated a rainy month. If stars were in the moon's circle, a storm of many days' duration was impending. If stars were bright and twinkling, fair and windy weather continued for the next twelve hours.

A brilliant sunrise overhung by clouds meant rain within a short time. If the sky turned yellow one-half hour before sunset, a hailstorm could be expected. A clear brilliant sunset generally signified fine weather on the following day. The Chippewa expressed their joy at the prospect by remarking: "Ma-dij-ikwe-wis, the vain woman, is painting her face and predicting fine weather." An orange-red sunset with a lavender haze presaged showers and unsettled weather conditions.

Thunder and wind, too, served as omens. When a loud peal of

thunder was heard in late November, it meant fair weather. If only rumbling was heard, the Chippewa said that the beaks of thunder birds were frozen, causing them to make mumbling sounds. Cold weather was then expected.

The Chippewa studied the direction of winds before starting on long water trips or marches. If the wind was from the northeast or northwest, Lake Superior was rough and it was not safe to venture out in canoes or boats. Northeast winds frequently brought a three-day rain in summer or a three-day storm in winter. Southeast winds were said to bring rain within twenty-four hours.

Such things as dew, moss, and echoes also played a role in weather predictions. If there was dew on the grass in the evening, the day following would be fair. In winter, the Chippewa regarded water seeping along the edges of ice on the river as a sign of an approaching storm. A heavy growth of moss on the north side of a tree indicated an early winter. When on an unusually quiet evening, echoes were clearly heard, rain was expected. As a weather vane, the Chippewa suspended a small dried sturgeon from the ceiling of their homes. Balancing it by means of a string fastened through its center, the fish shifted from one position to another and finally settled down, pointing its nose in the direction from which the wind would blow within a short time.

Even actions of children had weather significance. If a winter-born child, under seven years of age, suddenly went to the fire and warmed his hands, it was regarded as a sign of cold or stormy weather within the next twenty-four hours. If such a child made a snow-man, a cold snap was predicted.

Chippewa also prophesied or attempted to prophesy future events. According to Frank Scott, the coming of the pale-face had been prophesied long before America was discovered by Columbus. This prophecy was handed down from generation to generation. The Indian prophet pictured the first white men who landed on this continent as wearing chicken feathers. White feathers denoted humility; black, bravery.

The missionary foretold by Indian prophets generations ago was envisioned as a man wearing a cloak with a hat attached. This person was called "Wa-we-we-quan-nid," meaning a person whose outer garb and cap are in combination. The arrival of Father Allouez, followed by other missionaries, confirmed the prophecies of many years standing.

Angeline Cedaroot, "Nashinaquay," an old Indian, well-versed in Chippewa lore, was asked to explain the pictures of man wanting to fly that the Indians had drawn long before aircraft came into existence. She replied:

> The Indian knew about some of the modern inventions that you see today. When I was a little girl, I saw pictures of airships and that was long before they were ever heard of. The Indian foretold that some day we would have large objects flying through the air. Today we have the modern airship. He foretold voices coming from the sky, thousands of miles away; now we have radios.

An old Indian, recalling prophecies of long ago, said to his son: "You know, son, long ago, the Indian foretold that large objects would roam these woods. He told that large trails would wind through the country. Today, we have trains, autos, tractors, and other vehicles traveling through the country. Highways and railroads wind through the country, even through the Indians' last possessions." [2]

A Chippewa girl, living in Chicago, foretold Franklin Delano Roosevelt's death and other events. The following article regarding these prophecies appeared in a Chicago paper during the summer of 1945:

> Who is this Elinor Ross who foretold President Roosevelt's death and predicts our war with Japan will be over within the next eight months? the voice at the other end of the telephone demanded. "Where does she come from? What is she like? How does she make her prophecies?"
>
> So I borrowed a car and set off for the little West Side candy shop, where she is hidden from the world, to find out. But before I had gone more than half-way, my car broke down and I got my first clue to her vibrant and exceptionally friendly personality. When I telephoned to explain why I'd be late, she insisted on having her husband come and get me.
>
> She runs a typical neighborhood candy shop, the kind that has huge, pasteboard "coke" cuties ogling you through a thicket of bottled goods in the front window. And as we entered, a small and vivacious brunette in a smart black sleeveless dress glanced up brightly from ringing up a popsicle sale on the cash register, and said, "Hello."
>
> Elinor Ross suggested we "come back here where we can talk," and led the way to a booth for two against the wall. Above it, in large frames, hung yellowed newspaper stories

about some of her uncannily accurate predictions that dated back as far as 1920's.

"Now what do you want to know?" she asked agreeably.

As unique as her present background is her past history. Her birthplace was an Indian reservation at Odanah, Wis., and she was born with a veil over her face. The Indian midwife who attended her mother, a full-blooded Chippewa, incidentally, promptly adhered to the ancient superstition and buried it in an incision she made in the new baby's wrist.

Although she says she has "always been aware of things and events before they happen," her extraordinary extra-sensory perception first attracted the attention of outsiders when she was 6 years old. One day, she expounds, she "saw a coffin" with the chief of the reservation, then very much alive, stretched out inside, and ran around the Indian village announcing, "The Chief is going to die."

After he died, her native neighbors began to shun her, and were definitely relieved she says, when her father, a fur trader, moved his family to the neighboring town of Ashland. There she was known as "The White Voodoo," and went to school. When she was 16 (she's now 39), she came here to find a job.

In her scrapbook are clippings of 1928, which quote her as saying, "In 1932 a man named Roosevelt will be elected president of the U.S." Her prediction that "The U.S. will go to war late in 1941," made the newspapers in 1938. And she announced the forthcoming Big Three meeting in Berlin long before the announcement was official.

Among the future events she bids us to watch for are: The conclusion of the Pacific war by the end of 1945 or the beginning of 1946 . . . revolution and a great earthquake in Japan . . . the re-election of Anthony Eden . . . Russia's entrance into the Pacific war . . . the death of one of our leading publishers . . . the assassination of Franco . . . the serious injury of Gen. Stilwell in a plane crash . . . the movie debut of Mrs. Roosevelt in a screen history of her husband . . . and a wedding in the White House.[3]

How many of Elinor Ross's prophecies have been fulfilled is left for the reader to decide.

Indians are good weather prophets because of their natural heritage of discerning judgment. They, also, have the use of knowledge handed down for many generations.

FARMING AND GARDENING

chapter 38

BOOKS ABOUND WITH INFORMATION CONCERNING Indian utensils and implements and the red man's methods of hunting and fighting. He lives again in his dances, his feasts, his customs and his language; but he is seldom portrayed in the role of a farmer.

Yet, the Indian was Wisconsin's first farmer. Without his agricultural activities, the early exploration of Wisconsin would have been greatly retarded. Explorers such as Nicollet, Marquette, Joliet, and Carver were provisioned by the Indians. Soldiers on military expeditions relied upon the Indians for food. Traders who roamed the woodlands and sailed the waters of Wisconsin rivers and lakes, depended to a great extent upon the Indian for their sustenance. Moreover, when the first white settlers arrived in the state, they appropriated for their own crops the small cultivated plots of the red men. At the time of the final uprising of Wisconsin Indians in 1832, Black Hawk and his followers had 800 acres under cultivation in the Rock River area. In his autobiography, Black Hawk wrote: "The land being fertile, never failed to produce good crops of corn, beans, pumpkins, and squashes." [1]

Corn was the staple food among almost all North American Indians. They could truly say "Corn is king." Discoverers, explorers, traders, and early settlers found the red man cultivating corn from Montreal to Nova Scotia; from the New England States to Virginia; and from the Mississippi to the Gulf. New England Algonquins taught the early colonizers how to plant corn, and furthermore, how to insure vigorous plant growth by burying fish to serve as fertilizer within each hill of corn. Likewise, the Algonquins in Virginia saved the early settlers from starvation by providing them with baskets of corn in times of famine. [2]

Although the later Chippewa of northern Wisconsin grew different varieties of white man's corn, they were never without their traditional "calico" corn, also called squaw corn or Indian corn. Calico corn was a hardy species also known as ninety-day corn because it matured in ninety days.

Indian corn, "Anichinabe Mandamin," is in a class of its own. The stalks are usually from three to four feet in height, never attaining the height of common varieties. The ears are surprisingly large in comparison with the size of the stalk. Kernels are of different shades of red and blue, mixed with white.

Before planting the corn, the Chippewa usually soaked the grain overnight in water, and then placed it on damp grass until it showed signs of sprouting. During the growing season, soil water conservation was practiced. In the evening, when there was no sign of rain, smudges were built among the corn hills. The smoke served as a screen which prevented the soil moisture and the dew from evaporating as rapidly as it would have done otherwise.

American people owe a great debt to the Indian for corn, now almost universally known. Ash-cake, hoe-cake, succotash, samp, hominy, and various breakfast cereal preparations would not be known without corn. Perhaps greater, even than these, is the value of corn for beef cattle and swine.

Potatoes were another food crop grown by the Indians. Indians in Brown County cultivated a "very good kind of potato." In 1844, Increase Lapham wrote as follows:

> The potatoes, which are of an oblong shape, and not longer than a man's thumb, are partially boiled, and carefully peeled while hot, without breaking the pulp, and strung like so many beads upon a twine or tough thread of bark and then hung in festoons on the ridge pole of the wigwam, over the smoke of the fire, where they become thoroughly dry. This process renders the potato fit for transportation and use during the severest frosts without injury. The squaws take great interest in preparing this article of food which is about the only vegetable they cultivate.[3]

Ojibwe potatoes, "bugwudj apining," the so-called "wild potatoes," have been grown by the Chippewa for many generations. Though larger than Arrowheads, the Ojibwe potatoes never attained the size of common market species. An Odanah Chippewa, Qui-ka-ba-no-kwe, Mrs. Delia Diver, grew a supply of these potatoes from seed preserved from generation to generation for a period of almost a hundred years. Until 1938, when Mrs. Diver became too feeble to take care of this traditional custom, she personally attended to each spring's planting. Even then she gave a small sack of the potatoes to one of her relatives to plant, but they neglected to do this, and so Bad River Reservation has no more "Ojibwe" potatoes.[4]

Squash was another staple food among the Indians found by early settlers in eastern colonies. Roger Williams speaking of this vegetable said: "Askutasquash," the Indian vine-apples, was shortened by the English and called "squashes." Wisconsin Chippewa continued to raise and use this food of their ancestors.[5]

Squash, "okun ogwisiman," (bone squash) is a food that the Chippewa Indians claim as their own, so much so, that the term "Ojibwe squash" is a familiar name among them. In early days, it was planted in small clearings or near trees or stumps where nature annually fertilized the soil with decayed leaves and plants. The Chippewa planted enough for their needs. Seeds were carefully preserved for next year's crop. Even at the present time, squash is found in all Indian gardens.

The Chippewa of northern Wisconsin also grew tobacco and cured it for chewing and smoking. Tobacco that was prepared in plug form was sweetened to satisfy the individual's taste. Often tobacco used for pipe smoking was mixed with kinickinick. Many of the older Indians use this mixture today, not because it is more economical, but because it affords a cooler smoke. When French traders began selling tobacco to the natives, many Indians found it easier to purchase tobacco than to grow it. Finally tobacco production was discontinued.[6]

Because the Chippewa is a lover of nature, he takes delight in gardening. In 1832, when Schoolcraft ascended the Bad River, he visited Odanah then known as the Old Indian Garden. He also noticed that another Indian village, west of present Cable, had fine cultivated gardens producing an abundance of vegetables. That the Chippewa excels in gardening is evident from the following extract of the Minnesota Historical Society Collections:

> Contrary to what would be supposed, the Ojibway excels the white man in making a farm or garden when he wants to do it; not in wheat-farming, however, or such farming as he has not been used to, but such as he knows, vegetable raising. A skilled white farmer and gardener went on a journey of a hundred and twenty miles through the white man's country from Gull Lake Settlement to Hubbard and back; and he told me the best gardens by far that he saw on the road were Indians' gardens. The white man could not begin to equal them.
>
> Similarly a resident of Bemidji, an old farmer, told me that the best garden in all that region was that raised by Sheanawishkunk, the old Ojibway who had always lived on the town-

site of Bemidji. The Indian has genius; he can do anything he wants to — and his genius shows in the looks of his garden, even though it be a small spot he cultivates.[7]

Gardens among the Chippewa were of two types — individual gardens and community gardens. The former varied in size from the small garden patch to the acre or more size. The family had the necessary vegetables for summer use and also laid by a supply for winter consumption. Critics often claim that the Indian is not provident for the morrow. When winter closed in on the Chippewa and hunting and fishing were difficult, the Chippewa had a store of food carefully preserved. Famines sometimes occurred because of droughts which made it impossible for the Indian to store a supply of food for the winter.[8]

Perhaps the most interesting garden plant grown by the Chippewa was the cranberry pole bean or "miskodisi min." Indians are said to have cultivated these beans in aboriginal times and it is thought that many of our best commercial pole beans originated from this stock.[9] Even today, Chippewa Indians remember when their grandmothers raised these beans. Since the beans were a climbing variety, poles were arranged in trellis fashion from which the bright red blossoms of the bean gladdened the sight of onlookers.

WILD RICE GATHERING

chapter 39 WILD RICE[1] HAS BEEN ONE OF THE STAPLE FOODS of the Chippewa since their arrival in the Great Lakes area. The value of this grain as a tasty and nourishing food was discovered by the Indians so long ago that there is no authentic account of its earliest use. The struggle for rice fields was one of the principal causes for the Sioux-Chippewa feud.

Both early and late chroniclers have written of the importance of rice to the Indians. For example, in 1683, Father Hennepin wrote in his diary: "In the lakes grew an abundance of wild oats . . . provided that the lakes were not over three feet deep." Robert Dickson, in 1793, wrote about one crop of the Chippewa Indians near Portage: "On the lowlands by the river, great quantities of wild oats grow." Undoubtedly the wild oats was wild rice. In 1820, Schoolcraft reported that "all the interior of northern Wisconsin, from Lac du Flambeau, west, was known as the Folle Avoine country"; that is, all Wisconsin's area north of the bend of the Wisconsin River at Portage, was a wild rice country "par excellence." [2] Approximately a decade later, Lieutenant Jefferson Davis, then stationed at Fort Crawford, Prairie du Chien, Wisconsin, noted in his journal: "While on detached service in the summer of 1829, I think I encamped one night about the site of Madison. The nearest Indian village was on the opposite side of the lake. . . . The Indians subsisted largely on Indian corn and wild rice." [3]

William Warren gave rice gathering a prominent place in his Indian history. He wrote thus of the Rice Lake area:

> In the year 1798 a handful of Ojibway warriors fought a severe battle with the large party of Sioux, at Prairie Rice Lake. . . . During a two years' residence (1840-41) in the vicinity of this lake, and especially during a tour which the writer made through this district of the country, in the summer of 1850, circumstances happened which made him fully acquainted with this lake, and the country surrounding it.
>
> . . . The lake being miry-bottomed and shallow, is almost entirely covered with wild rice, and so thick and luxuriant does it grow, that the Indians are often obliged to cut passage ways through it for their bark canoes. From the manner in which they rice, and the quantity which a family generally collects during the harvesting season this lake alone would supply a body of two thousand Indians.
>
> In the fall of 1850, when the writer passed through it, he found it occupied by fifty wigwams of the Ojibways, numbering over five hundred souls. They were busily employed in gathering rice, camping separately in spots where it grew in the greatest thickness and abundance. . . . One single island about four acres in size and covered with a grove of beautiful elm trees, lies on the bosom of this picturesque lake. In times of danger the Ojibway "rice makers" have often pitched their wigwams on it for greater safety.
>
> From the earliest period of their occupancy of the Chippeway River country, the most fearless of the Ojibways came thither each fall of the year, to collect a portion of the abundant

rice crop, notwithstanding its close vicinity to the Sioux villages, and notwithstanding they lost lives from their sudden
attacks almost yearly.

In the year which has been mentioned, several wigwams
of the Lac Coutereille band, under the guidance of the war-
chief, Yellow Head, collected at Prairie Rice Lake, to gather
wild rice. . . .[4]

Annually, in midsummer, the Chippewa who lived in the wild
rice area, observed a festival of thanksgiving to the Great Spirit. The
first gathering from a new rice crop was parched, hulled, and win-
nowed for this feast. A portion of the rice was prepared for a meal,
duing which the head of the family or some prominent guest gave
a speech. The speaker exhorted the Indians to harvest the rice in a
respectful and thrifty manner. He also reminded them that rice,
"manomin," was a gift of the Manito and that it should be used in
accordance with the intention of the Giver.[5]

On their first trip to the rice fields,[6] the Indians customarily
made a peace offering to the underwater gods, "A-na-mibiggo-
munido." They addressed them thus: "Gods of the Underwater,
please accept our offering and do not molest us during this ricing
season." Each family made this offering so that the underwater gods
would not tip their canoes and plunge them into the water.

Still another custom was strictly adhered to. If a death had
occurred in a family, a feast in honor of the water gods was given
before the husband or wife went to the rice harvest. The Chippewa
believed that if any member of the bereaved family gathered rice
without first making this offering, bad luck would follow the path of
his canoe and rice would never grow again along the route he had
traversed.

About three weeks before harvest time, rice stalks are tied in
bunches to prevent birds from eating the grain. This process also
fosters the development of matured kernels. With one hand, the
Indian women hold the rice stalks and with the other, they wind
basswood twine around the stalk. The women tie all the rice stalks
in the area allotted to their respective families.

Although wild rice sometimes begins to ripen in the latter part
of July, the ricing season really starts only after the first frost. The
wild ricer's day begins early. On a typical day, mist ascends from
nearby streams, the rising sun throws its rays across the horizon,
and cumulous clouds float in the blue sky. Magic appears to be at
work. Along the shores of lakes and sloughs, tents, tar-paper shacks,
and in modern times, automobiles and even trailers emerge appar-

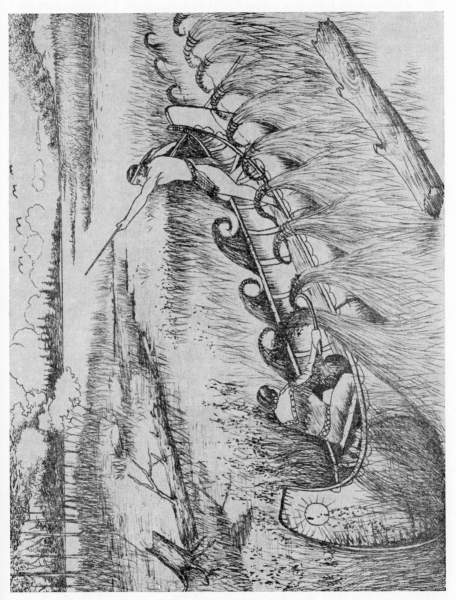

Harvesting Wild Rice

ently from nowhere. Smells and sounds fill the air. Echoes of voices
are a mixture of Chippewa and English. Dogs bark. Children scream
with delight. The smoke of cigarettes mingles with that of pungent
cedar from a nearby campfire where a juicy venison steak is frying.
Barefoot children race or amuse themselves by throwing sticks into
the water for numerous dogs to retrieve. Soon the real work begins.

The Indians make use of canoes in harvesting rice. The average-
size duck boat is large enough for two persons, the number required
to gather rice successfully. Canvas tacked along the inside edges of
the boat serves as a basket into which rice kernels drop. The
"knocker," generally a woman, sits as low as possible in one end of
the boat with the canvas drawn well over her lap. Her equipment
consists of a very sharp knife and two sticks about two feet long,
tapering from about an inch in diameter to a point at one end. Her
partner takes his position at the opposite end of the boat, facing the
"knocker." Holding a long pole, he stands and pushes the boat so
that the woman can reach the rice stalks. The "knocker" bends a
bunch of rice over the canoe and slits the wigub from bottom to
top. A slight tap with a stick causes the kernels to fall off the stalk
into the boat. If the rice has not been tied, a different procedure is
used. Holding a stick in each hand, the woman uses the right hand
to bend the stalks over the boat, while with the left hand, she strikes
sharply the heads of grain. Slight touches with a stick send showers
of ripe kernels into the boat. Half-ripe kernels require pressure and
green rice needs the full force of the stick.

The pilot, standing in the bow, can see good stretches of rice to
be harvested as well as bogs and other ricers to be avoided. If the
day is hot, he may add an extra shade of color to his already dark
skin. Meanwhile, especially if the rice is tall, the "knocker" almost
smothers in her cramped position and wonders if she will ever be
able to walk again. After "ricing" for sometime, a "knocker" develops
a rhythm as regular and apparently as effortless as that of a dancer;
that is, if the pilot moves steadily and smoothly through the rice
field. Sometimes the partners change work, but generally the woman
manipulates the sticks, "Bawa-igun-akon."

After from four to six hours labor, workers stop. Those who
camp nearby prepare a hearty meal. Others must return home. After
eating, a different kind of work begins. Parching of rice is begun on
the same day that the rice is gathered. This process kills the bugs
and worms that may be on the husks. Parching also prevents the
rice kernels from discoloring, a process that takes place if rice stands
in its raw state for some time. The day's gathering of a hundred

pounds or more is spread on birch bark to dry. A fire is started in a large hole and a kettle placed over the fire. Rice is put into the kettle and stirred constantly to prevent burning. The soft and rubbery kernels become crisp. If they snap when broken, the rice is parched sufficiently. The shrinkage is about one-third.

Hulling or threshing wild rice is the next process. Three methods used by present-day Chippewa are similar to those used by their forefathers. One method is to place wild rice in a buckskin bag and beat it with a club. Another method, more primitive, is to dig a hole in the ground and put the rice into the hole. An Indian steps into the hole and "dances" the rice. A third method used is trampling the rice. In trampling, the foot is borne down while the heel is pulled slightly inward. This produces a grinding effect. A traditional custom prevails that only men should trample rice. If the work of trampling is done thoroughly, all the chaff is loosened from the kernels. Machines bruise and break the kernels.

Winnowing is the final process in preparing the rice for food. A small amount of the threshed rice is put into a birch bark tray and tossed up into the air. Wind carries away the loosened chaff, leaving the rice grains free from any dirt. Rice is sorted and packed in birchbark mokuks, hardwood barrels, or bags woven of basswood twine.

Much of the wild rice grown in Wisconsin is sent to Minnesota for processing into three commercial grades. Burlap sacks of rice are soaked with water to keep the rice from heating and spoiling enroute. The commercial rice gets its dark color from maturing in the bags.

There are no accurate figures on the extent of the wild rice industry, but Minnesota producers set the value of one year's crop as high as $600,000. To protect the beds, Wisconsin and Minnesota prohibit the use of mechanical harvesting devices.[7] The Indians, using primitive methods, still harvest about 90% of the crop in Wisconsin. In areas not protected by law, white persons have gone into Chippewa country, bought green rice for about thirty cents a pound, threshed it, and sold it for a high price. Wild rice has become scarcer with the years and is no longer an important part of the Indians' diet. It has become a rare delicacy for the white man who now pays up to $3.00 a pound for it.[8] Some doctors prescribe wild rice for their patients. Mrs. Alfred Thayer, a rice-gatherer at Gordon, Wisconsin, has orders from many states.[9] The demand far exceeds the supply. The wild rice industry furnishes employment to thousands of Indians during the rice season.

BLUEBERRY, "MININ," PICKING IS ONE OF THE
chapter 40 leading industries of the Lake Superior Chippewa. Like other Chippewa occupations, it is seasonal. For centuries, the Chippewa people have looked forward to the blueberry season as a source of considerable income. Every summer, there is an exodus of Indians to the blueberry fields of the barrens near Washburn and Cornucopia, Wisconsin. Many Chippewa pitch their tents near the berry grounds, while others are content with merely a night fire and a blanket. Some Indians take advantage of rates offered to people who wish to pick berries only for their personal use. These groups leave early in the morning, pick for a day, and return to their homes in the evening.

In 1937, Marie Livingston recalled her experiences while blueberry picking in the following words:

> Forty-five years ago, the blueberries were so plentiful that it was a joy and a pleasure to pick them. The country was then, to a certain extent, uninhabited and in its natural wild state, the berries had a better chance to develop fully. One particular instance my mother delights to tell about is a comparison with the crops of recent years.
>
> It was in the vicinity of the little town of Gordon, Wisconsin, near Eagle Nest Lake. My father had come across a patch of berries which was approximately one mile square. It had originally been part of a Jack pine forest through which a raging fire had swept two years previous and had made it a real Eldorado for berry pickers. My parents went picking with some friends and they found berries so large and thick that it was impossible to avoid stepping on them. The clusters resembled grapes.
>
> Antoine Gordon, an Indian merchant, had a daily dray for the berries for which he paid $1.50 per bushel. At that time, they measured berries by bushels instead of the present system of measuring them in crates.

Far fetched as it may seem, it is nevertheless true, that one person picked six bushels in a single day. Two hundred bushels or one thousand three hundred and forty-four quarts represented the picking of one person per week.[1]

Florina Denomie, a contemporary Chippewa woman, found blueberry picking in northern Michigan both profitable and enjoyable. She told of her experience thus:

When the subject of blueberry picking is brought up, I can join in the conversation intelligently, as I have had considerable experience in that industry. Besides being a remunerative occupation, it may be considered a source of recreation, not only for children, but for adults as well.

Many years ago, late in the blueberry season, my Mother and all of us children, four in number, with John Hugo who is now residing with his family at Bear Trap, started out in his small sail boat from Assinins, Michigan, destined for the neighborhood of Keweenaw Point, in search of blueberries. Mr. Hugo knew a place where he thought no one had been that season. Sure enough when we landed at the camping place near Point Isabella, along the shores of Keweenaw Point, there were no signs of campers.

Next morning we started for the blueberry fields. Berries! That was one time I beheld blueberries growing on stems four to six inches long, in clusters like grapes. Three of us, my mother, a younger sister, and myself picked more than a hundred quarts in a few hours. I remember that I picked a pack-box full and also a large pailful. The capacity of a pack-box was from thirty to forty quarts; a pail, the standard measure used in the sale of blueberries, contained ten quarts.[2]

The importance of this crop was summarized in an article published in the Ashland *Daily Press*. An extract from the report states: "Every year the berry harvest proves to be a valuable aid to Indians, who, after scouting the fields, move with their families into the Barrens, and through their backbreaking efforts, realize enough profits to see them through the winter."[3]

In early days, the Chippewa brought rations to last the entire season. Convenient facilities about the camps now enable the Indians to exchange berries for food and other commodities.

THE MAPLE SUGAR INDUSTRY

chapter 41

AMERICAN PEOPLE ARE INDEBTED TO THE INDIAN for maple sugar. As early as 1663, journals of explorers record that Indians made maple sugar. Robert Boyle wrote: "There is in some parts of New England a kind of tree . . . whose juice that weeps out of its incision, if it be permitted slowly to exhale away the superfluous moisture, doth congeal into a sweet and sacharin substance, and the like was confirmed to me by the agent of the great and populous colony of Massachusetts.[1]

That the Algonquin Indians of Virginia knew how to extract the juice of the maple tree is evident from a report of Governor Berkeley who wrote in 1706: "It is said that the Indians make one pound of sugar out of eight pounds of liquor. It is bright and moist with full large grain, the sweetness of it being like that of good Muscovada."

Indians in Wisconsin still extract juice from maple trees as their ancestors from the East had done. For centuries, maple sugar has been an important food of the Chippewa. When the Jesuits arrived on an island in St. Mary's River area, they reported that Chippewa Indians annually harvested great quantities of syrup and more than a ton of maple sugar.[2]

The month of March generally found the Chippewa on their way to sugar camps. Warm, thawing days and frosty nights caused sap to flow freely during the day. If weather conditions were not favorable, the season was deferred. Sap that flowed in the early part of the season was considered the best.[3]

Sugar camps were permanent lodges about forty feet long and from ten to twenty feet wide. After the framework of the lodge was set up, the sides were covered with matting made from leaves of sweet-flag or from cattail. Matting was generally windproof. The roof of the lodge was made from large pieces of birch bark, overlapped to make it watertight. An opening, the size of the fireplace, was made for the smoke to escape. Along the side walls of the

Collecting Maple Sugar Sap

lodge, elevations about one foot high served as seats during the day and as beds at night.

Four large poles were planted in the ground. Cross pieces were nailed on top of the poles, and two pieces were also arranged lengthwise over the fireplace. Again, on top of these ridge poles were placed loose cross pieces two inches in diameter. These pieces held the chains from which large kettles were hung. Small kettles were hung on strong limbs of elm or maple with crotches serving as hooks. As protection against fire, short logs were laid on both sides of the fireplace. As soon as the logs were half burnt, they were pushed into the fire and replaced by others.

Much preliminary work was done before the trees were tapped. Early in March, Chippewa gathered birch bark for baskets. The baskets varied in capacity from one quart to two gallons. Small spouts called spiles, "o-ji-ga-i-ganan," were made of cedar, if basswood was not available. The spiles were driven firmly into incisions made in maple trees. Sometimes two to ten tappings were made on one tree; a small tree had only one tapping. Two or three days were required for tapping the trees and driving spiles into the gashes.

Sap containers or troughs were made from large basswood trees. About three feet of the trough was placed inside the sugar lodge to facilitate the handling of sap from trough to boiling kettles within the lodge. Sap was gathered and carried to the lodge daily. The boiling process was begun as soon as the sap was collected. The work often continued throughout the night to make the container available for the day's yield of sap.

The Chippewa used two methods for making maple sugar, hot and cold process. For the former, a fire was kindled and several large rocks were thrown into the fire. After the rocks were heated, they were placed one by one into a trough containing maple sap. As one rock cooled, another was substituted. Gradually the heated rocks caused the sap to boil. This process was continued until the sap reached the consistency of syrup. During the boiling process, a small piece of tallow was added as seasoning and also to help prevent the liquid from boiling over. The second method was to freeze the sap in shallow vessels. The ice was skimmed off and discarded. This process was continued until the sap had crystallized.[4]

Chippewa of the present day have replaced some of the former equipment. Sap is placed into barrels and hauled to the sugar lodge. Instead of the crude open fireplace, there is a brick or stone fireplace with an open grate. Large shallow tanks have replaced kettles.[5]

The finished maple product took one of three forms: syrup,

sugar, or cake. Sugar cakes were made by putting thick syrup into molds. After the sugar had hardened, the cakes were put into "mokuks" or birch bark containers. Today, glass jars or tin containers are used for storage purposes. If maple sugar cakes are kept in air-tight containers, they can be preserved almost indefinitely.

For centuries, maple sugar has been one of the staple foods of the Chippewa and was used in almost every kind of cookery. Instead of using salt on his meat, the Indian frequently used maple sugar. If maple sap was abundant, even fish were cooked in the liquid. The fish were said to have a delicious flavor. Early explorers found the Indians sustaining life with maple syrup and sugar, if fish and game were hard to procure. Maple sap was mixed with the sap of box elder or yellow birch and served as a beverage.

In modern times, the maple sugar industry is declining among the Chippewa, but the older men among them still feel that the year is incomplete without the annual excursion to the sugar camps where their mode of life for a short time approaches that of their forefathers.

LUMBERING ON CHIPPEWA RESERVATIONS

chapter 42   THE STATE OF WISCONSIN HAD A MAGNIFICENT endowment in her forests. Except for small scattered prairies, forests covered the entire area. The lumbering industry developed along four main streams, all tributaries to the Mississippi; the Wisconsin, the Black, the Chippewa, and the St. Croix. At first lumbering was carried on by men of moderate means. Because of fire and floods, their investment sometimes ended in financial disaster. However, between 1852 and 1857, the lumbering industry became prosperous because of the greater demand for lumber and the investment of new capital. After the Civil War, progress was amazingly rapid. Many persons found their livelihood in depleting Nature's bounty of trees. Some few amassed enormous wealth. Lumber operations determined the location of villages and cities, and the routes of many railways. Lumbermen also strongly influenced politics by causing the passage of bills that created problems of no mean proportions.[1]

Standing pine of Wisconsin 125 years ago is said to have amounted to 129,000,000,000 feet. To cut, saw, and bring to market this lumber was a colossal task that demanded long-continued efforts and great hardships. Only imagination can recreate the life called into existence by the lumber industry.[2]

Since many of the forests were on Indian lands, the white man carried on lumbering in these areas. In many instances, through treaty negotiations, the Indians permitted the white man to deplete their forests. The general pattern of the lumbering industry on other Chippewa reservations closely followed that of the Bad River Reservation.

The first sawmill in the Bad River area was built and operated in 1846 by Ervin Leihy at Bad River Falls, eight miles south of Odanah. Paddle wheels furnished power for the old vertical style saw. With such crude appliances, the sawing of six to ten logs was considered a good day's work. If weather conditions were favorable, lumber was placed on large cedar log rafts and guided down the Bad River. A long oar or sculler was used to propel the raft and to act as rudder.

From the mouth of the Bad River, the raft emerged into Lake Superior, along the south shore line to Chequamegon Point, and across to Madeline Island. Since the channel between the point and the island was considerably narrower at that time than it is at present, the lumber was transferred to other points on the lake by sailboats.

According to testimony of older residents of Odanah, another sawmill, located near the White River, was operated by "Wabi-gog," "White Porcupine." [3] During the winter season, the lumber from this mill was hauled on sleighs pulled by oxen to the present city of Ashland. This mill operated during the summer from 1846 until 1855. In 1864, it was torn down. By order of President Hayes, logging was begun on the Bad River Reservation in the autumn of 1878; thus permitting the Indians to cut timber from their allotments. Several million feet of logs were sold yearly to the highest bidder. In 1892, the Indians' permit to cut lumber was annulled, but permission was granted to the Stearns Lumber Company to build and operate a mill on the reservation.[4]

In 1894, Stearns Lumber Company completed a saw mill which produced a yearly output of 25 million feet. Later the mill was enlarged to the capacity of 60 million board feet a year. Two thousand logs were sawed into lumber every ten hours. The saw mill operated both day and night. The lumber yard covered an area of fifty-five acres with five and one-half miles of tramway. During the first eleven years of the Stearns Lumber Company operation, 36,250 carloads of lumber were shipped from Odanah and distributed to more than twenty-one states.[5]

The contract which the Indians signed with this company brought with it gross injustices. One of these injustices was the so-called 65-cent clause. It gave the lumber company the right to purchase from Indians all defective timber at 65 cents per thousand. From the finished product, the company received $1.50 per thousand. If a log had the slightest defect, it was classified as shingle timber and priced accordingly. This abuse prevailed for thirteen years and was discontinued only after many vigorous protests from the Indians. The shingle mills were then closed.

Another injustice was the $2.00 per thousand price for dead and down timber, including burnt timber. A committee of Indians, called the "Condemning Committee," examined timber on the reservation and condemned it, if spoiled by fire. But this committee condemned hundreds of acres of timber never touched by fire. Scorched timber was classified as "shingle timber," and the company paid shingle-timber prices for it. Thousands of acres of timber were also cut that were not covered by contract.[6]

Lands allotted under the so-called "Wooster Roll" contained approximately 42,800 acres of timber which was to be let out to the highest bidder. Although the Stearns Lumber Company was not the highest bidder, the timber was assigned to that company, probably because of political influence. According to the terms of their contract, Indians were to be consulted regarding scaling of their timber, but actually the Indians had no voice in the matter. Moreover, the Indians were obliged under the terms of the contract to pay 15% of the cost of scaling, regardless of the fact that they were represented by a government scaler.[7]

Another injustice inflicted upon the Indian was the coupon system. By the timber contract, the allottee was allowed five percent of the estimated value of his allotment. He seldom received this in cash. Instead, he was allowed credit which was given from time to time in the form of coupons. Since the lumber company operated a general store, the company received almost all the Indians' money.[8]

Gradually the great timber resources of Wisconsin were exhausted. In 1909, the original Mississippi River logging company was dissolved. The next year saw the last drive down the Chippewa, and in 1911, the largest mill in the world at the time sawed its last lumber.[9]

Logging activities on the Lac du Flambeau Reservation stopped in 1914; those on the Bad River, in 1922; and on the Lac Courte Oreilles Reservation, in 1925. Chippewa Indians today receive but nominal sums for lumber.[10]

In addition to the diminished lumber supply, the Indians have suffered other losses as a result of the timber industry. Before the exploitation of Wisconsin's northern forests, almost the entire livelihood of Indians inhabitating that area depended upon this natural resource. Nature's storehouse supplied bark and poles for homes; fuel for warmth; berries, nuts, and roots for food; leaves, roots, and herbs for medicine. Forests were the homes of wild animals from which the Indian obtained meat for food; skins and furs for clothing; and materials for handicrafts. Waters, sheltered and shaded by surrounding forests, conserved and maintained water tables. Trees falling into the waters of lakes and rivers attracted myriads of algae and insects which in turn provided ample food for fish. These "windfalls" also served as hideaways for fish. With the development of the logging industry, forests fell, and the Indian mode of living became more and more patterned after that of the white man. Today, former forest lands are pleasant, tillable fields or unkempt wildernesses of cut-over lands.[11]

CHIPPEWA INDIAN HUNTING PRACTICES

chapter 43

PERHAPS, THE NORTH AMERICAN INDIAN IS MORE often thought of in the role of hunter than in any other character. To this rule the Chippewa were no exception. In early days, hunting provided him with both food and clothing. Hunters respected all animals. Young hunters were advised never to belittle any animal or to boast that an animal was easy to kill. The Indians believed that all animals were endowed with a super-sense by which they knew if they were being disparaged. Generally they outwitted hunters who regarded them with levity.

The hunting season began about the middle of November and continued until sometime in March. Chippewa referred to the latter month as "the month of the broken snowshoes." [1] During the winter, the Chippewa hunted elk, deer, bear, wolf, fox, beaver, otter, muskrat, mink, marten, fisher,[2] and any fowl that chanced to make its appearance. When spring came, the Indians killed, if necessity demanded it, crows, owls, ducks, and even robins and blackbirds. When wild passenger pigeons arrived in prodigious flocks, settling in swamps and marshes, the Chippewa flailed them with long, untrimmed saplings.[3]

Primitive Chippewa had many superstitious practices connected with hunting. Potions concocted by medicine men were used to attract game. These preparations were also used by hunters who believed themselves bewitched, and therefore, unsuccessful in the hunt. Game that was killed while the hunter was using "medicine" was subject to many taboos. For instance, a woman was not to eat the head, liver, and kidneys of game. The meat was not to be given away, as this would destroy the efficacy of the charm.

A hunter never sharpened his knife just before hunting. This action showed over-confidence and ended in frustration. If a hunter forgot some of his accessories, he returned and called the hunt off. Turning back signified failure. Hunters who had killed no game during the day considered the hooting of an owl for three or four successive nights an omen of bad luck. They then broke camp and returned home. An Indian also considered it dangerous to lend his gun. An enemy might imperil the future success of the owner, either by re-setting the sights of the gun or by using bad "medicine." An old hunter preferred to give his gun away rather than to lend it.[4]

Some evil influence was usually regarded as the cause of a hunter's poor luck. To destroy such influence, Indian men held secret rites, known as the medicine hunt. Medicine men, the aged, and one youth from each family took part in this ritual. Youths erected a wigwam of cedar boughs and covered the floor with the same material. Incense compounded of cedar and "medicine" was added to the fire built in the center of the wigwam. Guns, bows, arrows, and all articles used in the hunt were held over the "medicined" smoke. Powdered "medicine" was sprinkled into gun barrels to insure accuracy. Braves and their clothing were also "smoked" to prevent game from scenting them.

After this ceremonial smoking, only hunters were allowed to

enter the wigwam or to touch the hunting implements. Hunters were not permitted to speak with members of their families until the hunt was over. The hunters lodged in the cedar wigwam, leaving for the hunt before dawn.

If an animal was seen, the hunters advanced toward their quarry in a semi-circle. Gradually they formed a complete circle. The Chippewa claimed that the "medicine" used in ceremonial smoking caused animals to become stupefied. If the hunters had scattered before an animal was sighted, a different procedure was followed. An initial shot was fired. Every hunter discharged the medicated cartridges or arrows into the air, and then advanced in the direction indicated by the shot. If an animal was killed, each hunter took his turn in carrying it the distance which the chief hunter had estimated for him. The carcass was not allowed to touch the ground from the time it was first taken up to the time the party reached the medicine lodge.

When the hunters arrived at the lodge, they built a fire and prepared a barbecue. Only hunters were allowed to partake of the meat. It was believed that if women or girls ate of meat killed in the medicine hunt, they would contract eczema. This disease, it was said, would first appear on the face, but it would spread until the entire body was covered.[5]

After the feast was over, the hunters returned to their homes. The following day, they resumed the hunt for family needs, feeling assured of success because of the medicine hunt. When they returned with the game, women showed their appreciation by immediately taking care of the meat. A notion that is still retained by some Chippewa is that the windpipe should never be cut in dressing deer. To do so, spoils a hunter's luck.[6] The Indians were very careful that meat was not wasted or allowed to decompose.[7]

The "first kill" of an Indian boy or girl was occasion for a feast. The meat of the animal was served as part of the main dish. Robert Wilson, a Chippewa from the Bad River Reservation, describes the feast thus:

> When I was six years old, my cousin Jack Couture and I saved up our scarce pennies until we had enough to buy a second-hand twenty-two calibre rifle. With this rifle we spent many happy days roaming the woods and fields in quest of "big game."
>
> After many days of unsuccessful hunting, during which many rounds of cartridges were wasted, I managed to shoot a

small chickadee which I prized very highly. When I arrived home, I proudly showed the "kill" to my mother who seemed rather amused over my "big game." She simply asked for the bird which I gladly gave to her. She took the chickadee, plucked the feathers, and stored it away to dry. Many a time while I was rummaging through a large cupboard, just for the fun of searching, I came across the dried-up bird. When I asked my mother the reason for saving it, she said that we would eat it some day. I was rather amused when I was told this, but I said no more about it.

When I reached my tenth birthday, I was at an age when I wanted to become a "big game" hunter. I often asked my father to take me on one of his hunting trips, but I always received the answer that I would be just a nuisance to him on such a trip. Finally my father agreed to take me with him on a trip up the White River. During the hunt, I succeeded in shooting a bear.

When I arrived home, my success was hailed with great joy. All the older men of the tribe were invited to a feast in my honor. The following day, the feast was in readiness. Soup, with thickening and seasoning, had been made of the bear meat. In the soup was my four-year old dried chick-a-dee![8]

Girls also experienced a thrill at their success in hunting. The following story told by Florina Denomie has its setting near Keweenaw Bay on the shores of Lake Superior:

I was in the sugar bush with my grandmother. One morning we were entirely out of meat. I told my grandmother that I was going to hunt for something to eat. With her consent, I went. I did not go far when I heard a whistle. I imitated the whistle and received a response. I wondered what this was; each time I whistled, I received an answer. To my surprise, it was a small porcupine, a "gog."

I picked up a stick and struck it on the head. A porcupine is one of the toughest animals in the woods and it was necessary for me to strike it repeatedly. I finally succeeded, as I thought, in killing it, and my next problem was to carry it to camp. Finally I took off my apron and tied the animal by the leg, and started to drag it back to grandmother.

When I sighted the sugar camp, I called, "Grandma, I got a 'gog'." She came running to meet me, and picked up a long stick and was ready to strike it when I told her it was already dead. To my surprise, it was still alive, and instead of dragging the animal, I was actually leading it! Grandma had to finish the killing.

Years later, my uncle came along with his rifle. I then had my first opportunity of learning how to shoot a rifle and how to carry a gun. It was necessary for me to do much target practice before I was able to shoot well enough to hit as large an object as a deer.

One day I went deer hunting. I was not far from home when I saw tiny holes in the snow. Examining them closely, I came to the conclusion that they must be deer tracks, and I became excited and began to shiver. In hunter's vocabulary, this is called "buck fever." After sometime, I thought "This will never do," and I continued my quest for deer. I became very tired, hardly able to lift my feet out of the snow. Finally, I tracked the deer through a small swamp. The tracks were getting fresher and my feet were getting heavier. But I managed to step over a windfall and just as I got one foot over, up came something like a white flash in front of me, and another, and another—three in all. I raised my gun and fired at the first flash, and it went up in the air and down. It might be well to explain that the flashes were the whites of deer tails. I took aim at the next one, but missed. I concluded that they were all gone, and that I had missed both shots.

Then I decided to go and see what I had done in the first shot. Imagine my surprise to find that I had succeeded in bringing down a small spiked-horn buck. There it lay, with such a pleading look in its eyes, that I turned away in sorrow and tears. Yet while the little creature had won my complete sympathy, it was necessary for me to complete the kill. Aiming at the head, I closed my eyes and pulled the trigger.

The deer was not very large, but by the time I got it home, I thought it weighed a thousand pounds. Later I skinned it, saved the hide, and had it tanned. The skin I used in making a blouse, and I still have this, which is part of my Indian costume.[9]

Many game animals still remain on the reservations. However, some species are almost extinct; one of these is the elk. Elk once roamed in the land of the Chippewa near the head waters of the Wisconsin River and also near the Chippewa, St. Croix, Rum, and Red Rivers. Elk on the run were a magnificent sight. They held their heads high, and curved their backs in such a manner that the large horns appeared to rest on them. In 1837, Copway wrote that he had seen a drove of five hundred.[10] In the mid-western part of the country, the elk is a rare specimen today. For several generations, no Chippewa remembered one being shot in their territory. In 1942, however, Jerome Arbuckle a Bad River Chippewa, succeeded in killing an elk. On October 13, the Ashland *Daily Press* reported the incident thus:

> So far as the annals of the history of the Chequamegon Bay region are concerned, the first elk ever shot in this region was downed by Jerome Arbuckle about six miles south of Odanah yesterday. He was hunting with his young son and daughter, when Jerry, aged 11, spotted the animal, thinking it was a large deer.
>
> Mr. Arbuckle says this is the second elk he has seen on the reservation. He saw one a month or so ago that was smaller than this animal. . . .
>
> Mr. Arbuckle had the horns of a 275 pound buck at his home and he placed them alongside of the antlers of this 500 pound elk. They certainly did look rather "pigmyish" in size.
>
> It was a beautiful animal with antlers measuring 47 inches long; these antlers were perfect with prongs matching exactly. The elk measured five and one-eighth feet to the shoulder and was a little more than eight feet long from the tip of his nose to the tip of his bob tail. The teeth were perfect. Elk are rarely seen in northern Wisconsin and the event is already breeding Paul Bunyan episodes in Odanah.

Although the Indian killed almost any animal or bird whose meat, hide, or feathers were of service to him, yet he seldom killed the bald eagle. The Chippewa have always held the bald eagle in highest esteem, but it was necessary occasionally to kill a number of these birds since their feathers and those of other rare birds were used for the Chippewa flag, "Mi-gwoni-giki-weum."

The capture of the eagle was a difficult task because few Chippewa were skilled enough to outwit the bird. The Chippewa sometimes resorted to primitive methods for guidance in selecting the proper person for this assignment as the following story told by Marie Livingston illustrates:

> By this method, (the shake lodge) they found that my father was one who had dreamed of killing eagles during his dream

trial. The juggler concluded that he was the logical person to get the much desired eagle. He was invited to partake of a meal with the juggler who gave him tobacco and much clothing. My father told his host that he would try his luck, but would not promise to bring the bird back.

On the following day, he turned westward, making the then uninhabited forest the vicinity of Moose Lake, Wisconsin, his objective. He built a cedar brush camp so constructed that it would not betray any human signs but it would afford him a good view of his surroundings.

After my father had completed his hide-out, he went hunting. He killed a deer and placed it at shooting distance from his lodge. He opened the deer and skinned a portion of it, so that the scent would be carried to the highly sensitive eagle. My father did not stay near the camp for a couple of days so that human scent would not mingle with that of the deer.

After a few days of watchful waiting, his patience was rewarded when he heard the whirring of wings. The eagle circled around his camp, then lighted on a nearby tree, expectantly scrutinizing the surrounding landscape. After the bird had satisfied itself, it flew to the ground a few yards from the bait, and cautiously walked to its prey. Standing on the carcass for a few minutes, it looked warily around before starting voraciously on the feast. The big moment had arrived for my father. He took careful aim, shot, and was rewarded to see the eagle drop to the ground.[11]

The modern Indian has a somewhat different attitude from that of his forefathers towards hunting. He hunts wild fowl both as a means of livelihood and as a sport. Because the shallow waters afford secluded hiding places, the many sloughs, streams, lakes, and rivers on the reservations are favorite resorts for wild fowl. The birds also find shelter from winds and excellent places for nesting. Thousands of these birds also feed on wild rice growing along the banks of these waters.

Some of the species that visit northern Wisconsin each year are the mallard, teal, and canvas back ducks, geese, skiff crows, mud hens, and hell divers. Occasionally swans have been seen in the area.[12]

One of the highly prized privileges of Wisconsin Chippewa Indians living on reservations is the right to hunt and fish with no restriction as to number or season.[13] Even today, venison and other game are important items in the Chippewa food supply. Venison is preserved by drying, smoking, or salting in brine, or by cooking and sealing it in glass jars. However, game is no longer as plentiful as it was a half century ago. After the lumbermen despoiled the forests and ruined the streams, much of the game was either killed or forced away from the reservations and surrounding areas. Then, too, some Indians, regardless of tribal affiliation, presume the right to hunt on any reservation. Indian blood does not give this right. Sometimes these "outside" Indians have been the chief offenders in the commercializing and wanton slaughter of deer and other animals. Many deer are also slaughtered by white settlers who live in close proximity to reservations.

FISHING ON CHIPPEWA RESERVATIONS

chapter 44

ANOTHER INDUSTRY CLOSELY ASSOCIATED WITH Indian life is fishing. From the earliest times when fishing nets were made of basswood twine or nettle stalks, fishing has been an important occupation among the Chippewa. Rivers, lakes, and sloughs on all Chippewa reservations are habitats of numerous fish. Some fishing areas can be reached by water, others by recently constructed roads or highways.

The magazine, *Outdoor Life*, described modern fishing possibilities of the Kakagon Sloughs on the Bad River as follows:

Reachable only by water, the Kakagon Sloughs give excellent fishing for pike, pickerel, and black bass. The sloughs are located about six miles northeast of Ashland, Wisconsin, and you can arrange in that place for someone to tow your small boat up there, leave you there, and then call for you at a designated time.

The stream, or slough, is about fifteen feet deep, and from fifty to seventy-five feet wide. The ground is marshy on each side, with only two or three places where the ground is firm enough to camp. Water for drinking purposes is taken out of the bay on the opposite side of the peninsula. Perch and large bullheads can be caught there almost by the boatload. There are no "No Trespassing" signs either.[1]

Kakagon Sloughs provided the older Chippewa with a variety of other fish, also, such as muskellunge,[2] sturgeon, and Lake Superior trout. Muskellunge, "muskies," considered a delicacy, are native to the Great Lakes and also northern Wisconsin inland lakes. "Muskies" weighing from 20 to 50 pounds have been caught either by trolling or by spearing. In order to control these large fish, it was sometimes necessary to shoot them. French fur traders found prodigious schools of sturgeon in all Chippewa territory reservations.[3] Sturgeon has always been a favorite food of many Chippewa, although the species is becoming rare in modern times.

Old residents of the Bad River Reservation affirm that at one time the waters of the area abounded with catfish, "ma-na-meg." These fish suddenly disappeared and they have never returned. The old Indians still believe that the fish emigrated en masse to other waters and that some day they will return to their former home.

A common method of catching catfish was to place baited hooks on poles in a river bank.[4] This was done in the evening. The next morning, each hook generally held a fish. This method required little effort on the part of anglers. Women often fished in this manner.

As a nonagenarian Chippewa, Joe Stoddard told of fishing in early days:

The amount of fish that abounded along the shores of Lake Superior seems fantastic when compared with the present time. An excursion in a canoe along the beach would reveal, if one looked into the water, huge schools of fish of all sizes and many species. Whitefish seemed to congregate in schools according to the size of the fish, thus the smaller fish were in a separate school from the larger fish.

An Indian selected a school of fish the size desired. Those along the shore assembled the net or nets which were often spliced together. The men got into a canoe with a net which they threw out of the boat as it encircled the school. After the net was set, the fish were in an enclosure of nets, bound on one side of the beach. Fishermen then hauled in the net from the beach, drawing the fish within reach of others who threw them upon the sands. After a sufficient quantity had been taken, they were dressed and cleaned. Fires were kindled under racks and the fish were smoked and dried.[5]

John Bardon corroborated Mr. Stoddard's statement regarding the abundance of fish: "Bradshaw Bros. and Bly packed as much as ten tons of trout and jumbo in one day." [6] Mr. Stoddard summarized the contrast between the Indian method of fishing and that of the white man with considerable acumen. He said:

It has been my good fortune to attain the age of ninety years and still to possess a sound mind, fair eyesight, good hearing, and freedom from decrepitude to the extent that I can still walk or paddle a canoe for many miles without tiring. I frequently ponder on the earlier years of my life. The changes wrought by the settlement of this region are both amazing and saddening.

I can state with authority and certainty that the arrival of the white man in this region marked the decline of wild life of the forests and waters and the virtual and complete extinction of many species. They came with pound nets and set them in Chequamegon Bay and along the shores of Lake Superior. Each day they lifted the nets, and removed thousands of pounds of sturgeon and threw them on the beach to rot. These fish, considered by the Chippewa to be the peer of fish, are now practically extinct.

After the sturgeon were removed from the nets, white fish which were the species sought, were scooped into boats in immense numbers. These were then salted in kegs, each keg weighing about a hundred pounds. Ten to fifteen kegs was an average catch for a day for many years until the drain became apparent by a marked decrease in catches.

Waste of fish in early days by white men was appalling. The excuse offered by fishermen for not liberating sturgeon was that they would catch them again. Therefore, they removed them forever, and a good job they made of it.

Contrast their method of fishing with that of the Chippewa. They cast their nets and took only what fish they could dry and smoke, liberating the others. Heads and certain intestines of larger fish were eaten in spite of the abundance of the species. These parts of the fish were not eaten by preference, but because Indians believed it sacrilegious to waste any game or part of game that was fit for food. Bad River Chippewa went to beaches where fishermen had dumped sturgeon and loaded their crafts with as much of the fresher sturgeon as they could handle, taking it home for food. This was to mitigate the waste. They could have taken the same species at their doors with less effort.

White men have no reason to accuse the Chippewa of being wanton destroyers of wild life. It was their race that leveled forests and depleted game and fish. Where Indians are left to their own resources, their locality is also the habitat of game.[7]

Mr. Stoddard's plea for conservation is heeded by Lac du Flambeau Chippewa. Through the cooperation of the Wisconsin Conservation Department and Lac du Flambeau Indians, a fisherman's paradise lies within the Lac du Flambeau Reservation. One hundred twenty lakes are within its boundaries. Thoroughfares connect the Flambeau chain of nine lakes which are navigable for small boats.[8] The Flambeau River, also known as Big Bear River, has its source in this chain of lakes. "Lazy Bend," a tributary of Bear River, offers some of the best "muskie" fishing in northern Wisconsin.

A fish hatchery at Flambeau is operated by the Wisconsin Conservation Department. This hatchery was second in the state to promote the propagation of black bass by artificial insemination. The hatchery annually plants 3,000,000 muskellunge and 45,000,000 wall-eyed pike in the waters of the Chippewa reservations.[9]

Fish is still one of the staple foods of the Chippewa. New methods of preservation have made it possible for the Chippewa to have fish at any time of the year. Because fishing is a favorite sport of many white men, tourists are also attracted to the reservations. The Indians, thereby, are the recipients of an additional income, especially on the Lac Courte Oreilles and Lac du Flambeau Reservations.

TRAPPING ON CHIPPEWA RESERVATIONS

chapter 45

ALTHOUGH HUNTING AND TRAPPING ARE CLOSELY allied industries, yet trapping did not become a major industry among the Chippewa until the advent of the fur trader. The trapping of fur-bearing animals is still a remunerative occupation for Wisconsin Chippewa. The low marshy lands on several reservations are favorite resorts for fur-bearing animals. Muskrats are especially numerous. From March to April, the fur of the muskrat is at its best. Mink, fox, skunk, and other fur-bearing animals are trapped during the winter months.

Systematically trapped for nearly 200 years before Wisconsin became a state, marten and fisher, two rare animals now, were the victims of man's greed! While stationed at Lac du Flambeau in the winter of 1804-1805, Victor Malhiot sent men to the Lake Superior area and to Lac Vieux Desert to buy fur. They brought back a total of 9 fisher and 159 marten taken in Vilas and Oneida Counties. In 1917, trappers reported 48 marten and 559 fisher taken; in 1918, 10 marten and 17 fisher; and in 1920-21, 3 fisher. In July, 1921, the hunting of marten and fisher was forbidden in Wisconsin.[2]

In early days, except for ruminant species, the deadfall, "mi-ti-go-ini-gun," was used to trap animals, small or large. The deadfall was contrived of heavy logs and stakes driven into the ground. At the entrance, four stakes were driven into the ground, two on each side. A log was placed on the ground between the first and second stakes at the front of the entrance. Directly above this, another log of the same size was placed, upon which were laid several heavy logs. The weight of these logs held the animal after the trap was sprung. The last log was called the "trip log." A stick baited at one end with meat or some other tempting morsel was placed on the trip log. After scenting the bait, the animal entered the pen through the only opening which was large enough to permit entry. As soon as the bait was disturbed, the trip log fell and trapped the animal. Generally the animal received a blow on its back which paralyzed it or crushed its vital organs. Death followed without injury to the

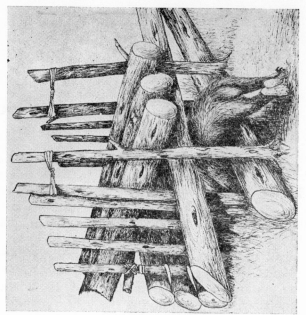

Trapped

Bear Trap

pelt. Bear, marten, and mink were the principal animals trapped in the deadfall. A bear trap was constructed proportionately larger.[3]

Rabbits were the principal animals snared by the Chippewa for both food and skins. The skins were sometimes cut into strings and woven into blankets or used for babies' garments. Florina Denomie told of her method of snaring rabbits in the following words:

An Indian is a hunter by nature, and, perhaps, the Indian in me has played an important part in the success I have had in hunting and trapping smaller animals, such as rabbits and muskrats.

There are different methods employed in snaring rabbits, and the one I describe is undoubtedly an old one, but I learned how to put this into successful execution from what I was told about its construction. That the method was not clearly illustrated to me is undoubtedly the reason why I encountered so much difficulty in snaring my first rabbit.

I used the spring-pole method. First, I secured a small pole, and bending this down, I tied the end with salted "wigub" to a peg in the ground. From the salted "wigub" I ran a "lead" made of a smaller strand of "wigub" across the rabbit's trail. About four inches from the end of the bent pole, I tied a loop made of copper wire, running the lead out through this loop, and onto the rabbit's trail.

As soon as the rabbit scented the salted lead, he lost no time in finding it, and he proceeded at once to satisfy his hunger. Following the lead and chewing vigorously all the while, he soon reached the spring-pole. But the rabbit is wise, and instead of attempting to pass through the loop and getting caught, it went around the snare, nipped the main strand of "wigub" and the spring-pole went flying into the air — with no rabbit on it!

I made many trips to see my snare, only to discover that "waboose," the rabbit, instead of going through the snare, had gone around it. By this time, I realized that the rabbit was smarter than I, so after some reflection, I built a brush fence around the anchor line and snare, leaving only a small opening so that the rabbit must put his head through the snare in order to eat the salted wigub. Then I returned home.

The next morning, I returned to the woods to see my snare, only to find that it had sprung again. But this time, to my intense satisfaction, there hung Mr. Rabbit high in the air. I had solved my problem.[4]

Since the decline of the fur trade, trapping is no longer a major industry among the Chippewa. Perhaps the largest returns from trapping are realized from muskrat fur.

CHIPPEWA ARTS AND CRAFTS

chapter 46

NATURE HAS LAVISHED UPON THE INDIAN A PRODIgal sense of design and color, and an eye for rhythm and proportion. According to eminent authorities, the richest source of art design is found in the arts and crafts of American Indians.[1]

Handicrafts of the Great Lakes Indians have not been so widely publicized and commercialized as those of Indians in other parts of the United States. Nevertheless, for centuries, these Indians have been producing many useful and attractive articles. This fact became more widely known at the centenary celebration of the city of Cleveland held in 1936. The Indians of the Great Lakes were asked to send exhibits of their arts and crafts to this celebration, which was dedicated to the advancement of the art, science, industry, and commerce of the Great Lakes area. Before these displays arrived, many persons questioned the wisdom of such a request. They had been accustomed to thinking that only the Indians of the Southwest were proficient in arts and crafts.

Within the brief period of two weeks, the superintendents and their helpers had collected a splendid assortment of handiwork. Visitors came and returned with their friends. The display included articles made of birch bark and leather. Among the crafts employed were carving, weaving, painting, and beading. Objects shown included costumes, weapons, utensils, pipes, baskets, and musical instruments. Critics praised highly the skills, the beauty, and the artistic workmanship of the Great Lakes Indians.[2]

Chippewa Indians are adepts in textile arts. These arts include basketry, weaving, quillwork, beadwork, and needlework. As prac-

Basket Weaving

ticed by the Great Lakes Chippewa, the finished articles abound in symbolic and decorative elements. Chippewa symbolism has its origin in mythology; whereas, the decorative elements grow out of the particular art itself. No other craft practiced by the early tribes called for such an exercise of artistic taste as did textile work.[3]

Basket-making is perhaps the oldest and most characteristic of the North American Indian arts. Roots, barks, twigs, wood splints, grasses, and reeds were the media used. Baskets were decorated with materials of contrasting colors and texture, such as bones, shell pendants, feathers, and quills. The construction of a basket by a Lac du Flambeau Indian was poetically described by John Parkey:

> A native of these virgin hills
> Came out and in the sunshine stood
> And told his wife beside the door,
> "I'll go and bring the basket wood."
>
> Then with his axe in supple hand,
> His gliding footsteps quickly sped
> Across the fields and over hills
> That to the verdant forest led.
>
> And there he sought the black ash tree
> Among its brothers tall and trim;
> The one that had a free strong grain
> From mossy ground to lower limb.
>
> Then with his axe, he felled the tree
> And bore away that part which grew
> From dun-brown earth to gray-barked limb
> Along the twisted paths he knew.
>
> At last he reached again his home
> And heaved his heavy burden down
> To wipe the sweat from off his brow,
> And sigh and sit him happily down.
>
> But when again the sun arose,
> Its light and warmth to bring,
> I heard the sledge's measured strokes
> Across the pleasant valley ring.
>
> As steadily he beat away,
> The pile of black ash ribbons grew
> Until his wife took them aside
> To strip and scrape them so and so,

And dip them in her pot of dye
Of red and green, and brown, and blue;
Of purple and of yellow light.
Each one some tint of rainbow hue.

And now the work of weaving starts;
And slowly splint by splint proceeds
From very base to pretty brim.
Till all that now the basket needs
Is sweet grass bound round the rim.

And there an Indian basket stands —
A test of patience, strength and skill;
A gift of art by Indian hands.[4]

The Chippewa of the Lake Superior region made several types of baskets from wooden splints dyed in various colors. Laundry hampers and clothes baskets were generally made from white ash and basswood. Strong, solid baskets for general use were made from elm bark. Because of the rugged material used in its construction, this type of basket could withstand exposure to any kind of weather. A tall water reed, "an-naka-na-shoise," was also used extensively by the natives for baskets.[5]

Since Wisconsin Chippewa belong to the Woodland Culture Indians, they utilized craft materials found in the area. Forest and field furnished materials for mats. For these, the Indians used reeds, rushes, cattails, black ash, and the inner bark of red and white cedar and basswood trees. Mats were used as coverings for tables, rugs for the floors, hangings for partitions, and side coverings for the wigwams. After the introduction of woven fabrics into Indian life, Chippewa women also turned old clothing to profitable use. Discarded clothing was made into attractive braided and loom rugs.[6]

The arrival of voyageurs in the Great Lakes area widened the scope of Indian crafts. Chippewa gladly exchanged furs for attractive garters and gaudy sashes worn by canoemen. Soon the Indians were making their own garters and sashes from woolen yarn obtained by unraveling blankets or other articles of clothing that had outworn their original purpose. Sashes and garters were woven in geometrical patterns and original designs.

Designs on the uppers of socks were frequently arranged in narrow encircling bands which gave a strata-like appearance to the finished article. Sashes were often decorated with interwoven beads. These brilliant-hued long-fringed sashes were generally worn about the waist at dances or social gatherings. Stockings, elaborately designed, were also worn at these times, especially during colder seasons.[7]

Bead work is not an exclusive Indian art since it was unknown to Wisconsin Chippewa before fur trading began. During the Renaissance, ladies in Europe had decorated brocades with beaded scrolls of flowers and leaves. European immigrants wore clothing decorated with beads. Their copper-colored neighbors were not slow in copying the patterns and in adapting the beads to suit their own needs.[8] For generations, the Indians had decorated their costumes, moccasins, head bands, bags, knife sheaths, pipestems, canoes, baby boards, and other articles with porcupine quills. But it was a difficult task to dye the quills and attach them with sinew thread to the respective objects. Hence Indian craftsmen turned readily to the use of beads and commercial thread, and soon became very skillful in beadwork. White traders always included beads with the commodities they exchanged for furs. When broadcloth and velvet goods were included in fur trading exchange, the Chippewa found these materials more adaptable to bead decoration than buckskin.

The question is sometimes asked: "Does the arrangement of beads have any significance?" James Scott, an Odanah Chippewa Indian, declared that in earlier days, these designs represented secrets which can be interpreted only by one familiar with this design language. Designs in Chippewa bead work of the present day follow the modern trend of conventional and geometric designs.[9]

Early Chippewa made thread and twine from deer sinews, animal hides, vegetable fibers, roots of Jack pine, and the inner bark of the basswood tree. The most commonly used twine, "wigub," was made from the inner bark of the basswood tree. The Chippewa used wigub for pack straps, for wigwam and canoe-making, for sewing and binding birch bark containers, and for fastening hides to frames for stretching and drying. Thin basswood fibers were also used for weaving bags, rugs, and toys.

The strongest thread was made from deer sinews. Coarse twine was made from the pelt of many animals. This twine was commonly used for pack straps, dog harnesses, and snow shoes. A strong durable cord made from nettles was used for fish nets, rabbit snares, and otter traps.[10]

The early Chippewa made warm, durable clothing from tanned hides of deer, elk, and bear. Skins of rabbits, weasels, beavers, and other small animals were used to decorate buckskin clothing. Many other articles such as drums, saddles, mide bags, and dance costumes were also made from skins. The difficult task of tanning hides fell to the lot of Chippewa women. Da-ba-sa-si-no-kwe, Cedar Root, was perhaps the last of the Chippewa women on the Bad River Reservation to practice the art of tanning hides in Indian fashion.[11]

Primitive Chippewa made dyes from plants and mineral matter. Vegetable substances frequently used were bloodroots, gold thread roots, butternut and hazel nut hulls, and various barks. Punk, usually gathered at night because of its phosphorescence, also produced various colors. Mineral substances were used as mordants. This mineral matter was obtained from lake shores and old river beds. The Chippewa skimmed the material from the surface of the water or scooped it from the bottom of water beds. Then they boiled it. The resultant dye was either a vermillion color, "wunamon," or a yellow ochre, "ozanamon." This substance was used either as a dye or as a fixative, but other vegetable and mineral ingredients were added to produce different shades and blends.

A red or black earth was usually found near springs. If rushes were to be colored black, they were buried in black earth for several days and a satisfactory black color was obtained. Black earth was also used as a coloring ingredient with other substances. Reddish earth was collected, dried, and baked in fire until it became hard as stone. The reddish bricks were pounded into a fine powder which was used as a dye and for painting the face. Grindstone dust was a mineral commonly used as a fixative.

Other colors could be obtained from plants. Red was obtained from white birch, oak, red-osier dogwood, willow roots, alder bark, hemlock, blood root, and wild plum. Red oak and quaking aspen yielded a blue color. Green was obtained from the punk wood of red oak and red maple. Yellow was obtained from spotted touch-me-not, speckled alder, punk wood, paper birch, black oak, and gold thread. Black was obtained from butternut, shell-bark hickory, red maple, and arbor vitae. Purple was obtained from hemlock and decayed maple wood.

Dyes were used for bodily decoration, for coloring skins, feathers, animal hair, porcupine quills, rushes, cotton, basket splints, yarns, blanket ravelings, drums, medicine bags, bows and arrows, and canoes.[12]

Primitive Indians started their fires by using punk, "sa-ka-ta-gon." Punk, a spongy, rust-colored substance, was taken from slowly decaying trees. This material was easily ignited by sparks struck from flint. Once a fire was started, it was carefully guarded, for it was easier to keep a fire burning than to start a new one.

Processing the Hide

Because of the difficulty entailed in starting new fires, Indians frequently transported fire. Dry cedar bark which had been frictioned into a fleecy substance was used for this purpose. Live coals were placed in the pulverized cedar bark. The bark was securely tied in bundles with wigub. When a quick fire was needed, a bundle containing coals was untied and kindling piled on it. In a short time a vigorous fire was burning. This method of carrying fire called "ic-ko-de-kan," employed the same principle as that of banking a coal fire with more coal.[13]

One of the most essential supplies required by early Chippewa was resin or gum. In spring, the Chippewa blazed and notched balsam, spruce, and other resin-yielding evergreen trees. The blazes acted as signs, and the notches permitted the gum to ooze. The notch was lower than the blaze and was made in such a position as to catch the oozings of the gum. Gum was gathered at intervals during the summer. Water was added to the gum, and the mixture was boiled until it was the right consistency. Cedar charcoal was added to the gum to make it thicker.[14]

Balsam pitch was the most popular of the resins. The gummy sap was boiled in water. Pure pitch rose to the surface and was skimmed off. During the boiling process, fat was mixed with the pitch to keep it soft and pliable. When the pitch was to be used, the substance was heated. Pitch was used for medicinal purposes, for torches, and for caulking holes in canoes.

Glue was made from spinal cords of sturgeons which were heated in a pan until they formed a sticky paste. A stick was dipped into the mass to which some of the substance clung. When needed, the glue on the stick was liquefied by exposing it to heat.[15]

The early Chippewa made their own soaps and scouring powders. Ingredients used in making soaps were lake sand, hardwood ashes, animal fats, and bones. Lye was prepared by soaking hardwood ashes in any kind of soft water. To this liquid were added sand together with fats saved from bear, deer, and other animals. This mixture was boiled and thoroughly stirred until the fats dissolved and a jelly-like substance formed. After the mixture had cooled, it was cut into cakes and was ready for use.

Soft soap was made by boiling the bones of large animals with hardwood ashes and sand for several hours. A substitute for soap was made from cambium taken from ash or maple trees. Cambium was cut into fine narrow strips about three inches long. These strips together with sand were put into water containing clothing to be washed, especially if the clothing was boiled.[16]

Lake sand was used with soap for scrubbing and scouring kettles. Sometimes a piece of sandstone picked from the lake beach was used for scouring purposes in much the same manner as modern scouring devices are used.

Powder for personal use was made from the inner bark of cedar trees. The bark was thoroughly dried and then pulverized. The powdered substance, brownish in color, had a natural fragrance. It was used for the same purposes as modern talcum powder.

Since Chippewa Indians lived in northern woods where the winters are long and severe and the snows deep and lasting, snow shoes, "a-gim-ug," were a necessity. Whether on the hunt or on the warpath, Chippewa Indians wore snow shoes when traveling in winter. The Chippewa claim that they were the originators of webbed foot-gear in that area.

Women and children wore a peculiar type of snow shoe, known as the "bearpaw," so-called because of its oval shape. Snow shoe frames were made of pliable wood from ash, birch, sugar maple, and tamarack trees. One or more crosspieces strengthened the framework. Narrow strips of rawhide were used for netting within the frame. Sinew and native twine were used for the finer netting at the ends of the shoes. Snow shoes were attached to the feet in hinge fashion by leather thongs which were inserted through the netting and wrapped across the instep from the front.[17]

The calumet is one of the most distinctive pieces of Indian handicraft. The Chippewa had two kinds of pipes, one for ordinary use and one for ceremonial purposes.

The ceremonial pipe was used in the ratification of all solemn engagements, both of war and peace. This calumet, as the French called it, was a symbol of the brotherhood of man. Presentation of the calumet meant more than friendship. It meant peace; the burying of the hatchet. It was a ritual which meant making the world a better place to live in. The bowl of the ceremonial pipe was made from red catlinite generally taken from the noted pipestone quarries in Minnesota. The long stem, made of wood or reed, was ornamented with feathers and porcupine quills.

The bowl of the common pipe was made of clay, limestone, pipestone, rocks, or bone. Many pipes were decorated with beads; others were painted. Some of the pipes had from four to seven stemholes around the bowl so that many persons might smoke at the same time.[18]

Before the introduction of firearms, the bow and arrow was the universal hunting weapon of the Chippewa Indians. The bow

Collecting Bark for Canoe

was usually made from a flat piece of ash, hickory, or ironwood trees. Bow strings were made from sinews of large animals, skins of snapping turtles, or nettle stalk fibers. The shaft of the arrow was made from the slender shoots of cherry or Juneberry trees. The arrow was feathered at one end and armed with bone or flint heads at the other.[19]

Arrow heads were of two kinds: blunt and sharp. Blunt heads were used for stunning birds or small game, thus preserving the pelt or plumage from cuts or blood stains. Sharp arrow heads were of two types—the lanceolate and the sagittate. The lanceolate was used in hunting when it was desirable that the arrow be removed entire. The sagittate was used in war so that it might rankle in the wound when the shaft was withdrawn.[20]

In making arrow heads, chips were successively removed by means of an awl-shaped tool made of bone or wood. Any Boy Scout can complete a perfectly formed arrow head of flint in about fifteen minutes. Contrary to the wide prevalence of the fiction, it was quite impossible to shape stone by heating it and dropping cold water on it. Glue for bow and arrow manufacture was made by boiling deer sinews and tops of antlers.[21]

Chippewa babies of past generations spent the first year of their lives on a cradle board. Cradle boards were made from straight-grained basswood. The main board, about two feet long and one foot wide, was padded with moss and feathers. A smaller board was placed at the bottom of the main board to serve as a foot rest, extending up on either side of the main board. A hoop protected the baby's head from injury in case of a fall. During the summer months, netting was thrown over the hoop to protect the child from flies and insects. In winter months, a blanket or an animal skin was hung over the hoop. When the baby was old enough to play, bright colored trinkets were hung from the hoop.[22]

The baby was held in position by a large piece of skin or a blanket folded over its body. Over this was placed a broad band of velvet or some other fine material, attractively embroidered with quills or beadwork. When long marches were necessary, pack straps attached to the cradle board were passed around the mother's forehead and the baby was safely and conveniently carried on her back.

When a child outgrew its cradle board, it probably slept in a swing bed, "we-wa-bi-sun." The swing bed paralleled the white baby's cradle. Two ropes were tied to hooks or nails driven into the walls. A blanket was folded crosswise over the ropes. Sticks placed at each end of the blanket in a horizontal position together with the weight of the baby kept the ropes the same distance apart. A pillow laid lengthwise on the blanket completed the swing and made a comfortable bed.[23]

Birch bark was an important item in the economic life of the Chippewa Indians. Bark was used for leaf transparencies, fans, dishes, trays, cooking utensils, mokuks, buckets, funnels or cones, torches, tinder, meat bags, canoes, and as covering for dwellings.

Birch bark buckets were not only water tight, but also fire-proof under certain conditions. Florina Denomie related that her grandmother made tea in a birch bark bucket and also cooked food in the same receptacle. Buckets were placed on sticks laid crosswise over a smouldering fire. The liquid contents prevented burning.[24]

Mokuks were made in different sizes and shapes according to their destined uses. The most common type was used to store maple sugar. Its capacity ranged from a few to forty pounds. Seams of mokuks were sewed with basswood fiber. A cover with slanting sides was sewed to the top. Mokuks were sometimes decorated with porcupine quills.

Storage mokuks were frequently made with one side over-lapping so that it could be bent over and tied. This type of mokuk was used for storing rice, nuts, berries, potatoes, and other dry foods.

Torches were made from oblong sheets of birch bark.[25] Each sheet was held over a blazing fire until it began to curl. The heat made the bark flexible and the sheets could be rolled and shaped without cracking. If the torch was rolled compactly, it burned with a steady light. Bark that was rolled loosely, flared up and burned out quickly. Indians, in early times, used torches extensively when hunting or canoeing at night. Women also used them when working around the camp.[26]

Before railroads were built, waterways were the main arteries of travel in northern Wisconsin. Birch bark canoes were the most important means of Indian travel and transportation. Canoes were also used by explorers, fur traders, and early settlers. Since the economic life of the Chippewa Indians demanded movement, the canoe was the "Ford car" of primitive times. Canoes took Indians to their hunting grounds in winter, to the sugar bush in spring, back to the Indian village in summer, and to the wild rice fields in autumn. Canoes were also used for fishing and trapping, for inter-tribal trading, for visiting friends and relatives, and for transportation in warfare.[27]

Canoes varied in size from small river craft that could be handled by two persons to large boats that required a crew of eight to ten men. These canoes were constructed entirely by hand with the aid of only a few simple tools. Only skilled men and women were employed in this work, for only dextrous hands could give the assurance of proper results. The Chippewa made a tobacco offering to Winabojo before they stripped the birch tree because this tree was regarded as one of the sacred trees.[28]

Careful selection of materials was no less important than choice of workers. Bark was usually collected in late June or July when it would peel off easily. The birch tree had to be free from any fungus growth and have a uniform diameter or from fifteen to twenty inches. After the tree was felled, a perpendicular slit was made according to the desired length of the canoe. The bark was stripped from the tree, rolled with the inner side outermost to overcome the natural curl of the bark, and put away in the shade.

White cedar was used to form the ribs, sheathing, thwarts, and gunwales.

Since more than one piece of birch bark was required for the canoe, the pieces were sewed with Jack pine roots. Pitch or resin was used to caulk holes in the bark. Native dyes furnished decorations. Usually the totem of the owners was the principal form of decoration.

After canoes were put to everyday use, any slight damage could cause an annoying leakage. Therefore, great care was always exercised in stepping in or out of the canoe or in loading it. The side of the canoe was always toward the shore. The canoeman usually carried a small repair outfit of pitch and a piece of dry pine root.

Two paddles usually made of cedar were used to propel the canoe. The exceedingly light material used in its construction adapted the birch bark canoe admirably for long portages; while its strength permitted the carrying of considerable weight, in some instances, several tons. The pointed ends of the canoe enabled it to ride safely over turbulent waters. Its speed was almost marvelous. Birch bark canoes in northern lakes and rivers have been paddled at the rate of seven and one-half miles per hour.[29]

The canoe is rapidly being replaced by motor boats and the art of canoe-making along with some of the other crafts is passing into oblivion.

Handicraft, as a means of income, is still of economic importance on the Lac du Flambeau and Lac Courte Oreilles Reservations; but many articles once commonly produced by Indians are being replaced by factory-made articles. Undoubtedly the Indian craft article is superior to the factory made commodity. However, the time entailed in its creation does not yield an adequate monetary return.

CHIPPEWA LODGES AND FURNISHINGS

chapter 47 CLIMATIC CONDITIONS DETERMINED THE METHOD by which the North American Indian provided for the basic human need of shelter. The Chippewa Indians had four types of homes; the domed and peaked wigwam for winter use, and the bark house and conical lodge for summer use.

Dome wigwams predominated. Poles and saplings set in the ground and bent over in a series of arches formed the sides of the structure. Horizontal poles encircled the vertical poles at intervals. Cattail mats were used for walls and roof. Sheets of birch, ash, or elm bark were laid over the mats to make them waterproof. The skin of some large animal served as doors.

The American Indian achieved the modern engineer's objective; a maximum of space with the least effort.

The peaked lodge had a long ridge pole connecting a series of A-shaped arches. The sides sloped straight to the ground. This type of lodge was also covered with cattail mats and sheets of birch or elmbark.

The bark lodge, one of the Chippewa summer homes, was a rectangular structure with a framework of pine, elm, or oak poles for walls and roof. Sheets of elm or cedar bark formed the outer covering. The conical lodge, also for summer use, had a framework of poles covered with birchbark, boughs, or cloth. This lodge resembled the tepee of the Plains Indians.

The fireplace was in the center of each lodge. Directly above the fireplace a hole cut into the roof provided an outlet for smoke. The fire was fed by four logs which radiated from the central flame like the spokes of a wheel. As each log burned, it was pushed inward toward the flame which was small, clean, and almost smokeless.[1]

There was little furniture in primitive Chippewa homes. A shelf about 18 inches in width and extending about one foot above the ground was built along the sides of the dwelling. This served as chair, table, work bench, or bed as the need required. Bark mats, woven rushes, or dressed skins were spread on these extensions. Pillows were made of skin cases stuffed with feathers and deer hair. Bearskin rugs served as seats of honor.[2]

The Chippewa used wooden dishes of oval or rectangular shape.[3] Dishes were made of burly sections of the elm, maple, and other hard woods. The wood was first charred and then scraped with bone or stone instruments.[4] Spoons, trays, and cones were also made of birch bark. Tiny cones were filled with hard maple sugar and hung on the baby's cradle board. Larger cones were similarly filled for the enjoyment of children.[5]

Vessels for serving food did not hold individual portions. The Chippewa ate in common. Small dishes held salt, maple sugar, or small quantities of delicate foods. Larger dishes contained preparations of corn or other vegetables. Trays and platters were for meats and breads.[6]

Shortly after the Chippewa settled on reservations, log cabins replaced wigwams, but few of these log houses remain today. Modern homes are similar to those of white people living in the same area.[7] Furniture is in keeping with the size and general appearance of the home.

CLOTHING AND ADORNMENT

chapter 48

CHIPPEWA INDIANS BELONG TO THE FULLY clothed Indian tribes of North America. In early days, they made their costumes from deer skins. The Indians often ornamented their clothing with beads, seeds, fish scales, porcupine quills, and sea or snail shells.

A Chippewa woman's costume was a single, sleeveless garment made of two deer skins, one skin forming the front and the other the back. The pelts were sewed together with deer sinews, allowing a four-inch extension strip in the seams for fringes. The garment was held together over the shoulders by strips of skins. A braided or beaded belt kept the dress in position. Ornaments frequently hung from the belt. Later, sleeves of the same material were added.

Deer skin leggings and moccasins completed the ordinary costume. The wide leggings extended a few inches above the knee and were fastened below the knee by a leather band. Some leggings were plain, others were decorated.[1]

Soon after the fur traders arrived in the Chippewa areas, broadcloth became one of the mediums of exchange. The Chippewa women found the material suitable for their costumes. Broadcloth costumes were sometimes heavily beaded.[2]

The Chippewa made three types of moccasins. The "sole-lapped toe," "abamin-gwe-ig-un," moccasin was apparently the most popular among the Indians of both sexes. The "seamed-toe moccasin," "dackingwe mukis'in," is, however, still made and preferred by some. "Partridge gizzard," "bine'odisi' mukis'in," a third type, was puckered and fringed, but is no longer made. Hunting and winter moccasins were made without ornamentation. Five to eight inch tops were sewed to the moccasin. The tops encircled the legs and were tied with tanned skin laces. The laces were interwoven at the seam which connected the top with the bottom, just below the ankle.

The "dress" or summer moccasins were made with low topped cuff. They were trimmed with beads, fish scales, porcupine quills, and sea or snail shells. Later, heavily embroidered black velvet was used for the cuff and tongue of the moccasin. When the moccasins were worn out, the embroidered yoke and cuffs were transferred to new ones.[3] Present-day Chippewa wear moccasins only on ceremonial occasions.[4]

The costume worn by Chippewa men consisted of a skin breech cloth, leggings, moccasins, and a deerskin robe worn over the shoulders. The leggings extended from the ankles almost to the hips. They were held in place by a leather strap tied to a belt, but they were also tied below the knee. After the introduction of commercially woven materials, a blanket replaced the skin shoulder robe. Velveteen or broadcloth leggings were worn with a beaded band or woven yarn garter below the knee.[5]

Personal adornment was practiced by both sexes.[6] Women considered their hair an ornament. In 1765, Alexander Henry, the English fur trader at Chequamegon, described the hair dress of Chippewa women as follows: "The women have agreeable features and take great pains in dressing their hair, which consists in neatly dividing it in the forehead and top of the head and in plaiting and turning it up behind."[7]

In the nineteenth century, women usually bound their hair

with some bright material. Bead work was often used. The hair was cut short across the forehead forming what is commonly called "bangs," while the remainder of the hair was bound and hung down the back. When in mourning, women cut some of their hair off in bunches and generally allowed the remainder to hang loose. If it was bound during the mourning period, the binding was of black material.

In early times, Indian men plaited their hair into two braids, one braid hanging over each shoulder. Sometimes they cut their hair short, imitating the white man's custom. Warriors are said to have plucked their hair. Marie Livingston asked her grandmother, then an old woman of ninety-four, if she had ever heard of Chippewa braves plucking their hair. Without hesitation, she replied: "I have never known or heard of any case where a Chippewa Indian plucked his hair by the roots." Indians cherished their wealth of hair as a gift from the Great Spirit and tried to stimulate its growth by oiling their scalps with bear fat or deer tallow.[8]

Many Chippewa painted their faces for personal adornment. Small red or blue dots were arranged in lines across the face of forehead, on each cheek, along the bridge of the nose, and between the eyes.

As a rule, both Chippewa men and women wore some form of ear adornment. Many had their ears ornamented for half their lower length with earrings and pendants of the "trade" variety, others used those of native manufacture. The trade earring was a flat crescent-shaped bit of shiny metal. A short wire which joined the points of the crescent was inserted through the ear. Originally the pendants were of native manufacture; later the design was copied by traders. Small wedge-shaped ornaments were fashioned from a metal resembling silver. Coins were frequently used for each ring; one or more being suspended from a wire to form a pendant.[9]

Copper-colored wire was obtained from traders for bracelets. Occasionally, women cut off some of their long hair which they made into narrow braids. These were worn on their arms as bracelets. Necklaces of trade beads, bear claws, and bones were also made by the Chippewa. Rice beads were made from wild rice kernels which were dyed in brilliant colors. Each color had a special message for the wearer. Green was for love. It represented Mother Earth in the blessing she gave the Indian in nourishing his body. Red signified spiritual blessing. It kept the red men walking in brotherly love with the Great Spirit and gave them spiritual light and understanding. Yellow represented the sun, the mother of life which gave the Chippewa life and heat. Blue typified material gain and represented prosperity and blessing. Purple was for social prestige, dignity, and love of fellowmen. The value of the rice necklace did not rest in its material substance, but in its significance.

CHIPPEWA FOODS AND THEIR PREPARATION

chapter 49 THE EARLY CHIPPEWA'S ABILITY TO ENDURE EX-treme hardship was partly due to his healthy and stalwart body. In many instances, the Indian's splendid physique could be attributed to the kind of food he ate. Although in early times, Indians knew little or nothing of calories, vitamins, and balanced diets, yet Nature supplied all these in a remarkable degree. Since the soil had not yet been depleted, the vegetable growth it produced was rich in minerals and other nutrients. The Indians were unconsciously good nutritionists. Their food habits compare favorably with present day standards. They traveled long distances to obtain foods they considered necessary for an adequate diet. In some instances, they made long pilgrimages annually to obtain salt. On the whole, however, the Chippewa preferred to season their food with maple sugar.[1]

There was no loss of vitamins in the foods eaten by the Indians because they consumed all edible parts of the plant: leaves, flowers, seeds, skins, roots, and bulbs. If plants were eaten raw, no food substances were lost by processing. Water used in cooking plants was consumed with the food or used in soups. Vegetables, grains, berries, fruits, and nuts provided abundant minerals and vitamins. Vitamin D was supplied by the use of fish and fish oils. Because wild animals roamed at will and fed on rich plant growth, their flesh was also rich in minerals. Freshly killed animals were eaten in their entirety. Even the bones were eaten, if they were not too hard to be masticated.

Carbohydrates were supplied by turnips, potatoes, parsnips, wild rice, maize, various berries, and the inside bark of spruce and hemlock. Maple sap and honey provided sugar. Proteins and fats

Preparing Homing

were supplied by rabbits, deer, bears, fish, and many species of wild fowl.[2]

Naturally the food supply varied according to season, but the Chippewa knew how to preserve food. Concentrated foods date back to Indians. Pemmican was made by cutting deer meat into thin slices and drying it in the sun or over the smoke of a slow fire. Then it was pounded into fine bits and mixed with fat.[3] Berries were sometimes added. Wild potatoes were cooked and dried, and then stored in mokuks for future use. Apples were also dried. Apple slices were strung on long strips of wigub twine and hung in a sunny, airy place. Berries were dried or they were preserved by boiling them in maple sugar. After the mixture had reached a heavy consistency, it was dropped into small cakes on sheets of birch bark for drying. "Berrycakes" were delicious; either in their original form or when re-boiled into jam or sauce.

If there happened to be a shortage of food, tanned deer hide was often toasted to a brown crispness. Then it was cut into small cubes and boiled. This constituted a meal which was strengthening and not unpalatable. In cases of extreme want, the Chippewa even toasted extra moccasins. Another food substitute during winter time was the climbing bitter sweet. The Indians gathered the vines, peeled off the outer bark, and then scraped the inner bark. From the inner bark, they made a bitter, unsavory soup. If it was available, maple sugar was added as a counter flavor. Lichens, "pugwa'kwak," also called "pine fish eggs" from their taste, were eaten in times of want. These plants were boiled until they formed a thick paste.[4]

Although salt was known to their ancestors, the old Chippewa claim that it was not generally used by them as a condiment. The difficulty and expense incurred in procuring salt made it somewhat of a luxury. The early Chippewa obtained their salt from other Indians living in the vicinity of Great Salt Lake. Before starting on their annual trip for salt, the Chippewa sent a messenger to the Indians of the "salt country" that they were coming. They also designated a place near the Mississippi to which the salt was to be brought. The Chippewa gave flint and pipestone in exchange. After a journey of several months, the Chippewa returned with the salt which they distributed to the various families. After logging camps had been set up in the Chippewa country, the Indians procured brine in which the white men had preserved pork. They evaporated this brine and obtained salt.[5]

Corn has always been a favorite food of the Indian. Green corn was boiled on the cob or roasted. Corn was also cooked in meat broths. The Chippewa always stored a sufficient quantity of corn for seed and winter use. The husks were turned back and braided, and the ears were hung to dry in an airy place. After corn was thoroughly dry, the kernels were removed from the cobs and ground into meal. Corn meal was boiled in meat broth or made into cakes.

Hominy has been and still is a favorite dish among the Chippewa. The first recorded use of the name occurs in Captain John Smith's account of *True Travels*, written in 1630.[6] The Chippewa much prefer Indian-prepared hominy, "yitchi-ko-na-e-si-ga-nag," to the commercially manufactured variety. Hominy is cooked in venison, beef, or salt pork broth.

Squash and pumpkin have long been staple foods among the Chippewa. Various methods were used in preparing these foods. One method was to cut or chop dried squash into medium-sized pieces. The pieces were placed in a shallow pan and sprinkled with maple sugar. Salt pork and a small quantity of water was added. The squash was baked in live coals or in an oven until the slices were brown and tender. Green squash was baked whole.

Two methods were used to store and dry pumpkins and squash. One method was to pare long strips and cut from stem to blossom. These strips were hung separately on a cord stretched across the wigwam and left hanging until perfectly dry. Another method was to cut squash and pumpkins into coils about an inch in width. Wigub was passed through the coils. The coils were dried and stored for future use.

Several varieties of roots were used as potatoes by the Chippewa. The Arum-leafed Arrowhead, or as the Chippewa termed it "wabisi pin" or white potato, was prepared by boiling; meat was added for flavor. At table, the potatoes were seasoned with maple sugar. The Indians also baked potatoes in campfires.

Wild leek has a pungent odor, but it has a mild taste. Leek was either boiled or fried. Sometimes it was used in stews. Leek greens were boiled and thickened with cornmeal. It was also used as a soup seasoning. Wild onions, "skunk plant," "jigaga winj," were prepared in the same manner as leeks.

Before the French introduced white bread among the Chippewa, they used ground corn for bread. Yeast was made from wild hops and lye. The Chippewa had never heard of wheat flour before they received it as part of their annuity payments. Since the early Chippewa did not know how to use flour as a food, many of them threw away their allotments of flour before returning to their settlements. Frenchmen who married into the tribe taught the Indians the use of flour. They used soda as yeast. The French called this bread "lugulate." Lugulate was also made from fish roe. The eggs were boiled, mashed, and made into a dough which was baked in a pan or on sticks over the campfire.

When Indians camped out, they shaped lugulate into round, flat loaves. They baked these loaves in a frying pan over hot ashes. Another method of making campfire lugulate was to flatten portions of the dough and fry them in a pan. Lugulate was served hot with maple syrup. Campfire cake was made by adding maple sugar and blueberries to the lugulate dough.[7]

Chippewa Indians were fond of soup. They boiled many of their foods and saved the liquid for soup. Fish soup was especially relished. After the fish had been boiled, ground corn was added to the broth. Sometimes squash blossoms and corn silks were used for flavoring and thickening soups. Rabbit soup was also greatly relished.

Meats were prepared in various ways.[8] Game, such as rabbit or partridge, was cleaned, then hung from a branch over a blazing fire. The fowl or rabbit was kept spinning over the hot fire until it was roasted. Care was taken that the spinning should not stop lest the meat be burned. The meat was seasoned with maple sugar.

Roast duck with dressing was considered a delicacy. Duck was plucked, singed over a flame, and then washed. Duck dressing was carefully prepared. The gizzard, liver, and heart were boiled in water for about thirty minutes. Then they were removed from the liquid and chopped fine. This meat was returned to the liquid and wild rice, onion, and seasoning were added. After the mixture had simmered for half an hour, it was used as dressing for the duck. The fowl was roasted until the meat was tender.

Smoked venison, "ba-ta-weos," was another favorite dish of the Chippewa. A frame about two and one-half feet high was made with a wire or green willow netting to hold the meat. A small fire was built underneath the frame. The meat was smoked for several hours over this frame. After salt became available, venison was soaked in salt water before it was smoked.

Woodchuck and porcupine were also eaten by the Chippewa.[9] The meat of both animals was boiled with any seasoning desired. In later years, salt pork was the usual seasoning.

That Indian women ever entertained their friends at a "tea" is doubtful, but that they served tea is a fact. Among the plants used by the Chippewa for tea were wintergreen, hemlock, choke cherry, and "mushkeegobug," a swamp root.

Wintergreen tea was brewed in much the same manner as

commercial tea. Green leaves of wintergreen were collected and boiled in a kettle from five to ten minutes. The mixture was strained and the liquid was sweetened with maple sugar. It was then ready to serve. Tea made from small branches of hemlock, or choke cherry, and swamp roots was prepared in a similar manner. The Chippewa considered these preparations delicious beverages.

Modern Chippewa eat with relish the same kinds of food that white people do. The supply and variety of their foods, however, is often limited by their straitened economic conditions. To a greater or lesser degree, natural foods on the reservations are supplemented by purchased foods.

PART

V . . .

CHIPPEWA SERVICE TO COUNTRY

CHIPPEWA INDIAN SERVICE IN AMERICAN WARS

chapter 50

BATTLEFIELDS BOTH IN NORTH AMERICA AND IN foreign lands bear testimony to the Chippewa Indian's loyalty to his country. Without questioning the white man's reasons for war, the Indian has fought and fights today to save the country which is his own by heritage. In evaluating the modern Indians' attitude toward war, it should be recalled that Indians, though conquered people, refused to submit to slavery. White colonists found on North American shores a proud race. Indians were sufficiently friendly to show white strangers how to cultivate the soil and to hunt wild animals, but they were utterly unwilling to accept the white man as master. When the Indians faced the alternatives of domination by virtual slavery or of moving westward, they chose the latter.

Despite the white man's former attempts to subjugate him, the Indian is willing to suffer and to die, if necessary, for American freedom. Uninformed persons explain this attitude by stating that Indians in pre-historic days were war-like, and that they have retained this propensity. They go to war because they like war. This explanation is not tenable in the light of actual conditions existing among the hundreds of tribes which lived in the United States before the white man's arrival.

For example, in the vast southwestern area of the United States, warfare among the tribes was regulated by an elaborate set of rules. Tribes in other areas fought exclusively in self-defense. The Great Plains Indians conducted war in the manner of medieval chivalry. The Apache and the Navajo were perhaps the only tribes which waged wars of conquest. Considering this background, the ancient love of war of some few Indians cannot explain the devotion of all the Indians to the United States in times of stress.[1]

It has been erroneously stated that the Chippewa, as a tribe, fought under the English flag during the War of 1812. A considerable number of Canadian Chippewa allied themselves with the English; but, on the whole, the Great Lakes Chippewa firmly withstood every effort made by the British to induce them to enter the war against the United States.

Colonel James Dickson, a prominent, active British agent, sent St. Germaine, an Indian, to the Pillager Chippewa in Minnesota to obtain their cooperation in the War of 1812.[2] After giving presents to Esh-ke-bug-ecoshe, (Flat Mouth), the chief of the band, St. Germaine presented him with a wampum belt and then delivered his messages. The Pillager chieftain returned the wampum belt with the laconic reply: "When I go war against my enemies, I do not call on the whites to join my warriors. The white people have quarreled among themselves and I do not wish to mingle among their quarrels, nor do I intend ever to be guilty of breaking the window glass of a white man's dwelling." [3]

Among the few Wisconsin Chippewa who helped the British in the War of 1812 were John Baptiste and Michael Cadotte, Jr., sons of Michael Cadotte of Madeline Island. Originally serving in the United States army, the British of Isle Drummond had given the option: Either go into confinement for the duration of the war or use their influence to recruit Chippewa for the British army. They accepted the latter alternative.

The British who were having slight success in recruiting the Chippewa Indians learned that their failure was due to the influence of Keesh-ke-mun, a Chippewa chief. English officers ordered the chief to appear before them at Fort Howard on Mackinac Island. Keesh-ke-mun, accompanied by some of his warriors, obeyed the order. Mr. Askin, a British agent, explained to the chief that his British father had sent for him because the red brethren had shut their ears against him. The red man's heart no longer belonged to the British. Furthermore, the British father was astonished that the chief dared to resist him. Michael Cadotte interpreted the British king's message to Keesh-ke-mun.

For a short time the chief quietly smoked his pipe. Then he arose, shook hands with the British commandant, and said . . .

Englishmen! you, Englishmen, you have put out the fire of my French father. I became cold and needy, and you sought me not. Others have sought me. Yes, the Long Knife has found me. He has placed his heart on my breast. It has entered there, and there it will remain![4]

Keesh-ke-mun extracted from his tobacco pouch a George Washington medal and placed it around his neck. Quietly he returned to his place. Incensed by the conduct of the chief, the British commander gave him an alternative: Either relinquish the medal or become a prisoner in the British fort. Keesh-ke-mun replied that he would not resign the medal. If he should be imprisoned, the Chippewa would fight for his release. After threatening to take the chief's life, the British dismissed him.

The following day, Keesh-ke-mun was again summoned before the British. The chief was given a large supply of tobacco and ordered to return to his people, but the Chippewa were warned that if they joined forces with the Americans, their villages would be burned in the same manner as fire burns dry grass on a prairie. Keesh-ke-mun accepted the presents and made no reply to the threat. The chief's influence was probably the principal factor in maintaining Chippewa neutrality during the war of 1812.[5]

During the Civil War, four regiments of Indian volunteers numbering 3530 served in the Union army. Casualty records show that 1018, or almost one-third of these Indians, lost their lives.[6] There are no complete Civil War records of Wisconsin Chippewa soldiers. Extant letters reveal that four grandsons of Michael Cadotte, sons of Charlotte Cadotte-Warren Ermatinger, served in the Union army. Charles and Isaac Ermatinger paid the supreme price. Elisha Ermatinger, after his return from the army, settled at Lac du Flambeau. George Warren served as orderly sergeant in Co. K, 36th Wisconsin Volunteers. Warren was seriously wounded at the battle of Cold Harbor — the same conflict in which his half-brother, Charles Ermatinger, was killed.[7] Among the Civil War veterans from the Bad River Reservation were John Scott, Joseph Scott, John Basna, Sr., Henry Condecon, George Armstrong, and George Madeiosh.

No records are available regarding Chippewa-Indian participation in the Spanish-American War.

When President Wilson called for volunteers in World War I, he found the Indian boy as ready as his white brother to defend his country's flag. During this war, the Indian ate and slept side by side with his white brother. Together they marched, they fought, they endured untold hardships, and together they died for a cause they were told was democracy.[8] For the first time, many Americans discovered that the Indian was a human being like themselves.

The day following the declaration of World War I, a group of patriotic Chippewa from the Bad River Reservation hastened to Ashland, Wisconsin, to offer their services.[9] These Odanah Chippewa helped to complete the National Guard Unit known as the Ashland Machine Gun Company. Chippewa Indians and white soldiers from the Wisconsin and Michigan National Guards were organized as the 127th Infantry Machine Gun Company. Later they were assigned as a unit of the 32nd Division in its overseas campaign.[10]

World War I records of Wisconsin Chippewa give the following data: Lac Courte Oreilles, 73;[11] Lac du Flambeau, 22;[12] Bad River, 58;[13] and Red Cliff, 10.[14]

Meanwhile, the Chippewa on the home front were not idle. Men above army age requirements worked in the lumber yards. Part of the proceeds which they received from the sale of timber was deposited in banks. The disposition of this money was under the jurisdiction of the Indian Agency at Ashland, Wisconsin. Much of this money was invested in Liberty Loan Bonds. The total quota allocated for the Bad River Reservation in the five Liberty Loan drives was approximately $150,000. The total amount given by the Bad River Indians reached the sum of $357,750. Regarding the Fourth Liberty Loan, the Ashland *Daily Press* carried the following item:

> The village of Odanah with a Victory Loan quota of $70,000 came across with $109,000. Some village, that village of Odanah. We are getting so used to her breaking all records that we hardly notice it, unless she smashed a record all to pieces, as she did this time in the Victory Loan.[15]

In addition to the Liberty Loan subscriptions, $58,880.31 was expended for War Savings Stamps purchases; $5,005.15 was donated to the Red Cross; and $3,851.15 was given to war service units, such as the Knights of Columbus and the Y.M.C.A. The Indian Office records at Ashland, Wisconsin, show a grand total of $425,736.61 contributed by the Bad River Chippewa for their country's defense during World War I. This amount does not include contributions and purchases made by Odanah boys in service, either at home or overseas.[16] Indians in the United States subscribed $15,000,000 for Liberty Loans, a per capita record of $50; the Odanah per capita was $358. The Chippewa on the other reservations displayed a similar patriotism.

Private Joseph Sky was the first casualty of the Ashland Machine Gun Company to be sent home. He had a leg shattered by shrapnel at Château-Thierry. His brother, John Sky, was killed in that battle. A third brother, Francis Sky, also served in the army. However, Joseph Sky was undaunted by his accident. Two days after his return to Odanah, he re-enlisted.[17]

Veterans, on the whole, were reluctant to speak about their war experiences. The *Evening Telegram* secured one story from Alex Cadotte. Two gold chevrons signified that he had distinguished himself in the army. In a quiet and unassuming manner, the young Chippewa reported his experiences while serving in the 127th Infantry. Cadotte was in all the battles fought by the 32nd. At Soissons, he was not wearing his mask when the Germans shot over sneezing gas. After he had donned his mask, he sneezed it off. Then he received a dose of chlorine gas which still caused him trouble. But he was soon back into the fray. At Argonne, a bursting shell sent shrapnel into his scalp. Six months of hospitalization followed. Cadotte also reported the following incidents:

> Up in the Argonne, I was a battalion runner between the lines. I hadn't had my shoes off for over two weeks and my feet were blistered and as sore as a boil, and I was just about exhausted all of the time. One night while running back from the front line, I fell exhausted into a huge shell hole, and after I hit the bottom, fell asleep immediately. In the morning, I woke up and in a half-dazed condition looked around in the hole. When I turned around, I saw a Hun who had been dead for about two weeks. Don't think for a minute I lost any time in getting back to my outfit.
>
> The 93rd division relieved us in the Argonne and they immediately started to press the Boches back. The Hun general in charge wired back to headquarters that the Yanks were punching him hard, and that they had used everything to stop their onrush but to no avail. The general at headquarters told the field general to gas the Yanks. "Gas 'em Hell! We've gassed them until they are black in the face and still they come," retorted the field general. The 93rd, you know, was composed of some Negroes from the South![18]

The number of Chippewa who served in the Engineers' Corps was small, but those who were identified with that branch of service distinguished themselves. One of these soldiers was Walter Sevalier, a Chippewa from Blueberry, Wisconsin. Sevalier was decorated with the Distinguished Service Cross. He swam across a river under heavy shell fire in order to anchor a rope. This enabled the soldiers to launch a pontoon bridge over which troops could cross. Carl Miller was another Chippewa who was mentioned for special merit, but he received no decoration. Miller served as a fireman with the railroad engineers. More citations were given, but the recipients were reluctant to give the reasons for the citations. When asked to display their decorations, the answer generally was: "I, alone, am not entitled to this, but all the men who were with us." [19]

The attitude of all the Indians in the United States throughout the war was one of uncompromising patriotism. Indians declared that they were only following the red man's traditional service to the white man which dates back to 1609. In his 1918 report, Cato Sells, Commissioner of Indian Affairs, wrote:

> I reluctantly withhold a detailed account of the many instances of tribal and personal patriotism and of individual valor and achievement by the Indian soldiers in the service of both Canada and the United States that came to my attention during the year, for no record here would seem fittingly impartial that did not include the hundreds of noteworthy and authenticated incidents on the reservations, in the camps, and in France that have been almost daily recounted in the public press. The complete story would be a voluminous narration of scenes, episodes, eloquent appeal, stirring action, and glorious sacrifice that might better be written into a deathless epic by some major poet born out of the heroic travail of a world-embattled era.[20]

In World War I, Indians were not citizens and were therefore not subject to drafting. However, more than 8,000 entered the military service. More than 17,000 registered for selective service, though they were not required to do so.[21] Sixty-four were commissioned officers and fifty-four received decorations. War records of Indians are rather fragmentary, but they include the names of 331 Indians killed and 262 wounded. The Indians distinguished themselves by their sagacity and alertness, their bravery and their scouting prowess. They furnished both more men and money per capita than any other racial group.[22]

Some Indians filled a position on communication lines that no one else could fill. Colonel A. W. Bloor, commander of the 142nd Infantry, said that one regiment of Indians possessed a company of Indians who spoke 26 different languages. Indians, speaking their own language, confused Germans who tapped American communication lines. On October 27, 1918, the Germans were reasonably sure that Americans were planning to attack in the vicinity of St. Etienne, but they did not know exactly where or when. They tapped American telephone lines. Although they heard Americans speaking loquaciously, they could not decipher their code. While the Germans puzzled over the words, Americans in the 36th Division stormed Forest Farm.[23]

Almost every general in the allied forces commended the red men for their heroism. They were the coolest men under fire. Few scientific studies have been made of Indian and white psychological differences. In 1927, one of these studies was published in the *Scientific American Magazine:*

In psychiatric tests applied to thousands of soldiers in the last war, the red men, of all four races, (white, yellow, black, and red) showed greater power to resist mental strain. An eminent authority insists this superiority is due to a spiritual poise that has come to the red man from a philosophy of life that makes God a universal, omnipresent, benignant force in nature giving to the Indian the ability to stand fast — a something which lies at the root of the race to which faith may be pinned, as well as this characteristic staunchness, dignity, self-respect, and strength of mind.[24]

In 1924, Congress asked the President of the United States to thank the Indian people for their assistance in World War I. Since this could not be done personally to each tribe, a certificate was issued to each band. Thus the gratitude of the nation was extended to all Indian tribes of this country.

On the Bad River Reservation, William H. Fordyce, a former army officer from Butternut, Wisconsin, presented the certificate to William Bigboy, a veteran. The certificate read in part as follows:

TO WHOM ALL THESE PRESENTS SHALL COME, GREETINGS —

The thanks of the Nation is extended through the President, Commander-in-chief of the Army and Navy of the United States, to the People of

THE CHIPPEWA OF THE BAD RIVER RESERVATION

for their unswerving loyalty and patriotism, The splendid service rendered, The willing sacrifices made, and The Bravery of the sons in the Military and Naval service of the United States, when the nation was in peril during the World War of 1917-1918.

July 4, 1924 (Signed) Calvin Coolidge.[25]

The Chippewa war record for World War II surpassed even that of World War I. Parents encouraged and aided their sons to enlist. Such was the case of seventy-year old Charles Burnell, a Chippewa, who went to a recruiting station to "give my son to white man's army." "Chief Little Cloud," resplendent in ceremonial dress, was a dramatic figure as he entered the "wigwam" of the Great White Father with his son, "Little Samson," John Burnell. Both father and son were proud to be of service to country. The father also seemed pleased for another reason. He remarked, "It's about time he gets out into the world to see what it is made of. He should come back big and strong." [26]

Chippewa Indians of the Great Lakes area are proud of several "firsts." The first student to register for the draft at the University of Wisconsin was Franklin Carroll, a Chippewa from Webster, Wisconsin. Michael Benedict Gunroe was the first person to register at Red Cliff Reservation. After the national lottery was held in connection with compulsory military training at Washington, D. C., Gunroe received No. 1 in the lottery. The first Great Lakes Indian casualty in World War II was Francis Soulier, 22, from Bayfield, Wisconsin.[27]

The first Indian in Florida to join the army was an Odanah Chippewa, Kenneth Arbuckle. After registering in Illinois, Arbuckle went to Florida as a winter resident of Bradenton Trailer Park.[28] Arbuckle expressed his reasons for leaving Illinois thus: "I wanted to see the state so many of my white neighbors had talked about." After Arbuckle's induction into the army at Camp Blanding, Georgia, he was assigned work as an army mechanic.[29]

Later in the war, Arbuckle was assigned to the medical corps and rose to the rank of Staff Sergeant. He and his wife, the former Mary Jane Bentley, also a Chippewa, were the first Indian couple from Odanah to serve in the army. Mrs. Arbuckle had joined the Women's Army Corps and was stationed at Miami, Florida.[30]

Chequamegon's first Chippewa commissioned officer, Arnold G. Smart, within the space of a few months, had experiences which removed all monotony from his army life. As navigator aboard a bomber, he was struck with flak which, as he said, "went clean through my left shoulder. I picked the piece off the floor of the plane. It was about as big as a shotgun slug." Shortly after this incident, Smart was promoted to first lieutenant. Later he received an Air Medal and two Oak Leaf Clusters for "exceptionally meritorious achievement while participating in sustained bomber operations over enemy occupied continental Europe.[31] The courage, coolness, and skill displayed by this officer upon these occasions reflects great credit upon himself and the armed forces of the United States." [32]

The army career of Oliver Rasmussen, 23, service man, was

also marked by eventful experiences. An outstanding first class naval aviation radioman, he attained prominence because for 65 days, he eluded Japanese pursuers on Hokkaido Island.

Rasmussen's adventure began on July 14, 1945. After strafing a train, the Helldiver in which he was riding crashed into a mountain side. Rasmussen reported the incident to Hazel Hartzog, United Press Staff Correspondent in Tokyo:

> I was strapped in my seat and had been slapped up under the edge of the crumpled wing, but I was still in one piece. I decided that I had to prevent shock, so I climbed out of the plane and lay down and went to sleep until nightfall. Then I got up and went to find the body of the pilot. He had been thrown some distance from the plane. I took the plane's emergency fishing gear, life raft and sail, and started for the coast.[33]

About September 15, Rasmussen noticed American aircraft flying extremely low. Deciding that something unusual had happened, he crept down to the beach and began to dig a "HELP" sign in the sand. Suddenly, a Japanese farmer stole up behind him and yelled that the war was over. The Japanese kindly offered Rasmussen a cigarette. Some time later, as military police escorted Rasmussen to the ship, they chided him: "Listen, fellow, have you been stealing milk from farmers?"[34]

Master Sergeant Joseph Marksman was a valiant soldier who did not survive to tell his story. Marksman, known as hero of Hill 609 in Tunisia, was later killed in action in Italy on January 10, 1944. As a member of the 133d Infantry Regiment, Marksman served in the African and Sicilian campaigns. When his platoon commander was killed in Tunisia, Marksman, according to the words of citation, "under heavy artillery and machine-gun fire advanced and immediately took command of the platoon. While advancing, his weapon was rendered useless. Without a weapon, he continued the attack and also the advance in the final assault. His leadership and devotion to duty assisted greatly in the capture of Hill 609." In forwarding the Division Commander's letter of citation to Sergeant Marksman, Lt. Col. Carley L. Marshall of the 133d Infantry wrote: "The Battalion is honored and the Battalion Commander is proud to have you as a member of his command."[35]

The Edward Dashner family of the Bad River Reservation contributed four sons to the service. Arthur, a graduate of Ashland High School, was the first son to enlist.[36] He was one of six men chosen to steal over to Nazi lines and bring back information. He always returned safe. Walter Dashner volunteered next and he was followed by twin brothers, Alfred and Wilfred. Walter's experiences were different from those of Oliver Rasmussen. In future years, if children ask their fathers to tell about the American soldiers of World War II, veterans of the 44th Division of the 324th Infantry, Seventh Army, France, may tell the story of Pfc. Walter Dashner, a Chippewa Indian from Odanah, Wisconsin. Here is his story as reported in a local paper:

> Dashner was just a tired, mud-caked half-frozen soldier fighting a bitter war somewhere in the Vosges area. His company had been fighting for endless days, and on this night, as on so many others, he had been selected to go on patrol.
>
> Halfway through a thick woods, the patrol was ambushed by a strong German force. Three machine guns pinned them down. Casualties were high. Every time an American moved, the machine gun coughed angrily.
>
> Then a voice came from the German positions: "Listen, Americans," it said in perfect Oxford English, "you know your position is hopeless. One by one, you'll be killed. Why not surrender now? We'll give you a hot meal, a warm bed, and treat you right."
>
> On and on the voice went — repeating the same warm promises. Suddenly Pfc. Dashner was on his feet. "God —— you," he shouted, "come and get me!"
>
> With his Browning automatic rifle at his hip, he sprayed three machine gun positions. He had six full clips and he emptied them at the Germans, shouting as he fired. His buddies caught the spirit of the Wisconsin boy and dashed forward. Within two minutes, all three machine-gun nests were wiped out. Dashner escaped without a scratch. The patrol continued to its objective.[37]

During World War II, General Douglas MacArthur publicly paid tribute to the Indians' fighting ability. He also expressed a desire to personally meet all the Indians who had served under his command. *Indians at Work* reported General MacArthur's cablegram from Australia:

> As a warrior, his [the Indian's] fame is world wide. Many successful methods of modern warfare are based on what he evolved centuries ago. Individually he exemplified what the line fighter could do by adaptation to the characteristics of the

particular countryside in which he fought. His tactics, so brilliantly utilized by our first great commander, George Washington, again apply in basic principle to the vast jungle-covered reaches of the present war.[38]

General MacArthur's opinion of the Indian was re-echoed by Major Lee Gilstrap. In 1942, the following article appeared in a Congressional Record:

Major Gilstrap knows Indians. He fought beside Indians in the World War, coached them football at Oklahoma Military Academy during peace years, and is "Big Chief" to 2,000 of them right now.

Some of the officers at this post assert that Secretary of War Stimson, himself, would vote the same way. They recall that Mr. Stimson was driving through the camp when his eye was caught by the grace and agility of an instructor in bayonet practice.

"Stop the car," ordered the Secretary. He watched in silence while the swift-moving bayonet flashed in the sun. "I want to meet the instructor," he said.

Secretary Stimson then complimented Sgt. Chauncy Matlock as "the finest instructor in bayonet practice I have ever seen" — an accolade to a full-blooded Indian who was a star football player and English scholar at Oklahoma College.

"The Indians love to use that bayonet," said Major Gilstrap, "and that probably explains why they are the best bayonet fighters. Indeed, they like the shining steel blade so well that it is a terrific job to make them remember that rifles carry bullets as well as bayonets.". . .

Indians may prefer to use the bayonet but it is a fact also that they are the best rifle shots in their division. About half of them have an expert's rating, and most of them are particularly adept at long-range rifle shooting.

"At scouting and patrol work," Major Gilstrap adds, "the Indians stand out like a sore thumb. During recent combat maneuvers one Indian, single-handed captured a tank and its crew; another Indian came back with 87 'scalps' or identifying arm bands."

The sense perception of many Indians is so acute that they can spot a snake by sound or smell before they can see it. They have an uncanny faculty at weaseling over any kind of terrain at night, and there is a saying that "The only Indian who can't find his way back to his own lines is a dead Indian."

Physically most Indians have the qualifications for a perfect soldier. Their long, sleek muscles are built for endurance. Some Indians at this post have been known to come in from a 25-mile hike and then walk 2 or 3 miles to a United Service Organizations' hut to a dance.

Not only is the Indian well-nigh indefatigable but he also has better muscular coordination than any other race. "I coached athletics for 15 years and I never saw an Indian who lacked that rhythm, timing, coordination that golfers like to call 'form,'" Major Gilstrap says.

The real secret which makes the Indian such an outstanding soldier, in Major Gilstrap's view, is his enthusiasm for fighting. . . . This fighting spirit is attested by many a semi-apocryphal tale. One concerns a portly Indian who tried to join the Army, and, told by the recruiting officer he was too fat to qualify, tartly replied: "Don't want to run. Want to fight."

The great classic on the Indian's fighting attitude, however, was made 25 years ago by John Rat, a Cherokee. When he came home from France in the last war, he was asked by his friends how he liked the Army. His answer is still echoing in this war, "Too much salute, not enough shoot."

As a matter of fact, that Indian talk business of "Me ketchum," "Me strong, silent man," is heard no more. Once there might have been Indians like the Cherokee soldier who saluted his colonel in the morning but refused to do so in the afternoon because, as the Cherokee put it: "Back where I live, speak to men in morning. No more that day." [39]

The attitude of the Great Lakes Chippewa toward World War II compares favorably with that of the entire Indian population. Jesse Cavill, Superintendent of the Great Lakes Indian Agency, reported:

It is our belief that at least 75 per cent of those listed in military service have volunteered and have not waited to be drafted. . . . We are very proud of the Indian boys. A considerable number of them are non-commissioned officers, many holding the rank of sergeant and several have higher ratings.[40]

In 1943, during a year and a half of participation in World War II, there was a greater proportion of Chippewa young women

and men in the armed forces and critical war industries than any
other community.of comparable size or population.[41]

The experience and training of many of the older men qualified them for work in strategic war industries. Many Chippewa men
left the reservations to work in war plants. The Globe and Butler
Shipyards in Superior, Wisconsin, employed many Indians as weld-
ers and burners. Indian men who had formerly worked on Civilian
Conservation Construction work obtained jobs in Army and Navy
projects. A former construction worker helped in the building of an
air base in Newfoundland and two others were on the construction
crew of the newly opened Alaska highway. Canadian war projects
attracted many Lake States' Indian workers. Several Chippewa
worked on war jobs in Vancouver. Many Indians also worked in
the woods to supply lumber for the nation's needs.[42]

The fidelity of the Indians and the quality of their service im-
pelled one shipyard official to say: "The Indians are 100% loyal.
Where they are, there is never any worry about sabotage. Their
patriotism is taken for granted. They are making a record for industry and loyalty." [43]

The Vocational school at Superior, Wisconsin, conducted a
National Youth Administration war training center. Approximately
50 Indian boys and girls from the Great Lakes area finished the
courses offered and obtained positions in war plants. Young women
from reservations found jobs as sheet metal workers in Minneapolis
and Detroit.

That Chippewa women were as anxious to help their country
as were the men is shown by the fact that forty Chippewa women
formed a rifle brigade for home defense. Indian women performed
much work in the forests — work previously considered exclusively
"a man's job." Outstanding among the work done by women was
treatment for blister rust given to 80,182 acres of forest, principally
in the lake states. In the Red Lake forests of Minnesota, crews consisting of two women and one man planted young trees to replace
those cut down. During one spring period alone, 90,700 trees were
planted on 238 acres of land. On Lac du Flambeau Reservation, ten
Indian women also received Red Cross pins for 150 hours of knit-
ting and sewing. Many women qualified for other awards.[44]

With most of the men engaged in war work, women and children took over the planting and care of home gardens. Under the
guidance of Indian Service Workers, boys and girls were taught
the fundamentals of farming. On scores of newly-seeded plots of
land, the "4-H Victory Garden" posters were displayed.[45]

Thus in many ways the Chippewa Indians responded to their country's needs. To the Chippewa, the winning of the war was the first and most important business of life.

But to all Indian tribes, much credit must be given for the outstanding part they played in the final victory. In some respects, the Indian sacrificed more than most white men who participated in the war. Frequently the Indian left the only land that he had ever known. He traveled to strange places where people often did not understand him and his way of life. He worked under supervision in a way that was new to him. These were adjustments more difficult for the Indian than for the white man.

The proved devotion of all Indian people on the home front, and the conspicuous courage shown by their sons and daughters in the various branches of armed service, entitles the Indians to share all the honors bestowed upon their white comrades. The story of the Indians' contribution to the winning of the war has been told only in part. A Sioux veteran succinctly summarized the case thus: "As a rule nowadays, the fellows don't go in for heroics." [46]

Chippewa service to country is not a thing of the past. On March 3, 1954, Mr. and Mrs. Edward Dashner, whose four sons served in World War II, received the following letter from Major General William Bergin, USA, in recognition of the military service of their SEVEN sons:

Dear Mr. and Mrs. Dashner:
My attention has been called to the fact that all seven of your sons served in our Armed Forces during World War II or since that time. Four served during World War II, one of whom has been reenlisted and is again serving on active duty, one has served since, and two are currently in service. I immediately inquired into this matter and found that their names are Arthur, Walter, Wilfred of the Army; Robert and Edwin of the Air Force; Alfred of the Navy; and Burton of the Marine Corps.

I can fully realize the pride which you take in these fine young men. For my part, I should like to assure you of the deep appreciation of the nation which accepted their service with gratitude and a strong sense of responsibility.

The no-greater contribution to the preservation of the American way of life in this troubled world should be a source of gratification to you both.

During the anxious days of World War II when all our resources were directed to victory, you gave in abundance.

Now, the freedom of this country and of the rest of the free world is threatened again, and you are contributing immeasurably to its security.

Please accept my congratulations on your noteworthy contributions to the success of our common cause.

William E. Bergin,

Major General, USA.[47]

APPENDIX . . .

APPENDIX.

THE RESERVATION SYSTEM

appendix A MUCH CONFUSION EXISTS REGARDING THE MEANing of the term "reservation." An Indian reservation is a tract of land or land and water, owned by the Indians themselves as individuals under the Allotment Act, or sometimes by an entire tribe. In the latter instance, the governing body of the tribe may assign the use of portions of the land to individual members of the tribe. Before the inauguration of the reservation system, the Indians, in general, practiced group ownership; but, if an individual Indian used a plot of land satisfactorily, no one in the tribe could take it from him. The title of the land, however, belonged to the tribe.[1]

Usually, under the reservation system, the government purchased for a nominal sum a relatively small tract of land from the larger area originally owned by the Indians. This portion, because it was "reserved," became known as a reservation.[2]

The United States government considered the reservation system necessary in order to provide the Indians with homes, to avoid disputes in regard to boundaries, and to bring the natives more easily under Federal control.[3] A similar policy had been followed in Canada under both French and English control and was inaugurated by the United States in 1786.

The Act of March 3, 1871, which brought transactions with the Indians under immediate control of Congress terminated the setting aside of reservations by treaty. Congress assumed control of future transactions by substituting simple agreements for treaties. Subsequent laws placed the subject of reservations under the President's jurisdiction. Prior to 1887, reservations established by executive order without an act of Congress were not held to be permanent. Under the 1887 Allotment Act, some reservations apportioned the land to individual Indians. The title was held in trust by the government, and in some instances, the individual Indian was not allowed to sell his allotment.

All reservations, whether created by executive order, by act of

Congress, or by treaty, are permanent. Strangely enough, it has been singularly difficult for many white people to understand that Indian communities have a right to exist as entities or that the Indians themselves ought to have anything to say about their own affairs.[4] In 1820, John C. Calhoun, the champion of States Rights, said:

> The Indians must be brought gradually under our authority and laws, or they will insensibly waste away in vice and misery. It is impossible with their customs, that they should exist as independent communities, in the midst of civilized society. They are not in fact an independent people (I speak of those surrounded by our population) nor ought they to be so considered. They should be taken under our guardianship; and our opinion, and not theirs, ought to prevail, in measures intended for their civilization and happiness.[5]

There is a strange inconsistency in this statement of Calhoun's. The Indians fared quite well before the white man came; in fact, so well that they kept the white man from starving when the latter tried to eke out an existence from the soil.

In 1825, President Monroe concurred with Calhoun's policy by presenting to the Senate a formal "plan of colonization or removal" to western areas, of all tribes then residing east of the Mississippi. Again, this was a strange inconsistency. The champion of the Monroe Doctrine wished to remove the threat of harmful foreign influence from the Americas, but he requested that native Americans be driven from their lands![6]

The government maintained schools on some of the first reservations, and tried to prevent traders from selling firearms and liquor to the Indians. In fact, the government dealt with the natives as if they were children who must be fed and clothed, and kept restricted in order to prevent mischief. The idle, useless, and dependent life which the reservation Indian led created trouble both for the Indian and for the government.

Frequently, another defect of the reservation plan was its lack of stability. After the Indians had settled down for a few years, the government ordered them to move again. In 1810, Tecumseh complained to General Harrison of this state of affairs, saying: "You are continually driving the Red people; at last you will drive them into the great lake where they can't either stand or work."

The Indian was driven farther west across the prairie, but soon he saw and heard strange sights and sounds. Covered wagons loomed on the horizon. The creak and strain of their wheels, and the chatter and laughter of their occupants perplexed and annoyed the Indian. Strange guns spoke against his buffalo and, before long, the bones of thousands of these animals lay strewn on the ground. The prairies became rutted and sometimes the white men's bones were left for the Indian and his horse to stumble over.

Then another sound, the heartbeat of civilization itself, broke upon the Indian's ears. The earth began to quiver under the thrust of the shovel and the plow. Strange plants began to push up from the soil. Lowing of cattle and bleating of sheep replaced the thud of buffaloes' hoofs. As the number of buffalo dwindled before the white man's gun, the red man faced hunger and starvation. In 1830, Speckled Snake, a Cherokee, raising his voice in protest, delivered the following speech before President Jackson:

> Brothers, we have heard the talk of our great Father; it is very kind. He says he loves his red children. Brothers! When the white man first came to these shores, the Muscogees gave him land, and kindled him a fire to make him comfortable; and when the pale faces of the South made war on him, their young men drew the tomahawk, and protected his head from the scalping knife. But when the white man had warmed himself before the Indian fire, and filled himself with Indians' hominy, he became very large; he stopped not for the mountain tops, and his feet covered the plains and valleys. His hands grasped the eastern and even the western sea. Then he became our Great Father. He loved his red children but said, "You must move a little farther lest I should by accident tread on you." With one foot he pushed the red man over the Oconee and with the other he trampled down the graves of his fathers.
>
> But our great Father still loved his red children, and he soon made them another talk. He said much; but meant nothing but "Move a little farther, you are too near me!" I have heard a good many talks from our Great Father, and they all began and ended the same. Brothers! When he made us a talk on a former occasion, he said, "Get a little farther; go beyond the Oconee, and the Ockmulgee; there is a pleasant country." He also said, "It shall be yours forever."
>
> Now he says, "The land you live on is not yours; go beyond the Mississippi; there is land; there is game; there you may remain while the grass grows or the water runs." Brothers! Will not our fathers come there also? He loves his red children and his tongue is not forked." [7]

The reservation Indian is sometimes looked upon as a person who receives much but gives little in return. Hence, the question is frequently asked: Do Indians on reservations pay taxes? Every Indian pays some taxes, both federal and state. Indians pay state and federal income taxes, inheritance taxes, sales taxes, excise taxes of all kinds, and personal property taxes on unrestricted property. But Indians do not pay taxes on some restricted personal property. Indian tax exemption was incorporated in many statutes and early Indian treaties with the United States. It was often part of the promised price for the lands which the Indians relinquished to the white man. This tax-free status is usually an established property right.[8]

Another reason why Indian land on reservations is not subject to taxation is that, originally, Indians lived on a subsistence economy. They raised their own food, made their own clothing, and built their own dwellings. They sold a modicum of what they produced and consequently had limited cash with which to buy articles or to pay taxes. If their lands had been subject to taxation, they would have suffered the loss of these lands as the white people did during the depression.

Since Indian land is in trust status, it could not be pledged as security for debt prior to 1934. This was a serious handicap to the Indian because he found it difficult to borrow money for farm improvement or for the expansion of business. The Indian Reorganization Act of June 16, 1934, removed this disadvantage by its credit provisions. Through this Act, substantial sums of government money are now available to Indians as loans.

The government protection of title to Indian lands has for its purpose to safeguard the Indian. When Indians were given free title to their lands, many were victimized by disreputable white people who secured possession of Indian lands for a fraction of their value. When the Indian was dispossessed of his lands, he usually became dependent upon the government. New steps had to be devised to rehabilitate him. By the Allotment Act of 1887, individual allottees were authorized to obtain fee title and to dispose of their holdings, if they so desired. Thus between 1887 and 1934, by reason of this legalized alienation, Indian lands decreased from 138 million to about 52 million acres. With few exceptions, the land sold was the most desirable farming and lumbering land. During this same period, the Indian population increased from 240 thousand to approximately 400 thousand.[9]

Reservation lands were not lost only by individual sales. When death overtook the older allottees, state inheritance laws were allowed to take their course. Ownership soon became so divided and confused that the only equitable solution lay in the sale of the allotment, and the distribution of the sale price to the heirs.

Since 1933, the government has purchased approximately four million acres of land, bringing the total holdings for Indian use to fifty-six million acres. This has not been from any desire to force the Indian back to the land, but to rehabilitate the Indian on the reservation where he lives. Some people demand that the reservations be abolished, thereby intimating that the Indian is compelled to remain on the reservation. Such is not the case. Only about two-thirds of the Indians in the United States live on reservations.[10] Sitting Bull in his memorable conversation with General Nelson A. Miles, said: "God made me an Indian, but not an Agency Indian." [11]

It is a well-known fact that many Indians are living on lands that do not adequately support them. The Indian Service is endeavoring to train the Indians who remain on the land to use its resources as effectively as possible, but frequent changes of superintendents have worked havoc with this plan. The following story was told by an Indian:

> Years ago, a superintendent came to our reservation and developed a cattle, horse, and garden program. He was followed by a superintendent who said, "Get rid of your livestock and take up farming." The second man was followed by a third who advised, "Take up sheep farming." He in turn, was followed by another man who said, "Plant flowers." [12]

Although the reservation system is not an ideal solution of the so-called "Indian problem," yet, it would not be a wise move to abolish the system at the present time. The Indian must be prepared to meet world conditions before he can shift for himself.

In a symposium on "The Indian in Modern America," sponsored by the Rockefeller Foundation held at a meeting of the Wisconsin State Historical Society at Madison, Wisconsin, on June 26, 1954, the consensus was that if the Indian is deprived of all government control, he will become a wandering, landless dependent, similar to the Negro after the Civil War.[13]

MADELINE ISLAND IN THE TWENTIETH CENTURY

appendix B

A COMPARISON BETWEEN MADELINE ISLAND OF Indian Chippewa trading post days and Madeline Island in the mid-twentieth century is in place here.

Palefaces are more numerous than dusky ones. The tepee and the trading post are replaced by tourists' summer homes and cottages. A nine-hole golf course supplants the sporting grounds of numerous deer which once enjoyed this animal haven, although enough deer remain for hunting during the open season. The sandy beach near the Old Mission Inn, where dusky boys and girls once frolicked after a swim in the lake, is now patrolled by a registered life guard. "Deep sea" fishing boats and motor launches now displace the birch bark canoes that once glided gracefully over the sky blue water.[1]

Square dances replace the ceremonial dances of the Chippewa. Sport and country clothes are the fashion instead of the blankets and deer-skin that once covered the bodies of the aborigines. Telephone and telegraph lines replace the Indian runner. Catholic and Protestant churches provide houses of worship instead of the Midewiwin lodge. A beauty parlor dispenses one from the necessity of resorting to various plants and muds for facial decoration.

Pasteurized milk has replaced rum, but whitefish and trout and berries fresh from the woods are still a part of Madeline Island fare. These are some of the changes wrought by time on Madeline Island, once the headquarters of the Chippewa Indian world.

One of the interesting spots on Madeline Island is the Old Mission Inn which was built in 1831-1832. This inn has been the scene of several literary works of note. Here the New Testament was translated into the Chippewa language by Mrs. Sherman Hall, the wife of the island's first missionary. Wisconsin's first book, a Chippewa speller, was written by Frederick Ayers, the schoolmaster of the island. One of the most authentic histories of the Chippewa, *A History of the Ojibwa*, was written here by a native Wisconsin author, William Whipple Warren, son of Lyman Warren. The Mission was also the home of the Reverend and Mrs. Leonard Wheeler, whose son Edward founded Ashland Academy, later known as Northland College.[2]

For many years after the beginning of the century, the Old Mission Inn was operated as a summer resort by Edward P. Salmon, a classmate and a personal friend of Edward P. Wheeler, eldest son of the missionary, Leonard Wheeler. Edward Salmon was a man of intellectual power and earnest religious convictions. In the development of the mission, he gave a prominent place to its religious history, thus preserving the spirit of the men and women who founded it. He maintained Sunday services during the summer season, always ringing the church bell himself.[3]

For a time, the Mission property was in the possession of the Angus family of which Nels Angus, the caretaker in 1943, was a member. Then the property was acquired by Edward Salmon of Beloit, Wisconsin, who deeded it to Beloit College in memory of his uncles. For a number of years, Beloit College conducted the old Mission House as a summer resort.[4]

In 1953, the old Mission Inn and the adjoining land was purchased by Mrs. Thomas Vennum, the wife of a Minneapolis attorney. For some years, the island had been the rendezvous of a group of St. Paul and Minneapolis people interested in the arts. The island, with its fishing industry and rugged shores, combines the scenery of the Maine coast and Massachusetts' Cape Cod, both of which have attracted many artists, professional and amateur, every summer. An art colony was established on the island in 1954. The center is not to be a formal art school, but a place where anyone interested in art can meet others interested in the same field, either for instruction or for creative work.

Malcolm Lein, director of the St. Paul Gallery and School of Art, said that the quiet island was conducive to serious study and work. He further stated that the center might be staffed from a variety of art schools in the midwest, perhaps from the Universities of Wisconsin and Minnesota. In addition to painting, Lein intimated that the center planners hope to have work done in drawing, weaving, ceramics, clay modeling, and possibly music. They also hope to have a children's art program.[5]

A tour of the island discloses summer cottages of unusual attractiveness. Chateau Madeline, with its 15-acre grounds, combines old-world charm with new-world comfort. The grounds, mostly heavily-wooded, contain a three-tiered formal garden. The Sea

Cottage was designed by outstanding architects to take full advantage of its beach location. Large sliding windows in the rooms provide a spectacular view of bay and hills beyond. Another charming summer home is Brittany Cottage, an ideal family unit, quaintly decorated throughout. Nine of the cottages located near the Old Mission Inn are the property of Twin City residents interested in the arts.

Famous Indian chiefs and pioneer settlers lie buried in the old burial grounds which attract many tourists who are interested in the island's history. The wooden houses which cover some of the old Indian graves are rapidly deteriorating. However, not all of the Indians are buried in a cemetery. Under an old tree is a marker bearing the date 1858, with most of the inscription obliterated by time. Only the following is decipherable: age 61, Chief . . . Chippewa, Last S . . .[6]

Among the interesting people living on the island at the present time, (1954), is William Gordon, a son of John Gordon at whose home Father Chrysostom frequently read Mass. William Gordon, friendly and decidedly French in appearance, is always ready to relate tales of by-gone days.[7]

Another interesting person is Mrs. Madeline Stahl-Albright, named after Madeline Island, whose father, Thomas Stahl, came to the island in 1862. For 60 years, Mr. Stahl was caretaker for the Catholic Church. A special feature of an August, 1922, issue of the Milwaukee *Journal* was an article written by a staff writer who came to Madeline Island for the express purpose of interviewing Thomas Stahl, then in his eighty-fourth year. The information desired centered around a famous painting, "The Descent From the Cross," that stood in St. Joseph Church before it was destroyed by fire. Tradition related that Father Marquette had brought the painting with him on his first visit to the Chippewa. When the Chippewa were driven back to Mackinac by the Sioux, Father Marquette was supposed to have given the painting to his successor. But records do not indicate that Marquette had any successor in the Chequamegon area until Father Baraga came to Madeline Island more than a hundred years later.[8] Father Baraga's *Memoirs* state that he brought the painting with him.

Thomas Stahl, the oldest settler on the island at the time of the interview, reported that in the eighties, while he was sexton of the church, there came to Madeline Island a famous Italian artist who begged leave to see the painting. The artist sat for an hour studying it, then he exclaimed: "It is the same, the very same!" Then he explained that in St. Peter's Church in Rome, there was a painting exactly like this one which had puzzled artists for years, for it bore no trace of the painter's identity. Learning of the painting on Madeline Island, the artist had come from Rome to see if there might be some trace of the artist's name on the canvas. But this trip proved fruitless, for there was no mark of identification. When the church burned in 1901, many of the old residents on the island believed that the building had been destroyed by thieves who stole the painting. There is, however, no proof to substantiate the claim.[9]

The story of Madeline Island would be incomplete without reference to several "grass roots" white families who settled there in the early days. In 1944, Mrs. Thomas Martin, who was then 82 years of age, was the oldest woman member in the "Old Settlers' Club" of the Chequamegon area. Her grandfather, Antoine Pernier, came from Montreal to Madeline Island in 1835 in company with a colony of laborers and professional men as part of the American Fur Company which John Jacob Astor had organized in Montreal. Upon his arrival at La Pointe, Mr. Pernier assisted Father Baraga in the building of St. Joseph Church.

Since Antoine Pernier was a shipbuilder, he found much work awaiting him for all boats available at the time were hand built. He erected a workshop on the beach and provided living quarters for his family a short distance away. In 1854, Mr. Pernier acquired title to the property and built a new home for his family on the present dock site. The title to this property remained in the Pernier family for three generations.

Mrs. Martin's father, Antoine Pernier, Jr., was born in 1837. He lived on Madeline Island with his parents until he was 21 years of age. For sometime after his marriage, he worked at Grand Island, Michigan, as a boat builder. In 1869, he returned to La Pointe with his family; Lillie (Mrs. Martin) was then seven years of age. Mrs. Martin recalls that she used to look across the bay in the direction of what is now Ashland and ask, "What is over there?" Invariably the answer was, "Nothing is over there." Two years later the family moved "over there," and Lillie discovered that the answer to her oft-repeated question was almost correct — only a few homes of a ghost settlement remained. From that time on, Lillie Pernier became a part of Ashland County.[10]

Among others who came to La Pointe at the same time as Antoine Pernier was John Bell, a young Englishman who was in the employ of the American Fur Company as a clerk or agent. This intelligent and strong-minded man was the dominating spirit in the history of La Pointe and Ashland County for nearly 60 years. He held almost every office in the village, town, and county, and was Justice of Peace for 45 years. He was the "legal light" of the community and his word was law. Bell was called "King of La Pointe," or "King Bell." The settlement and final signing of the Treaty of 1854 was effected in Judge Bell's office.[11]

Then there are the O'Briens. Dillon O'Brien, the earliest novelist of the island, came to Madeline Island from Ireland in the 1850's and served as a teacher for the Indian children. Shortly afterward, his wife and four children — Christopher, John, Susan, and Mary came to the island. A son, Thomas, was born on Madeline Island on February 14, 1858. About 1859 or 1860, the Protestant Indians of La Pointe moved to Odanah and the Catholic Indians went to Red Cliff. Dillon O'Brien accompanied the Indians who went to Red Cliff and continued his work as a teacher. Here was born the sixth O'Brien, Henry, who later became Dr. Henry O'Brien.

During his teaching days on Madeline and at Red Cliff, Dillon O'Brien wrote two well-known novels of the early days — *The Dalys of Dalytown* and *Tom Blake*. After teaching a few years at Red Cliff, Mr. O'Brien and his family moved to Minnesota, where Mr. O'Brien became editor of *The Northwest Chronicle*. He also spent much of his time on the lecture platform crusading for temperance.

Two of Dillon O'Brien's sons, Christopher and John, have built summer cottages on Madeline Island where they and their children are summer residents. In 1945, there were nine persons of the immediate branch of the O'Brien family in the service of their country.[12]

There is also an imposing row of summer homes on Madeline Island known as "Nebraska Row." The history of "Nebraska Row" begins with the arrival of the late Colonel Fred Woods, an internationally known livestock auctioneer who went to Madeline Island in the early 1890's seeking relief from hay fever. The first Woods' cottage was built near the old mission property. Since Colonel Woods' chief recreation was bowling, he decided to build a bowling alley alongside his cottage. This arrangement was too worldly for Edward Salmon, proprietor of the Mission. To Edward Salmon's protests, Colonel Woods delivered this ultimatum: Either buy the Woods' property or endure the bowling alley. Mr. Salmon bought the property. The Colonel moved to the other end of Madeline Island where he could enjoy his bowling alley in peace.

The second, third, fourth, and fifth generations of the Woods' family now occupy homes on Nebraska Row. These homes, built on the northwest corner of the island, are the first that the visitor sees as he approaches the island from Bayfield, Wisconsin.[13]

Recently the Woods revived an old family custom. More than 400 regular and summer guests on Madeline Island were served an outdoor feast at the home of Tom Woods. This custom was begun by Colonel Woods and was continued by his son, the late Frank H. Woods.[14]

One of the "must" persons whom tourists are advised to meet is "Gram" Johnson, born Emma Mansell, daughter of an iron puddler in England. In 1891, Emma Mansell came to Madeline Island to visit her uncle, Alfred Terry. Since there were only five families living on the island, Emma became homesick. One day, in her loneliness, she said to her uncle: "The waves are calling me, Uncle; I must go back." Emma was then seventeen. Her uncle consoled her and asked her to remain a little longer. She did. Later she met Captain Charles Russell whom she married. The Russell family was blessed with six sons. One son, Howard, maintains the family tradition by operating the ferry between the island and the mainland.[15]

In 1915, Captain Russell drowned when the ice closed in on his boat which was heavily laden with mail sacks. Eight years later, "Gram" married William S. Johnson, for many years postmaster on the island and later caretaker of the Old Mission.

"Gram" has seldom left the island since she made it her home. One of the highlights of her life was the visit of President and Mrs. Coolidge to Madeline Island in 1928. The annual concert given on the island by Elizabeth Terry, Mrs. Johnson's cousin, is one of "Gram's" joys.[16] Both Mrs. Johnson and Elizabeth Terry are cousins of the renowned English actress, Ellen Terry.

What "Gram" means to the island is well expressed in verse by a granddaughter, Sally Russell:

> The Queen of the Island, they call her
> Now who on earth could it be?
> My own darling Gram Johnson
> And truly a queen is she.
>
> She has no castle nor palace
> Her kingdom is smaller than small,
> For a throne she has but a kitchen
> And from that she rules over all.

She's also the queen of the cook stove.
Her dinners are the pride of the isle,
For some of her bread and biscuits
The people come many a mile.

Her kingdom is in Lake Superior
She rules the isle Madeline,
And even without a castle
She is the world's best queen.[17]

CHIPPEWA TREATY CENTENNIAL

Wisconsin Chippewa celebrated 100 years of peaceful relationship with the United States government, September 5 and 6, 1954, on the Red Cliff Reservation.[1] The opening of the centennial began with the celebration of Mass by Bishop Joseph Annabring of the Superior diocese. After this ceremony, the Chippewa pledged allegiance to Christ the King and to all men without distinction.

The colorful pageant and re-signing of the 1854 Treaty, directed by William E. Dormady of Ashland, Wisconsin, was the finest and most impressive spectacle of its kind ever presented in northern Wisconsin. Mr. Dormady was ably assisted by Chairman John Soulier and other members of the Red Cliff centennial committee.[2] The pageant and the re-enactment of the treaty was followed by the Pow-wow Dance, a Flag Song, the Victory Dance, and the Star-Spangled Banner.

Admiral William D. Leahy, Chief of Staff to two presidents and the highest ranking American, next to the president, attended all the ceremonies as guest of honor and represented the 1854 Commissioner, David B. Harriman.[3] Assistant Area Director of the United States Indian Bureau, R. G. Fister, Minneapolis, Minnesota, represented Henry C. Gilbert, another United States Commissioner of the 1854 Treaty.

The celebration included induction ceremonies into the Chippewa tribe conducted by Chief Martin Buffalo of Red Cliff, Chief Antoine Starr of Ashland, Wisconsin, and Chief Sam Frogg of Hayward, Wisconsin.[4] The men thus signally honored by the Chippewa were Bishop Joseph Annabring of Superior, Wisconsin; Father Justus Nelles, O.F.M., pastor at Red Cliff; R. G. Fister, Assistant Area Director of the Indian Bureau; Emmett J. Riley, United States Indian Agent, Ashland, Wisconsin; Lieutenant Paul Jarecki, who fled the Communist Polish air force at the risk of his life; Henry Wachsmuth, mayor of Bayfield, Wisconsin; and William E. Dormady, pageant director.

Other persons honored by the Chippewa were Admiral Leahy, already an honorary Chippewa through his adoption in 1938, and Congressman Alvin O'Konski, also an adopted Chippewa. These men were presented with an honorary headdress. Women, also, received tokens of esteem. Sister M. Victoria who has given 64 years of unremitting toil among the Red Cliff Chippewa; Sisters Cordula, Eustacia, Patrick, and Alfred, also of Red Cliff; and Mrs. Alvin O'Konski, wife of Congressman Alvin O'Konski, were presented with beaded novelties.

The Chippewa drum beats reverberated into the night as the evening crowds returned home after the two-day ceremony and tribal dancing in the lovely setting of Indian tepees, bonfires and evergreens, all illuminated by the harvest moon shining over the rippling waters of Lake Superior.[5]

One of the thrills following the centennial celebration was the appearance of pageant highlights on the Bob Ball's Television Program over WDSM-TV, both at six o'clock and at ten o'clock P.M. Bob Ball attended the Red Cliff celebration in person, took the pictures, and processed them in time for the television. Thus ended the centennial celebration.[6]

FOOTNOTES . . .

CHAPTER 1

1. Ales Hrdlicka, *Anthropological Survey in Alaska*. Publication 3134 of *Explorations and Field-Work of the Smithsonian Institution 1927-1931*. Washington, D.C., 1932, p. 99.
2. John P. Harrington, "Across the Bering Strait on the Ice: New Documentation on the Siberian Origin of the American Indian," *Indians at Work*, V (January, 1938), 10-14. This periodical was published by the Education Department of the United States Indian Service, Department of Interior, from 1933 to 1945.
3. Hrdlicka, "Kodiak Island Gives Clue to Prehistoric Indians," *The Indian Leader*, XXXVII (January, 1934), 1. This is a publication of Haskell Institute, Lawrence, Kansas, Department of Indian Service.
4. P. Chrysostomus Verwyst, O.F.M., *Life and Labors of Rt. Rev. Frederick Baraga*. Milwaukee: M. H. Wiltzius and Co., 1900, pp. 3-4. Hereafter cited as Verwyst, *Bishop Baraga*.
5. New York *American Weekly*, October 8, 1938, p. 11.
6. Charles J. Rhoads, Commissioner of Indian Affairs, Washington, D.C. Broadcast over Station WRC and Nation-wide Network, November, 1932. Not until June 2, 1924, did the 68th Congress enact a law (Public No. 175) which conferred citizenship on all Indians born in the United States.
7. Tom St. Germain, "Post-War Planning," *Indians at Work*, X (No. 2-6, 1943), 38.
8. Rt. Rev. Henry B. Whipple, "Civilization and Christianization of the Ojibways in Minnesota," *Collections* of the Minnesota State Historical Society, IX (1901), 137-138. Hereafter cited as MHS *Collections*.
9. Irwin S. Cobb, "Just a Minute," *Indians at Work*, III (October 1, 1935), 47.
10. "Columbus Likes Indians," *ibid.*, V (October 15, 1937), 9.
11. William Frazier, "We are a People Alive," *ibid.*, VIII (March, 1940), 12-13.

CHAPTER 2

1. The word "Algonquin" is here used in its broadest signification. It was originally applied to a group of tribes north of the St. Lawrence River. The difference in language between the original Algonquins and the Abenaquis of New England or the Ojibways of the Great Lakes corresponded to the difference between the French and the Italian or Italian and Spanish. Each of these languages again had its own dialects, like those of different provinces of France. Francis Parkman, *The Jesuits in North America*. Boston: Little, Brown and Co. 1887, Part II, p. xx.
2. *Ibid.*, p. xx.
3. David Bushnell, Jr., *Tribal Migrations East of the Mississippi*. Vol. LXXXIX of *The Smithsonian Miscellaneous Collections*. Washington, D.C., 1924, pp.2-3.
4. Mark R. Harrington, *Cherokee and Earlier Remains on Upper Tennessee River*. No. 24 of *Indian Notes and Monographs*. New York: Museum of American Indians, 1922, p. 167.
5. William W. Warren, "History of the Ojibways," *History of the Ojibway Nation*, MHS *Collections*, V (1885), 30.
6. Parkman, *op. cit.*, p. xxi.

CHAPTER 3

1. Warren, *op. cit.*, p. 36. See also F. W. Hodge, *Hand Book of American Indians,* Bulletin 30 of the Bureau of American Ethnology, United States Department of the Interior, Office of Indian Affairs, 1910, Part I. Hodge lists a large number of variants of the word "Ojibway." The two forms commonly used are Ojibway and Odjibwa; the former is preferred. The correct pronunciation is preserved in both the singular and plural by ending the word in *y.*
2. Henry R. Schoolcraft, *The Indian in His Wigwam or Characteristics of the Red Race of America.* New York, 1848, p. 205. Henry Schoolcraft had extensive dealing with the Indians. His publications describing these experiences extended from 1820 to 1857.
3. Warren, *op. cit.,* pp. 79-83.
4. Smith, Huron H., *Ethnobotany of the Ojibwe Indians.* Bulletin of the Public Museum of Milwaukee, Wisconsin. Milwaukee, 1932, IV, 337-338.
5. A marker placed at the mouth of Fish Creek, near Ashland, Wisconsin, shows the location of the first house. It was unveiled in October, 1931, by two Indian girls, Lucile Buffalo and Dorothy Cadotte. The principal address was delivered by Joseph Schafer of the Wisconsin State Historical Society.
6. Reuben Gold Thwaites, *The Story of Wisconsin.* Boston: D. Lothrop Co., 1890, p. 37.
7. John G. Shea, *History of the Catholic Missions Among the Tribes of the United States, 1529-1854.* New York: P. J. Kennedy, 1854, p. 364.

CHAPTER 4

1. When the lake traveler approaches the islands from the east, he sees only twelve divisions of land. The term may have originated in the missionary custom of giving religious names to new places.
2. Guy M. Burnham, *The Lake Superior Country in History and Story.* Ashland, Wisconsin, 1930, p. 99.
3. "Papers of James Duane Doty," *Wisconsin Historical Collections,* XIII (1895), 201. Hereafter cited as WSHS *Collections.*
4. Verwyst, "A Glossary of Chippewa Names," *Acta et Dicta,* IV (July, 1916), 263, translates "Mon-in-wan-e-kan-ing" as "The place where there are many lapwings." Father Verwyst is perhaps the best authority on Chippewa place names.
5. "Malhiot's Journal," WSHS *Collections,* XIX (1910), 175, n. 44.
6. "The Wisconsin Island," Ashland *Daily Press,* August 8, 1945.
7. Warren claims that some of the medicine men poisoned their enemies and ate the bodies. Later they demanded children as victims.
8. Philip Ainsworth Means, *Preliminary Survey of the Remains of Chippewa Settlements on La Pointe Island, Wisconsin.* Vol. LXVI of *Smithsonian Miscellaneous Collections.* Publication 2438, No. 17, p. 99.
9. *Wisconsin in Three Centuries, 1634-1905.* 4 vols.; New York: Century History Co., 1906, I, 161.
10. Warren, *op. cit.,* p. 131.
11. *Wisconsin in Three Centuries,* I, 241.
12. Means, *op. cit.,* p. 99.

13. Edward D. Neill, "History of the Ojibways," MHS *Collections,* V (1885), 448.
14. Warren, *op. cit.,* p. 213.
15. "The Mackinac Register," WSHS *Collections,* XIX (1910), 69-70.
16. "Malhiot's Journal," *op. cit.,* p. 175.

CHAPTER 5

1. Nathan Cohen, "Arrowhead Boast Lusty Pioneering Background," Duluth *News-Tribune,* Cosmopolitan Section, July 24, 1938. See also, "Swashbuckling Traders once Ruled Supreme at Lake Port," *ibid.,* November 20, 1938.
2. Louise Phelps Kellog, *The French Regime in Wisconsin and the Northwest.* Madison: State Historical Society of Wisconsin, 1925, p. 51.
3. Parkman, *The Pioneers of France in the New World.* Boston: Little, Brown and Co., 1887, p. 409.
4. Russel H. Austin, *The Wisconsin Story.* Milwaukee: *The Milwaukee Journal,* 1948, p. 24.
5. *Wisconsin in Three Centuries,* I, 109.
6. Schoolcraft, "An Incident of Chegoimegon, 1760," WSHS *Collections,* VIII (1908), 224-225.
7. "Bark of Forty Tons Was First Ship to Sail on Lake Superior," Superior *Evening Telegram,* June 11, 1940. Sailing vessels for the fur trade were not used until 1784, when the Northwest Company petitioned for the privilege of building a vessel, appropriately called the "Beaver."
8. Neill, *op. cit.,* pp. 447-448. When Johnston solicited permission from Waubo-jeeg to marry his daughter, the chief replied: "White man, I have noticed your behavior; it has been correct, but, White man, your color is deceitful. Of you, may I expect better things? You say you are going to Montreal; go, and if you return I shall be satisfied of your sincerity, and will give you my daughter." When Johnston returned from Montreal, the chief fulfilled his promise. Johnston's children were educated in Dublin. One of his daughters married Henry Schoolcraft, the explorer and historian. *Ibid.*
9. "Fur Trade on Upper Lakes," WSHS *Collections,* XIX (1910), 361.
10. "Malhiot's Journal," *ibid.,* p. 171.
11. William Bartlett, *History, Tradition, and Adventure in the Chippewa Valley,* Chippewa Falls, 1929, p. 97.
12. Warren, *op. cit.,* pp. 279-282. It was not difficult for Cadotte to secure employment since his abilities as a clerk and Indian trader were known; then, too, his expedition to the sources of the Mississippi had established for him a reputation of great fearlessness and hardihood. The closing chapter of John Baptiste Cadotte's life remains in obscurity.
13. "Malhiot's Journal," *op. cit.,* p. 173.
14. "The Apostle Islands, Madeline, Chequamegon—What These Names Signify," Ashland *Daily Press,* August 8, 1945. The Warren family, descendants of the General Warren of Bunker Hill fame, came to Madeline Island from Vermont in 1818.
15. Bartlett, *op. cit.,* p. 97.
16. *Ibid.,* p. 95. Annie Ermatinger, granddaughter of James Ermatinger, has the andirons and the fireshovel used by her grandfather in the old trading post of Jim Falls. She has also in her possession letters written on Madeline Island

dated as early as 1833; two of these letters are in the Chippewa language. Directly across the lake from Miss Ermatinger's home in Jim Falls is the former residence of Mrs. Charlotte Cadotte-Warren-Ermatinger, daughter of the Indian princess for whom Madeline Island was named.

17. Thwaites, *op. cit.*, p. 157.
18. Ebenezer Childs, "Recollections of Wisconsin Since 1820," WSHS *Collections,* IV (1859), 156.
19. James H. Lockwood, "Early Times and Events in Wisconsin," WSHS *Collections,* II (1904), 130-131.

CHAPTER 6

1. Thwaites, *op. cit.*, pp. 24-31.
2. Warren, *op. cit.*, pp. 130-31.
3. *Ibid.*, p. 132.
4. Parkman, *The Conspiracy of Pontiac.* 2 vols., Boston: Little Brown and Co., 1887. I, 175.
5. Warren, *op. cit.*, pp. 349-50.
6. "Governor Cass at St. Marie 1820," WSHS *Collections,* V (1907), 412.
7. *Indians—Yesterday and Today.* Chilocco: Information Pamphlet, 1, July, 1941, p. 33.
8. Warren, *op. cit.*, pp. 132-133.
9. John Bardon, "Half Breed Public Men and Office Holders," Personal Collection of Short Stories, No. 72. Bardon's father was an Indian Agent and early pioneer of Superior, Wisconsin. Hereafter cited as Bardon's MS.

CHAPTER 7

1. Bartlett, *op. cit.*, p. 13.
2. *Ibid.*, pp. 10-35.
3. *Ibid.*, pp. 86-87.
4. Frank Smart, "Encounter Between the Chippewa and Sioux," Great Lakes Indian Agency, Ashland, Wisconsin, W.P.A. Project on the Chippewa Indians, 1936-1940. Folder I, Item No. 25. All references to this project follow the classification of a copy of this project as filed in St. Mary's Indian School, Odanah, Wisconsin where the project was assembled. Hereafter cited as WPA Historical Records, Odanah.

   Mr. Webster was a child at the time of the incidents related. His memory of the battle was re-enforced by details related by his grandparents. He gave this information of the battle to Frank Smart, an Odanah Chippewa, employee of the United States Indian Service as Easement Clerk, Law and Order Enforcement Officer, and Field and Enrolling Agent. Mr. Smart reported that: "One day, during the course of my duties, I approached the village of Solon Springs from the south and was traveling in a leisurely manner with the memories of the old Indian's narrations fresh in my mind. I came to a high hill and as I broke over the crest, I was amazed and delighted to see before me an exact reproduction of the mental picture I had obtained from the narratives and descriptions of the older Indians. . . . Lying there before me was a panoramic view of this Indian battlefield." *Ibid.*

5. The association of the Chippewa with wild rice became so marked that a large portion of the tribe were called "Wild Rice Indians."
6. Bartlett, *op. cit.*, p. 1. The name Sioux, given by the Chippewa to this tribe of Indians is an abbreviated form of the word "Naudouessioux," signifying "enemy." The Sioux designated themselves as Dakotahs. In 1680, they occupied the area of the Great Lakes, but claimed an indefinite territory extending westward to the Rocky Mountains. They were of the open country and excelled in horsemanship.
7. Jerome Arbuckle, "Prowess of the Chippewas as Warriors," WPA Historical Records, Odanah. Folder I, Item No. 16.
8. Burnham, *op. cit.*, pp. 26-29.
9. *Ibid.*, p. 26.
10. *Ibid.*, pp. 26-27.
11. *Ibid.*, pp. 28-29. The Chippewa showed many signs of civilization. Most of them were well-clothed and not a man among them was a "blanket" Indian.
12. "Father Gordon to Unveil Chippewa, Sioux Memorial," Superior *Evening Telegram,* September 23, 1939.

CHAPTER 8

1. As late as 1938, a very aged woman was visited on New Year's Day by many persons of the Bad River Reservation. According to an Indian custom, the elderly visitors greeted the old woman as a "manitou" in consequence of her great age.
2. George Copway, *The Traditional History and Characteristic Sketches of the Ojibway Nation.* Boston: Benjamin B. Mussey & Co., 1851, pp. 147-48.
3. *Ibid.*, p. 159.
4. *Ibid.*, pp. 148-49, 159-160.
5. Schoolcraft, *Indian in His Wigwam*, p. 206.
6. Warren, *op. cit.*, pp. 63-64. If an Indian wanted to give vent to his anger, contempt, or bitter feeling, he might call his offender "animosh," dog or "ginebi," snake.
7. *Ibid.*, p. 73.
8. *Ibid.*

CHAPTER 9

1. Parkman, *Conspiracy of Pontiac*, I, pp. 52-53.
2. Celestine Bittle, O. M. Cap., "Three Flags—One Faith," Milwaukee *Catholic Herald,* December 20, 1934, p. 15.
3. Verwyst, *Bishop Baraga*, pp. 11-12.
4. *Ibid.*, pp. 15-16.
5. Bittle, "Three Flags—One Faith," *op. cit.*, p. 16.
6. Verwyst, *op. cit.*, p. 18.
7. Bittle, *op. cit.*, p. 16. Some years ago, a party of hunters traversing the fire-swept bluffs along the Wisconsin River, above the city of Merrill, Wisconsin, came upon a pile of stones heaped in the form of a rude cairn. The heat of the fire had failed to disintegrate the crumbling mass. The careful observer found evidences which indicated that at some time in the long-forgotten past, an

effort had been made to perpetuate some outstanding event. What that event may have been is pure conjecture, yet there is a possibility that in the immediate vicinity of this bluff, the brave and dauntless missionary, Father Menard, gave his life in the cause of Christianity. At any rate, northwest of Merrill, near the Copper River a Pere René Menard monument has been erected.

8. Verwyst, *op. cit.,* p. 21.

9. Bittle, *op. cit.,* p. 16. Many erroneous claims have been circulated concerning the location of the chapel erected by Father Allouez. It is a common but mistaken opinion that the chapel was built at La Pointe on Madeline Island. Allouez gave the name "point" to the place, not because it was a point of land, but because of the neighboring Chequamegon Point which forms a part of the eastern shore of Chequamegon Bay. The latter juts out into the lake like a pointing finger and was observed by the westward voyaging missionary as the most prominent feature of the area.

See also *Jesuit Relations and Allied Documents,* 1896-1901. The exact location of the chapel can be ascertained from the account in the *Jesuit Relations* for the years 1666-1667: "This part of the Lake where we have halted is between two large villages, and forms a sort of center for all the nations of these regions because of its abundance of fish which constitutes the chief part of these people's sustenance. Here we have erected a little Chapel, where my entire occupation is to receive the Algonkin Ottawas and Huron Christians, and instruct them; baptize and catechize the children; admit infidels, who hasten hither from all directions. . . ." *Relations,* L. p. 273.

Oral traditions of both Indians and white men, together with scientific investigation, prove beyond a doubt that at Fish Creek, between Ashland and Ashland Junction, there had been an ancient clearing on which stood a large Indian village. Historians who write of the problem are convinced that this is the site of the large village of the Ottawa. Allouez wrote that the "grand bourg" was one and seven-eighths miles from his dwelling; therefore his abode was near Whittlesey Creek. Verwyst, "Historic Sites in Chequamegon Bay," WSHS *Collections,* XIII (1895), 430.

10. Verwyst, *Bishop Baraga,* pp. 22-23. About 4,000 feet beyond Whittlesey Creek is a Lourdes grotto on the property of Mr. William Nohl's summer camp. On a granite slab in front of the shrine is carved this inscription: "In Memory of Fathers Menard, Allouez, and Marquette." This grotto was erected in 1924 by Father Louis Charron. Mr. Nohl was assured by an old Sioux Indian that the seventeenth century mission was on this land. Some years ago, the foundation of an ancient building was discovered near the grotto, but it crumbled to dust when disturbed by the spade.

11. *Ibid.,* pp. 24-25.

12. Parkman, *La Salle and the Discovery of the Great West.* Boston: Little Brown & Co., 1879. p. 33.

CHAPTER 10

1. Ashland *Daily Press,* December 2, 1938. On April 1, 1831, Harriet Hall was born at La Pointe; the first white child born in the Lake Superior country.

2. *Ibid.,* May 4, 1945.

3. The lumber for the Old Mission was whip-sawed according to the custom of the day. A trench was dug and then a log was placed on supports above the

trench. One Indian in the trench and another on top of the log performed the sawing.

4. Burnham, *op. cit.*, pp. 111-12. See also Ashland *Daily Press,* May 12, 1943. The Old Mission Church, built in 1839, during its more than a century of existence, has been visited by thousands of people from all over the world. The original site of the church was near Crescent Bay, south of the Captain Angus home. It was moved on the hillside overlooking the Old Mission House in 1901 by Edward Salmon. In 1915, the interior of the church was decorated with cedar and birch bark. Until the church was wrecked by a heavy wind on May 12, 1943, the original stove and bell were still in use. After the demolition, the old organ was moved to the Mission House.

5. Ashland *Daily Press,* August 8, 1945.
6. Arthur Gunderson, "Frontier Bishop," Duluth *News-Tribune,* April 13, 1941.
7. *Ibid.*
8. *Ibid.*
9. Verwyst, *Bishop Baraga,* p. 113.
10. *Ibid.,* pp. 114-171.
11. *Ibid.,* p. 174.
12. *Ibid.,* p. 177.
13. *Ibid.,* p. 181.
14. *Ibid.,* pp. 186-187.
15. *Ibid.,* pp. 189-190.
16. "Father Baraga May Be Beatified," Duluth *News-Tribune,* August 28, 1938.
17. Verwyst, *op. cit.,* p. 196. Later, when Mrs. Lacomb married Mr. A. Corbin, she received a particle of the true Cross from Father Baraga. This relic is now kept with reverential care in the church at Lac Courte Oreilles.
18. Vincent Roy was one of the most widely known and highly respected Indians of the Head of the Lakes in pioneer days. His father was a French Canadian; his mother a Chippewa. Vincent followed the traders, serving in various capacities, and he eagerly sought every opportunity to secure an education. He was always reliable and trustworthy. He established a line of trading posts at points along the international border, extending as far west as Lake of the Woods. Then he opened a general store in Superior. His business ability made him an outstanding figure in the area. He is said to have been "better than most white men—reliable, intelligent, and cheerful." Duluth *News-Tribune,* January 21, 1945.
19. Verwyst, *op. cit.,* pp. 203-04.
20. Well-meaning persons have made an error as to the builder of the church at La Pointe. In the book *The Catholic Church in Wisconsin* (1895-1898), p. 268, there is a picture of St. Joseph's Church at La Pointe, Madeline Island, with this caption: "This is the oldest church in Wisconsin; originally built by Father Marquette, about 1666; rebuilt by Rev. Frederic Baraga, 1835. It contains many precious relics of old paintings to the present day."
21. Verwyst, *op. cit.,* p. 204.
22. *Ibid.,* pp. 206-09.
23. Gunderson, "Frontier Bishop," Duluth *News-Tribune,* April 13, 1941. This event is commemorated by a 12-foot granite cross erected by the combined efforts of the historical societies of Cook, Lake, St. Louis and Douglas Counties together with those of Bishop Welch, the clergy, and several societies of the Duluth Catholic Church Diocese.

24. Rt. Rev. John Zaplotnik, O.S.F.T., "Father Otto Skolla, O.F.M., Indian Missionary," *Franciscan Herald and Forum,* XIX (1940), 653-54.

25. Bischop Baraga died at the age of 70 years on January 19, 1868. His ceaseless activity has been described as "sanctity in action." Duluth *News-Tribune,* April 13, 1941.

26. Verwyst, "Brief Sketch of the Indian Missions of Lake Superior Region: La Pointe Mission," MS, Provincial Archives, St. Louis, p. 15.

27. *Indians at Work,* II (December, 1934), 2.

28. *Ibid.,* VII ((September, 1939), 9.

CHAPTER 11

1. Charles Kappler, *Indian Affairs. Laws and Treaties.* Washington: Government Printing Office, 1904. Volume II lists the total number of treaties between the Indians and the United States government as 367, the Chippewa participating in 44. See an account of this compilation in "389 Old Indian Treaties and 4,267 Laws Compiled Recently After Years of Need," *Indians at Work,* VII (June, 1940), 6-7.

2. James M. Scott, "Kish-ke-tuh-wug and the Treaty of 1795," WPA Historical Records, Odanah, Folder 1, Item No. 34.

3. Consult Kappler, *op. cit.,* for such promises in the various treaties of the United States with the Indians.

4. *Congressional Record,* LXXXVII, Part 10, A33-34.

5. Prairie du Chien was neutral ground and thousands of redskins from within a radius of 300 miles came to barter their furs and pelts with the traders. White men had been encroaching upon Indian territory and adventurers were particularly menacing the Winnebago country through which most of them passed. Many white people held the "naked Indians" in great contempt and these usually encroached upon the Indian rights in the lead mines of Wisconsin.

6. Neill, *op. cit.,* pp. 467-70. The graphic description of this meeting was drawn from the manuscript "Collections of Frank Setter," Lac Courte Oreilles Reservation, Stone Lake, Wisconsin.

7. *Ibid.*

8. Taggart Brown, "Wisconsin Indian Land Cessions," *Wisconsin Archeologist,* XVI (September, 1936), 53-54.

9. Bartlett, *op. cit.,* pp. 67-68.

10. *Ibid.,* p. 68.

11. *Ibid.,* pp. 119-120.

12. *Ibid.,* pp. 69-70.

13. *Ibid.,* pp. 70, *passim.*

14. *Ibid.,* pp. 80-81. Chief Nay-gon-ab-nay survived the 1854 treaty by eleven years. In the autumn of 1855, the chief was hunting in the vicinity of Prairie Farm with a party of 50 Chippewa. Suddenly they were attacked by more than 100 Sioux who had come from Wabasha, Minnesota, to avenge the killing of a Sioux party two years before at Battle Island, south of Durand, Wisconsin. Chief Nay-gon-ab-nay, past 60, carrying a heavy pack, was the first to be killed when the Sioux war whoop sounded. His picture is in the museum at Madison. *Ibid.,* 64-65.

15. Neill, *op. cit.,* p. 502.

CHAPTER 12

1. Shirley McKinsey, "An Economic Survey of the Bad River Indian Reservation," (typewritten) Ashland, Wisconsin, 1938, p. 1.
2. Jesse C. Cavill, "Report of Great Lakes Indian Agency," (typewritten), Ashland, Wisconsin, March 20, 1944, p. 1.
3. Verwyst, "A Glossary of Chippewa Names," *op. cit.,* IV (1916), 255.
4. John J. Teeple, "Rivers of the Bad River Reservation," WPA Historical Records, Odanah, Folder 1, Item No. 33.
5. In 1852, the discovery of an antique silver crucifix which had been buried in the garden of an old Indian woman offered confirmatory evidence of such visits. The finding of this crucifix occasioned considerable excitement among the Indians. Perhaps the crucifix had been lost by Jesuit missionaries while at Bad River. It is equally plausible, however, that the crucifix was a gift of the missionaries to some Indian chief who had the treasure buried with him upon his death. Warren, *op. cit.,* p. 117.
6. "Beloit College to Preserve Historic Old Mission Property," Superior *Evening Telegram,* July 21, 1941.
7. Franciscan Clerics, "Franciscan Missions Among Indians of Wisconsin Mission Groups: Bad River Reservation," *Franciscan Herald,* XXIII (1935), 539-40.
8. Verwyst, *Bishop Baraga,* p. 322.
9. Bertrand Mitchell, O.F.M., "St. Mary's Church, Odanah," Milwaukee *Catholic Herald Citizen,* March 6, 1954.
10. Franciscan Clerics, "Father John Gafron," *op. cit.,* XXIV (1936), 156. Although Father John Gafron's principal mission was Bad River, he also cared for the Indians in surrounding areas. During winter months, when the lakes and rivers were frozen but not yet covered with snow, the trips were easy and even pleasant. The dog teams drew the missionary's sled swiftly across the glassy surface. Unfortunately this weather condition did not continue for long. Soon the whole country was wrapped in snow. Then it was not only toilsome, but even dangerous to make these journeys. Shod with snow shoes and accompanied by a sturdy Indian guide, Father John braved sickness and death in his apostolic zeal to minister to the needs of his red children. During spring rains, the trips were equally dangerous and more fatiguing since the lakes were unfit for sled or boat. During one of these trips, Father John traveled in a steady downpour of rain which drenched him through and through. The missionary contracted a severe cold which necessitated his removal to a more suitable climate. But the little friar returned to the Indians. He came back to Ashland, Wisconsin, in 1897 and died there. His funeral was the grandest that the town had ever witnessed. To the Indians, the memory of the evenings spent around the fire stretched like a golden cord between the past and the present. *Ibid.,* 156-57.
11. Verwyst, "Reminiscences of an Indian Missionary," *Franciscan Herald,* XV (1927), 392-93.
12. A lifelong interest in Indians and their spiritual and economic uplifting lies behind the career of Reverend Browne. He is the seventh generation of his family in the clergy to serve the Indians.
13. Attendance records of St. Mary Indian School, Odanah, Wisconsin. Soon two classrooms were added to the original St. Mary School. In 1889, the old Presby-

terian Mission was purchased by the Catholic Mission to furnish accommodations for the ever increasing number of school children. Further additions were later made to the school buildings until they resembled a "patch upon a patch." Due to the wear and tear of time, these buildings finally became unsuitable for school use. In 1941, a new St. Mary School building was begun. It was completed the following year. The two-story brick structure has a frontage of 102 feet, with the main structure extending 78 feet back, with an additional 35 feet for gymnasium purposes. See the account "New Building at St. Mary's Indian School Marks Big Step from Early Log Cabin Start," in Superior *Evening Telegram,* August 23, 1941.

14. Records of St. Mary's Indian School, Odanah, 1909. Visit on September 24, 1909.
15. Letter of Jesse Cavill to Odanah Parents. December 10, 1937. Mention was made by Mr. Cavill of the fine attendance at St. Mary School. As noted previously, when St. Mary's opened its doors, or door, one of its greatest problems was to keep the Chippewa in school, a nation-wide problem in Indian schools. At certain seasons, unless preventive measures were taken, the "call of the wild" was heeded. The "sugar bush" season generally caused an exodus of a dozen or more pupils. To forestall this, it was ascertained who intended to go and a friendly chat with the parents sometimes prevented absences. If this proved unsuccessful, a warning that pupils would forfeit promotion by their absence, sometimes secured results. When Gladys Cloud completed the eighth grade in St. Mary School, she had missed only one day in eight years. See "160 Rural Children Graduated," Ashland *Daily Press,* May 21, 1941.
16. "The Chippewa in St. Mary's School," *Ibid.,* February 1, 1946.
17. More than a quarter of a century of devoted service has been given to St. Mary's School by each of the following Sisters: Sister Macaria Murphy, 46 years, Sister Eustella Olbertz, 45, Sister Chrysostoma Dorweiler, 43, Sister Catherine Buckley, 38, Sister Clarissima, 28, and Sister Heriberta still working (1956), 47 years.
18. Log houses were built on the reservation in the 1880's. In 1953, but two of these remained—the home of Mrs. Florina Denomie near St. Mary's School and the one occupied by Mike Couture across the Kakagon River.
19. McKinsey, "Report: Living Conditions on Bad River Reservation," 1938, p. 30.
20. Cavill, "Report," 1944, p. 6.
21. *Ibid.*
22. *United States Statutes at Large,* Washington: Government Printing Office, 1953, LXVII, 588-590.
23. Cavill, "Report," 1944, p. 9.
24. *Ibid.* See also "Indians in Boats Harvesting Rice," Milwaukee *Journal,* August 30, 1953.
25. Verwyst, *Bishop Baraga,* p. 211.
26. McKinsey, "Typical Types of Farm Organization," MS Survey, p. 25.
27. The industry and versatility of the four brothers, John, Alex, George, and Dan was responsible for much of their success. John, quiet and soft-spoken, explained that when they started they knew nothing about bees. They liked the work and learned as they went along.
28. See report of the Land Field Agent "Indian Bee Keepers at Bad River Reservation," *Indians at Work,* IV (January 1, 1937), 31.
29. "Our Red Clay for Pottery," Ashland *Daily Press,* March 19, 1940.

30. "Odanah 4-H Club," *ibid.,* May 5, 1939.
31. The Odanah Boy Scouts were the featured attraction of the Superior Boy Scout Circus held at the State Teachers' College, Superior, in 1946. Dressed in their Indian costume they participated in three dances and in the evening parade. According to the scoutmaster, Patrick Clement, they carried off all the honors and were the most popular participants in the show. A trophy of appreciation was presented to Mr. Clement by the Douglas County scoutmasters. See "Odanah Scouts at Superior," *ibid.,* May 17, 1946.
32. "Recreational Program Launched at Odanah," Superior *Evening Telegram,* December 2, 1936.
33. "Celebration at Odanah," *ibid.,* July 1, 1938.
34. Ashland *Daily Press,* July 5, 1938. Mr. Smart is well-known both in the Chequamegon area and in Florida for his extensive work in pageantry. He attended Northland College and graduated from St. Paul College where he was prominent in athletics and served in the capacity of athletic coach. During the pageant, his interpretation of an aged Indian chief meeting a government agent, was one of the highlights. In 1937, two of the pageant dancers, John Smart and Wallace Mayotte, toured a number of the middle western states performing the hoop dance.
35. "Tom-toms Forgotten by Odanah Group," Superior *Evening Telegram,* July 25, 1939.
36. "Massed Indian Band Fete Set," Ashland *Daily Press,* December 7, 1938.
37. "Tribute Paid by Centurama Official," *ibid.,* August 15, 1946. These Indians made their appearance in Green Bay, Milwaukee, Chicago, Detroit, Cleveland, South Bend, Evanston, Boston, New York, Philadelphia, and cities in the south. They performed in theaters and colleges, and before social gatherings, gave educational lectures on Indian costumes, and displayed valuable exhibits.
38. "Chippewa Dancers in Chicago," *ibid.,* August 16, 1951. The invitation to this outstanding event was due to the adoption of Colonel Robert McCormick, editor of the Chicago *Daily Tribune,* into the Chippewa tribe a few months previously. The title "Me-Gee-See," "Eagle," was given to Colonel McCormick by Chief Me-Gee-See, hereditary head of the Chippewa nation. Incidentally, the Chicago *Tribune* fought for the rights of the American Indians almost one hundred years ago.

    Chief Antoine Starr and family and the Vincent Bender family with their four gifted children remained another day in Chicago to appear on the Russ Davis Television Show.

    At the Chicago festival, white persons who had rendered outstanding services to the Chippewa on the Bad River Reservation, received special decorations. Sister M. Francetta, F.S.P.A., superior at the Odanah mission school, was given a head band and the rank of "Friend and Helper of Indian Children." Mr. John B. Chapple, editor of the Ashland *Daily Press* was given one head band and rank of "Friend Who Has Signally Honored Us," and a second band and rank of "One Who is Greatly Honored by Us All."

CHAPTER 13

1. Cavill, "Great Lakes Indian Agency Survey," 1943, p. 1.
2. Warren, *op. cit.,* p. 193.

3. *Ibid.*, p. 191. That the settlement was originally the home of Mound Builders is evident from the mounds on the reservation. Two medium-sized oval mounds are near Reserve, the principal town on the reservation.

4. *Ibid.*, pp. 324-35.

5. In 1894, Mr. Wright, a Protestant missionary, again made an unsuccessful attempt to Christianize the Lac Courte Oreilles Indians.

6. It is not certain that Father Chebul read Mass on his visitations. Father Chrysostom Verwyst, then a secular priest, is usually credited with the honor of celebrating the first Mass at Lac Courte Oreilles in 1878.

7. Mr. Corbin made full amends for the "wife-beating" incident.

8. Franciscan Clerics, "Franciscan Missions: Lac Courte Oreilles," *op. cit.*, XXIII (1935), 564.

9. *Ibid.*, p. 565.

10. Cavill, "Report," 1943, p. 12.

11. Franciscan Clerics, *op. cit.*, p. 565.

12. Superior *Evening Telegram*, December 24, 1937.

13. Cavill, "Report," 1943, p. 6.

14. J. H. Mitchell, "Pipe Stone Quarry-Restoring an Ancient Indian Shrine," *Indians at Work*, II (December 1, 1934), 25-27.

15. Ashland *Daily Press*, April 2, 1951. That the art of dancing is not a lost accomplishment on the Lac Courte Oreilles Reservation is evidenced from the performance of 95 year-old John Frogg. In 1951, on the occasion of the adoption of Colonel McCormick of Chicago into the Chippewa tribe, Mr. Frogg's dancing was one of the outstanding entertainments at Ashland, Wisconsin. During the early days of the resort area, Mr. Frogg originated the first Indian pageant held in the area. His son, Sam, continues to uphold Indian lore and the traditions of the Chippewa; likewise, his son, Alvin, is a worthy successor of his grandfather.

16. Superior *Evening Telegram*, October 29, 1937.

CHAPTER 14

1. Cavill, "Economic Survey of Chippewa Reservation," 1942, p. 1.

2. Warren, *op. cit.*, p. 192.

3. Cavill, "Economic Survey," 1942, p. 3.

4. *Ibid.*, 1943.

5. Verwyst, "Reminiscences of An Indian Missionary," *op. cit.*, XVI (1928), 58.

6. Letter of Rev. Charles Goldsmith cited in J. A. Anderson, *Goldsmith, Late Pastor of Notre Dame*, Chippewa Falls, 1895, p. 324.

7. Verwyst, "Indian Missions; Flambeau Farm," MS Provincial Archives, St. Louis, pp. 65-66.

8. Franciscan Clerics, "Franciscan Missions: Lac du Flambeau," *op. cit.*, XXIII (1935), 565.

9. J. H. Mitchell, "Field Day at Lac du Flambeau IECW Camp," *Indians at Work*, II (August, 1934), 30-32.

10. Superior *Evening Telegram*, July 30, 1937.

11. P. D. Southworth, "Recreation at Lac du Flambeau," *Indians at Work*, II (August, 1935), 41.

12. Albert Huber, "Meeting at Lac du Flambeau," *ibid.*, IV (October, 1936), 26-27.

13. Benjamin Gauthier, "Rustic Furniture," *ibid.,* III (April, 1936), 37.
14. "Lac du Flambeau," *Handbook of Wisconsin Indians,* Madison: Governor's Commission on Human Rights, 1952, pp. 18-19.
15. Milwaukee *Journal,* March 12, 1953.
16. Robert Trier, "The Pokegama Bridge," *Indians at Work,* VI (December, 1938), 19. The designer never saw the completed bridge, for he became ill and died before the bridge was completed. His last words to Trier, Highway Engineer, were: "I hope I don't miss my chance to do the plans for the Bad River Bridge." Chief Drumbeater recalled that during Indian occupancy of this untouched wilderness, a canoe battle between the Chippewa and Sioux Indians had taken place at this site.
17. "Lac du Flambeau Chippewa Build Summer Colony," *ibid.,* V (August, 1938), 30.
18. "For Summer Travelers in Northern Wisconsin," *ibid.,* VIII (May, 1941), 18-19.
19. One of these guides, John H. St. Germaine, had an unusual experience on July 6, 1940. With St. Germaine as guide, three prominent men from Illinois, Arthur B. O'Brien, secretary to the late Governor Henry Horner, John H. Hallihan, director of the Illinois Department of Education, and Martin J. O'Brien, Cook County Public Administrator, were in a motor boat on Crawling Stone Lake. Suddenly a squall arose and the boat sank at a point one-half mile from shore. However, St. Germaine succeeded in towing each of the three men to shore. Arthur O'Brien died shortly after the rescue from a heart attack. The two rescued officials showed their gratitude by giving St. Germaine a scholarship to the University of Wisconsin—a life-long wish of the Indian. Ashland *Daily Press,* July 12, 1941. Germaine's heroism was also rewarded with a bronze medal from the Carnegie Hero Fund Commission. See "Indian Hero Wins Medal and Scholarship," *Indian Leader,* XLIV (April, 1941), 3.

    At a meeting with Mr. J. Cavill at Lac du Flambeau, the author was informed that two of St. Germaine's brothers, Benedict and Fred, are graduates of Haskell Institute, Lawrence, Kansas. The father, now dead, was a graduate of Yale and a prominent attorney. It was said of him that at a meeting held to improve Chippewa conditions, a certain Indian opposed the proposed reform. In disgust the attorney exclaimed: "You are an Indian who wears a moccasin on one foot and a shoe on the other." Meeting on "School Programs" August, 1941.

CHAPTER 15

1. A great-granddaughter of Chief Buffalo, Mrs. George Duffy, lives at Red Cliff. Five of her sons were in service of their country in 1952. One of them had paid the supreme sacrifice. Mrs. Duffy, pleasingly youthful in appearance, is a charming hostess and a worthy descendant of the illustrious Buffalo.
2. Cavill, "Indian Agency Survey," 1942, p. 1.
3. Ashland *Daily Press,* August 8, 1945.
4. Cavill, "Survey" 1942, p. 1.
5. Verwyst, "Reminiscences of an Indian Missionary," *op. cit.,* pp. 345-46. Before he had mastered the Chippewa language, Father Chrysostom employed Joseph

Gordon (Gaudin has been anglicized to "Gordon") as his interpreter. Gordon helped the missionary to read the Gospel in Chippewa and to make his church announcements. During the sermon, Gordon, his black hair shining with grease, stood a short distance from the pulpit and repeated the missionary's words.

The necessity of an interpreter is evident from the following incident which happened during Father Chrysostom's absence from the mission. His house-keeper, Miss Annie Bird, an elderly white woman, requested Angelique Gordon, Joseph's twin sister, to stay with her during the missionary's absence. During a conversation one evening, Angelique who had a limited command of English, innocently told Miss Bird that her folks had caught a "girl" (squirrel) and that they had killed "her" and she had tasted so good! Miss Bird, thinking she was in the midst of a race of cannibals, became extremely excited. In her terror, she said: "You would not eat me, Angelique, would you?" Angelique, noticing the agitation of Miss Bird, replied, "I go home." But Miss Bird was alarmed at the prospect of remaining alone and, in spite of her fears, she prevailed upon Angelique to remain.

6. Ashland *Daily Press,* July 17, 1953.
7. Oscar Rascher, O.F.M., "The Evergreen and the Mission," *Franciscan Herald,* XXIII (1935), 318.
8. Franciscan Clerics, "Franciscan Missions: Red Cliff and Buffalo Bay," *op. cit.,* XXIII (1935), 566.
9. *Ibid.*
10. "54 Years at Red Cliff, Sister Victoria's Record of Service," Ashland *Daily Press,* October 16, 1944. Sister Victoria is one of the best informed persons alive today regarding the famous Chicago fire of 1871. Ida Steidl (now Sister Victoria) lived but two doors from Mrs. O'Leary, whose cow, according to legend, kicked over the lantern that set Chicago ablaze. But Sister Victoria affirms that it was the O'Leary boys smoking behind the barn who caused the trouble for which the cow received the blame. Sister Victoria, although but three years of age at the time, remembers vividly that her father and older brother came speeding home with a horse and wagon—just in time to help the family escape from the flames. That the children set fire to the barn was a generally held belief in the neighborhood at the time. Later someone started the cow legend which seemed a more romantic explanation for the fire.
11. *Indians at Work,* III (May, 1936), 46.
12. *Ibid.,* IV (November, 1936), 39.
13. *Ibid.,* IV (December, 1936), 16.
14. Cavill, "Survey," 1942, p. 4.

CHAPTER 16

1. Cavill, "Mole Lake or Sakaogon Reservation," Report of Great Lakes Indian Agency, 1944, p. 1.
2. Charles Rhoads, "Tribal Enrollment," *Annual Report* of the Commissioner of Indian Affairs to the Secretary of the Interior, for the Fiscal Year Ended June 30, 1931, p. 33.
3. Since Mole, Pelican, and Post Lakes are in close proximity, the Indians living in that area are interchangeably called Mole, Pelican, or Post Lake Indians. Antigo *Daily Journal,* January 9, 1935.

4. Ki-chi-waw-be-sha-shi is buried on the north bank of the Wolf River at its outlet, Post Lake. In the middle of the lake, the "Narrows," a tree or shrub which resembles a post, was held sacred by the Chippewas. According to Chippewa lore, Post Lake was the site of one of the largest Indian settlements in that area. There is also archeological evidence that this region was once a large Indian settlement, even in prehistoric times. Charles E. Brown, former curator of the Wisconsin State Historical Society Museum, found quartz arrow chips on a field south of the Narrows bridge and also fragments of Indian pottery.

5. Shortly before his death, Mee-gee-see gave the map and a medal given him by the commissioner, to his son, Wau-bi-ski-ba-nase.

In 1953, Williard Ackley, "Ga-bay-is-gon," or "Walk Around the World," a grandson of Chief Mee-gee-see, slowly raising his eyes from the top of Spirit Hill where the north wind was moaning through the tree tops and the branches were writhing as if in agony, sadly remarked:

The spirit of Gitche Mee-gee-see is troubled. Another winter is on its way. One hundred years have passed since the treaty. The white man's promises are still unfilled. Yet they have grown wealthy on the lands of our birthright while we are left with only a medal to gnaw on. There is no nourishment in the silver coin.

The Chief had finally traced the precious piece of paper. After a jubilant journey to Duluth where he engaged the aid of four lawyers, Chief Ackley went back home to await results. Finally the government purchased a segment of land for these Indians. But, according to the Chief, it was too late to prevent the desecration of their burial mounds or the exploitation of their timber.

The Sakaogons are not interested in gaining ownership of the land originally promised to them. They hope to obtain a financial settlement for the missing timber which will enable them to finance a reservation project to expedite their self-sufficiency. Olive Glasgow, "Chief Carries on Long Campaign for Property of Lost Chippewa," Green Bay *Press Gazette,* December 28, 1953.

6. Charles Ackley linked present day Antigo with its prehistoric past. Antigo *Daily Journal,* April 1, 1947.

7. *Ibid.,* February 27, 1952. Charles Ackley worked on logging drives at the early age of fifteen years. He recalled one log jam at the Eau Claire River that extended from three to four miles up river. To break the jam, an immense head of water was accumulated at a dam upstream. When the jam broke, the logs surged forward with such force that they spilled over the banks and knocked down trees.

Two or three canoes were always kept at the Ackley cabin for use on the Eau Claire River. For trips to Wausau, oxen were hired or the trip was made on foot. Supplies brought from Wausau were loaded into canoes and sent up river to their destination.

The first logs on Ackley's camp were floated down to the Kelly mill. Later, some were drifted to Schofield by way of the Eau Claire and Wisconsin Rivers. Oxen pulled travois loaded with logs from Stevens Point. Later horses were used. But logging was not profitable. Prices paid for pine were so low that sales yielded little more than enough to pay for supplies.

8. Letter of Grace S. Ross to Sister M. Macaria, Odanah, June 2, 1937.

9. *Ibid.* In 1883, Mr. and Mrs. Samuel Shaw and two daughters arrived at what

is now Crandon, Wisconsin. After selecting a home for his family, Mr. Crandon returned to Madison, Wisconsin, to complete his year's contract with the school board, having served as city superintendent of schools for eleven years. Mr. Shaw was instrumental in organizing Forest County which had been a part of Langlade and Oconto Counties. At the time, he founded Crandon as the county seat, also naming it. Forest County was named by Mrs. Shaw, the first white woman in the county and the first county superintendent of schools.

10. *Indians at Work,* VI (December, 1938), 3.
11. Cavill, "Report," p. 3.
12. *Ibid.*

CHAPTER 17

1. Superior *Evening Telegram,* June 8, 1937.
2. Ellen Bannister, "A Lost Tribe is Restored," *Indians at Work,* VII (June, 1939), 38.
3. Superior *Evening Telegram,* December 10, 1937.
4. While gathering data for the government, Mr. Smart gleaned much information regarding Chief Buck or Chief Ya Banse. Chief Buck was a notable character in this area. He was recognized by his people as an able warrior, a courageous, shrewd, cunning, and aggressive leader, having exceptional oratorical ability. His life's interests centered around those of his people. He was leader in the massacre of the Sioux in the vicinity of present day Solon Springs. His descendants describe him as follows: Chief Ya Banse was five feet, eight to ten inches tall; weighed about 180 pounds; wore his hair shoulder length; and always wore a band of cloth around his head, usually a large black silk handkerchief. Due to an injury received in his younger days, he walked with a slight limp. His complexion was very dark. A special chart showing the genealogy of this Indian chief is now a part of government records. The present descendants are five generations removed from the chief. *Ibid.*
5. Frank Smart, "Chief Ya Banse and the Lost Tribe," WPA Historical Records, Odanah, Folder 1, Item No. 29.
6. Chief Little Pipe, or "Cut Lip" as he was nicknamed, was a colorful character in the area. "Cut Lip" had an inch-wide scar which he had received in his youth as the result of a disagreement with a logging foreman. He had many friends among the Cumberland people and often borrowed money from them. His word was as good as his bond. He paid the loan when he could. But he might return the next day to borrow more money.

"Cut Lip's" regard and courtesy for the white man is shown by the following story. One day, he called on the Hodgkin family and asked to see the baby. This was the first white child born on the island and was called by the Indians "Lily of the Woods." When Mrs. Hodgkin gave "Cut Lip" the child, she noticed that the chief fumbled with the baby's feet. A few days later, the chief returned with a pair of quaint beaded moccasins that were a perfect fit. He had measured the baby's feet with his hand.

"Cut Lip" lived to an advanced age, but his death was a sad one. According to legend, he and his wife had been to town. On their homeward trip in their canoe, they had a disagreement which ended in blows, causing the canoe to overturn. The squaw, although an old woman, swam to shore. "Cut Lip" was drowned. A picture of the old Chief hangs in the Cumberland library. The portrait was painted by Mrs. Foote, a daughter of Dr. Pease. *Evening Telegram,* June 8, 1937.

7. *Ibid.*

8. Cavill, "Agency Report: St. Croix Reservation," 1944, p. 2. See also Duluth *News-Tribune,* August 17, 1938, for the following interesting account: John Matrious was a typical member of the "Lost Tribe." Matrious lived in a house in Minnesota built on land which he did not own. However, he received his mail at Danbury, Wisconsin. He also bought his food there. For more than thirty years, John Matrious, his three married sons, and other Chippewa lived as "squatters." Their tar-paper shacks consisting of one or two rooms were in need of paint and flooring. These Chippewa raised a few potatoes, some vegetables, and a little corn. With an old-age pension of $18 a month, Matrious supported himself, his wife, a young daughter, and two orphaned grandchildren. When questioned if he ever visited Duluth, old Matrious replied in conversational English, "I come to Duluth maybe once a year."

CHAPTER 18

1. Oscar Lipps, "Retrospect and Prognosis," *The Indian Leader,* XXXVII (January 12, 1934), 5.

2. White Cloud, Kansas, *Globe Tribune,* May 26, 1939.

3. Willard Beatty, "The Overstuffed Chair," *Indian Education,* XXXIV (1939), 1-2. It is an open question whether the Indian needed an upholstered chair. But the point is that he developed a desire and reorganized his own life so that he satisfied that desire by his own efforts. The acquisition of the chair, the clothes, the food, the house, or whatever the Indian needs is of less importance than the training given the individual with regard to the satisfaction of his needs. *Ibid.*

4. Florina Denomie, "The Chippewa Indian Was Always Self-Supporting," WPA Historical Records, Odanah, Folder 8, Item No. 1.

5. Charles Carter, "Indian Laziness," *Indian Leader,* XXXVIII, May 1, 1935.

6. A. C. Cooley, "Extension Work Among the Indians," *Indians at Work,* XIII (May-June, 1945), 2-3.

7. "Recent Legislation," *ibid.,* III (September 15, 1935), 41.

8. William Obern, "Lumbering Among the Chippewa," WPA Historical Records, Folder 8, Item No. 43.

9. Emmet Riley, "Placement and Relocation Program for the Indians of Northern Wisconsin," Great Lakes Indian Agency Report, July 16, 1953.

10. *Ibid.*

11. Ashland *Daily Press,* July, 1952. The men who moved to Manitowoc are employed in the Manitowoc Shipbuilding Company of that city. On May 9, these men all took part in the launching of the steamer, John J. Boland, the second largest boat ever built for Great Lakes traffic. It was built at a cost of nearly $8,000,000, requiring more than a year for its construction. Riley, "Report," July 16, 1953.

12. *Congressional Record,* LXXXIX, Part II, 2100.

13. *Ibid.,* p. 2099.

CHAPTER 19

1. Willard Beatty, "What to Teach? How to Measure Success?" *Indian Education,* XV (September 15, 1937), 3.
2. *Indians at Work,* II (January 1, 1934), 9.
3. *Ibid.,* VIII (April, 1941), 31. One Indian CCC worker, a 65 year old man, took the test receiving a rating which made him eligible for the seventh grade. In his earlier schooling, this Indian had only completed third grade. His goal then became to win an eighth grade diploma through further study. *Ibid.,* VII (1940), 33.
4. Dr. Arthur Grace, "An Experience in Testing Indian Children," *ibid.,* IX (November, 1941), 3.
5. *Ibid.,* pp. 3-4.
6. *Ibid.,* p. 1.
7. *Ibid.,* p. 4.
8. Juanita Bell, "Little Indian Speaks," *Indian Education,* X (1946), 137. Mrs. J. Bell died June 11, 1946 in Phoenix, Arizona. Her husband, Christopher G. Bell, is an accountant and auditor in the Indian Service.

CHAPTER 20

1. *Handbook of Wisconsin Indians,* p. 41.
2. Milwaukee *Journal,* October 21, 1923.
3. Ashland *Daily Press,* April 24, 27, 1930.
4. Dr. Sincock's Indian name was "Wa-say-gaw-ne-be," meaning "Shining White Feather." At the time of his adoption into the Chippewa tribe in 1920, Dr. Sincock was given a full medical outfit. The feather of a white eagle graced the headgear. This was an unusual honor since previous to that time, only six other white men had received this unusual symbol. Letter of Dr. Henry Sincock to Sister M. Carolissa, October 25, 1954.
5. In 1936, three public health nurses, financed by the State Board of Health, were working among all the Wisconsin Indians. Unfortunately some of the nurses did not understand the Indian and even mis-represented conditions on the reservations. These nurses reported that the Indian would rather own a dog than a cow and live in a makeshift tent than in a new frame house. They charged that more than once a government built house had stood unoccupied while the owner and his family, by preference, lived in a nearby tent that boasted not even a floor. The Indians' love for gypsying probably increased his reluctance to burden himself with a cow, with the result that young children had little or no fresh milk to maintain their health. Seasonal occupations and mere whims combined to make the Indians indifferent to civilized ways and made the Indian nurse's routine a hectic one. Ashland *Daily Press,* April 10, 1939.

   These charges raised a number of protests from the Indians. John Soulier, spokesman for the Red Cliff Indians, wrote thus: "We of the Red Cliff band of Chippewa Indians read with much interest the article under the caption that some INDIANS PREFER WIGWAMS TO WELL-BUILT HOMES.

   It is indeed pathetic to try and stress upon the reading public such rot. The reports would have our well-wisher believe the exaggerated narratives as contained in your article of April 10.

My memory reaches back a half century, and we have long been naturalized. To this day, many of us have never seen a wigwam or whatever our ancestors may have had for their abodes.

In regard to keeping a dog rather than a cow, it's a known fact that it is only a minority of my race that become farmers. The average Indian would rather work at other trades and labor than on a farm, as for keeping a dog, I see no disgrace in owning one.

Are not our White Brethren endowed with whims and fancies? And why should my people be different for possessing said whims to cause our Nurses' routine to be a hectic one? I might state emphatically that the routine of our Nurse is NOT a hectic one, because she is seldom seen on our reservation.

Gypsying in this community has never existed, though when the annual harvest is on and the relief is cut off, they move to the plains for their livelihood. . . . We are not a perfect people, but we do try to manage the best we know how." Ashland *Daily Press,* April 14, 1939.

Referring to the Nurses' report, Mary Jane Livingston, from the Bad River Reservation, wrote in part:

I grant that dogs are many and cows are few. But must we Indians be ridiculed because of this deficient population of bovine friends, which, incidentally, is no fault of ours? Has this so-called trio of silent workers ever given serious consideration to the fact that bovines cost money? How then are these unfortunate Indians expected to own cows for the milk they can give, when money is an item as scarce as the whiskers on a sucker's head? Possibly this so-called trio of silent workers have been active in formulating benevolent plans, but in all probability they have been pipe dreaming and therefore expect poor Indians to perform the miraculous feat of pulling the cow out of the proverbial plugged hat. . . .

Regarding our preference for floorless tepees to that of new frame houses, I can only say that it is downright false. True, a large portion of Indian homes are ruined and dilapidated, but that is no grounds for assuming that our homes are floorless. As a member of the Bad River Tribe of Chippewa Indians, I vigorously repudiate such a statement, and openly challenge the authoresses to bring forth proof and cite a single instance in which the Bad River Indians out of the 13,000 Indians of Wisconsin prefer the humble shelter of the floorless tepee to that of newly-constructed government frame houses. If such proof cannot be given, then I demand a sincere apology for the insidious, prejudiced reference to the Wisconsin Indians. *Ibid.,* April 15, 1939.

6. Bad River Reservation Health Records, Odanah, 1939.

7. *Handbook of Wisconsin Indians,* p. 64.

8. "Health Conditions on the Lac du Flambeau Indian Reservation," Letter of Dr. Edward Seaforth to Sister M. Carolissa, July 28, 1952.

9. Special mention is due to Miss Margaret Gebhardt, a state nurse. Her unselfishness, self-sacrifice, and devotedness are exemplary. An official report stated that in two months, in addition to her assistance at health centers and clinics, Miss Gebhardt had made 180 field visits, and given 14 talks and lectures. Her field visits were not mere inspection trips to see how the Indians were living. On her visits, she did not hesitate to do work that would cause many a person to shrink from in disgust.

10. *Handbook of Wisconsin Indians,* pp. 41, 49-50.

CHAPTER 21

1. William Obern, "Fur Trade and Liquor," WPA Historical Records, Odanah, Folder 4, Item No. 4.
2. Superior *Evening Telegram*, January 1, 1945. Ruth Underhill has well characterized the effect of this discrimination. "Give a dog a bad name and hang him," is an ancient proverb based on true psychology. Social scientists of today would word it: "Give a whole group an inferior position and it is very hard for any individual to overcome it." *Indian Education*, VIII (November 1, 1944), 2.
3. Ashland *Daily Press*, May 13, 1946.
4. *Indians at Work*, IX (March, 1942), 23-24.
5. *United States Statutes at Large*, LXVII, 586-87.

CHAPTER 22

1. Wayne Morse, "Crime Prevention Among Indians," *Indians at Work*, IV (July 15, 1937), 16-26.
2. Ashland *Daily Press*, August 3, 1939, gives this interesting data. Sometimes these court cases of Indians taken into custody assumed a humorous turn. Fifty-year old Joe Sky of Odanah was weaving an intricate pattern on Highway 53 one evening. The deputy sheriff happened along and took the protesting Indian to Ashland. Joe had been brought before Judge Parker on a similar charge the week before and had confessed that this was the first time that he had been drunk in "50 years," and that it wouldn't happen again for another 50 years. When he appeared before Judge Parker a second time, the judge intimated that a workfarm sentence might be in order. The Indian, bobbing in nervous fright, asked for leniency. Finally, the judge dismissed Joe with a warning. Tearfully grateful, Joe replied: "No happen no more, Judge!" But this time, he did not repeat his promise not to get drunk again "for 50 more years."
3. Letter of Charles Picard, President of Keweenaw Bay Tribal Council, L'Anse, Michigan, to Sister Carolissa, February 17, 1956, containing statement of the case by Francis Kotila, Baraga County Clerk. Spruce appeared before a local justice three times, but each time, no one appeared against him. Citing his rights as an Indian, he told tribesmen he would like to prosecute the mysterious officers since they had violated a Federal law prohibiting the sale or giving of liquor to Indians. A tribal spokesman, withholding his identity for fear of what he termed "persecution," charged the tricked arrests were only a continuation of the practice of "getting" the Indians.
4. Ashland *Daily Press*, November 8, 1939.
5. *Ibid.* The joint appearance in Federal court of the only two Indian attorneys in Wisconsin was unique. Kershaw, whose appearance belied his 74 years, had practiced law for more than 40 years. He had passed the state board examination in Wisconsin in the nineties and had practiced law ever since. He was widely known throughout the country and had handled numerous cases for both white people and Indians. *Ibid.*, October 6, 1939.
6. *Indians at Work*, IV (November 15, 1936), 35.
7. *Ibid.*, IV (July 15, 1937), 20-21.
8. Mark Burns, "Indians and the New Deal," *ibid.*, II (December 15, 1934), 42.

CHAPTER 23

1. Gilfillan, *op. cit.,* pp. 57-58.
2. *Ibid.,* p. 58.
3. Marie Livingston, "Admonitions to an Indian Girl," WPA Historical Records, Odanah, Folder 6, Item No. 23.
4. Livingston, "Divorce and Marriage Customs," WPA Historical Records, Folder 6, Item No. 20.
5. The husband worked out a schedule for his wives who lived in separate wigwams. They took turns in cooking, sewing, and washing for him. As time went on, both wives sometimes lived, worked, and traveled together. If a wife went visiting and remained away too long, she sometimes found another in her place on her return.
6. *Journal of Rudolph Kurtz,* Bureau of American Ethnology, Bulletin 115 (1937), p. 155.
7. *Indian Education,* IV (1941), 5-6.
8. Schoolcraft, *Indian in His Wigwam,* p. 230.
9. Gilfillan, *op. cit.,* 64.
10. *Ibid.,* pp. 62-63.
11. *Ibid.,* pp. 65-66. It is alleged by some people that Indians are greedy and consume enormous quantities of food. The Chippewa stopped eating after his appetite was sated and did not eat for the mere pleasure of his palate. Since the Chippewa did not always have an adequate food supply, when food was available, it was partaken of in large amounts.
12. Sister Inez Hilger, *Chippewa Child Life and Its Cultural Background,* Bureau of American Ethnology, Bulletin 146 (1951), p. 103.
13. "Captain John Smith, Chippewah, Died At Age of 129 Years," *The American Indian,* June, 1939, p. 4.
14. Letter of J. G. Morrison to Sister M. Macaria, August 5, 1937. When John Smith, "Gah-be-nung-we-way," was asked to what he attributed his long life, he replied that he had reached his years through abstaining from the use of liquor. His questioner "mulled" over this reply, recalling that he had seen Smith "in his cups" in times past. Then he questioned further, "When did you quit the use of intoxicants?" The old man chucklingly replied, "About two years ago!" *Ibid.*
15. Ashland *Daily Press,* November 26, 1940. Mrs. Margaret Akiwense died on the Bad River Reservation at the age of 93. Her father, Chief Mazhinaway, was a signer of the 1854 Treaty, at which Margaret was present. Among her prized possessions were the peace pipe used in the 1854 Treaty; a document dated May 1, 1850 recounting the splendid qualities of her father, signed by an Indian Subagent; a medal presented to her father by President Franklin Pierce, dated 1853; and a small part of an American flag also presented to her father. *Ibid.,* April 19, 1939.
16. Gilfillan, *op. cit.,* pp. 56-57.
17. *Ibid.,* pp. 90-92.

CHAPTER 24

1. Jerome Arbuckle, "Old-Time Chippewa Names," WPA Historical Records, Folder 2, Item No. 3.

2. Schoolcraft, *Indian in His Wigwam,* p. 213.
3. Arbuckle, "How Surnames Were Acquired by the Chippewa," WPA Historical Records, Folder 2, Item No. 4.
4. *Ibid.*

CHAPTER 25

1. Warren, *op. cit.,* pp. 42-46. Because of this symbolic tie, it was seldom, if ever, that marriages took place between two persons of the same totem. Beliefs and teachings handed down to each succeeding generation, by the older Indians, held that such marriages brought grief and sorrow to the participants and deformity to the offspring. Marriages of this kind were sometimes punished by death.
2. Arbuckle, "Totems," WPA Historical Records, Odanah, Folder 5, Item No. 2.
3. *Ibid.* The Chippewa sometimes used the word "dodaim" instead of "totem." In addition to the tribal totem, each warrior had a personal totem. During his period of fasting, when entering maturity, the totem was given to him in a dream. Because of this totem, the warrior became a blood-brother to all others who had seen the same totem under similar circumstances. An Indian hundreds of miles from his own band, and among strangers of his own tribe, was regarded as a brother and treated accordingly by the members of his totem clan. In 1952, on the Lac du Flambeau Reservation, slender poles were planted near homes located on the outskirts of the village. A non-descript piece of cloth fluttered midway from each pole. The totem poles were those of Indian youths who had undergone a period of fasting. Drawings of animals and plants that the boys had seen in their dreams were sketched on the cloths attached to the poles.
4. James Scott, "Repairing an Insult," WPA Historical Records, Odanah, Folder 5, Item No. 5.
5. Livingston, "Respect for Dodem or Totem," *ibid.,* Folder 5, Item No. 6.
6. August Whitebird, "Ogeemageezshig," *ibid.,* Folder 5, Item No. 6. This type of totem pole must not be confused with the totem pole of Alaskan Indians. The totem pole of the latter bore a symbolism of two distinct types. One in which the carved symbol represented a legend often repeated to children, a story with a moral which formed an important part of their education. The other symbol represented the totem of its owner, a secret of the powers usually known only to the person to whom it belonged. The Alaskan totem pole is a genealogical family tree; each branch has its animal or some other symbol to identify it.
7. Scott, "Totem Pole Ceremony," *ibid.,* Folder 9, Item No. 6.
8. *Ibid.*
9. An interesting totem pole was carved by Willard L. Martinson, a Boy Scout of Billings Park, Superior, Wisconsin. This pole depicted the history of Superior. Reading from top to bottom, in customary Indian fashion, a figure of the Wise Old Owl represented the Indian who first inhabited the Lake Superior area. A "Frog" represented the coming of the French. The arrival of pioneers was shown by a beaver—symbolic of the courage and energy needed to found a community. The last figure signified the capture of slaves. It represented Superior's ultimate capture of the commercial supremacy of inland seas. Bardon's MS Collection of Short Stories. Story No. 54.

CHAPTER 26

1. Robert Wilson, "Personal Recollections of Adoption," WPA Historical Studies, Odanah, Folder 6, Item No. 29.
2. Superior *Evening Telegram,* September 18, 1937.
3. *Ibid.,* November 26, 1937.
4. Admiral Leahy had mingled in the games and sports of the Chippewa boys of this area. His father was Indian Agent of the Great Lakes area. Shortly after the Adoption Ceremonies, Admiral Leahy wrote to Guy Burnham of Ashland, Wisconsin, requesting information regarding the ceremonies held there. Mr. Burnham requested Sister M. Macaria, F.S.P.A. of Odanah to furnish him with the information. In return for this information, Admiral Leahy wrote the following letter:
   "Please accept this expression of my appreciation of your kindness in looking up the matter of adoptions as practiced by the Chippewa Indians and in sending me a copy of the result of your study via Mr. Guy Burnham. I have read the paper with much interest and will keep it with a record of my interesting experiences and prized honors." Letter of Admiral W. D. Leahy to Sister M. Macaria, January 3, 1939.
5. Superior *Evening Telegram,* August 15, 1938.
6. *Ibid.,* June 7, 1939.
7. Ashland *Daily Press,* March 26, 1951.
8. *Ibid.* Colonel McCormick was given this recognition because of his uncompromising fight for the welfare of the United States, for honesty in public office, for freedom of speech, and for freedom of the press. Indian spokesman also said that a debt of gratitude was due Colonel McCormick for his inflexible battle against criminal and political racketeering and his repeated denunciation of traitors and official bunglers.
   There is a remarkable parallelism between the ideals carved in stone into the Tribune Tower in Chicago and the traditions and religious ritualism of the Chippewa people. The beautiful carved stone screen above the Tribune Tower doorway is called THE TREE OF LIFE: Perched among the branches of this Tree of Life are the fox, the bear, the owl, the eagle, and the crow. The animals perched on the tree are the animal totems of the Chippewa. The foundation of the ancient religion of the Chippewa was based on the Tree of Life. According to this religion, there is one straight road to follow in life— the straight trunk of the tree of life. Unknown to the Chippewa, Colonel McCormick had enshrined in stone much that reflects the faith and beliefs of the Chippewa before the coming of the white man to America. *Ibid.*
9. Superior *Evening Telegram,* October 9, 1938.
10. *Indians at Work,* VIII (1940), 35.

CHAPTER 27

1. Hodge, *op. cit.,* I, 455.
2. Gilfillan, *op. cit.,* p. 82.
3. Livingston, "Requirements of a Guest at a Feast," WPA Historical Records, Odanah, Folder 6, Item No. 39.
4. Caroline Parker, "Conferring Names," *ibid.,* Folder 6, Item No. 26.
5. Peter Halfaday, "A Feast for the Dead," *ibid.,* Folder 6, Item No. 29.
6. Smart, "New Year's Day Feast," *ibid.,* Folder 6, Item No. 48. It was at New

Year that the Indians of early days took an inventory of their supplies to ascertain whether they had enough food for the remainder of the winter. If they had, they rejoiced with a thanksgiving feast which lasted during the week between Christmas and New Year. The Chippewa said: "The backbone of the winter has been broken and we can survive until the maple sugar season."

If it was known that some members of the tribe did not have sufficient food, a small group of Indians made personal calls on the other members of the community and collected food. The food was apportioned according to the needs of the family.

The custom of going from house to house is called Ani-mo-ka-ga-win. The derivative of this word is Ani-mosh or dog. To the Indian, the dog is an animal symbolic of humility and fidelity. Therefore, when a person enters a home, he is said to be Ani-mo-ka-ga, assuming the role of a dog. This word indicates that the person is entering the home with the utmost humility and fidelity to those who are within. *Ibid.*

7. John Teeple, "Feasts of Thanksgiving," *ibid.,* Folder 6, Item No. 13.

8. Livingston, "Feast of the Bear Paw," *ibid.,* Folder 6, Item No. 12.

9. William Newell, "Ta-ka-ra-kwi-ne-ken-ne," *Indians at Work,* IV (December, 1936), 28-29.

CHAPTER 28

1. Frances Densmore, *Chippewa Music,* Smithsonian Bulletin 45 (1910), 2.

2. Schoolcraft, *Indian in His Wigwam,* pp. 391-392.

3. Densmore, *op. cit.,* Bulletin 53 (1913), p. 53. At the age of 89, Odjib-we still possessed a voice of unusual strength and sweetness. The first phonographic records of his songs were made in 1909. For purposes of comparison, a second set of records was made two weeks later. It was found that the songs were accurately repeated. At the expiration of several months, some new songs were sung and others recorded a third time. In these repetitions, it was noted that certain tunes which were shortened or prolonged in the original rendition were again similarly shortened or prolonged. A slight sharping or flatting of certain tones was repeated. The records occasionally vary in unimportant melody progressions or in note values but the variation does not affect the length of the measure.

A few songs show changes in words, Odjib-we stated that it was permissible to alter the words, but that the "tune" and the meaning of the words must not be changed. Seventy of his songs were recorded. These were only part of the melodies at his command.

Odjib-we died in April, 1911. In generalship, Odjib-we was distinguished for sound judgment and steadiness of purpose, rather than for reckless daring. His war expeditions were successful, and he boasted that he was never wounded by a Sioux. His hand was never lifted against white men. His preeminence in music was unquestioned by his tribe throughout northern Minnesota. *Ibid.,* pp. 59-60.

4. Mary Wiggins Killoren, *Poems for Life,* Superior: Evening Telegram Printing Office, 1954, Poem No. 15. After spending three years at an Indian craft school at Flandreau, South Dakota, Mary Wiggins, "Princess O-Mi-Mi," entered the United States Indian Service. Miss Wiggins left the Indian service to prepare

herself for a career on the concert stage. She studied voice under the direction of Stella Prince Stocker at Duluth, Minnesota. Later, Miss Wiggins studied voice and dramatic art at the Hinshaw Conservatory, Chicago. Her final training was at the Scaffi Grand Opera School.

Miss Wiggins' stage career was one of continued success. She was perhaps the only Indian who sang and recited epics of Indian life. Playing leading roles in Indian pageants, she delighted thousands. Her interpretation of Indian life was one of the outstanding attractions at the World Fair held in St. Louis. Princess O-Mi-Mi has sung over radio stations WLS, WMAQ, WHT, KYW of Chicago, and KDKA of Pittsburgh. She also modelled at art schools in Chicago, St. Louis, and Pittsburgh. Princess O-Mi-Mi has devoted her later years to the teaching of folklore, Old Chippewa songs, and chants. In 1942, she was forced to abandon her career because of an automobile accident. In private life, Princess O-Mi-Mi is Mrs. James Killoren. She resides in Superior, Wisconsin.

5. Violet Brown, "Music of the American Indian," *The Indian Leader,* XLIV (March 28, 1941), 2.

6. An old Indian said of his tribal music: "We have looked at them both, O Father. There may be something wrong with the Indian's drum dance, but— I do not like the white man's fiddle dance." T. C. McGee, "Indian Music," *The Indian Leader,* XLI (April, 1938), 7.

7. Benjamin Armstrong, adopted son of Chief Buffalo, reported the incident thus: It was in the spring of 1878, I think, that considerable excitement was caused in and around Ashland, Wisconsin, over a report in circulation that Indians were dancing and having powwows further west and were working their way toward reservations in this part of the country. . . . There were between 60 and 70 in the party, which consisted of a young Sioux girl and her interpreter, the balance being made up of Chippewa from this immediate neighborhood. . . . She represented herself to be of the Sioux tribe and a member of a band of the tribe that were massacred by Custer's army on the Little Big Horn about May, 1876, in which all of her people were killed except herself; she saved herself by jumping into the water on the approach of the soldiers and hiding herself by clinging to roots and bushes of an overhanging tree or upturned roots until the slaughter was over and she could make her escape; that she was in the water about 20 hours; that she reached a band of her tribe and told them the story. . . . She said that spirits had told her she must teach a new dance and to teach it to all the Indian tribes; that she had taught her own tribes and had come to this reservation to teach. She taught that Indians must put away the small pipe dances and practice only the one she was teaching. She said the small drum was no longer large enough to keep away the bad spirit and the larger one must be used on all occasions. Her nation, the Sioux, she said, had given up all other dances since the massacre of her own little band. B. Armstrong and T. Wentworth, *Early Life Among the Indians.* Ashland: A. Bowron Press, pp. 156-158.

8. The Chippewa chose Chief May-qua-ne-kwe, "Red Hair," as first custodian of the drum. In 1917, James Scott, on the Bad River Reservation, became the custodian. The custody of the drum has passed from one Lake Superior band to another. James Scott, "Origin of the Ceremonial Pow-wow Drum," WPA Historical Records, Odanah, Folder 2, Item No. 10.

The ordinary dance drum is made from a bass log, hollowed out by charring and scraping. The ends are closed with deer skins. Rattles are made from wild gourds, sometimes from animal bladders. Small stones or shot inside the rattles produce the sounds. Sometimes the dried hoofs of a deer are attached to a stick and used as a rattle. The Chippewa lover accompanies his songs with a flute. The flute is commonly made of two semi-cylindrical pieces of cedar, united with fish glue. A wet snakeskin is drawn tightly over the instrument to prevent it from cracking. Densmore, *op. cit.*, Bulletin 45 (1910), 11-12.

9. It was quite opportune that the Chippewa should be the first or among the first to be thus favored by the Sioux since they were their most formidable enemies. The Sioux had possibly originated this dance as a pacifier to their immediate enemies, the Pawnees, the Crows, and the Chippewa. This accomplished, they could devote their entire strength to fight against the white people and the United States army. The adoption of this ceremonial by the several tribes eliminated them as enemies of the Sioux and as potential allies of the United States army.

10. The glory and the romance surrounding the calumet belong to history. Sioux tribes claim that it was given to them in a vision and thus was heaven-sent. The Pawnee claim that they were the originators of the idea and they passed it northward. Be that as it may, when the French explorers entered the Mississippi Valley, they were received ceremonially, the chief feature being the "dance of the calumet," during which a pipe was presented to them.

11. The difference between the dance of the white man and that of the Indian was quaintly expressed by a red man: "The white man dances with his legs; the Indian with his individual muscles." Julia Buttree, *The Rhythm of the Redman.* New York: A. S. Barnes and Co., 1930, p. 67.

12. When epidemics occurred, this medicine was used to destroy the germs. It was taken internally or used for bathing. Modern Indians resort to injections when epidemics occur.

13. Among Civil War veterans of the Bad River Reservation who took part in the Scalp Dance were Joseph Scott, John Scott, John Basna, Sr., Henry Condecon, George Armstrong, and George Madweiosh. Veterans of World War I usually participated in the Scalp Dance on Armistice Day. Some of the performers were William Bigboy, Henry Martin, Charles Mannypenny, Francis Wiggins, Sam Wiggins, Joseph Sky, Archie Shinaway, Alex Davidson, and Charles Cadotte.

14. James Scott, "Indian Dances," WPA Historical Records, Odanah, Folder 11, Item No. 8.

15. *Ibid.*

16. Lawrence Marksman, "Lone Feather," a Bad River Chippewa, was considered one of the best hoop dancers in the United States. His career was cut short by his untimely death, the result of an automobile accident. Marksman was an outstanding student and graduated in 1932 from De Padua High School, Ashland, Wisconsin. He performed the Hoop Dance in 1933 at the World's Fair in Chicago. At the time of his death, he had been appearing in an Indian pageant at the Wisconsin Dells. Ashland *Daily Press,* August 31, 1940.

17. Caroline Parker, "The Forty-Nine Dance," WPA Historical Records, Folder 11, Item No. 9.

18. This dance has spread from reservation to reservation and is a general favorite. It is one of the few Indian dances in which women are allowed to participate.

The original song must not be confused with the many versions of the "49" which nearly every tribe now has. The Indians in the far west, middle west, and the southwest, all have their version of the song, usually using English words in certain parts of the song. Some of these versions take away the beauty of the original song and serve to obscure, if not totally destroy, the true meaning and ideal for which the song stands. Joe Wilson, "The Song of the Forty-Nine Dance," *ibid.,* Folder 11, Item No. 11.

19. Scott, "Indian Dances," *ibid.,* Folder 11, Item No. 8. Antoine G. Starr, formerly of Odanah, Wisconsin, is considered one of the best performers of the Horse Dance in this area. Mr. Starr's surname is not a mis-nomer. He is well known as the dancing star who performed the Horse Dance at the Milwaukee Centurama in 1946. In 1951, his gifted children, George and Joan, danced and sang in the Chicago-land Music Festival at Soldiers' Field in Chicago. Later Starr and his family appeared on the Russ Davis Television Show.

20. Frank G. Smart has left this information about Indian Dance Houses. Since dancing played such an important part in the lives of the Chippewa, a dance house was almost indispensable among the earlier Indians. The building took the form of an octagon having an opening in the roof to permit "Gi-ji-ma-ni-do," the god who dwells in the air, to come and go at his will.

Dance houses are fast disappearing. The dance houses in the Chippewa area are at Balsam Lake, Lac du Flambeau, and Lac Vieux Desert. The Lac du Flambeau dance house, constructed of modern materials, is used principally as a council house. However, the Indians use it for their annual ritual dances. *Ibid.,* Folder 11, Item No. 12.

CHAPTER 29

1. Hodge, *op. cit.,* I, p. 483.
2. The French gave the game its name, probably from the fact that the lacrosse racquet resembles somewhat a bishop's crosier. It was not until 1840 that it was played by white people. About 1860, the game became popular in Canada. Seven years later, Dr. W. George Beers, of the Montreal La Crosse Club, formulated rules which, with slight changes, are in general use today. The game was introduced into Great Britain by visiting Canadian teams, and annual championship matches are played between England and Ireland teams. In the United States, the game has become popular among colleges, and is promoted by intercollegiate matches.

   At one time in colonial history this game led to an Indian massacre. Lacrosse or Bag-ad-away or Baga-udowe, as the game was sometimes called, cost the English Fort Mackinac in 1763. The Chippewa offered to play the game in honor of King George's birthday. The soldiers, excited over the prospect of the game, bet heavily among themselves upon the outcome of the sport. About 400 Chippewa took part in the contest. Indian women, with weapons concealed under their blankets, were posted near the entrance of the fort. During the course of the game, the ball was repeatedly thrown inside the fort and it was left for the garrison to retrieve. At a pre-arranged signal, the ball was again thrown inside the fort. As the Indians rushed in after it, the women handed them the weapons which they had concealed. The entire garrison was killed, with the exception of Alexander Henry, a fur trader who had been friendly to the Chippewa. Warren, *op. cit.,* pp. 202-204.

3. Lacrosse is still played by Great Lakes Chippewa in much the same manner as it was played hundreds of years ago. In 1948, this game was one of the highlights of the Wisconsin State Centennial celebration at Copper Falls State Park. Frank Gishkok, age 99, as drummer, opened the game for the Bad River Chippewa. Ashland *Daily Press,* August 1, 1948.

At an Indian celebration held in Odanah about 20 years ago, a game of lacrosse was played between the Chippewa of Odanah and Red Cliff. The game was played in the primitive manner with no recognized boundaries and no set rules. A beverage, supposed to strengthen the players, was given to the Odanah team and the medicine men also "loaded" the local team's racquets with "Indian medicine." Red Cliff was defeated.

Later, a trophy was offered by the Ashland *Daily Press.* Odanah and Red Cliff again played, and again the Odanah team was victorious. The victors challenged any band to engage in a contest. No one accepted the challenge. They are still the proud possessors of the trophy.

4. Jerome Arbuckle, "Women's Game," WPA Historical Records, Odanah, Folder 11, Item No. 4.

5. Arbuckle, "Moccasin Game," *ibid.,* Item No. 11. Sometimes the moccasin game is played with but one bullet. The player puts his hand under each of the four moccasins in hiding the bullet.

6. Marion Gridley, *Indians of Today.* New York: M. A. Donahue & Co., 1936, p. 15. Chief Bender died on May 22, 1954. The obituary in the Milwaukee *Journal* reads as follows:

There were two things they always said about Charles Albert (Chief) Bender, the famous Philadelphia Athletics pitcher who died here Saturday of cancer and heart disease at the age of 71.

Connie Mack, his manager throughout his major league career, always said that if there were one game he had to win, he would rather have the Chief pitch it than anyone else. And players and fans both agreed that the rangy, forthright Indian never made an enemy, in or out of baseball.

Bender joined the Athletics fresh from the famous Carlisle Indian School but later got his degree from Dickinson College. Connie Mack saw him shut out the Chicago Cubs, 3-0, in an exhibition game at Harrisburg and signed him for $1,800 a year. He never got more than $2,400 a year as one of baseball's all-time greats. Although he also had been a football star and could play golf and billiards with all but the top professionals, baseball was Bender's true love.

The Chief's major league record showed 212 victories and 128 defeats, and a world series record of six games won and four lost. Just before the 1913 world series, Connie Mack called him to his office and said: "I'm banking on you to win. By the way, how much of a mortgage do you carry on your home?" "That's a little personal, isn't it?" replied the Chief, who never was one to make capital of his troubles.

The A's won the series, with Bender beating McGraw's Giants twice, and the club gave him a bonus check of $2,500 to pay off the mortgage. Bender's best season was the 1910 in which he won 23 games, lost only five and pitched a no-hit game against Cleveland. He missed a perfect game by walking one batter. The runner was thrown out stealing, and Bender faced only 27 men.

Despite the fact that he was an expert on textiles, a tailor, and a diamond appraiser as well as scout and part time coach for the Athletics, Bender ran into financial difficulties due to medical expenses in later years. Once baseball asked for cash and the Red Cross called for blood for him. Fans, including former teammates and rivals, came through with more than enough of both. The Chief was elected to baseball's Hall of Fame only in September, 1953. It was his proudest moment.

"Practice, and then keep on practicing, if you want to be a pitcher—it's the only way to get control," the Chief always advised youngsters. "Connie Mack used to have to steal the ball from me to keep me from throwing." Despite his emphasis on control, the Chief in his prime had a fast ball that was generally regarded as second only to Walter Johnson's in the major league.

Bender was a full blooded Chippewa Indian and one of 13 children born on a reservation near Brainerd, Minnesota. He never had any children of his own. His wife, to whom he was devoted for more than 40 years, was with him when he died. Milwaukee *Journal,* May 25, 1954.

7. The Odanah *Star,* November 15, 1912, quoting the *Spokesman Review* of Spokane, Washington.
8. Superior *Evening Telegram,* August 9, 1939.
9. Ashland *Daily Press,* March 21, 1939.
10. *Indian Leader,* XLVII, April 28, 1944. The Haskell team not only boxed, but they also inspected the Paramount studios in Los Angeles. They rubbed elbows with the cinema's great in the studio cafe and even lunched at Joe di Maggio's famous restaurant. The young Chippewa said the trip was a most interesting one.
11. Ashland *Daily Press,* August 18, 1944.
12. *Ibid.,* November 4, 1941.
13. *Ibid.,* May 15, 1944.
14. *Ibid.,* May 29, 1944.
15. *Ibid.,* June 1, 1945.

CHAPTER 30

1. Florina Denomie, "The Indian Doctor," WPA Historical Records, Odanah, Folder 9, Item No. 12.
2. Mathew Stirling, "Some Misconceptions About the American Indians," *Indians at Work,* IV (December 15, 1936), 32.
3. *Ibid.,* IV (March 15, 1937), 26.
4. *Ibid.,* p. 27.
5. *Ibid.,* pp. 27-28.
6. Smith, "Ethnobotany of the Ojibwe," *op. cit.,* IV (1932), 348. In primitive days, Indians lived close to Nature and had the benefit of fresh air. This, together with vigorous exercise necessary for the hunt, warded off the dread white plague, Tuberculosis. There were, however, exceptions.
7. Caroline Parker, "Wabadow—Herbs and Medicine," WPA Historical Records, Odanah, Folder 6, Item No. 41.
8. *Ibid.* See also Livingston, "Chippewa Appellations for Herbs and Roots," *ibid.,* Folder 9, Item No. 2.
9. Arbuckle, "Chippewa Remedies—Surgical," *ibid.,* Folder 9, Item No. 4. Dried fish bones were used as needles.
10. Bardon MS, Story No. 65.

11. According to John Gordon, a Chippewa from the Red Cliff Reservation, special sweat houses were constructed for warriors. These lodges were built in a "long" fashion and called "bear baths." Bear root was used in the liquid for steaming and when the warrior left the sweat house, he walked like a bear. This bath was a ceremonial or rite in preparation for war. WPA Historical Records, Folder 9, Item No. 4.

12. *Ibid.*

CHAPTER 31

1. Hodge, *op. cit.*, I, p. 946.

2. Observations of the author at Lac du Flambeau Reservation. For detailed description of burial customs see WPA Historical Records, Folder 6 in particular, Items Nos. 7-11.

3. *Ibid.*, Item No. 3.

4. *Ibid.* Instead of planting flowers on the grave, the Chippewa placed thereon whatever the departed had liked most while living. They believed that the deceased received the benefit of the food, even if it was consumed by the living. The relatives always informed others when these edibles were to be found there, so that they would be eaten. This was done frequently until after the first death anniversary of the departed. It was understood that the first person "happening along" had the privilege of taking anything edible that he found on the grave. The gifts varied with the season—in spring, maple sugar; in late summer, wild rice and berries; in autumn, clothing necessary for the winter; in winter, hunting equipment that the man had owned during his life—were placed on the grave.

   The ancient Chippewa believed that the northern lights, Aurora Borealis, were the Chippewa spirits dancing. They regarded this phenomenon with mingled feelings of joy and awe—joy, in the belief that the departed could thus conduct and enjoy themselves; awe, at the grandeur of the heavenly display.

   Superstitions associated the fear of a heavy death toll for the ensuing year with the opening of a new cemetery. Consequently the Chippewa did not prepare their burial plots. When a burial was to be made, a place was selected in the most casual manner and the plot enlarged when necessary.

   To move the corpse from one house to another meant death to one of the occupants of either home. To weed and freshen an old grave also indicated the death of a relative. Indians never disturbed a grave once the dead was buried. They also believed that a "high mounded" grave was an indication of a death in the family of the deceased. *Ibid.*

5. "Services of an Undertaker," *ibid.*, Item No. 9.

6. *Ibid.*, Item No. 5.

7. *Ibid.*

8. *Ibid.*, Item No. 10.

9. In 1937, while engaged on a Works Progress Administration road project at Odanah, a group of Indians unearthed three adult skulls, other remains of adult bodies and bones of young children. Religious articles were found buried with these bones, as were also beads, knives, teaspoons, and a glass mug. The graves were not more than a foot and a half deep, implying that the dead had been buried in early reservation days. *Ibid.*, Item No. 4.

CHAPTER 32

1. Hodge, *op. cit.,* I, p. 400.
2. Livingston, "Significance of Charcoal," WPA Historical Records, Folder 6, Item No. 2.
3. Hodge, *op. cit.,* I, p. 453.
4. Robert Wilson, "Dreams—Their Significance," WPA Historical Records, Folder 6, Item No. 1.
5. *Ibid.,* Folder 9, Item No. 14.
6. Parker, "Windigo," *ibid.,* Folder 6, Item No. 40.

CHAPTER 33

1. Warren, *op. cit.,* pp. 66-69.
2. *The American Indian,* June, 1939, p. 35. The word "Gijie Manido," Kind Spirit, noted often by both early and later missionary writers, meant the Chippewa god. No Indian used the term "Gitchi Manido," Grand Medicine Spirit. Four Manido, one at each cardinal point, were under his jurisdiction, together with a large number of other deities who assumed the form of animals. The Manido most closely connected with the Midewiwin was an animal which lived in the water. The Mide Manido resembled an old man who had lived on the earth one hundred years. The Mide Manido taught the Midewiwin the use of herb remedies.
3. Densmore, *Chippewa Music,* Bull. 45, 1910, p. 13.
4. *Ibid.,* p. 14.
5. Warren, *op. cit.,* pp. 77-78. The Midewiwin had a cross connected with it, a symbol of the fourth degree of the society. The cross was used before the Christian white men came. Its use was not divulged because the members did not disclose the secrets of the Midewiwin. See Smart, "The Mide Cross," WPA Historical Records, Folder 6, Item No. 15.
6. Copway, *op. cit.,* pp. 161-162.
7. *The American Indian,* June, 1939, p. 35.
8. Copway, *op. cit.,* pp. 162 *passim* holds that an indentation was made in the center of the candidate's breast for entrance of the medicine or shell. It was blown by the medicine man himself to the candidate and was to remain with him for life. Other writers affirm that when the candidate received this shell he became unconscious. Upon recovering consciousness, the shell was expelled from his mouth. *The American Indian,* June, 1939, p. 35.
9. Warren, *op. cit.,* pp. 77-79. An entrance into the lodge itself, while the ceremonies were being performed, was sometimes granted through courtesy. It was related that a gentleman travelling in a Sioux village, near St. Paul, was told by a waggish Indian to go into the lodge and smoke with the old men. He went in and then a tug of war began. One Indian jerked off his hat, another pushed him out of the lodge, sending his hat in advance. Undaunted, the man attempted to enter again, but was met at the entrance and thrown down. In the scramble, an Indian lad adroitly cut off the tail of his coat. He could not comprehend the meaning of the treatment and thought the Indians rude. He finally saw the humorous side of it, especially when he saw the fit of his coat

and the condition of his hat. Cf. Copway, *op. cit.*, p. 162.

One initiation song was as follows:

> The weasel skin
> Through it I shoot the white shells,
> It never fails
> The shells go toward them
> And they fall.
> My brother is searched
> In his heart is found
> That which I seek to remove
> A white shell.
>
> *The American Indian,* June, 1939, p. 35.

10. Livingston, "Zinso-O-Win-Protective Medicine," WPA Historical Records, Odanah, Folder 6, Item No. 44.
11. *Ibid.*
12. *The American Indian,* June, 1939, p. 35.
13. WPA Historical Records, Folder 9, Item No. 5.
14. Black Hawk had a mide roll which he gave to his son, Mountain, who later transferred it to his son, Gagewin. The latter presented the roll to Miss Frances Densmore in 1918. Black Hawk's roll represented four degrees of the society, each degree's teaching was given separately. Beginning at the reader's right, the instructions for entering the first degree were as follows: In taking this degree, the candidate provided one dog which lay over the entrance to the lodge. The candidate was obliged to step over the dog in entering. Evil spirits, represented by two men, were stationed outside the lodge. Before the candidate entered the lodge, these men tried to dissuade him from entering. Although the doorkeeper did not permit these two men to enter the lodge, they attempted to distract the candidate. If the aspirant was diverted or discouraged by these taunts, his life would be shortened. Within the lodge, four men constantly advised him how to conduct himself. He must look at the sacred pole and pay no attention to his tempters. He must lead a moral life, be quiet, and speak gently. Then these men threw the "shell" into him. According to Chippewa lore, this small white shell appeared on the surface of the sea when the Manido caused the waters to seethe. *The American Indian,* June, 1939, p. 36.

CHAPTER 34

1. Parkman, *Jesuits in North America,* p. lxxxiv.
2. Among the American Indians, a fetish was an object, large or small, natural or artificial, regarded as possessing consciousness, volition, and immortal life. "Orenda," or magic power, was the essential characteristic which enabled the object to accomplish in addition to those that are usual, abnormal results in a mysterious manner.

   A fetish might be a bone, a feather, a carved or painted stick, a stone arrow head, a curious fossil, a tuft of hair, a necklace of red berries, the stuffed skin of a lizard, the dried hand of an enemy, a small bag of charcoal mixed with human blood—anything, in fact, which the owner's medicine dream or imagination might suggest, no matter how uncouth, provided it was easily portable and attachable.

No matter how insignificant in itself, it had always, in the owner's mind, some symbolic connection with occult power. It might be fastened to the scalp-lock as a pendant, attached to some part of the dress, hung from the bridle bit, concealed between the covers of a shield, or guarded in a special repository in the dwelling. Mothers sometimes tied the fetish to a child's cradle board.

A fetish was acquired by a person, a family, or a people for the purpose of promoting welfare. In return, the fetish acquired worship from its owner in the form of prayer, sacrifice, feasts, and protection. It received good or ill treatment in accordance with its behavior towards its votaries. Some fetishes were regarded as more efficacious than others. The fetish which lost its repute as a promoter of welfare gradually became useless and degenerated into a sacred object—a charm, an amulet, or a talisman—finally into a mere ornament. Then other fetishes were acquired and subjected to the same test of efficiency in promoting the well-being of their possessors. Hodge, *op. cit.*, I, pp. 456-458.

3. Arbuckle, "Evil Medicine Men," WPA Historical Records, Odanah, Folder 6, Item No. 52.

4. It was said that those who practiced the "bear walk" buried their medicines in a kettle, covered this kettle with another kettle, and then covered these with earth. This was done when the leaves had all fallen from the trees. In spring, when the trees began to bud, the buried medicine was dug out of the ground. It was said that on one occasion, a life was sacrificed to test the efficiency of the medicine. A person was "bear walked" by a medicine man.

Only those who were far advanced in "Grand Medicine" could manipulate the mysteries of the fire ball. When the first degree was conferred, the person was given a squirrel hide; at the second degree, a weasel skin; at the third degree, a robin's skin (feathered) or some other small bird. When the person had reached the eighth degree, an entire outfit to walk or to fly with the fire ball was conferred. The "bear walker" could transform himself into the image of an animal or a bird. Generally he was seen on the ground in the form of a bear; in the air, as an owl. The fire-like illumination was really a piece of phosphorus wood that the medicine man or woman carried and upon which he or she breathed medicated breath at regular intervals. Denomie, "The Bear Walk," *ibid.*, Folder 6, Item No. 47.

5. Livingston, "Bad Medicine Man's Fragility," *ibid.*, Folder 6, Item No. 48.

6. Morrison, "My Family's Experience with the Fire Ball," *ibid.*, Folder 6, Item No. 43.

7. Condecon, "Fire Ball," *ibid.*, Folder 6, Item No. 49.

8. Livingston, "The Fire Walker, Ma-gi-dens," *ibid.*, Folder 6, Item No. 50.

9. Denomie, "The Indian Fire Ball," *ibid.*, Folder 6, Item No. 51. Various other notions were connected with the fire ball. Some Chippewa contended that the fire ball made its appearance after the death of a tribal member who had lived an evil life or was in some manner connected with witchery. The ball of fire which left the dead body was, supposedly, the spirit.

10. Arbuckle, "Crafty Medicine Man," *ibid.*, Folder 6, Item No. 53.

11. MHS *Collections*, IX, 221-222.

12. WPA Historical Records, Odanah, Folder 12, Item No. 9.

CHAPTER 35

1. WPA Historical Records, Odanah, Folder 12, Item No. 9. See also Folder 9, Items No. 15-17.

2. The Chippewa had a strange belief that every Indian at birth received an animal miniature; a perfect likeness of some living creature. This manito was seen only in rare cases, as when a djisaki man regurgitated it with medicine bones or when the small animal was ill. The person often had the same habits and characteristics as those of the animal. For instance, if a person was born with a miniature bear within his body, it would be impossible for him to eat the flesh of a bear, neither could he endure its odor. When one was aware of such an endowment, he knew that particular animal was being cooked. The odor was repulsive to him. The Indians never urged anyone to eat under such circumstances. A legend originated among the lower St. Croix Lake Indians that an Indian endowed with a miniature fish at one time ate the forbidden fish. He developed such a craving for water that he went to a lake and drank such a great quantity of water that he became a fish. Thereafter, this fish was seen only on cloudy days.

3. The djisaki man did not claim to cure or give medicine to anyone who came to him. He stated that he was only the medium through whom the wise counsel of the spirits acted. He affirmed that during his youthful fasting, the manitoes had taken pity on him and had given him the assurance of their help and guidance. The djisaki man also had a helper who beat a drum at certain times.

   Youths aspiring to become djisaki were cautioned not to impair their health by assuming the responsibilities of a djisaki man. The jugglers claimed that the ceremonies were a great drain on one's vitality. The aspirants were advised to wait until they had reached the age of fifty or sixty years before they took up the profession. Among the djisaki, the leaders were called jugglers.

4. "A Skeptic and the Djisakin," WPA Historical Records, Odanah, Folder 9, Item No. 16.

5. "The Wrath of a Juggler," *ibid.,* Item No. 18.

6. Robert Wilson, "Power of the Shake Lodge," *ibid.,* Item No. 19.

7. Parkman, *The Conspiracy of Pontiac,* II, 165-166.

8. Bash-kwo-dash was an animal that resembled a wolf. This animal had no hair on its body except for the ridge on its back, extending from head to tail. It was believed to be a sort of a god or spirit that answered the juggler's call for help.

9. "My Experience with the Shake Lodge," WPA Historical Records, Odanah, Folder 9, Item No. 15.

10. "Cures of the Shake Lodge," *ibid.,* Folder 9, Item No. 13.

11. The end of the jugglers who had performed the shake lodge ceremony was unfortunate. One was found frozen to death, another was drowned, and the third was found with his head extending above the waters of a shallow lake, his mouth full of moss.

12. "Occult Power of the Shake Lodge," *ibid.,* Folder 9, Item No. 13.

13. "Messages Through the Djisakin Lodge," *ibid.,* Folder 9, Item No. 17.

14. Parkman, *Jesuits in North America,* p. 85.

15. Parkman, *Pioneers of France in the New World,* II, 167.

16. Verwyst, "Indian Jugglery and Witchcraft," WPA Historical Records, Folder 9, Item No. 19.

CHAPTER 36

1. Hodge, *op. cit.,* II, 956.
2. The next day the child died. Sometime in the past, the parents of this child had incurred the displeasure of the witch. She wreaked her revenge upon them by causing the deaths of children. Four other members of this family had previously fallen victims to her witchery.
3. Letter to Sister M. Macaria, July 8, 1937. This information is a direct contrast to that given by Mrs. Grace Shaw Ross, a resident of Crandon, Wisconsin, for fifty-four years. She wrote as follows:

   I have never heard anything about any witchcraft or any woman being tried in court for same. My father studied law, and was admitted to the bar and practiced in circuit and supreme court for many years before his death in 1917, so I would have been apt to hear of this had there been anything in it. It might have been a myth of the Indians. Letter to Sister M. Macaria, June 2, 1937.
4. Livingston, "Bewitched Indian at Lac Courte Oreilles Reservation," WPA Historical Records, Odanah, Folder 6, Item No. 45.
5. Smith, *op. cit.,* IV (1932), 426.
6. Livingston, "Magic Ritual of Making Charms," WPA Historical Records, Odanah, Folder 6, Item No. 16.
7. Ashland *Daily Press,* August 20, 1940.
8. *Ibid.,* August 31, 1940.
9. Belief in witchcraft still exists among nearly all Indian tribes. Investigation of an ax murder on the Colorado River Indian Reservation near Parker disclosed that "witchcraft" remains a potent factor in the lives of southwestern tribesmen.

   Ronald Jones, 36, an educated Yuma Indian, calmly told Federal authorities that he had hacked John Elee Stokes, 58, to death because he feared Stokes would "bewitch" him and his family.

   "It is something like hypnotism," Jones said in describing the sorcery attributed to Stokes. "They just have to look at you to bring death." Jones asserted that Stokes caused the death of his own son through witchcraft because he had disapproved of the young man's marriage to a relative of Jones. Milwaukee *Journal,* April 25, 1937.

CHAPTER 37

1. Parker, "Chippewa Weather Predictions," WPA Historical Records, Odanah, Folder 6, Item No. 21.
2. Robert Wilson, "Father's Prophecy," *ibid.,* Folder 6, Item No. 46.
3. Chicago *Sun-Times,* July 1, 1945.

CHAPTER 38

1. Racine *Wisconsin Agriculturist and Farmer,* August 13, 1938.
2. Hodge, *op. cit.,* I, 791.
3. Racine *Wisconsin Agriculturist and Farmer,* August 13, 1938.
4. In reply to an inquiry why the name "Chippewa" was given to a variety of potato, J. G. Milward, Extension Potato Specialist at Madison, Wisconsin,

quoted a paragraph from a letter received from F. J. Stevenson, Senior Geneticist, Beltsville, Maryland:

"If you will look over the names that we have given our new varieties of potatoes, you will know that most of them are Indian—Katahdin, Chippewa, Warba, Pontiac, Sequois, etc. The suggestion was made by Dr. C. F. Clark a number of years ago that we give all of our new varieties Indian names. This suggestion was strongly supported by Dr. William A. Taylor who was then chief of the Bureau of Plant Industry. In fact, he was responsible for naming the Katahdin and Chippewa varieties. We suggested a list of Indian names, but he chose these two. The name 'Chippewa' was chosen because that variety seemed to do so well in northern Michigan, Wisconsin, and northern Minnesota, which, I believe is Chippewa Indian territory." Letter of F. J. Stevenson to J. G. Milward, October 29, 1940.

5. Hodge, *op. cit.,* II, 629.
6. Frank Gishkak, "Tobacco Cultivated on the Bad River Reservation," WPA Historical Records, Odanah, Folder 8, Item No. 9. Kinickinick is usually made from two species of willow, the red and the spotted green. The outer bark was removed and the inner bark was scraped into a pan. The willow scrapings were then dried over a fire or spread on a piece of cloth and dried in the sun. When perfectly dry, they were ground and mixed with tobacco.
7. Gilfillan, *op. cit.,* pp. 107-108.
8. The Indians on the Bad River Reservation had a good market for their farm produce during the operation of the Stearns Lumber Company. With the termination of the lumbering industry, the market for Odanah farm products ceased. The Indians failed, not as producers, but because they were unable to sell their produce. Since they had no cooperative associations, they could not enter into competition with their white neighbors.

That these Indians raised good crops is evident from a newspaper account in 1919 of a fair held in Odanah. "Several hundred automobile parties left here (Ashland) yesterday for Odanah, where they witnessed the sixth annual fair on the Indian reservation. . . . This year's fair at Odanah eclipses anything that has as yet been put on there. The stock exhibits are better than ever, and the vegetable exhibit is one of the finest seen in this section of the country. The Fair closes today with a large stock parade. The Indian farmers on the reservations are known to have the best working horses that can be found." "Odanah Fair," Superior *Evening Telegram,* September 26, 1919.

9. Smith, *Ethnobotany of the Ojibwa,* Bulletin, Public Museum, Milwaukee, IV, No. 3, 394.

CHAPTER 39

1. Wild rice, Zizania Aquatica, an aquatic plant of the grass family, when ripe, resembles a stalk of oats. Ripe kernels do not remain on the stalks long, but drop into the water. The kernels anchor themselves in mud and thus produce next year's crop.

In the spring, the plants shoot up from the water, grow rapidly, and may attain a height of from six to seven feet above the surface. Wild rice blossoms in the latter part of May or early in June, and matures from the beginning of late July until about the middle of September.

The kernels are black and long, varying in length from one-half inch to nearly an inch. The plant grows chiefly around the edges of shallow lakes, sloughs, and slow-flowing streams which have a mud-alluvial bottom. Proper water levels are of great importance for growth of the plant. If the water is too high, the stalks are lifted off the stems and float. If the water is too low, rushes, weeds, and cattails crowd out the rice. Weather conditions also exert considerable influence on the rice crop. Storms thresh the ripened grain; frosts may kill the plant, if it has not reached maturity. *Indians at Work,* VI (January, 1939), 26-27.

2. The term "Folle Avoine," wild rice, was especially applied to the St. Croix region where the Indians were frequently known as "Wild Rice Makers." This branch of the Chippewa was frequently spoken of as the "Folle Avoine Sauteur" in contradiction to the "Folle Avoine" of Menominee tribesmen. (Sauteur was the French name for Chippewa.) The Chippewa, or Sauteur of northwestern Wisconsin, therefore, were known as the "Wild Rice Chippewa."

3. Racine *Wisconsin Agriculturist and Farmer,* August 13, 1938.

4. Cited in Bartlett, *op. cit.,* pp. 47-48.

5. Mark Burns, " 'Manomin,' The Wild Rice of the Lake Country," *Indians at Work,* VI (January, 1939), 26.

6. See various methods of rice harvesting in "Wild Rice," WPA Historical Records, Odanah, Folder 8, Item No. 38.

7. Milwaukee *Journal,* October 3, 1954.

8. *Ibid.* How widespread the market for wild rice has become may be estimated from the following newspaper account published in 1940:

The Indians of northern Minnesota had a huge wild rice crop this year. Not until the last decade has the wild rice industry, which dates back long before the coming of the white men, reached proportions where it has come to be regarded as one of the most important pursuits in this section of the country. First, the demand for the parched rice for table use has increased every year for the past ten years; and secondly, more interest has been created in the last decade in the conservation of wild life, making lakes more attractive for water fowl. This latter trend has brought about an increase in the planting of wild seed. The outstanding market in the United States for the product is said to be on the Pacific coast. Duluth *News-Tribune,* September 1, 1940.

9. Milwaukee *Journal,* October 3, 1954. The propagation of wild rice is not left entirely to nature. In 1936, two hundred twenty-five bushes of giant wild rice was planted in the Kakagon Sloughs. Over 7,000 pounds of rice were gathered the next fall. This project, sponsored by the Indian Service, was a precedent for later plantings. The Northern Wisconsin Rod and Gun Club carried out a similar project in the spring of 1942 to offset a disastrous flood which threatened the rice crop. This later undertaking was to help both the Indians and the wild game. Letter of Dwight Kenyon to Sister M. Carolissa, October 25, 1954.

CHAPTER 40

1. Livingston, "Blueberrying Forty Years Ago," WPA Historical Records, Odanah, Folder 8, Item No. 11.

2. Denomie, "Picking Blueberries in Northern Michigan," *ibid.,* Item No. 10.

3. Ashland *Daily Press,* August 20, 1940.

CHAPTER 41

1. *The Indian Leader,* XL, February 12, 1937.
2. Ivan Stretten, "Indians Invented Maple Sirup," *ibid.,* XXXVIII (May 24, 1935), 37.
3. Arbuckle, "March Notes," WPA Historical Records, Odanah, Folder 8, Item No. 33. The Ashland *Daily Press,* April 6, 1939 mentioned that several families moved their sugar camps as late as April 4.
4. Peter Halfaday, "Maple Sugar Industry," WPA Historical Records, Odanah, Folder 8, Item No. 34.
5. Peter Marksman, "Maple Sugar Making," *ibid.,* Item No. 35.

CHAPTER 42

1. William Raney, "Pine Lumbering in Wisconsin," *Wisconsin Magazine of History,* XIX (1935), 71-83.
2. *Ibid.*
3. Arbuckle, "First Sawmills on the Bad River Reservation," WPA Historical Records, Odanah, Folder 8, Item No. 4.
4. *Ibid.* "Wabi-gog" frequently made trips on foot to St. Paul via a trail that intersected the "Military Road." On one of these trips, "Wabi-gog" failed to arrive at his destination. No trace of him was ever found. Since he usually carried a considerable sum of money to purchase necessities for his mill, it was surmised that he had been waylaid and murdered.
5. Matthew Schumacher, "Lumbering Industry on Bad River Reservation," MS Report, June 19, 1906. Files of St. Mary's Indian School, Odanah.
6. Morrison, "Lumbering on the Bad River Reservation," WPA Historical Records, Odanah, Folder 8, Item No. 43. Morrison maintains that it was through the efforts of a Mr. Cushman, an Indian lawyer representing the Stearns Lumber Co., that a contract to operate a saw mill on the Bad River Reservation was approved by the Bureau of Indian Affairs.
7. *Ibid.*
8. *Ibid.* In 1906, Lucius Baker was president of the Stearns Lumber Company, having served as secretary and treasurer of the company from 1893 to 1907. According to the 1916 *Who's Who in America,* this millionaire lumberman was connected with at least seventeen like business concerns.
9. Raney, *op. cit.,* p. 75 *passim.*
10. Cavill, "Lumbering on the Lac du Flambeau Reservation," Great Lakes Indian Agency Report, 1943, pp. 7-8.
11. C. N. Nelson, "Indian Forests," Report, Lac du Flambeau Agency, May, 1943.

CHAPTER 43

1. In March, snowshoes finally deteriorated from their continuous use in the winter's hunt. The crust which formed on the snow at this time of the year was also destructive to the rawhide meshwork of the shoe.
2. The fisher is a rare animal today. It was killed mainly for its fur.

3. It is asserted that the pigeons were once so numerous that they darkened the sun in their flight. By sheer weight, they broke branches of trees in which they roosted. For several years, in the latter part of the nineteenth century, they became so scarce that not a single bird could be seen. Arbuckle, "March Notes," WPA Historical Records, Odanah, Folder 8, Item No. 33.

4. Livingston, "Hunter's Superstitions," *ibid.*, Folder 6, Item No. 30. Some Indians still believe in the potency of "hunting medicine" and carry it on their person while hunting, or smoke their guns over coals upon which some "medicine" is being burnt. Hunting "medicine" is smoked in a pipe while hunting, in the belief that the fumes will attract game within its range.

5. Livingston, "The Medicine Hunt," *ibid.*, Item No. 32.

6. Livingston, "Hunter's Superstitions," *ibid.*, Item No. 30.

7. The Indians had the first game laws. Two hundred years ago, Indians in Kentucky set aside large areas as "beloved bear grounds." Only a limited number of animals could be killed each year. *Indian Leader,* IX, September, 1935.

8. WPA Historical Records, Odanah, Folder 7, Item No. 7.

9. *Ibid.,* Item No. 13.

10. Copway, *op. cit.,* p. 42.

11. WPA Historical Records, Odanah, Folder 7, Item No. 14.

12. Both Indian and white hunter disregard conservation laws in regard to wild fowl. One Chippewa claims that a hunter killed 165 ducks in one season. Shooting from fast motor boats and using high-powered repeating guns is a highly destructive practice which accounts for the rapidly diminishing number of wild fowl. *Ibid.,* Item No. 5.

13. This unrestricted privilege was granted in the Treaty of 1854. On August 1, 1914, Congress passed a law creating the final roll on the Bad River Reservation, known as the "Wooster Roll," which states that the enrolled members ʋre entitled to hunting and fishing privileges on the reservation.

CHAPTER 44

1. *Outdoor Life,* LXXXV (April, 1940), 15.

2. There are various spellings of the Indian name "muskellunge"; others being muscalonge and muscallenge. The first is the most popular.

3. Sturgeon were once so common that the French cast them aside as too common. Heaps of decaying fish could be seen along banks or shores, the oil seeping through the sand.

4. These catfish are not to be confused with a related species, known as "bullheads," which never attain to the size of catfish. These latter are rather numerous in reservation waters.

5. WPA Historical Records, Odanah, Folder 7, Item No. 1.

6. Bardon MS, Story No. 25. Jumbo was the commercial term for whitefish of four pounds or over, the choicest fish of the markets in early days.

7. WPA Historical Records, Odanah, Folder 7, Item No. 2.

8. These lakes contain some of the largest bass, pike, and muskellunge fish to be found in any of the Wisconsin lakes. W. E. Stimson, keeper of Ojibway Lodge, on Fence Lake published the following letter on ice fishing: "I found out from the Indians that our system of ice fishing was all wrong. After talking

with Frank Wildcat (one of our Indian guides), I cut a hole through the ice and then built a wigwam over it. First some sticks are put up in tent fashion over the hole and tied together at the top, then two or three blankets are wrapped around the sticks and a small box put inside to sit on. This makes it dark inside and you can see down to the bottom even in fifteen feet of water. This also keeps the light from shining through the hole so bright, which has a tendency to scare the fish away.

I put up a rig of this kind, and then went down to the spring and got out some large sucker minnows I had kept over from last fall. All the tackle you use is a short stout pole about two feet long with six or eight feet of line, and an ordinary pike hook. After baiting up, I had sat in the wigwam perhaps ten minutes when out shot a pike after that minnow and I was so startled that I pulled the bait right away from him, but then I settled down and caught three nice ones, the largest weighing six pounds and one ounce.

After this there was nothing doing for a long time, and just as I was getting ready to quit a muskie came swimming up real slowly and swallowed my minnow and stayed right there until I sunk the hook and right there was where my troubles began. He ran around and around the hole and all I could do was to hold on. I tried a dozen times to pull him out, but every time I got him where I thought I could head him up through the hole, he would shoot on past.

By this time I had become desperate, I kicked over the wigwam and for the first time in my life I yelled for help to land a fish. My man, who was at the barn, came out to the lake shore to see what was up and I told him to bring down a gaff. After several attempts we finally gaffed Mr. Muskie, and, although he weighed only sixteen pounds, I am here to tell you boys that if you want to work up a sweat in the winter time just try to pull a muskie out of a twelve inch hole in the ice." Chicago *Daily News,* March 21, 1924.

9. Ben Gauthier, "The Flambeau Hatchery," *Indians at Work,* VI (September, 1938), 34-35 citing the *Flambeau Blue Book.*

CHAPTER 45

1. The fisher was trapped mainly for its fur, but the Chippewa found that its meat was very palatable. When boiled with potatoes, pork and dumplings, it was considered a choice dish. John Gordon, a Red Cliff Chippewa, reported that he saw a fisher, "ojig," on August 5, 1937.

2. *Wisconsin Conservation Bulletin,* IV (October, 1939), 21.

3. A conservation measure was taken by Indian Commissioner Collier on February 16, 1937. He issued an order abolishing the use of steel-jawed traps in the I.E.C.W. predatory animal control program on Indian lands. Instead of the old-fashioned steel jaws which mangle and injure the animal trapped, modern traps employ a noose or chain which catch and hold the animal securely without injury. If the animal caught is desirable for its fur or meat, it can be given a sure and clean death. Harmless and useful animals are not injured in the trap and may be set free. *Indians at Work,* IV (March 1, 1937), 43.

4. WPA Historical Records, Odanah, Folder 7, Item No. 11.

CHAPTER 46

1. Rene D'Harnoncourt, "Indian Art," *Indians at Work,* VIII (December, 1940), 18. This author, former director of Indian Arts and Crafts in the United States Office of Indian Affairs, said: "Real Indian art is kept hidden from the average tourist in Indian Territory. Because the traveler cannot afford to pay for the real art objects of our Indians, he is given a cheaply and hastily made souvenir." *Ibid.*

2. Cleora Helbig, "Indian Participation in the Great Lakes Exposition," *ibid.,* IV (September 15, 1936), 20.

3. *Library Bulletin,* Office of Indian Affairs, 1927, p. 3.

4. *Indians at Work,* VIII (February 15, 1936), 15.

5. Scott, "How Baskets Were Made by Indians," WPA Historical Records, Odanah, Folder 8, Item No. 25.

6. Parker, "Mat Weaving With Different Materials," *ibid.,* Folder 8, Item No. 6.

7. Arbuckle, "Weaving," *ibid.,* Folder 8, Item No. 5.

8. Marion Gridley, "Crafts of Our Northern Indians," *Indians at Work,* II (July 15, 1935), 7-10.

9. James Scott reported that he was present at a medicine dance held in Odanah, June 30, 1937. The Master of the Secret Order and his associates present wore beaded costumes. A wheat design signified a knowledge of herbs. He did not reveal the significance of other designs.

   Two processes were used by the Chippewa in bead work decoration. In one process, the beads were strung on threads and sewed to the material. In the second process, more intricate and beautiful, the beads were woven with the material.

10. Denomie, "Wigub," WPA Historical Records, Odanah, Folder 8, Item No. 24.

11. Isabelle Nevieux and Caroline Parker, "Tanning a Hide," *ibid.,* Folder 8, Item No. 7.

12. Denomie and Parker, "Chippewa Dyes," *ibid.,* Folder 8, Item No. 2. Antoine Soulier accidentally discovered the value of alder bark as a dye. He owned a little white dog which became very soiled and covered with fleas. Antoine knew that boiled alder bark killed fleas. Hence he boiled some bark. After the liquid had cooled, he gave his dog a bath. The animal went into the sun to dry. Sometime later, Antoine looked for his dog. But no white dog was in sight; just a red one. The Indian gave his customary whistle, but only a red dog responded with a happy bark! His "leetle" dog had changed to a redskin!

   The Chippewa used bloodroot in its fresh or raw state for painting their faces and for marking different clan signs on their bodies. After being dried and powdered, reddish earth was mixed with grease and applied to the face. Charcoal made from cedar wood was also used. For ceremonial rites and when on the war path, the Indians usually painted their bodies with grotesque designs in red and white.

13. Livingston, "Fire Making and Fire Transportation," *ibid.,* Folder 8, Items Nos. 14 and 18. Producing fire by friction was known and resorted to. The Indian hunter carried his stone flint for this purpose. Florina Denomie related that her grandmother solved the light problem thus: Night approaching, and with the kerosene supply exhausted, the old lady took a large button and tied it to a piece of cloth. She soaked this in melted deer tallow, lit the cloth, and

there was a fairly good light. The button anchored the cloth which served as a wick for the tallow.

14. Livingston, "Resin, or 'Kwani Bigu,' " *ibid.*, Folder 8, Item No. 22.

15. Marksman, "Pitch," and Arbuckle, "Glue," *ibid.*, Items Nos. 23 and 21.

16. Denomie and Nevieux, "How the Chippewa Made Soap," *ibid.*, Item No. 28. In laundering, the garments were immersed in water on a beach and a portion of soap, together with lake sand, was rubbed on the clothing. Then the clothing was beaten with a stout stick.

17. Arbuckle, "Snow Shoes," *ibid.*, Item No. 21.

18. Frank Gishkak, "Indian Pipes and Pipestone," *ibid.*, Item No. 29. Frank Smart, Chippewa Indian, owns a pipe used by Chief Sitting Bull at General Custer's last stand at Little Bighorn. Smart believes that it was made of human bone. Since its exposure to air, the pipe has turned a light brown. This is a characteristic of human bones; animal bones turn white upon exposure. The pipe is about 10 inches long and upon close contact, one can detect tobacco odor. Mr. Smart obtained the pipe from Sitting Bull's granddaughter in recognition for special services given to her. Superior *Evening Telegram,* July 10, 1939.

19. Arbuckle, "Bows and Arrows," *ibid.*, Item No. 43. Stories regarding the certainty of aim and piercing power of Indian arrows are greatly exaggerated. The hunter or warrior got as near to his victim as possible. In shooting, he drew his right hand to his ear. His bow register scarcely exceeded sixty pounds, yet arrows are said to have gone quite through the body of a buffalo.

20. Hodge, *op. cit.*, I, p. 91.

21. *Wisconsin Conservation Bulletin,* VI (March, 1941), 18. When Mr. Halver Skavlem began making arrows in 1912 with tools of primitive man, his summer home at Carcajou Point on Lake Koshkonong, Wisconsin, attracted visitors from all parts of the United States and Canada. Many of these wrote articles for publishers about this "charming arrow maker," and protested that making flint arrowheads is not a "lost art." One article written by Charles Stewart for the *Atlantic Monthly* is of interest in this history. The author related in his article that when Skavlem visited some of the Chippewa Indians in northern Wisconsin, they had no tradition about either the use of stone arrowheads nor the way in which they were made. Only one old squaw could be found who was even willing to give a genuine Indian arrowhead a name, namely a "Thunder Stone." These Indians were as curious and as interested in watching Skavlem make arrowheads with stone and bone tools as any of his white visitors had been. Stewart commented: "I would say that if no Wisconsin Indian thinks of making flint implements with bone, and would not know how to set about it, if he did; and if this is true of North American and other Indians in general . . . that would about fill the definition of a 'lost art' to anyone who knows what an art is." *Atlantic Monthly,* XIII (June, 1923), 799, cited in *Logan Museum Bulletin,* Beloit College, XI, No. 1, 12-14.

22. Scott, "How Indian Cradles are Made and Why," WPA Historical Records, Odanah, Folder 8, Item No. 26. When the child was placed in the cradle board, its legs were bound together and its arms held down on each side of the body with finely tanned buckskin. The baby lay flat on its back and remained in the cradle board in this position for several hours each day. The child must have been comfortable because when it was released for feeding or change of clothing, it often cried until it was returned to the board. While the

Indian mother performed her tasks about the home, the baby was secure in its cradle board. The safety of the cradle board was demonstrated by Frank Smart at an Indian pageant given on Apostle Islands in 1922. A Chippewa baby was placed in a cradle board and thrown into the air several times. Each time the cradle landed on the protective hoop, with the baby's face towards the ground. The baby suffered no injury.

23. Nevieux, "Swing Beds," *ibid.,* Item No. 44.

24. John Bardon stated that birch bark buckets, if filled with water or any liquid, can withstand heat from a bed of coal. The hot stone would be placed in the contents of the bucket. Interview with Bardon, Meeting of the Douglas County Historical Society, October 28, 1937.

25. Chippewa Indians also made torches from cedar bark, hazel brush, and basswood. For the cedar-bark torch, bark was crushed into sheets of loose fibers, rolled, and tied securely with strips of wigub. The rolls were then dipped into melted pitch to which powdered charcoal had been added to insure firmness and durability. The torches, each the size of a man's forearm, were stored away until needed. Before being used, however, they were again dipped into pitch. Hazel brush and basswood torches were made in a similar manner. Cedar blocks split into thin boards, often served as reflectors and also as shields to conceal occupants in a canoe.

26. Halfaday, "Birch Torch—How Made," WPA Historical Records, Odanah, Folder 8, Item No. 17.

27. Robert Ritzenthaler, *The Birch-Bark Canoe in America,* Milwaukee: Public Museum Bulletin, 1950, pp. 59-61.

28. Lyford, *Crafts of the Ojibwa,* pp. 49-51. According to Chippewa tradition the birch is never struck by lightning.

29. Morrison, "How to Construct a Canoe and a Dugout," WPA Historical Records, Odanah, Folder 8, Item Nos. 30, 31. In their light bark crafts, the Chippewa forefathers fearlessly trusted themselves to be pulled into the rapids. Flashing onwards, they shot through cataracts, and after being hidden some moments in mist and foam, they emerged from the seething waters a few hundred feet below, dancing on the heaving pool like some great sea bird.

James La Fernier, Bad River Chippewa, told of a canoe feat that he had witnessed on St. Mary's River in 1865. The canoe carried six men, one to guide, one to steer, and the other four to paddle. They covered a distance of one and one-half miles in six minutes.

Another type of water craft used occasionally by the Indians was the "dugout." According to the Chippewa Indians, the proper name for a dugout is boat. The term "dugout" is derived from its peculiar construction. In order to avoid confusion with the common troughs used for watering cattle, the term used in speaking of dugouts is boat. Dugout boats were used before the days of the saw mills when lumber was difficult to obtain.

Construction of a dugout required skill since it was made from one solid piece of white pine designed along the general lines of ordinary flatbottom boats of today. The size of timber required depended upon the width and the depth of the boat desired.

Dugouts could either be poled or rowed. Wooden pins were used as oar locks. Another method used for moving the boat was "sculling"; a process used only by experienced rivermen and sailors. A deep notch was cut in the center of the stern of the boat into which an oar was fitted. By a peculiar

twist of the oar, back and forth, the craft moved along at a satisfactory rate.
Ibid.

CHAPTER 47

1. Lyford, *Crafts of the Ojibwe,* pp. 17-19.
2. Hodge, *op. cit.,* I, 476.
3. *Ibid.,* p. 392.
4. Lyford, *op. cit.,* p. 31.
5. Densmore, *Uses of Plants by the Chippewa,* Forty-fourth Annual Report, Bureau of American Ethnology, 1928, p. 389.
6. Hodge, *op. cit.,* I, 392.
7. Modern designers are beginning to appreciate the building sense of primitive peoples. The lack of pretentiousness in the shelter of early Indians tended to obscure its superior design. These shelters kept the Indian families dry and comfortable in regions with extremes of climate. *Indians at Work,* VIII (October, 1940), 12-15.

CHAPTER 48

1. Livingston, "Chippewa Women's Costumes," WPA Historical Records, Odanah, Folder 10, Item No. 4. An amusing story is told of a Chippewa woman who purchased a pair of store leggings. A band of Chippewa returned to their encampment from a trip to a newly established trading post. Among the group was an old woman who seemed unusually delighted over her purchases which were contained in a large bundle. She immediately retired to her own wigwam from where came a joyful exclamation, "Oah! Apitchi winin-aji-wiwad!" "Oh, aren't they nice!"

   With a new supply of provisions on hand, a feast for the community was in order. Then, too, an occasion of this kind also furnished an opportunity to display any newly acquired article of adornment. Fire was kindled in a large fireplace and women reputed to be proficient in culinary arts were summoned to demonstrate their ability. The old woman who had been heard extolling the qualities of her goods, was requested to assist as she was noted for her ability to make a bread termed "lugulate."

   The assemblage anxiously awaited her arrival. Presently she was seen leaving her wigwam, walking slowly and laboriously; apparently she had suddenly become lame. A murmur of concern was heard from the gathering until it was noticed that, as she drew near, she was beaming with pride and self-satisfaction. The cause of her lameness was discovered to be two lengths of stove pipe which she had purchased and was wearing for leggings! Exclamations of admiration, not unmixed with envy, were now heard from the crowd as the bread-making got under way. Arbuckle, "The Height of Style," *ibid.,* Item No. 9.
2. A beaded broadcloth costume made by Mrs. Benjamin Gauthier, a Lac du Flambeau Indian, is in the Smithsonian Institute, Washington, D. C.
3. Indian influence in foot wear is found in the type of shoe called "loafer." This shoe emphasizes comfort and color. The laces are rawhide and the shoe is brightly beaded. *Milwaukee Journal,* February 8, 1953.

4. Arbuckle, "Moccasins," WPA Historical Records, Odanah, Folder 10, Item No. 10.
5. *Ibid.,* Item No. 2.
6. With the caption, "Borrowing From Indians," The Milwaukee *Journal,* August 8, 1954, printed the following: "Fashion stories are revealed in authentic reproductions of Wisconsin Indian costumes on display in a Milwaukee department store. Warriors wore elaborate dress; ceremonies when Indians prayed for rain and good crops were occasions for brightly beaded reds, blues, greens and yellows. . . . The first Americans were fond of jewelry, too, and the fashion minded woman would do well to add sparkling touches of her own to dresses in Indian colors."
7. Milo M. Quaife, *Wisconsin Its History and Its People,* 1634-1924, 3 vols. Chicago: S. J. Clark, 1924, p. 267.
8. WPA Historical Records, Odanah, Folder 6, Item No. 34.
9. *Ibid.,* Folder 10, Item No. 7. The "ear piercer," usually a woman, rubbed the ear lobe vigorously between thumb and forefinger, causing a tingling sensation. She used a sharp instrument to pierce the ear and drew a thread through the incision. This thread was allowed to remain in the ear. During the healing process, the thread was moved frequently to keep the cord free. After the wound had healed, a wire of the ear ring was inserted through the small opening. Ears of children were pierced as early as the age of five or six years.

CHAPTER 49

1. Cleora Helbing, "Indian Foods," *Indian Education,* VII, January 15, 1944. There are a few old Chippewa today who still follow the custom of seasoning their food with maple sugar used much as we do salt. They use the maple sugar to flavor their soups, wild rice, and hominy, and sprinkle it liberally over boiled fish or meat.
2. *Ibid.*
3. Hodge, *op. cit.,* II, 283.
4. WPA Historical Records, Odanah, Folder 8, Item No. 42.
5. *Ibid.,* Item No. 37. Consult Kappler, *op. cit.,* for the Salt Treaty of August 21, 1847, by which the government agreed to supply the Chippewa Pillagers with five barrels of salt annually for five years.
6. Hodge, *op. cit.,* I, 558.
7. Lugulate was adopted by the Chippewa as a universal food and is still eaten by them. The present-day process of making lugulate is similar to that used in making baking powder biscuits, except that the dough is baked in one cake.
8. WPA Historical Records, Odanah, Folder 8, Item No. 42.
9. John Gorden tells us that white men also relish porcupine. When he and the Indian cook served a lawyer vacationing in northern Wisconsin, they served themselves porcupine while the lawyer was served meat. When the lawyer learned that Indians ate porcupine, he stated disgustedly that he would not eat such meat for anything in the world. Mr. Gorden wagered $25.00 that he would eat it and relish it. So he caught a young "porky" and after preparing it with onions and seasoning, served it to the unsuspecting lawyer who ate it with great relish. After being told, the lawyer admitted that the "porky" was exceptionally good, and willingly paid the wager. *Ibid.,* Folder 12, Item No. 11.

CHAPTER 50

1. *Indians at Work,* XII (July-August, 1944), 2-4.
2. Neill, "History of Minnesota," MHS *Collections,* I (1883), 390.
3. Warren, *op. cit.,* p. 369.
4. *Ibid.,* p. 373.
5. *Ibid.,* pp. 375-376.
6. Letter of C. G. Lindquist, Attorney at Law, Duluth, Minnesota, to Ralph Case, Attorney at Law, Washington, D. C., p. 6. Copy of letter in the WPA Historical Records, Odanah.
7. Bartlett, *op. cit.,* p. 109.
8. Frazier, "We Are People Alive," *Indians at Work,* VIII (March, 1940), 12-13.
9. Bigboy, "Indians in World War I," WPA Historical Records, Odanah, Folder 2, Item No. 16.

All passed the physical examination except James Bachand whose height was below requirements. The men were instructed to return home to await further orders. Sometime later, some of these Chippewa were called to Ashland for induction. James Bachand, who had been rejected, was undaunted. He reported to Ashland under Arthur Duscharme's name and was sent to Kelley Field, Texas. (Duscharme had passed the physical examination for entrance in the air force).

After the training period in Texas, Bachand was assigned to an overseas squadron. Subsequently, the squadron was air-raided in France with heavy casualties. Among the seriously wounded was the Indian lad who had stolen his way to do his "bit" for his country.

Arthur Duscharme, the Odanah Chippewa who had passed the examination, finally approached the draft board and inquired the reason for his induction delay. After he had given his name, he was told that he had been furnished transportation to Kelley Field, Texas, he had been sent overseas, and furthermore, that he was in a hospital in France! In consternation, the young Chippewa wondered if he was himself or if he wasn't! Then it occurred to the army officials that someone had entered the army under Duscharme's name.

When the shell-shocked James Bachand, alias Arthur Duscharme, was able to give an account of himself, he admitted the deception. By that time, the war was almost over and nothing was done to discredit him. But difficulty ensued when Bachand tried to receive benefits accruing from the veterans' bonus and hospitalization fund. Eventually, Bachand was given recognition as a veteran under his own name and was given credit for his service in the army. *Ibid.*

10. *Ibid.*
11. Riley, "Veterans of World War I, Lac Courte Oreilles Reservation," Indian Agency Report to Sister Carolissa, July 10, 1953.
12. Dorothy Stewart, "Veterans in World War I, Lac du Flambeau Reservation," Sub-Agency Report to Sister M. Carolissa, July 28, 1952.
13. Bigboy, "Indians of Bad River Reservation in World War I," WPA Historical Records, Folder 2, Item No. 19.
14. Sister Victoria Steidl, O.S.F. Data on soldiers from Red Cliff Reservation in World War I in a letter to Sister M. Carolissa, October 22, 1954.
15. Ashland *Daily Press,* April 21, 1919.
16. Among the enlisted Chippewa who subscribed to Liberty Loans, Frank Antoine

led the list with $7,500. Other Liberty Loan bond-minded soldiers were Joe Wilson, $5,000; Edward Starr, $4,500; Sam Shebinco, $3,000; Francis Sky, $2,000; William Bresette, $1,700; and seventeen year-old Francis Shebinco, $600. Superior *Evening Telegram,* January 19, 1919.

17. *Ibid.*

18. *Ibid.,* May 13, 1919.

19. Bigboy, "Indian Preferences, World War I," WPA Historical Records, Folder 2, Item No. 16.

20. *Indians at Work,* X (January, 1942), cover page citing Cato's report.

21. Eleanor Williams, "A Memorial Day Tribute," *ibid.,* XI (May-June, 1943), 17.

22. *Congressional Record,* LXXXIX, Part II, 2100.

23. Williams, "Indian Warriors of Today and Yesterday," *Indians at Work,* XI (May-June, 1943), 17.

24. *Ibid.,* citing the *Scientific American Magazine.*

25. Bigboy, "Indians of Bad River Reservation in World War I," WPA Historical Records, Odanah, Folder 2, Item No. 21.

26. Duluth *News-Tribune,* February 23, 1941.

27. Ashland *Daily Press,* October 16, 1941.

28. Brandenton *Herald,* March 25, 1941. At Brandenton Park, where he acted in the capacity of entertainer, Arbuckle was known as "Chief Whirling Thunder." He was a star performer of the double hoop dance and a skilled musician on string instruments. He was also widely known as an amateur pugilist.

29. *Ibid.* Arbuckle was not a mechanic by chance. He studied mechanics in Superior, Wisconsin, after completing high school. Arbuckle knew more about the sputter of a "cranky" motor than he did about trapping wild animals. Among his army friends, some called him "Ken"; others called him "Chief"; but none ventured to call him by his Indian name, "Gi-ji-ba-ami-mi-ka." Ashland *Daily Press,* January 13, 1942.

30. *Indians at Work,* XI (September-October, 1943), 15.

31. Ashland *Daily Press,* July 19, 1944. Arnold Smart was graduated from Northland College with a degree of Bachelor of Arts. Later he was employed in the U.S. Indian Service at Ashland, Wisconsin, and also at Tomah, Wisconsin. Before enlistment in the army, Smart was fire inspector at Fort Sheridan, Illinois. *Ibid.*

32. There is also the story of Ronald Frost, a Bad River Chippewa, who did not see the front lines of the battle field, but his attempt to do so featured a three-column space in a Milwaukee newspaper which carried this bold headline: ODANAH MAN WITH WOODEN LEG SENT BY DRAFT BOARD. Despite a home-made peg leg which replaced the right leg which he had lost in a train accident two years earlier, Ronald Frost, 24, father of two children, appeared at the Milwaukee induction center.

After a brief examination, he was rejected. The State Draft Board ordered the Selective Service Board at Ashland, Wisconsin, to check why Frost had been classified in 1-A and ordered to report to the Milwaukee Induction Board.

Frank Clock, chief clerk of the Ashland Selective Service Board, reported that Frost had registered for draft in 1941. He gave a scar on his left thumb as his only identifying mark and mentioned no physical disabilities. In September, 1943, Frost had filled out a second questionnaire and returned it without naming any serious physical defect. The Draft Board did not know that in November of the same year, Frost's right leg was badly crushed while he was attempting to board a train. The injured limb was amputated by a local physician. The November, 1941 classification had placed Frost in 3-A because he was the father of two children. In 1943, he was given a 2-B occupational deferment because he was working in a Superior shipyard. Frost received his first 1-A classification on April 3, 1944 and was ordered to notify the board of any physical defect. Frost neglected to do so.

Seemingly, Frost meant to hide his defect since he boarded the train at Odanah instead of leaving at Ashland with the other men. After his return to Ashland, he was asked how he was almost "drafted." Frost's explanation was, "I didn't want anyone to say I was a draft dodger or slacker. If they thought they could use me, I was ready to go." Milwaukee *Sentinel,* May 11, 1944. See also Ashland *Daily Press,* April 11, 1944.

33. See article, "Rasmussen, Odanah, a War Hero; Lived 68 Days Uncaptured after the Crash in Japan," in Ashland *Daily Press,* September 24, 1945. Rasmussen's island adventures were not unmixed with humorous incidents. On his way to the coast, he found a few bird eggs which "tasted like steak." This was lean fare for a fighting man; consequently, Rasmussen was exhausted after he reached the beach. Suddenly his trained-farmer's eye saw something familiar. A cow! A Japanese cow, to be sure, but it had everything in the right places. The soldier staggered over to the cow. He lived principally on milk and its by-products during the remainder of his almost Robinson Crusoe days. He even made his own butter and cheese.

The Japanese farmer was confused because of the cow's dwindling milk supply. He muzzled the cow's calf. Then he freed the cow, hoping that the animal would find more food and increase her milk yield. Rasmussen continued to thrive and the farmer continued to wonder.

During the night of August 10, the Indian tried to escape in a fishing boat, but he failed. After two more attempts, he gave up the idea because each time the Japanese fishermen almost captured him.

Rasmussen also made night raids on Japanese gardens. One night he was discovered. He used his high school track training experience and escaped. Then he caught frogs and ate their legs raw. Sometime later, Rasmussen fortunately stumbled on a dugout containing rice, butter, and potatoes. He stayed in the dugout for five days, but was obliged to flee when Japanese arrived to investigate.

Then he wandered to several farms during the night, and drank cream from the milk cans. Once the farmers "ganged up" to seize him. From their place of concealment, they all sprang out at one time. "I was scared to death," admitted Rasmussen, "but I used a few football tactics and got away from them."

Rasmussen received two checks from newspapers that publicized his feat— the *Chicago Tribune* and the *Wisconsin Agriculturist.* The latter paper stressed the fact that Rasmussen owed his life to his knowledge of dairying.

When Rasmussen's uncle, Joe La Fernier, of Ashland, Wisconsin, learned of his nephew's safety, he remarked: "Oliver always liked reading adventure stories and among his favorites was *Robin Hood.*"

The good news was broken to Grandfather La Fernier in Odanah by John B. Chapple and George Bassford from Ashland. They found the 79 year-old man with his son, Pfc. Frank La Fernier, also a World War II veteran. The old grandfather listened attentively to make certain that he had understood the message correctly. Then he extended his hand to each of his guests, saying: "Put it there, put it there." The La Fernier history has been one of devotion to country. Oliver Rasmussen's great grandfather had been a Civil War veteran.

Grandfather La Fernier was of French-Canadian and Indian extraction. His father was one of the early pioneer Frenchmen who came from Montreal into Michigan and helped to construct the Houghton-Hancock Michigan bridge. He was married to the daughter of the ruling Indian chief of Bear County, Michigan. Ashland *Daily Press,* September 24, 1945; February 2, 1946.

34. *Ibid.*

35. "Hero of Hill 609 Killed," *Indians at Work,* XI (March-April), 13. Mrs. Angeline Rice, Marksman's mother, received her son's posthumous Silver Star award. Later she received a letter from Corporal Joseph R. La Goy of which the following is an extract:

> Should the censor permit, Mrs. Rice, I'll tell you the story the way I heard it of Joe's death. He was leading a patrol (as he always did for the company, and we were always in good hands) and the patrol drew some heavy fire from the Germans. A few of the boys managed to get out but poor Joe and the Acting Company commander were killed. From the reports, I gather Joe didn't suffer much as his death was instantaneous. I'm sure he made a confession before going into combat as he was the good Joe for going to church. I'm sure God has him in Eternal Peace, and that his cause was not in vain.
>
> Joe was a dear friend to all of us and his sayings being known throughout the division. He was known far and wide by all the men, too. I remember during parades or marches in Ireland, the civilians would yell, "Hello, Joe." He was a great man, Mrs. Rice, and is the type for people to be proud and say, "I know him.". . .
>
> Please, Mother Rice, accept my sincere sympathy in your recent loss and believe me, when I say, "They didn't come any better than Indian Joe Marksman." Ashland *Daily Press,* July 19, 1944.

Joseph Marksman was a graduate of St. Mary's School at Odanah and later attended an Indian government school at Tomah, Wisconsin. In 1930, he enlisted at Fort Snelling, Minnesota, and was assigned to Company C of the Third Infantry. Upon completion of his first year army-life, Marksman was promoted to the position of head bugler for his company. Later he qualified at rifle range, first as marksman, then as sharp-shooter, and in his second enlistment, became an expert rifleman. In March, 1941, Marksman re-enlisted and was promoted from private to corporal. He attained the rank of sergeant in one month. Marksman was the only Indian in the company. *Ibid.,* May 29, 1941.

36. Arthur Dashner and a "Buddy," John Shipuleski of Long Island found a rabbit on their advance into Normandy. They kept the rabbit as a mascot and gave it a prominent place on the vehicle. The rabbit brought them luck, so they thought. Superior *Evening Telegram,* August 21, 1944.

37. Ashland *Daily Press,* January 2, 1945. On March 20, 1945, Walter Dashner returned to Odanah from the Schick General Hospital, Clinton, Iowa. He had undergone treatment for a hand wound and other shrapnel injuries received from an enemy hand grenade four days after his conquest of the machine gun nest in which he had miraculously escaped injury. Dashner, towering six feet, three inches, did not give the slightest impression of the fighting spirit he so

dauntlessly displayed in the army. Hesitatingly, he told of his journey back to the States after his hospitalization of several months duration in England:

The hospital ship I was returning on carried about 500 other injured soldiers and was due to dock in the States some time in January. However, as we approached Bermuda, a British isle, the bottom of our ship struck an enormous rock underseas, practically upsetting us. This naturally delayed us. Another boat nearby, gave us a hand and within eight hours, all the fellows on our boat were transferred safely to it. After being taken to the hospital at Bermuda, which by the way is as up-to-date as some of ours, we stayed there for almost a week.

It was quite an experience for us, too. As you know, cars were never used on the island until the army came and at that, they aren't too plentiful. We fellows would often go riding around in those horse and buggies they use for transportation, and no kidding, we had fun. Some of us acted like kids having our first ride.

After a while, another ship was brought to Bermuda to get us underway on our journey. So it wasn't until February when we landed in the States, and, believe you me, we were darn glad to be back. *Ibid.*, March 20, 1945.

All the Dashner boys were graduates of St. Mary School at Odanah. Walter also attended De Padua High School, Ashland, Wisconsin.

38. Williams, "Indian Warriors of Today and Yesterday," *Indians at Work,* XI (May-June, 1943), 18.

39. *Congressional Record,* LXXXVIII, Part 10, A 4125-4126. There were 2,000 Indians at the post mentioned above, representing 50 different tribes. Many of these Indians had a college education and the number who hadn't at least a high school education were few. Yet some people still persist in using "ugh" and one-syllable words on their first conversational approach to an Indian. Such was the case of a young woman, a radio program announcer, who had asked some Indians to sing native songs. She wanted informational background about these songs so that she could introduce them intelligently to her listening audience. The job of informing the young lady fell to the lot of the bayonet specialist, Sergeant Matlock. The tall, somberfaced sergeant with a couple of football scars on his head was convincing evidence to the lady that she was addressing a real Indian. Timidly she intimated to him with two-syllable words and sign language gestures that she would like to have him explain the background of his native songs. "Madam," said Sergeant Matlock, with a combination of soft southern and slow western drawl, designated as a 'mellifluous Oklahoma tone,' "the easiest way for me to explain our Indian songs is to tell you they are similar to a series of progressions in Chaucer's Canterbury Tales." Then the *Indian* proceeded to quote examples from the prologue while the young lady's jaw dropped.

40. *Indians at Work,* XI (September-October, 1943), 15.

41. *Ibid.*

42. *Ibid.*

43. *Ibid.*

44. *Indians in the War,* Chicago: U.S. Department of Interior, Office of Indian Affairs, 1945, p. 49.

45. *Indians at Work,* XI (September-October, 1943), 15-16.

46. *Indians in the War,* p. 1. Chippewa records of World War II show that the

reservations contributed the following numbers of men and women engaged in the actual conflict: Bad River Reservation, 157. WPA Historical Records, Odanah, Folder 2, Item No. 21. Courte Oreilles Reservation furnished 95. Letter of Rev. E. Fox, Stone Lake, to Sister Carolissa, October 22, 1954. Lac du Flambeau records list 110. Report of D. Stewart to Sister Carolissa, July 28, 1952. The Red Cliff Reservation supplied 40. Chief Martin Buffalo, Letter to Sister Carolissa, October 26, 1954.

47. Superior *Evening Telegram,* March 3, 1954.

APPENDIX A

1. Willard Beatty, "What is an Indian Reservation," *Indian Education,* VIII (December 15, 1944), 1.
1. *Ibid.*
3. The Federal Government administers Indian affairs through the Indian Bureau, established in 1826 as part of the War Department and transferred to the newly created Department of Interior, in 1829. The Bureau is subject to orders of the President. The objectives set for it dealt with the making of treaties with the Indians whereby the natives would relinquish the lands which White settlers wanted; the provision for removals of Indians from these lands; the regulation of trade with the Indians; and the civilization of Indians through instruction in manual training, agriculture and mechanics. Theodore Haas, *The Indian and the Law—1.* United States Indian Service, 1949, p. 5. (Pamphlet)
4. *Handbook of American Indians,* II, p. 1.
5. *Indians at Work,* II (January 15, 1935), 33. General Sherman is said to have cynically described an Indian reservation as "a tract of land entirely occupied by Indians and entirely surrounded by white thieves." Haas, *op. cit.,* p. 14.
6. *Handbook of American Indians,* II, p. 1.
7. *The American Indian,* June, 1939, p. 2.
8. *Answers to Your Questions on American Indians.* Pamphlet II, Haskell Institute, Lawrence: United States Indian Service, 1952, pp. 16-17.
9. William Zimmerman, *The Federal Indian Service,* Washington: Department of Indian Affairs, 1949, pp. 6-7. (Pamphlet)
10. *Answers to Your Questions on American Indians,* II, p. 16.
11. *The American Indian,* June, 1939, p. 50.
12. D. W. Murphy, "Memorandum to the Commissioner," *Indians at Work,* III (December 15, 1935), 45.
13. Sister M. Carolissa, Meeting of the Wisconsin State Historical Society at Madison, Wisconsin, June 26, 1954.

APPENDIX B

1. The next world record lake trout may be taken by one of the boats fishing waters surrounding the Apostle Islands, according to Joseph W. Le Bel, third generation fisherman who has been captain of his own trolling boat for 24 years. Commercial fishermen have netted trout weighing 72 pounds. The world record laker caught on rod and reel weighed 63 pounds 2 ounces, caught in Lake Superior.

Le Bel's one regret is that he and other trolling captains did not have the equipment 25 years ago that the boats have today. Le Bel explained that trollers then used handlines woven of cotton wound to a foot-long stick. "If we hung up on bottom, we just threw the stick away," explained Le Bel. "If we got hold of a fish we couldn't handle, we did the same and then picked the stick up later. In those days, we used to quit trolling by July 1 because we thought the trout had quit hitting. When we got metal lines and could go deeper, we discovered they hadn't quit hitting, but had only moved out to deeper water." Milwaukee *Journal,* September 5, 1954.

2. Ashland *Daily Press,* February 4, 1954.

3. *Ibid.*

4. Superior *Evening Telegram,* August 21, 1941. Nels Angus, the former owner, was the son of the late Captain Russel Angus, a sailor, and the grandson of the original Captain Nels Angus, the old "sea dog," who sailed the seven seas and later the Great Lakes.

5. Milwaukee *Journal,* November 8, 1953.

6. Sister M. Carolissa, Visit to Madeline Island, 1952.

7. Sister M. Carolissa, Interview with William Gordon. The town of Gordon, northern Wisconsin, was named after Antoine Gordon.

8. On August 9, 1935, Catholic and Protestant, Christian and non-Christian, native islanders and visitors, white men and red men, assembled on Madeline Island to pay homage to the "Apostle of the Chippewa," Bishop Baraga, on the occasion of the centennial celebration of his arrival on the island.

   Before an outdoor altar of ivory and gold silhouetted against a green background of cedar and fir trees, a solemn High Mass was celebrated. Father Emeran Fox, O.F.M., from Odanah, celebrant, wore a set of vestments which had been worn by Bishop Baraga.

   A glowing tribute was paid to the saintly bishop by Father Peter Crumbley, noted Franciscan missionary, a native of Ashland, Wisconsin. Attorney C. A. Lamoreaux of Ashland, also delivered an encomium to the bishop. Governor Robert M. La Follette was represented by Assemblyman J. C. Sibbald of Bayfield County and Hugh Harper of Grant County.

   John Bardon, pioneer and historian of Superior, Wisconsin, brought to the island an extensive collection of historical material which was displayed in the Old Mission Inn. The collection included a Chippewa-English Dictionary written by Bishop Baraga, letters from the Bishop to members of the Bardon family, and the key to the original church erected on the island by the bishop.

   The celebration also included a pageant depicting the arrival of Bishop Baraga on Madeline Island and the signing of the Treaty of 1854. The latter was presented by the Chippewa from Odanah. William Dormady of Ashland directed the pageant. Ceremonial dances performed by the Odanah Chippewa were also an interesting feature of the pageant. Ashland *Daily Press,* August 10, 1935.

9. Milwaukee *Journal,* August 13, 1922. In an interview with Mrs. Stahl-Albright, the author learned that Thomas Stahl had died in 1922, and that the family had, during succeeding generations for a period of nearly hundred years, taken care of the Catholic Church on the island. She was also informed that the old silver chimes in the church built by Father Baraga, were damaged in the fire of 1901, and after repair in St. Louis, were restored to the Catholic Church on the island.

10. Mention should also be made of Michael Cadotte who carried on the traditions of the Cadotte family, although he does not live on Madeline Island at the present time. Cadotte is the only name in this area that has come down in an unbroken line from 1765 when the United States was still under British sovereignty. In 1945, there were sixteen of the Cadotte lineage serving in World War II; among these were Vincent "Jack" Cadotte, father of the present Michael Cadotte. Since the untimely death of the father who drowned on Long Island, possibly the original LaPointe, on May 25, 1946, the family no longer lives on the island. Ashland *Daily Press,* May 25, 1946.
11. *Ibid.,* February 4, 1954. Mrs. Pernier Martin used to recall that her grandmother, a native of Bristol, England, often described to her grandchildren the signing of the 1854 Treaty. Since the Pernier home was between the beach and Judge Bell's office, the Pernier lawn was part of the camping ground of the Chippewa who arrived in boats and canoes.
12. *Ibid.,* September 11, 1945.
13. *Ibid.,* June 21, 1945.
14. Milwaukee *Journal,* September 6, 1953.
15. *Ibid.,* April 13, 1954.
16. In private life, Miss Terry is Mrs. John J. Kardon of Superior, Wisconsin. In 1944 she was soloist of St. Paul's Episcopal Church in Duluth, Minnesota. She also gave vocal lessons in her studio in Superior.
17. Ashland *Daily Press,* August 25, 1944.

APPENDIX C

1. Although all the Chippewa reservations conducted some type of celebration, the principal commemoration of the 1854 Treaty was held on the Red Cliff Reservation.
2. Other members of the Red Cliff band who worked on the committee were Mr. and Mrs. George Gurnoe, Mrs. Rose Duffy, Mrs. Frank Basina, John Daly, and Louis Vandervenier.
3. James M. Gordon acted as aide to Admiral Leahy at Red Cliff. At one time, Mr. Gordon, in order to attend an American Legion convention at Miami, Florida, made the entire trip almost by canoe, via the Mississippi River.
4. Chief Martin Buffalo is a great-grandson of the illustrious Chief Buffalo.
5. For an account of this celebration see "Bishop, Admiral Leahy, Congressman Alvin O'Konski, at Historic Ceremony," Ashland *Daily Press,* September 7, 1954.
6. *Ibid.*

INDEX

374